LIBRARY OF NEW TESTAMENT STUDIES

463

formerly the Journal for the Study of the New Testament Supplement series

Editor
Mark Goodacre

PAUL AND JUDAISM

Crosscurrents in Pauline Exegesis
and the Study of Jewish-Christian Relations

Edited by
REIMUND BIERINGER
and
DIDIER POLLEFEYT

t&t clark

Published by T&T Clark International
A Continuum imprint
The Tower Building, 11 York Road, London SE1 7NX
80 Maiden Lane, Suite 704, New York, NY 10038

www.continuumbooks.com

British Library Cataloguing-in-Publication Data
A catalogue record for this book is available from the British Library

ISBN: HB: 978-0-567-07280-1

Library of Congress Cataloging-in-Publication Data
A catalog record for this book is available from the Library of Congress

Typeset by Free Range Book Design & Production Limited
Printed and bound in Great Britain

CONTENTS

LIST OF CONTRIBUTORS

Michael Bachmann is Professor of New Testament at the University of Siegen, Germany.

Reimund Bieringer is Professor of New Testament Exegesis at the Catholic University of Leuven, Belgium.

Michael F. Bird is Lecturer in Theology and New Testament at Crossway College, Queensland, Australia, and is Honorary Research Associate at the University of Queensland.

Thomas R. Blanton, IV is Visiting Assistant Professor in Religion at Luther College, Decorah, Iowa, USA.

William S. Campbell is Reader in Biblical Studies at the University of Wales Trinity St David, Lampeter, UK.

Philip A. Cunningham is Professor of Theology specializing in Christian-Jewish Relations and Director of the Institute for Jewish-Catholic Relations of Saint Joseph's University, Philadelphia, USA.

James D. G. Dunn is Emeritus Lightfoot Professor of Divinity at the University of Durham, UK.

Hans Hermann Henrix is Director Emeritus of the Episcopal Academy of the Roman Catholic Diocese of Aachen, Germany, Honorary Professor of Theology at the University of Salzburg, Austria, and Consultant to the Holy See Commission for Religious Relations with the Jews.

Mark D. Nanos is Soebbing Distinguished Scholar-in-Residence at Rockhurst University, Kansas City, Missouri, USA.

John T. Pawlikowski is Professor of Social Ethics and Director of the Catholic-Jewish Studies Program at Catholic Theological Union, Chicago, USA.

Didier Pollefeyt is Professor of Pastoral Theology, Theology of Jewish-Christian Relations and Post-Holocaust Theology at the Catholic University of Leuven, Belgium.

Hans-Joachim Sander is Professor of Dogmatic Theology at the University of Salzburg, Austria.

LIST OF ABBREVIATIONS

AB	Anchor Bible
ACJD	Abhandlungen zum christlich-jüdischen Dialog
AGJU	Arbeiten zur Geschichte des antiken Judentums und des Urchristentums
AHST	Arbeiten zur historischen und systematischen Theologie
ATANT	Abhandlungen zur Theologie des Alten und Neuen Testaments
AYBC	Anchor Yale Bible Commentary
BETL	Bibliotheca Ephemeridum Theologicarum Lovaniensium
BEvTh	Beiträge zur evangelischen Theologie
BibInt	*Biblical Interpretation*
Bijdr.	*Bijdragen*
BJRL	Bulletin of John Rylands University Library of Manchester
BThSt	Biblisch-Theologische Studien
BZ NF	*Biblische Zeitschrift Neue Folge*
Cath(M)	*Catholica (Münster)*
CBNT	Coniectanea Biblica, New Testament Series
CBQ	*Catholic Biblical Quarterly*
CBR	*Currents in Biblical Research*
CRINT	Compendia Rerum Iudaicarum ad Novum Testamentum
EdF	Erträge der Forschung
EDNT	Exegetical Dictionary of the New Testament
EWNT	*Exegetisches Wörterbuch zum Neuen Testament*
FES	Finnish Exegetical Society
FRLANT	Forschungen zur Religion und Literatur des Alten und Neuen Testaments
GlLern	*Glauben und Lernen*
HBS	Herders Biblische Studien
HTR	*Harvard Theological Review*
ICC	International Critical Commentary
Int	Interpretation
ITQ	*Irish Theological Quarterly*
IVP	Intervarsity Press
JAOS	*Journal of the American Oriental Society*
JBL	Journal of Biblical Literature
JECS	Journal of Early Christian Studies
JGRChJ	*Journal of Greco-Roman Christianity and Judaism*
JSNT	*Journal for the Study of the New Testament*

JSNTSup	Journal for the Study of the New Testament: Supplement Series
JSOT	Journal for the Study of the Old Testament
JSQ	*Jewish Studies Quarterly*
JTI	*Journal for Theological Interpretation*
JTS	*Journal of Theological Studies*
Jud.	Judaica
KuD	*Kerygma und Dogma*
KuI	*Kirche und Israel*
LNTS	Library of New Testament Studies
LThK	*Lexikon für Theologie und Kirche*
NCCS	New Covenant Commentary Series
NIB	*New Interpreter's Bible*
NICNT	New International Commentary on the New Testament
NovT	Novum Testamentum
NSBT	New Studies in Biblical Theology
NTL	The New Testament Library
NTOA	Novum Testamentum et Orbis Antiquus
NTP	Novum Testamentum Patristicum
NTS	*New Testament Studies*
NZZ	Neue Zürcher Zeitung
PAST	Pauline Studies
PrST	*Perspectives in Religious Studies*
RGG	Religion in Geschichte und Gegenwart.
RSR	*Recherches de science religieuse*
SBB	Stuttgarter Biblische Beiträge
SBL DS	Society of Biblical Literature Dissertation Series
SBL.SBibSt	Society of Biblical Literature Sources for Biblical Studies
SCJ	Studies in Christianity and Judaism
SHR	Studies in the History of Religions (supplement to *Numen*)
SKI	Studien zu Kirche und Israel
SNTS	Society for New Testament Studies
SNTS MS	Society of New Testament Studies Monograph Series
SRivBiB	Supplements to Rivista Biblica
ST	*Studia Theologica*
StTAC	Studien und Texte zu Antike und Christentum
StUNT	Studien zur Umwelt des Neuen Testaments
stw	Suhrkamp Taschenbuch Wissenschaft
TBei	*Theologische Beiträge*
ThHK	Theologischer Handkommentar
ThLZ	Theologische Literaturzeitung
ThRv	*Theologische Revue*
ThZ	*Theologische Zeitschrift*
TQ	Theologische Quartalschrift
TSJ	Texts and Studies in Judaism
TUAT.NF	*Texte aus der Umwelt des Alten Testaments Neue Folge*
TynBul	*Tyndale Bulletin*

UTB	Universitätstaschenbücer
WBC	Word Biblical Commentary
WUNT	Wissenschaftliche Untersuchungen zum Neuen Testament
ZNT	Zeitschrift für Neues Testament
ZNW	*Zeitschrift für die Neutestamentliche Wissenschaft*
ZThK	Zeitschrift für Theologie und Kirche

ACKNOWLEDGEMENTS

In 2007 the Research Foundation Flanders (FWO) awarded a research grant to us for the project entitled 'New perspectives on Paul and the Jews: A critical investigation into the significance of the Letters of Paul in light of the historical parting of the ways between Judaism and Christianity with particular attention paid to 2 Cor. 3.6,7-18 in light of Jewish-Christian dialogue' (2007–10). Two PhD students, David Bolton and Emmanuel Nathan, joined our research group. They took up the tasks of researchers in our project. Emmanuel took the responsibility for the exegetical dimension of the project in view of Jewish-Christian dialogue. The title of his dissertation is 'New Perspectives on Paul and the New Covenant in 2 Cor. 3.6,7-18: Hermeneutical and Heuristic Considerations on Continuity and Discontinuity' (promoter: Reimund Bieringer; co-promoter: Didier Pollefeyt). It was defended on 22 December 2010 and is being prepared for publication in WUNT. David focused on the study of Jewish-Christian dialogue in relation to the interpretation of the Letters of Paul (promoter: Didier Pollefeyt, co-promoter: Reimund Bieringer). He defended his dissertation entitled 'Justifying Paul Among Jews and Christians? A Critical Investigation of the New Perspective on Paul in Light of Jewish-Christian Dialogue' on 14 February 2011. We are grateful to Emmanuel and David for the highly professional and enjoyable cooperation in the project and for their contributions to the completion of this book. We acknowledge that the work that went into completing this book would not have been possible for us, had it not been for the grant by the Research Foundation Flanders.

The papers contained in this book have their origin in an international conference held in Leuven on 14–15 September 2009. They were revised and edited for publication in the present volume. Like the project, the conference and the book bring together different perspectives and approaches from the areas of biblical exegesis and Jewish-Christian dialogue. This intradisciplinary approach offers a rather unique perspective on the subject of 'Paul and Judaism'. The first five contributions to the book offer an exegetical perspective, the remaining four a Jewish-Christian dialogue approach. The prologue and the epilogue try to foster the dialogue between both perspectives.

We are grateful to the contributors for a very challenging conference and for their texts which appear in this book. Special thanks are due to James D.G. Dunn who was not able to attend the conference but generously offered to write the epilogue. We express our gratitude to Andrey Romanov for making the indices. Finally, we thank the editors of the Library of New Testament Studies for accepting this book into the series and the publisher T&T Clark International for their efficient cooperation.

Reimund Bieringer
Didier Pollefeyt

Leuven, 25 January 2012
Feast of the Conversion
of Saint Paul

January 27, 2012
International Holocaust
Memorial Day

PROLOGUE:
WRESTLING WITH THE JEWISH PAUL

Reimund Bieringer and Didier Pollefeyt

The relationship of the early followers of Jesus to contemporary Judaism is one of the central issues of the New Testament, particularly the letters of Paul. This relation became controversial when non-Jews started to join the group of Jesus followers. The conflict that arose was not only one of membership criteria but it also raised fundamental theological questions concerning early Christian self-definition, especially in relation to the Judaism(s) of the time. The conflict played itself out as a dispute on the meaning of justification and the issue of salvation. In subsequent centuries, the New Testament texts that deal with this conflict shaped the ensuing theological discussions on who has access to salvation and how access to salvation is made possible. These soteriological discussions determined the self-understanding of the Christian churches and their relationship with the Jewish people. Since the Reformation, a consensus had developed under the influence of Protestant exegesis that Paul is at the origin of an antithesis between contemporary Judaism and Christian faith, an antithesis between works and grace, law and gospel. Consequently, Paul was seen more and more as the actual founder of Christianity while Jesus was presented as having stayed completely within the boundaries of Judaism. In this way, the traditional reading of the letters of Paul became one of the cornerstones of the Christian perception of the Jew as the 'unsaved other' which have had destructive consequences for the Jewish people. One of the key questions of the present volume is whether the traditional understanding of the process of separation of Judaism and Christianity indeed has exegetical and theological support from Paul.

1. From the Old to the New Perspective and Back

In historical perspective it was above all the traditional Lutheran doctrine of justification which determined the way scholars interpreted Paul's understanding of the relation between Judaism and Christianity. Justification means in this context that human persons are not saved by their own merits, but exclusively by God's grace made available by Christ's merits in his death on the cross. Paul's emphasis on justification by grace alone was seen as a reaction against

Judaism. Luther rejected the Roman Church of his time because in his conviction she promised salvation on the basis of works, that is, precisely for the same reason for which Paul, according to Luther, had rejected Judaism. Judaism is here understood and rejected as a legalistic religion which makes salvation dependent on human merits. In light of the dramatic events of the twentieth century, especially the Shoah, this theology of justification came under pressure. James D. G. Dunn, one of the leading scholars in the field, points out how this post-Shoah perspective made possible new developments in the field of New Testament exegesis and theology: 'Post-Holocaust theology could no longer stomach the denigration of historic Judaism.'[1]

In Pauline studies the most important developments happened in the context of the so-called 'New Perspective'[2] which cleared the Judaism contemporary to Paul of the accusation that it is a religion based on works righteousness. Sanders introduced the term 'covenantal nomism' into the debate to summarize his understanding of Judaism as a religion based on the grace of the covenant, seeing works of the law as signs of loyalty and gratitude. Sanders stressed that Judaism like Christianity was based on God's unmerited grace. Sanders' study caused a major shift in Pauline studies because of the 'sharp contrast he drew between his restatement of Palestinian Judaism and the traditional reconstructions of Judaism within Christian theology'.[3] This implied a totally new understanding of the relationship between Paul and Judaism. According to Sanders the major difference between Judaism and Pauline Christianity is not the antithesis law and grace, but the (more fundamental) difference between covenantal grace (Judaism) and the grace of the new creation in Christ (Christianity). Thus for Paul it would not be enough for Christ to undo the consequences of human sin by renewing the covenant. Rather the whole creation needs to be renewed. According to Paul this more fundamental goal can only be realized through the death and resurrection of Christ and through dying and rising with Christ (what Sanders calls 'participatory union').[4] Dunn took 'New Perspective' theology a step further by replacing the antithesis between law and grace which was traditionally seen in Paul's theology by the antithesis between national (exclusive) and universal (inclusive). Dunn is convinced that in the theology of Paul the renewal of the covenant of Judaism in Christ takes the central position. Through the Messianic gift of the Spirit, the national borders of Israel are opened for the nations. 'It is the law understood in terms of works, as a Jewish prerogative and national monopoly, to which he [Paul] takes exception ... It is works which betoken racial prerogative to which he objects.'[5] According to

---

1.   James D. G. Dunn, *The Theology of Paul the Apostle* (Grand Rapids: Eerdmans, 1998), p. 338.

2.   E. P. Sanders, *Paul and Palestinian Judaism* (London: SCM Press, 1977); James D. G. Dunn, 'The New Perspective on Paul', *BJRL* 65 (1983): 95–122; Krister Stendahl, 'The Apostle Paul and the Introspective Conscience of the West', *HTR* 56 (1963): 199–215.

3.   Dunn, *The Theology of Paul the Apostle*, p. 5.

4.   Sanders, *Paul and Palestinian Judaism*, pp. 513–14

5.   Dunn, *Jesus, Paul and the Law: Studies in Mark and Galatians* (London: SPCK, 1990), p. 200.

Dunn the conflict concerning the works of the law has to be understood as an intra-Christian clash between 'Pauline' and 'Jewish' Christianity.

The 'New Perspective' which was developed by authors such as Sanders and Dunn in order to free the relationship between Paul and Judaism from the stereotypical, potentially anti-Jewish patterns was, however, put under critique from two very different sides. Some authors try to undo the 'New Perspective' completely at the risk of reintroducing the sharp opposition between Judaism and Christianity. Gundry, for instance, tries to undermine the shift which Sanders caused in Pauline research by claiming that it is irrelevant whether Judaism at Paul's time taught works righteousness or not. According to him the only thing that counts is that Paul understood (and rejected) the Judaism of his time as a religion which taught works righteousness.[6] At the other end of the spectrum, some authors come to the conclusion that even the shift brought about in the work of Sanders and of Dunn does ultimately not transcend the anti-Jewish character of the theology of Paul. According to them, the 'New Perspective' runs the risk of introducing new, potentially anti-Jewish patterns into the relationship between Judaism and Christianity. They accuse Sanders of replacing works righteousness by an exclusive christomonism and Dunn of replacing works righteousness by national exclusivism. The 'New Perspective' is critiqued for presenting Judaism as a religion which lacks the Spirit and which is unfaithful to its divine mission for the nations. Mark Nanos points out that the supposed intra-Christian character of the conflict is in no way able to dispel its anti-Jewishness: the same things for which Paul reproaches Jewish Christians ultimately also concern Judaism itself.[7]

In our analysis the fundamental problem in this discussion is the question of continuity and discontinuity between Judaism and Christianity and its assumed implications for Jewish-Christian dialogue. We note that it is commonly assumed that continuity is automatically favourable for the dialogue and discontinuity is automatically an obstacle for dialogue. While the traditional approach to Pauline studies emphasized strong discontinuity and had potentially anti-Jewish implications, the 'New Perspective' was commonly perceived as the rediscovery of continuity between (Palestinian) Judaism and (early) Christianity. The 'New Perspective' is usually seen as a constructive contribution to Jewish-Christian relations by those who experience the post-Shoah rapprochement of Jews and Christians as something positive. It was, however, criticized and rejected by those who see the rapprochement only as a threat to the Christian (and particularly Protestant) identity.

Next to the discussion on the continuity or discontinuity between Judaism and Christianity in the thought of Paul, a second central dimension of the relationship between Jewish and Christian identity in Paul's work concerns Paul's understanding of salvation as exclusive, inclusive or pluralist. This

---

6.   Robert H. Gundry, *The Old is Better: New Testament Essays in Support of Traditional Interpretations*, WUNT 178 (Tübingen: Mohr Siebeck, 2005), pp. 195–224, here 223.

7.   See Mark D. Nanos, *The Mystery of Romans: The Jewish Context of Paul's Letter* (Minneapolis: Fortress Press, 1996).

discussion is closely linked with the theological debate between the one and two covenant theories. Some authors will argue that there is only one covenant and that Christianity is an extension of the original Jewish covenant. Jews and Christians are included in the same covenant. However, authors differ as to how this inclusion is realized, sometimes understanding the original covenant as the true covenant, and the inclusion of Christians as the tail end of Judaism; sometimes, Judaism as the precursor and prefiguration of the (true) Christian covenant; sometimes, Judaism and Christianity as two modalities of the same covenant both being of equal value (inclusivism). Other authors will argue for two different covenants. Sometimes authors will argue for two successive, even mutually exclusive covenants (exclusivism); others will argue for two parallel covenants, both being of equal value and enduring legitimacy (pluralism).

Within this matrix of continuity and discontinuity on the one hand (the historical dimension) and exclusivism, inclusivism and pluralism on the other (the soteriological dimension), various positions are possible. We have grouped the various contributors in this volume according to where we think their work is positioned on this historical-soteriological axis. After categorizing the different approaches, albeit in summary fashion, we will then primarily focus on presenting our own position on the matter.

1.1. *Historical continuity with Judaism and soteriological inclusivism*

Paul was in historical continuity with Judaism and advocated soteriological inclusivism. This position covers those who argue that Paul's gospel was compatible with the common Judaism of the Second Temple period and that Paul did not set out to start a new religion called Christianity. Rather, Paul was reforming and extending the Mosaic covenant in new ways based on the new revelation made known to him through Christ. Further, this position usually includes those who hold that Paul was soteriologically inclusive of non-Christian Jews, seeing an eventual acceptance of Christ by ethnic Israel at some point in the future.

Such a stance obviously questions E. P. Sanders' emphasis on Paul's discontinuity and his related claim that Paul transcended covenantal categories altogether through his wider stress on the 'new creation'. In this volume, Thomas Blanton, in his study 'Paul's Covenantal Theology in 2 Cor. 2.14–7.4', could be located within this approach. He contends that it is a false dichotomy to play off the particularity of the covenant against the universality of new creation, as if Paul replaced one with the other. He maintains that the covenantal nomism of Second Temple Judaism already contained the seeds for universalism within itself as standard practice.[8] Was not the God of ethnic Israel also the maker of heaven and earth and did not the prophets proclaim that all nations would eventually look to this God for their own well-being and salvation along with Israel? Paul's use of universalistic language, such

---

8.   Thomas Blanton, 'Paul's Covenantal Theology', pp. 61–71.

as 'new creation' or cosmic reconciliation did not then transcend covenantal categories. On the contrary, Paul's discourse in 2 Cor. 2.14–7.4 was a type of covenantal nomism itself that continued the prophetic hope for covenantal renewal.[9] His gospel included the basic elements of covenant, obedience, reconciliation and judgement in a similar way to Sanders' covenantal nomism. In light of this, 'Paul's theology in 2 Cor. 2–7 is to be classified as a subset within the broader category, Judaism.' From this perspective, Paul was in historical continuity with Judaism and his own theologizing was broadly inclusivistic.

In a similar way to Blanton, W. S. Campbell, in his study 'Covenantal Theology and Participation in Christ: Pauline Perspectives on Transformation', seeks to emphasize aspects of 'commonality and continuity in Paul's understanding of covenant rather than those of opposition and discontinuity'.[10] He understands Paul to regularly engage in comparative theology, comparing covenantal nomism (Second Temple Judaism) with what he now had in the gospel of Christ. In this regard Paul quite frequently employed *qal wahomer* arguments, meaning that he argued from the lesser (e.g., the ministry of death in 2 Cor. 3.7) to the greater (e.g., ministry of the Spirit in 2 Cor. 3.7). Contrary to common scholarly opinion, Paul was not thereby denigrating Judaism per se; he was rather upholding the value of Judaism in its covenantal nomistic form but pointing to something even greater that had arisen out of it.

At the same time, Campbell notes that though Paul operated out of a covenantal context, he did not construct a separate covenant for the gentiles or call them 'Israel' as James Dunn has argued.[11] Paul allowed gentiles to share in the promises of Israel through Christ, but he did not allow them to enter into Israel's covenant itself. The inclusion of the gentiles was primarily a christological issue (based on their belief in Jesus as Messiah) and not a covenantal one. What is often overlooked is that by acting in this way, Paul was actually protecting and preserving Jewish identity as a good thing. Rather than demolishing or abolishing it, Paul was actually valuing it highly enough to preserve it. That is, he sought to keep Jewish believers as Jews and gentile believers as gentiles within the one, shared church community.[12]

So Paul's comparisons with Judaism implied an underlying continuity with Judaism. Seemingly discontinuous statements made by him were not statements of ultimate value but of comparative value only. Sanders was wrong to say that Paul had transcended covenantal categories altogether. Paul still operated out of them, though he reserved covenant membership proper for the Jews alone. Gentile believers were 'in Christ' rather than 'in the covenant'.

---

9.   Ibid.

10.   W. S. Campbell, 'Covenantal Theology and Participation in Christ: Pauline Perspectives on Transformation', p. 41.

11.   Dunn's comment, 'A Christianity which does not understand itself in some proper sense as "Israel" forfeits its claim to the scriptures of Israel', *The Theology of Paul the Apostle*, p. 508, cf. also pp. 509–13. Cited in Campbell, p. 12.

12.   See the similarity here with Paula Fredriksen's 'Judaizing the Nations: The Ritual Demands of Paul's Gospel', *NTS* 56 (2010): 232–52.

1.2. Historical continuity with Judaism in terms of Torah observance and soteriological inclusivism

Paul was in historical continuity with Judaism in terms of Torah observance and advocated a soteriological inclusivism. This position is similar to the one above, but goes deeper in that it stresses the historical continuity in terms of Paul actually keeping the Torah after coming to believe in Jesus as the Christ. This is reflected in the study by Mark Nanos, entitled 'Paul's Relationship to Torah in Light of his Strategy "to Become Everything to Everyone" (1 Corinthians 9.19-23)'. In this study Nanos takes Paul's ongoing Torah observance for granted (as a matter of covenant fidelity) and contends that his letters reflect an intra-Jewish debate about the correct interpretation of Torah and the role of those gentiles who were associating with the Jewish community. From that perspective Nanos highlights Paul's rhetorical adaptability in 1 Cor. 9.19-23 to argue from the point of view of different interlocutors in order to persuade them to come to his Torah-respecting conclusions. Paul argued according to whatever context he found himself in, for example from the standpoint of those outside the law, or from the viewpoint of those who are under the law in order to highlight his own position of being in Christ. By being in Christ one is able to 'fulfil the law', rather than be 'without it' or 'under it'. Paul attempted to sustain this position as the only truly valid one for both Jew and gentile alike. Paul was thus setting out to sanctify both the nations and the Jews who came across his path by helping them all attain the goal of the Torah, that is, righteous living. Such a reading kept Paul firmly within Judaism, even though Paul hoped that all would adopt his christocentric form of Judaism.

1.3. Historical discontinuity within a greater continuity and soteriological inclusivism

Paul had elements of historical discontinuity, but always within a greater continuity vis-à-vis Judaism. Once more the apostle advocated soteriological inclusivism. Hans Hermann Henrix, in his study entitled 'Paul at the Intersection between Continuity and Discontinuity: On Paul's Place in Early Judaism and Christianity as well as in Christian-Jewish Dialogue Today', presents such a position of discontinuity within continuity. The discontinuity is to be found in Paul's quite radical and new understanding of the Torah as now being communicated through Christ and as being embodied by him. Embracing this new insight Paul then went to the nations as a Jewish apostle to testify to this message. However, despite the seeming disjuncture with his own religious heritage, this model underlines the fact that Paul was actually 'called' to a christocentric form of Judaism rather than 'converted' to a new religion called Christianity. In a way similar to Nanos, Henrix is also open to seeing Paul and other Jewish Christians continue to live in a 'loving correspondence with the Torah'[13] and considers that it is misguided to imagine Paul as bringing a Law-free gospel. On the contrary, this approach maintains that such a re-evaluation of the relationship between Christ and the Torah is a very important development and one that will help overcome the negative historical view of Paulinism vis-à-vis Judaism and the Jewish people.

In a similar vein Michael Bachmann also champions a discontinuity within continuity model. In his study on 'Paul, Israel and the Gentiles: Hermeneutical and Exegetical Notes', he presents Paul as seeking to overcome the boundary markers that separated Jews from gentiles and thus to relativize the importance of the Law. However, Bachmann is keen to point out that Paul was generally positive in his comments on the Law though he was aware of how sin abused it to increase human desire for what was prohibited. Paul's problem was ultimately not the Law but rather the shortcomings of human nature that could not perform adequately under a nomistic framework. For Paul the Christ-event revealed this powerlessness and offered a spiritual transformation in a way that the Law could not. The Christ-event therefore continued at a higher level what the Law was attempting to achieve.

As a corollary this approach does not see Paul as replacing Israel with the church but as complementing Israel by the church. In Bachmann's analysis Paul retained the nomenclature 'Israel' exclusively for the Jews. Gentiles joined the 'church (of God)' but not Israel. The Pauline church could not therefore be interpreted as an anti-Judaic reality because it arose in Judaism and emerged out of Judaism. It was something like the universalization of the Jewish people. More explicitly than several of the other models presented above, this approach also touches on the soteriological question of the status of non-Christ-believing Jews. Yet in tandem with what we can assume from the trajectories of those previous approaches, this stance likewise argues that for Paul the 'salvation of all Israel' did not mean a salvation without Christ. Paul expected Israel to acknowledge Christ at the *parousia*. Nonetheless, in Bachmann's view, Paul was not responsible for disinheriting Judaism by claiming this. The church and Israel were two elect groups which would ultimately be reunited eschatologically.

1.4. *Historical continuity and discontinuity: inclusivism*

Paul had elements of historical continuity with Judaism but only within a greater discontinuity. The church today should realize that the Jews are already in a related saving relationship with God. Approaches in this vein have attempted to address the hermeneutical question regarding the gap between Paul and the contemporary church and have sought ways to understand Paul

---

13. Hans Hermann Henrix, 'Paul at the Intersection between Continuity and Discontinuity', p. 205, here citing from Michael Bachmann's contribution, 'Paul, Israel and the Gentiles', p. 97.

for the twenty-first century. Philip Cunningham, in his contribution 'Paul's Letters and the Relationship between the People of Israel and the Church Today', has put forward a dialectical hermeneutic that seeks to do just that. This is understood as a hermeneutic that highlights the relation between textual explanation (with a focus on the past) and textual meaning for the contemporary reader (with a focus on the present). Textual explanation includes the historical-critical and literary-critical readings which ground all legitimate interpretations. Textual meaning on the other hand includes the engagement of the reader with the text, producing the meaning of the text for today.

On the historical-critical and literary-critical levels, Paul can be shown to hold together various (paradoxical) statements. He simultaneously held to (1) the irrevocable election of all the People of Israel and the inevitable fulfilment of God's promises to them; (2) Israel's current failure to perceive these promises as being fulfilled in Christ; (3) the significance of Christ for all humanity; and (4) Christ's imminent *parousia* and the dawning of the New Creation.

On the level of textual meaning, various discrepancies between Paul's perspective and today's (Western) Christian reader come to the fore. The contemporary reader usually does not share Paul's end-times expectations. Christians also have a radically different 'effective history' vis-à-vis Judaism than in Paul's day. They now often have to learn from Jews about Judaism and Christianity's own Jewish roots. Further, in difference to Paul, the Christian religion is for all purposes a gentile Church. Any Jewish Christians that there still are usually assimilate into the gentile environment and are in any case considered non-Jews by their former co-religionists.

In dialectically contemporizing Paul through bringing these two perspectives into dialogue, Cunningham comes up with a series of guidelines, or pointers for a twenty-first-century post-Shoah Christian response and relationship to Judaism. These include the affirmation that God intends for both Judaism and Christianity to have complementary, if different, roles in the world. Their covenantal life is to be lived out in two distinct but related modalities. As a result of this, the church should no longer seek to baptize Jews, even if Paul was open to do this in his day.

1.5. *Historical continuity and discontinuity: inclusivism with pluralistic tendencies*

Paul had both historical continuity and discontinuity vis-à-vis Judaism. He was an inclusivist with pluralistic tendencies. John T. Pawlikowski takes this position in a study entitled 'A Christian-Jewish Dialogical Model in Light of New Research on Paul's Relationship with Judaism', related to Cunningham's approach. This position notes that thanks to the New Perspective we now have a Paul who is 'still very much a Jew, still quite appreciative of Jewish Torah with seemingly no objection to its continued practice by Jewish Christians so long as their basic orientation is founded in Christ'.[14] This model holds Christ and Torah together in an unresolved tension, though Christ takes the role of *primus inter pares*. Yet by continuing to uphold Torah, Paul was both a faithful Jew as well as the de facto 'founder' of 'Christianity' since the gentile form of his movement eventually became the norm for the whole church. Any critique Paul had on the Law was not against the Law itself but against any fellow Jewish or gentile believers who were extreme Judaizers, that is, who put Torah above and before Christ.

Pawlikowski also addresses the soteriological issues regarding non-baptized Jews and argues that Paul was not a pluralist, that is, he did not hold that Judaism and Christianity were two different ways to salvation. Yet nor was he an exclusivist who said that all peoples, including the Jews, had to confess Christ now in order to be saved. Paul in fact was an inclusivist, that is, he saw Israel and the church as ultimately enjoying the same salvation through Christ without showing how this would really come about. However, by Paul's holding onto Israel's eventual redemption even though Israel did not regard Jesus as the Messiah, Pawlikowski thinks it is best to see Paul as an inclusivist with pluralistic tendencies. From that point of view it is better to talk of 'distinctive but not distinct' paths to salvation for both Jews and Christians as 'the best current linguistic option'.[15]

1.6. *Historical continuity within a greater discontinuity and soteriological pluralism*

Another possible position is that represented by Hans-Joachim Sander in his chapter, 'Sharing God with Others or Dividing God from Powerlessness: a Late-Modern Challenge by the Heterotopian Experience of the New Paul'. This approach champions the New Perspective on Paul from a unique angle. It sees Paul as one who challenges religio-cultural binary oppositions that divide people. Paul sought to overcome the binary presupposition that separated Jew and gentile and he did this not by force but by presenting Christ's powerlessness. Contrary to the Lutheran reading of Paul that stressed the role and power of the individual, this new approach relativizes the power of the individual by highlighting that the fate of the individual depends on others. For example, Paul came to the insight that justification could only truly come about when both Jews and gentiles saw themselves as equal citizens in God's kingdom. Such a mutual justification does away with the binary code between 'us and them'.

This model also picks up on the turn to Paul within philosophy by writers such as Badiou, Agamben and Žižek, who explore the

---

14.　John T. Pawlikowski, 'A Christian-Jewish Dialogical Model', p. 168.
15.　Ibid., p. 171.

meaning of Paul in a post-modern context. Here Žižek's stress on the powerless of Paul's gospel and the challenge this presents to institutions and civilizations that base themselves on seeking power in perpetuity is especially highlighted. For Sander, Paul dangerously deconstructed the binary codes of inclusion and exclusion on which power is usually built by means of his message of the cross. This is what he calls Paul's heterotopian perspective that goes beyond the utopias of artificial binary constructs, whether theological, political, cultural, and so on: 'By the new perspective and by the new philosophy on Paul, Paul's canonical letters are turned into a heterotopos.'[16]

In terms of soteriology, this understanding of the apostle's message translates into the full acceptance of Jewish otherness, foregoing the need to have any Christian mission to the Jews. Mission, he argues, is based on a binary view of justification, that God can only save through a certain group's own salvific means. Overcoming that binary code of the 'saved' and the 'unsaved' lets God be God once more and lets him justify anyone and everyone in his own way.

1.7. *Sharp historical discontinuity and soteriological exclusivism*

A last position is that modelled by Michael F. Bird in his contribution 'Salvation in Paul's Judaism?'. Here he seeks to compare how Paul described salvation in Judaism with salvation in Christ. He argues that while Paul is a Jew, he is an 'in-Christ' Jew whose reconfiguration of eschatology, identity transformation and christology could no longer be accommodated within common Second Temple Judaism. Bird actually thinks that the new group of Jesus believers could be conceived of as a third race.

As regards the Law, this position holds that since it has fulfilled its goal in the life of Christ, its operation is terminated. Salvation has moved on from the Mosaic covenantal framework to faith in Christ directly. This means that Paul was largely behind the parting of the ways between Judaism and Christianity, though what he was advocating was a surpassing of Judaism rather than setting it aside altogether.

So while Bird is in favour of advocating Paul's discontinuity with Judaism, it is a qualified discontinuity because Paul sees faith in Christ as an extension of Judaism's own scriptural heritage. On the other hand, since Paul sees Christ as the goal of Judaism, Bird is content to say that for the apostle 'salvation is of Judaism only in so far as Judaism is of Jesus Christ'.[17]

---

16.   Hans-Joachim Sander, 'Sharing God with Others', p. 191.
17.   Michael F. Bird, 'Salvation in Paul's Judaism?', p. 40.

2. *The Future Perspective as a New Norm for Pauline Theology*

The above overview of the positions offered in this book highlights that several scholars primarily focus on the historical question of continuity/discontinuity regarding Paul's relationship with Judaism (i.e., Blanton, Campbell, Henrix and Nanos). On the other hand, several scholars also focus on the soteriological question and the issue of whether Jews need to be baptized in order to be saved (e.g., Bachmann, Bird, Cunningham, Pawlikowski and Sander). Our above analysis has shown how the two axes of historical continuity/discontinuity on the one hand and soteriological exclusivism, inclusivism and pluralism on the other come into play.

In our own analysis of the above positions we note that there are several premises at work, often interlocking and more often than not taken for granted. These are as follows.

Premise one: historical continuity is necessary between Paul and Judaism in order to justify (save) Paul in a post-Shoah context. Premise two: historical discontinuity between Paul and Judaism is bad for dialogue in a post-Shoah context. Premise three: soteriological inclusivism, and to a lesser degree exclusivism, are espoused to guarantee the christological finality of salvation history. That is, both maintain that Christ is necessary for the fullness of salvation to be achieved and enjoyed. Premise four: soteriological pluralism is generally considered theologically less attractive because it does not do full justice to either Jewish or Christian particularism.

In light of these premises, it is perhaps not surprising that we end up with the largest group of scholars covered above having a bias towards historical continuity and soteriological inclusivism. When these axes are crossed we have a picture of Paul as a Jew operating from within common Jewish theological loci and presenting a gospel that is complementary with rather than antithetical to Judaism. In this scheme of things, the Jews will still eventually need to acknowledge Christ as saviour, since the *eschaton* is the dénouement of the whole salvation historical enterprise. Only a few of the authors question that consensus. Cunningham, for example, cautions against assuming that the eschaton will be homogeneous and opens the door to eschatological pluralism. In a similar vein, Pawlikowski warns against assuming that Jews will have to acknowledge the coming messianic event in explicitly christological terms. Further afield, Sander contends for a de facto pluralism, limiting the meaning of Christ's universal significance to Christians alone, while Bird argues at the other end of the spectrum for a christological exclusivism that applies universally to Jews as to Christians.

This grouping of most scholars around historical continuity-cum-soteriological inclusivism actually reflects on the impact the New Perspective on Paul has had within Pauline studies over the last generation. As mentioned at the beginning of this chapter, the New Perspective is largely responsible for challenging and even overturning the classical Baurian inspired Old Perspective that explicitly positioned Paul against Judaism, based on the Lutheran rubric of Law versus Grace. Dunn has succeeded in replacing a clear discontinuity paradigm with a revitalized continuity one. In terms of soteriology, Dunn is also an advocate of soteriological inclusivism, to be made apparent in the eschatological era.[18] His influence on the axial positioning of our contributors is therefore significant.

In our opinion, however, several of these underlying premises can be questioned. Historical continuity is not necessary in itself to justify Paul after the Holocaust. It remains a pertinent question in its own right based of course on critical historical reconstructions. We ourselves are persuaded that the move towards seeing Paul as continuing within a Jewish theological context is to be welcomed as a historically credible reading of the apostle (here broadly in agreement with the New Perspective). We are further persuaded that Paul continued to operate out of given Jewish theological premises concerning, for example, God, the covenants, the election of Israel and so on, but that is not the same thing as saying that he remained within Judaism itself.

In our opinion, the focus of Paul's gospel was ultimately the embrace of all in the new creation, which if it does not abrogate covenantal categories, certainly transcends them in its goal. While Paul does mention the new covenant in Christ (1 Cor. 11.23-26; 2 Cor. 3.6), he takes it as a starting place rather than an end in itself. For Paul, the new covenant leads to new creation (2 Cor. 3.6; 5.17). The former is indispensable for the latter, but the latter remains the ultimate goal. By new creation (Gal. 6.15; 2 Cor. 5.17) we mean Paul's understanding of God's dream to establish justice, well-being and life for all, the earth included (Rom. 8.19-21; 1 Cor. 15.28). Such a horizon, or rather the joining of the two horizons of heaven and earth, cannot easily be contained within a covenantal framework since covenants are normally particular expressions of the divine–human relationship and can only with difficulty capture the universal outworking of what they themselves represent. The new covenant, for example, points towards the eventual justice of God on the earth, which remains an eschatological dream, and to a large extent the sign of an unrealized signified. But it is that very dream that is at the heart of Paul's message, rather than the re-establishment of a covenantal framework. So while there is undoubted historical and theological continuity between Paul and Judaism, it is our understanding that such continuities take place within a more fundamental discontinuity, since what is signified in Paul's new covenant in Christ points to a transformative future that for Paul was already dawning and which was all-embracing.

Paul's vision was ultimately not christocentric nor even pneumatocentric but theocentric. His furthest horizon was God becoming 'all in all' (1 Cor. 15.28), a view that surpassed Jewish distinctives and particularities, as well as Christian ones. The reality of the new creation was all-absorbing for Paul (though he was admittedly inconsistent in how he lived out its ideal) and in our opinion it still presents challenges for any type of covenantal language to mediate it.

18.   Dunn, *The Theology of Paul the Apostle*, p. 508; idem, 'Two Covenants or One? The Interdependence of Jewish and Christian Identity', in eds Hubert Cancik, Hermann Lichtenberger and Peter Schäfer, FS M. Hengel, *Geschichte-Tradition-Reflexion* (Tübingen: Mohr Siebeck, 1996), pp. 97–122, here 117.

Further, we are persuaded hermeneutically that we do not need to stay encamped at the last place Paul visited in his own developing understanding of the relationship between 'Judaism' and 'Christianity' or the church and the synagogue. While it is clear that Paul held elements of both exclusivism and inclusivism together without working out the systematic relationship between them, we, two millennia later, can certainly re-evaluate that relationship according to our own vision for the now in light of how we understand the future. Without a doubt there has been much that could be considered tragic in the *Wirkungsgeschichte* and *Auslegungsgeschichte* of both Pauline and New Testament texts in general vis-à-vis the Jewish people. We realize that the mediation of all revelation comes through soiled hands and that ours today are no different. We cannot divorce ourselves from our previous tradition, nor stand in judgement over it from some Archimedian point. We are rather an extension of our ongoing tradition in its totality and, in dialogue with it, we take up responsibility for how we continue its witness in our generation and beyond.

This is where a closer analysis of the hermeneutical approach known as Normativity of the Future may come in useful.[19] In this perspective the stress is laid upon the 'dialogical dimensions of the theology of revelation' as expressed, for example, in the Dogmatic Constitution on Divine Revelation of the Second Vatican Council *Dei Verbum* 2.[20] This dialogical aspect puts an emphasis on the contemporary reading community and their ability, through engaging with the Spirit who transcends the text, to go beyond the limitations of the biblical text and 'write their own fifth gospel'.[21] This future-orientated hermeneutic 'look[s] at texts from the perspective of their future and ... [sees] the locus of revelation in that future'.[22] The future unfolded by the texts is an alternative world. The criteria for discerning which elements of that alternative projection could be used as building blocks for better representing God's ultimate dream for humanity is expressed as 'those things which allow for or even create a future for all humanity without exception', that is, 'a vision of a just and inclusive community'.[23]

---

19. Reimund Bieringer and Mary Elsbernd, 'Introduction: The "Normativity of the Future" Approach: Its Roots, Development, Current State and Challenges', in idem, eds, *Normativity of the Future: Reading Biblical and Other Authorative Texts in an Eschatological Perspective* (Leuven: Peeters, 2010), pp. 3–25.

20. Ibid., p. 4. See further, *The Dogmatic Constitution on Divine Revelation* (*Dei Verbum*, 18 November 1965), no. 2, which includes the words: 'Through this revelation, therefore, the invisible God (see Col. 1.15; 1 Tim. 1.17) out of the abundance of His love speaks to men as friends (see Ex. 33.11; John 15.14-15) and lives among them (see Bar. 3.38), so that He may invite and take them into fellowship with Himself.' Available online at http://www.vatican.va/archive/hist_councils/ii_vatican_council/documents/vat-ii_const_19651118_dei-verbum_en.html (accessed 26 October 2010).

21. Reimund Bieringer, 'Biblical Revelation and Exegetical Interpretation According to *Dei Verbum* 12', in eds M. Lamberigts and L. Kenis, *Vatican II and Its Legacy*, BETL 166 (Leuven: Leuven University Press; Dudley, MA: Peeters, 2002), pp. 25–58 (52).

22. Bieringer and Elsbernd, 'Introduction: The "Normativity of the Future"', p. 5.

23. Ibid., p. 7.

While being aware that the future per se is not necessarily superior to the present or the past, and that ideological distortion may still be present in one's understanding of a biblically inspired future, the position is taken that the future vision contained in the texts could certainly make ethical and theological claims on the present.[24] In that sense, the texts are not to be taken as simple scripts to be slavishly followed, nor are they even to be endlessly reinterpreted in a search for their permanent core principles. Rather they have a 'paradigmatic value' which means that 'the reading community has the task of reading and internalizing the ancient text as the first chapters of a chain novel of which they have to write the next chapter'.[25]

The reading community is encouraged to write that new chapter in light of what they discerned as the Normativity of the Future, since its association with God's vision for humanity entails a certain hermeneutical privilege over the present and the past. Moreover, the future's inclusive justice as the horizon of the biblical texts and of the texts of Paul in particular ('God become all in all' in 1 Cor. 15.28) is to take precedence over any conflict of values encountered in the historical or literary dimensions of the text.[26] In other words, marginalizing, discriminating, or of course in our case, supersessionary elements in the biblical story and in Paul's letters in particular, could be openly challenged in the name of what that story ultimately pointed towards – the inclusive and life-giving reign of God. Here the text certainly takes a privileged place vis-à-vis the author, but for their part the reading community is not just asked to re-engage with the text in a new way, rather it is asked to write a new text, in line with what the biblical text had taught the community about God's dream. In that sense the Bible is not to be treated as a closed canon but as an open narrative to which each generation has its own contributions to make. All authors, of course, whether past or present, have to take responsibility for the consequences of their writings including any effects it may have (or had had) on others. 'Scholarship is a political act.'[27]

In our understanding, from a Normativity of the Future approach we are encouraged by our vision of the future to position ourselves on the borderlands of inclusivism-pluralism, certainly as it concerns the Jewish-Christian relationship. God is in a permanent relationship with the Jewish people. That guarantees their salvation. Where Paul lost sight of that in his writings, the contemporary church community needs to enter into constructive dialogue with him in light of his own future vision. We can also agree with those who, like Sanders, critique the all too common power plays attendant to soteriological debates. Christ does not need to save everybody directly in order for him to remain as the Christ. God has many ways to express his commitment and love to creation. Regaining a theocentric vision, the real *telos* of Paul's new creation, is actually continuing the Pauline project and exploring further the avenues he all too vaguely mapped out.

24.   Ibid., pp. 6–9.
25.   Ibid., p. 10.
26.   Ibid., p. 12.
27.   Ibid., p. 16.

Chapter 1

SALVATION IN PAUL'S JUDAISM?

Michael F. Bird

1. Introduction

The title of this study is deliberately ambiguous. Obviously there is the initial puzzle of what 'salvation' meant to Jews, Christians, Greeks and Romans. Apart from that there is the more perplexing issue of the referent in the phrase 'Paul's Judaism'. Does that mean (a) the Judaism known to Paul, or (b) the Judaism expressed in Paul's own *Christian* beliefs?[1] And therein the questions begin on either option: is Paul a reliable witness to the Judaism of his time and are Paul's theological and religious beliefs to be situated within Judaism or external to it? I am interested in both of these questions. First, I am concerned in this study with how Paul described salvation in Judaism. Second, I am concerned with how that description is both continuous and discontinuous with Paul's articulation of salvation in his Christ-believing faith. As we will see, the rhetoric and reality of Paul's description of salvation in Judaism is much debated (especially by Jewish interpreters of Paul)[2] and the degree to which Paul and his communities are enmeshed in the matrix of 'common Judaism' is likewise varyingly understood. In light of that, it is the task of this study to explore the relationship between Paul and Judaism in relation to salvation. That requires pursuing how to situate Paul in relation to the Judaism of his own time and identifying how Paul's story of salvation in Jesus Christ relates to his narration of the story of Israel. The way in which I will proceed is by: (1) briefly surveying key nodes in scholarship about Paul's relationship to Judaism, and (2) discussing the socio-religious position of Paul and his gentile Christ-believing communities in relation to Judaism.

2. Paul and Judaism in Scholarship

There have been various proposals as to what kind of Judaism Paul knew and how well he knew it. In each case there is a different understanding of

1. I owe this to Mark Nanos, 'Paul and Judaism: Why Not Paul's Judaism', in *Paul Unbound: Other Perspectives on Paul*, ed. Mark Given (Peabody, MA: Hendrickson, 2009).

what Paul thought of salvation in or from Judaism. What follows is a brief summary of the main respective views.[3]

2.1. Paul and Jewish legalism

A first perspective is that Paul, in his post-conversion period, rallied against Judaism which in the post-exilic period had degenerated into a form of legalism, merit-theology and synergism.[4] This led Günther Bornkamm to say that: 'Paul's opponent is not this or that section in a particular church, but the Jews and their understanding of salvation.'[5] While it is no doubt true that in some schemes performance of the Law could be emphasized as the basis of approval before God's throne or the condition of entering the future age (e.g., Wisd. 5.15; 6.18; *Pss. Sol.* 9.3-5; 1QS 3–4; *4 Ezra* 6.5; 7.77; 8.33, 36; *2 Bar.* 14.12; 51.7), we cannot escape the fact that other schemes can also emphasize grace, election and covenant as the efficacious force in salvation (e.g., 1QH 11.11-15; 1QH 15.18-20; *m.Sanh.* 10.1). Philo also attests to debates among Alexandrian Jews about the degree to which God's blessings are earned or freely bestowed (*Sac.* 54-57 (= Deut. 9.5)). By no stretch of the imagination can *all* Judaism be lumped into the one soteriological pattern regardless of whether some label that pattern 'legalism' or 'synergism'. Paul's critique of works, Law and works of Law (for whatever reason) is certainly critiquing perceived abuses or failures with the Jewish religion in his opinion, but he is still doing so using the framework, tradition and grammar of the Jewish religion itself. As long as Jewish teachers remained in dialogue within their own sacred literature and traditions, they cannot have removed grace and covenant from their thinking. Even Paul's opponents in Galatia would claim that their soteriological pattern was one of grace (Gal. 2.21). The issue was the nature and mechanism of divine grace for Paul (not the fact of divine

2.   Michael F. Bird and Preston M. Sprinkle, 'Jewish Interpretation of Paul in the Last Thirty Years', *CBR* 6 (2008): 355–76.

3.   Cf. other surveys in Douglas A. Campbell, *The Quest for Paul's Gospel: A Suggested Strategy* (London: T&T Clark, 2005), pp. 139–40; Frank Thielman, *From Plight to Solution: A Jewish Framework for Understanding Paul's View of the Law in Galatians and Romans* (Leiden: Brill, 1989), pp. 1–27; W. S. Campbell, 'Perceptions of Compatibility Between Christianity and Judaism in Pauline Interpretation', *BI* 13 (2005): 298–316.

4.   F. Weber, *System der altsynagogalen palästinischen Theologie aus Targum, Midrasch und Talmud* (Leipzig: Dörffling & Franke, 1880); Rudolf Bultmann, *Primitive Christianity in its Contemporary Setting* (trans. R. H. Fuller; London: Thames and Hudson, 1956 (1949)), ch. 2; Stephen Westerholm, *Perspectives Old and New on Paul: The 'Lutheran' Paul and His Critics* (Grand Rapids, MI: Eerdmans, 2004), pp. 332–5; see discussion of 'legalism' and 'synergism' with references in Michael F. Bird, *The Saving Righteousness of God: Studies on Paul, Justification, and the New Perspective* (Carlise, UK: Paternoster, 2007), pp. 89–90.

5.   Günther Bornkamm, *Paul* (trans. D. M. G. Stalker; New York: Harper & Row, 1971), p. 95.

grace) in light of a particular eschatological and messianic configuration in his own telling of the story of salvation. What is more, there is no term in antiquity that is translatable as 'legalism' so its imposition upon ancient Jewish and Christian texts is somewhat anachronistic. Even if one prefers the more fashionable term 'synergism', that still raises the question as to what it means and how is it that Paul's own soteriological scheme,[6] which has its own articulation of divine sovereignty and human responsibility, avoids becoming equally synergistic in some sense.[7]

2.2. Paul and diaspora Judaism

In another depiction, Paul did not experience true Judaism; rather, he knew only its Hellenistic counterpart which was impoverished when compared to the Talmudic Judaism of Palestine.[8] The obvious problem here is that it assumes that diaspora Judaism was lax whereas there is a great amount of proof that Jews outside of Palestine were no less loyal to the pillars of Judaism than their Palestinian counterparts, even if they lived away from the land and far from the temple, even if they faced a different array of external pressures, and even if they expressed their piety in a different cultural idiom.[9] It also assumes an unhelpful dichotomy between Hellenism and Judaism whereas it is now axiomatic that all Judaism of the first centuries BCE and CE was permeated by Hellenism in some form.[10] The notion of a liberal and Hellenized Judaism, as opposed to that of Palestine, which was a foil for Paul's argumentation, is a scholarly myth.

---

6. Against the designation of 'synergism' is James D. G. Dunn, *The New Perspective on Paul* (Grand Rapids, MI: Eerdmans, 2008), pp. 77–89; Kent L. Yinger, 'Reformation *Redivivus*: Synergism and the New Perspective', *JTI* 3 (2009): 89–106.

7. Cf. Mikael Winninge, *Sinners and the Righteous: A Comparative Study of the Psalms of Solomon and Paul's Letters* (Stockholm: Almqvist & Wiksell, 1995), p. 334; Kari Kuula, *The Law, the Covenant and God's Plan: Paul's Treatment of the Law and Israel in Romans* (FES 85; Göttingen: Vandenhoeck & Ruprecht, 2002), p. 5; Douglas Harink, *Paul among the Postliberals: Pauline Theology Beyond Christendom and Modernity* (Grand Rapids, MI: Brazos, 2003), pp. 32–8; Chris Vanlandingham, *Judgment and Justification in Early Judaism and the Apostle Paul* (Peabody, MA: Hendrickson, 2005). But see objections of Peter T. O'Brien, 'Was Paul a Covenantal Nomist?', in *Justification and Variegated Nomism: Volume 2 – The Paradoxes of Paul*, eds D. A. Carson, Peter T. O'Brien and Mark Seifrid (Grand Rapids, MI: Baker, 2004), p. 265.

8. Samuel Sandmel, *Judaism and Christian Beginnings* (Oxford: OUP, 1978); idem, *The Genius of Paul* (Philadelphia: Fortress, 1979); C. G. Montefiore, *Judaism and St. Paul: Two Essays* (New York: Dutton, 1915); H. J. Schoeps, *Paul: The Theology of the Apostle in the Light of Jewish Religious History* (Philadelphia: Westminster, 1961).

9. The ubiquity of Jewish loyalty to their native customs throughout the inhabited world is stated frequently in Jewish and non-Jewish writings, e.g., Josephus, *Ant.* 17.26; 18.84; 19.290; Tacitus, *Hist.* 5.5.

2.3. *Paul's misrepresentation of Judaism*

On another account, Paul's view of Judaism was jaundiced and skewed as he was unfair in his description of it.[11] In favour of this view we can say: (1) there is undoubtedly an element of rhetoric and caricature of Paul's polemics against his Judeo-Christian opponents and his lament at the failure of Israel to embrace the Messiah; (2) he also reconfigures his biography to emphasize the inadequacies of his pre-conversion life in pharisaic Judaism; and (3) his theological critique of Torah is somewhat atypical in Judaism. However, the content of Paul's language is hardly anti-Judaistic per se, as the form and content of his language reflects typical intra-Jewish disputes. His conversion was, in its immediate setting, a transference from one Jewish sect to another even if he led his converts away from common Judaism in the end. Paul's remarks about the Torah oscillate between hostility and veneration depending on the argumentative context (e.g., from Galatians to Romans) and Paul still remains far from a Gnostic perspective on the Torah as intrinsically unjust. What is more, the New Testament generally and Paul specifically simply are among our best sources of knowledge for pre-70 CE Judaism.[12]

2.4. *Paul and covenantal nomism*

Probably the most influential proposal in studies on Paul and Judaism in the last 30 years has been E. P. Sanders' construal of Palestinian Judaism as 'covenantal nomism'.[13] This 'pattern of religion' is now well known and is expressed by the dictum 'grace to get in and works to stay in'. In Sanders' own words: '*obedience maintains one's position in the covenant, but it does*

---

10.   Martin Hengel, *Judaism and Hellenism* (2 vols; trans. John Bowden; London: SCM, 1974), 1.104; I. Howard Marshall, 'Palestinian and Hellenistic Christian: Some Critical Comments', *NTS* 19 (1973): 271–87; Troels Engberg-Pedersen (ed.), *Paul Beyond the Judaism/Hellenism Divide* (Louisville: Westminster John Knox, 2001); Anders Gerdmar, *Rethinking the Judaism-Hellenism Dichotomy: A Historiographical Case Study of Second Peter and Jude* (CBNTS 36; Stockholm: Almqvist & Wiksell, 2001).

11.   Joseph Klausner, *From Jesus to Paul* (Boston, MA: Beacon, 1939); Hyam Maccoby, *Paul and Hellenism* (London: SCM, 1991).

12.   Cf. Alan F. Segal, *Paul the Convert: The Apostasy of Saul the Pharisee* (New Haven, CT: Yale University Press, 1990), p. 48: 'Paul's text provide information about first-century Judaism and Jewish mysticism, as important as the Jewish texts that have been fond to establish the meaning of Christian texts. Indeed, Paul's letters may be more important to the history of Judaism than the rabbinic texts are to the interpretation of Christian Scriptures.'; idem, 'Conversion and Messianism: Outline for a New Approach', in *The Messiah: Developments in Earliest Judaism and Christianity*, ed. James H. Charlesworth (Minneapolis, MN: Fortress, 1992), p. 299): 'The New Testament is … much better evidence for the history of Judaism [in the first century] than is rabbinic Judaism for the origins of Christianity.'

13.   E. P. Sanders, *Paul and Palestinian Judaism: A Comparison of Patterns of Religion* (London: SCM, 1977), p. 422.

not earn God's grace as such. It simply keeps an individual in the group which is the recipient of God's grace ... obedience is universally held to be the behaviour appropriate to being in the covenant, not the means of earning God's grace.'[14] Paul's problem with the Torah was that it had simply been superseded by Christ, and Paul himself reasoned from Christ's Lordship to the human problem; that is, from solution (Christ) to plight (Law).[15] There has been an industry to critique Sanders' portrayal of Judaism and Paul and I include only a few points. (1) There are undoubtedly documents from antiquity that exemplify the pattern that Sanders proposes (e.g., *Testament of Moses, 1 Esdras*, Pseudo-Philo, Romans 2 and 1QH). Yet it is hard to compress all narrations of the basis and means of salvation in Judaism into a single religious descriptor because the emphasis could fall upon either the 'covenant' or the 'nomism' depending on the peculiar dynamics of a given writing.[16] While covenantal nomism is 'a very flexible pattern',[17] the efforts of some to suggest that it can still accommodate highly nomistic praxes is to make the concept so broad as to be meaningless.[18] (2) I would also maintain that the discussions of the *basis* for persons entering the future eschatological age, sectarian disagreements over whose interpretation of the Law counts, and debates over the rites of entry for outsiders within Jewish groups led to soteric patterns that placed an incredible amount of gravity on nomistic observances.[19] We are confronted then with varied and variegated degrees of nomism in first-century Judaism. (3) It is likewise a matter of contention as to whether or not what Paul found wrong with Judaism was merely its *heilsgeschichtlich* obsoleteness. It is equally contestable that Paul's own

14. Sanders, *Paul and Palestinian Judaism*, pp. 420–1.

15. Ibid., p. 552.

16. D. A. Carson, 'Summaries and Conclusions', in *Justification and Variegated Nomism: Volume 1 – The Complexities of Second Temple Judaism*, eds D. A. Carson, Peter T. O'Brien and Mark Seifrid (Grand Rapids, MI: Baker, 2001), pp. 543–8; Brendan Byrne, 'Interpreting Romans: The New Perspective and Beyond', *Int* 58 (2004): 248; Bird, *Saving Righteousness*, pp. 93–4; Francis Watson, *Paul, Judaism, and the Gentiles: Beyond the New Perspective* (rev. edn; Grand Rapids, MI: Eerdmans, 2007), pp. xvii, 12–15.

17. Richard Bauckham, 'Apocalypses', in *Justification and Variegated Nomism: Volume 1 – The Complexities of Second Temple Judaism*, eds D. A. Carson, Peter T. O'Brien and Mark Seifrid (Grand Rapids, MI: Baker, 2001), p. 174.

18. C. F. D. Moule, 'Jesus, Judaism, and Paul', in *Tradition and Interpretation in the New Testament*, eds G. F. Hawthorne and O. Betz (Grand Rapids, MI: Eerdmans, 1987), p. 48; Douglas J. Moo, *The Epistle to the Romans* (NICNT; Grand Rapids, MI: Eerdmans, 1996), pp. 215–16; Timo Eskola, *Theodicy and Predestination in Pauline Theology* (WUNT 2.100; Tübingen: Mohr/Siebeck, 1998), p. 56; Bird, *Saving Righteousness*, pp. 94–5. But see the objections of Bruce Longenecker ('On Critiquing the "New Perspective" on Paul: A Case Study', *ZNW* 96 (2005): 266–9) who understands 'staying-in' as a multi-temporal signifier that includes an eschatological component and believes that covenantal nomism comprises an element of eschatological nomism.

19. Cf. Michael F. Bird, 'What if Martin Luther Had Read the Dead Sea Scrolls? Historical Particularity and Theological Interpretation in Pauline Theology: Galatians as a Test Case', *JTI* 3 (2009): 107–25.

pattern of religion was, despite his participationist eschatology, essentially in agreement with covenantal nomism simply because Paul exhibits a stronger anthropological pessimism than his compatriots and has a more radical perspective on the operation of divine agency in salvation.[20]

2.5. *Paul and ethnocentric Judaism*

A further perspective is that Paul never changed the mode of salvation in Judaism, he never doubted the efficacy of Israel's election, nor did he criticize Israel for anything other than rejecting the notion that the good news had come to gentiles.[21] This perspective is typified by two aspects: postulating a Pauline *Sonderweg* for Israel and regarding Israel's misstep as denying God's salvation to the gentiles. Israel's failure, according to John Gager, is: '[I]t has nothing to do with accepting Christ as Israel's saviour. What Israel missed was understanding the goal of the Torah as it relates to the gentiles.'[22] In the specific case of Rom. 11.25-27 it is said, 'Es ist nicht die Rede von Israels Bekehrung, sonder vons Israels Rettung durch Gott.'[23] Although the *Sonderweg* perspective is appealing to post-modernists, pluralists and post-Holocaust interpreters, it is historically and theologically objectionable.[24]

---

20.   Sanders, *Paul and Palestinian Judaism*, pp. 514, 543, 552; cf. M. D. Hooker, *From Adam to Christ* (Cambridge: CUP, 1990), pp. 155–64; Peter T. O'Brien, 'Was Paul a Covenantal Nomist?', in *Justification and Variegated Nomism: Volume 2 – The Paradoxes of Paul*, eds D. A. Carson, Peter T. O'Brien and Mark Seifrid (Grand Rapids, MI: Baker, 2004), pp. 249–96.

21.   Cf. e.g., Klaus Haacker, 'Das Evangelium Gottes und die Erwählung Israels. Zum Beitrag des Römerbriefs zur Erneuerung des Verhältnisses zwischen Christen und Juden', *TBei* 13 (1982): 70–1; Lloyd Gaston, *Paul and the Torah* (Vancouver: University of British Columbia Press, 1987); John Gager, *Reinventing Paul* (Oxford: OUP, 2000); Stanley K. Stowers, *A Rereading of Romans: Justice, Jews, Gentiles* (New Haven, CT: Yale University Press, 1994); Eung Chun Park, *Either Jew or Gentile: Paul's Unfolding Theology of Inclusivity* (Louisville, KY: Westminster John Knox, 2003). See the particular construal of this position by Mark D. Nanos, *The Mystery of Romans: The Jewish Context of Paul's Letter* (Minneapolis, MN: Fortress, 1996); idem, 'The Jewish Context of the Gentile Audience Addressed in Paul's Letter to the Romans', *CBQ* 61 (1999): 283–304; idem, *The Irony of Galatians: Paul's Letter in First-Century Context* (Minneapolis, MN: Fortress, 2002); idem, 'How inter-Christian approaches to Paul's rhetoric can perpetuate negative valuations of Jewishness – Although proposing to avoid that outcome', *BI* 13 (2002): 255–69; idem, 'Paul between Jews and Christians', *BI* 13 (2005): 221–316.

22.   Gager, *Reinventing Paul*, p. 135.

23.   Bernhard Mayer, *Unter Gottes Heilsratschluss. Prädestinationsaussagen bei Paulus* (Würzburg: Echter, 1974), p. 290.

24.   Cf. Richard H. Bell (*Provoked to Jealousy: The Origin and Purpose of the Jealousy Motif in Romans 9–11* (WUNT 2.63; Tübingen: Mohr/Siebeck, 1994), pp. 354–5): 'Paul's theology *demands* a mission to the Jewish people. Provoking Israel to jealousy is no replacement for mission. It is just one possible precursor for mission. The gospel must be preached for it is only the gospel, God's reconciling word, which can make someone a Christian (Rom. 10.17) … I would maintain that evangelism to Jews is not antisemitism;

(1) In the logic of this view Jewish Christianity becomes a mistake, though perhaps a necessary one, to force the issue of gentile inclusion. (2) It does not make sense of Paul's statement about the gospel being for the Jew first (Rom. 1.16), or his assumption of a continuing mission to the Jewish people (Rom. 10.14-21; cf. 11.14; 1 Cor. 9.20; Gal. 2.9), nor why Paul celebrates the existence of a current remnant of Jewish believers in Jesus (Rom. 9.27-29; 11.1-10). (3) For Paul there is no διαστολή between Jew and gentile in either condemnation (Rom. 3.22-23) or justification (Rom. 10.12), as both therefore need faith in Jesus Christ.[25] Likewise, while Paul undoubtedly critiqued ethnocentric interpretations of the Torah as requiring gentiles to become Jewish proselytes in order to become Christ-believers (e.g., Gal. 2.11-15; Rom. 3.21-31) and he mentioned Jewish resistance to his gentile mission (1 Thess. 2.15), one cannot properly regard Jewish ethnocentrism as the sum total of Paul's critique of the place of the Torah in redemptive-history and his anguished concern over Israel's failure for several reasons. (a) Paul did not need the word of the cross to learn that God was the God of the gentiles too, since God's concern for the nations is attested from Genesis to Isaiah and in various other Jewish writings with various patterns and modes of univeralism emerging.[26] (b) To what extent is it valid to call ancient Judaism ethnocentric or exclusivist? Jews did indeed accept gentiles into their communities as proselytes (Philo, Josephus and the Rabbis speak glowingly of them).[27] In addition, is not Christianity just as exclusivistic as Judaism in some respects in forbidding intermarriage with pagans, censuring sexual immorality, expulsion of apostates, avoiding pagan religious associations, and displaying a sectarian social perspective that rejects the values of their surrounding cultural environment?[28] (c) Paul also deals with a more

---

rather to renounce preaching the liberating gospel to Jewish people is anti-Semitism.'; N. T. Wright ('Romans', *NIB*, ed. Leander E. Keck (12 vols; Nashville, TN: Abingdon, 2002), 10.697): 'to imagine that Jews can no longer be welcomed into the family of the Messiah ... [that] for Paul, would be the very height of anti-Judaism'.

25.   While interpreters of this 'new Paul' are trying to avoid supersessionism, in many ways, they imply a supersession of Jewish ethnocentrism and of Israel's role to be a light to the gentiles by Paul. Cf. Bruce Longenecker, 'On Israel's God and God's Israel: Assessing Supersessionism in Paul', *JTS* 58 (2007): 26–44.

26.   Cf. Terence Donaldson, *Judaism and the Gentiles: Jewish Patterns of Universalism (to 135 CE)* (Waco, TX: Baylor University Press, 2007).

27.   Cf. Michael F. Bird, *Crossing Over Sea and Land: Jewish Proselytizing Activity in the Second Temple Period* (Peabody, MA: Hendrickson, 2009).

28.   Francis Watson, *Paul, Judaism, and the Gentiles: Beyond the New Perspective* (Grand Rapids, MI: Eerdmans, 2007), pp. 53, 232; N. A. Dahl, 'The One God of Jews and Gentiles (Rom. 3.29-30)', in *Studies in Paul* (Minneapolis, MN: Augsburg, 1977), p. 191; E. P. Sanders, *Paul, the Law, and the Jewish People* (Philadelphia, PA: Fortress, 1983), p. 160; idem, 'Jewish Associations with Gentiles and Galatians 2.11-14', in *The Conversation Continues: Studies in Paul and John in Honor of J. Louis Martyn*, eds Robert T. Fortna and Beverly R. Gaventa (Nashville: Abingdon, 1990), p. 181; Anders Runesson, 'Particularistic Judaism and Universalistic Christianity?: Some Critical Remarks on Terminology and Theology', *ST* 54 (2000): 55–75.

fundamental issue, viz., what is the problem with humanity that Judaism and its covenants cannot solve, that is, the Adamic self.[29] (d) As uncongenial as it might be to Jewish-Christian relations, Paul clearly sees the gospel as something that Israel needs to embrace in order to avoid a cataclysmic judgement (see Rom. 1.16; 10.1-13; 11.7, 23). Nonetheless, while Paul does not have a *Sonderweg* for Israel he does foresee a *Sonderplatz* for the Jewish nation in God's eschatological plans.[30]

We must be careful not to turn intra-Jewish debates into anti-Jewish accusations. Paul never denied belonging to or representing the Jewish people, but his continued engagement with his Jewish contemporaries served only to solidify his own disparity with them and that, to later readers of Paul especially, became a definitive matter for relations between the two communities. Paul's matrix of eschatology, christology and a proselytism-free gentile mission could not be accommodated within a 'common Judaism' and later many gentile Christians rather liked it that way.[31] Moreover, we can also say that during the later stages of his Aegean mission Paul had become somewhat sectarian in terms of adopting an attitude of separation from Jewish communities in the aftermath of the failure of Jewish communities to receive the gospel. A major concern of Paul was the integrity of gentiles *qua* gentiles and not their integration into non-Christ-believing Jewish groups.

2.6. Summary

From this survey we have seen that according to some authors Paul thinks of salvation as consisting of freedom from a legalistic Judaism whereby Judaism and the Law are the antithesis of grace and mercy. Alternatively, others think that Paul did not really understand Judaism and its mode of salvation as he caricatures its beliefs and practices. More recently there have been efforts to situate Paul's thought within Judaism, to reinterpret the rhetoric and polemics in Paul's letters as intra-Jewish affairs, and to postulate the church as remaining as part of Israel's gentile clientele with due allowance made for its unique Christ-centred faith. Others see Paul as remaining in the orbit of Judaism but engaging in some creative configurations of Jewish beliefs around his christocentric faith, shifting from a renewal movement within Judaism to a sectarian ecclesiology beside Judaism in the course of his missionary career, and postulating an ideological legitimation for the freedom

29.   Mark A. Seifrid, *Christ, Our Righteousness: Paul's Theology of Justification* (NSBT 9; Downers Grove, IL: IVP, 2000), pp. 19–21; Bruce Longenecker, *The Triumph of Abraham's God: The Transformation of Identity in Galatians* (Nashville, TN: Abingdon, 1998), pp. 120–1.

30.   Cf. further critiques in Reidar Hvalvik, 'A "Sonderweg" for Israel: A Critical Examination of Current Interpretation of Romans 11.25-27', *JSNT* 38 (1990): 87–107; Terence L. Donaldson, 'Jewish Christianity, Israel's Stumbling and the *Sonderweg* Reading of Paul', *JSNT* 29 (2006): 27–54.

31.   Cf. Magnus Zetterholm, *The Formation of Christianity in Antioch* (London: Routledge, 2003).

of his converts from proselytism. Nonetheless everyone admits that Paul still has some degree of tension with his Jewish compatriots in general and with his Jewish Christian contemporaries in particular. In modern interpretation these tensions seem to revolve around various conceptions of nomism, supersessionism and ethnocentrism and they can be configured with a Paul external to Judaism or with a Paul still within Judaism.

Israel's Problem	Nomism	Supersessionism	Ethnocentrism
Paul *contra* Judaism	Paul possessed a Law-gospel antithesis developed in contrast to the religion of Judaism.	Paul conceived of Christians as a replacement for or fulfilment of Israel as God's people.	Paul established Christian communities separate from Judaism and resisted attempts at bringing them into closer socio-religious proximity to Judaism.
Paul *intra* Judaism	Many Jews and Judeo-Christians would concur with Paul's critique of nomistic stances, and nomism only arises in the context of admitting gentiles into mixed Jew–gentile fellowships.	Paul conceived of Jewish and gentile Jesus believers as a remnant within Israel who occupy a special place within an irrevocably elected Israel.	Paul believed that the eschaton had dawned in Jesus' resurrection and Jesus had become the way for gentiles to enter into Israel without having to actually become Jews themselves, and Israel must accordingly accept this fact.

Most of these perspectives imply some kind of disjunction between Paul's articulation of salvation in Jesus Christ and his perception of the scope and means of salvation according to his fellow Jews. It is the degree of discontinuity that is debated and whether that discontinuity removes Paul from common Judaism altogether.

My own view is that Paul very much straddles the 'contra' and 'intra' Judaism fence depending on what part of his career one looks at, what we make of the gravity of his rhetoric, and contingent upon what social pressures he was facing at the time. Paul is intra-Judaism insofar as most of his community debates can *normally* be paralleled in halakhic discussions and they are often analogous to similar debates that took place among Jews in the diaspora (Paul was not the first Jew to argue about food and circumcision and the gentiles!). On top of that, Paul's rhetoric fits the sectarian context of Second Temple Judaism with rancorous polemics between sects and Paul never intended to set up a new religious entity. Yet Paul can also be seen to be contra-Judaism in a very radical sense as he seems to be willing to go where very few Jews would wish to follow by lowering the currency of

Israel's election through the inclusion of gentiles as part of the 'Israel of God'. Indeed, Paul's exegesis of Lev. 18.5, his anthropological pessimism, placing Jesus *within* the Shema, the triadic link of Law–sin–death that he makes, and attributing the giving of the Torah to angels are too raw and radical for most of his contemporaries to accept as 'in-house' debates. In any case, Paul's contrariety will depend entirely on which salvation scheme in Judaism we are talking about for it seems that Paul knew several. In Rom 1.18-32, his critique of idolatry and pagan immorality mirrors the 'ethical monotheism' of Philo, Wisdom of Solomon and Sirach yet Paul doubts the existence of pagan philosophers who, by the pursuit of virtue and assent to monotheism, have a soul that is on a sojourn towards God and the heavenly Jerusalem. Paul evidently knows of a 'covenantal nomism' whereby grace is embedded in the covenant and obedience is merely the appreciative response to maintain one's election, yet his objection remains that covenantal grace is only efficacious in the context of covenantal obedience which is precisely what Israel lacks (Romans 2–3; 9–10). Paul responds most virulently to an 'ethnocentric nomism' (Gal. 2.1–3.29; Phil. 3.1-9) whereby Christ is merely an add-on to the Sinaitic covenant so that Christ tops-up rather than displaces the salvific function of portions of the Torah. This effectively keeps the butterfly in the cocoon and locates salvation exclusively within the Jewish constituency. Paul strenuously objects to the view that the gospel is the good news that pagans can be saved by becoming Jews. Paul also responds to a 'sapiential nomism' (1 Cor. 1.10–3.23; 2 Corinthians 3) that I postulate as a scheme arising in Corinth that perceives in Christ and the Torah a means to wisdom, power and glory. Finally, Paul opposes an 'apocalyptic mysticism' that locates salvation as something acquired through Law-observance coupled with visionary ascents to heaven couched in the language of Hellenistic philosophy (Colossians).[32]

If we are to try to understand the context and rationale for Paul's continuities and discontinuities with the various schemes of salvation in the Judaism that he knew, then I think that we need to identify the particular socio-religious location of Paul and his converts and the theological texture of his argumentation. Only then can we place Paul's soteriology in relation to that of Judaism.

3. The Identity of Paul and the Socio-Religious Location of Paul's Communities

In Gal. 1.13-14, Paul writes: 'You have heard, no doubt, of my former way of life in Judaism [ἐμὴν ἀναστροφήν ποτε ἐν τῷ Ἰουδαϊσμῷ]. I was intensely persecuting the church of God and was incessantly trying to destroy it. I advanced in Judaism beyond many among my kinsmen of the same age, for I was far more zealous for the traditions of my ancestors.' The crux of the issue is how Paul's current life (ἐν Χριστῷ) differs from his former way

---

32. Cf. Michael F. Bird, *Colossians and Philemon* (NCCS; Eugene, OR: Cascade, 1999), pp. 15–26.

of life (ἐν 'Ιουδαϊσμῷ). In his conversion/call Paul shifted from a pharisaic sect to a messianic sect *within Judaism*. Even so, I sense that Paul, by the 50s at least, did not regard the formal structures of Judaism as the most determining aspects of his identity and mission.[33] Yet Paul did not cease thinking of himself as a 'Jew', 'Israelite' or 'Hebrew'. Thus, the subject of Paul's identity (and Christian and Jewish identity in antiquity for that matter)[34] is incredibly complex.[35] In what follows, I want to analyze Paul's own conception of his identity and the socio-religious location of the Pauline communities in relation to Judaism. I intend to look at several aspects of Paul's letters that point to continuities and discontinuities with his Jewish milieu under the headings: Pauline identity, christology and covenant, and church and synagogue.

3.1. The Pauline identity

Paul's biography was a matter seismic changes in personal identity: beginning life as a diaspora Jew, then Palestinian Pharisee, and finally Jewish Christian apostle of Jesus Christ to the gentiles. So who was he? Paul's representation of himself in his letters is that he is just as Jewish as his Jewish Christian contemporaries and he also holds ethnic descent from Israel (cf. Acts 21.39; 22.3). Paul's rebuke to Cephas in the Antioch episode included the comment that 'we who are Jews by nature and not gentile sinners', which clearly marks Paul and Cephas as Jewish Christians rather than gentile adherents to faith in

33.   Cf. Georg Strecker, *Theology of the New Testament* (trans. M. E. Boring; Louisville, KY: Westminster John Knox, 2000), pp. 21–2; Giorgio Jossa, *Jews or Christians?* (WUNT 202; Tübingen: Mohr/Siebeck, 2006), pp. 12, 95–102; Watson, *Paul, Judaism, and the Gentiles*, pp. 96–9.

34.   Cf. e.g., E. P. Sanders et al. (eds), *Jewish and Christian Self-Definition: Vol. 2: Aspects of Judaism in the Graeco-Roman Period* (London: SCM, 1981); W. C. van Unnik, *Das Selbstverständnis der jüdischen Diaspora in der hellenistisch-römanischen Zeit* (Leiden: Brill, 1993); S. J. D. Cohen, *The Beginnings of Jewishness: Boundaries, Varieties, Uncertainties* (Berkeley, CA: University of California, 1999); Jörg Frey, Daniel R. Schwartz and Stephanie Gripentrog (eds), *Jewish Identity in the Greco-Roman World* (AGJU 71; Leiden: Brill, 2007); Judith Lieu, *Christian identity in the Jewish and Graeco-Roman World* (Oxford: OUP, 2004); Bengst Holmberg, *Exploring Early Christian Identity* (Tübingen: Mohr/Siebeck, 2008).

35.   Cf. K.-W. Niebuhr, *Heidenapostel aus Israel: Die jüdische Identität des Paulus nach ihrer Darstellung in seinen Briefen* (WUNT 62; Tübingen: Mohr/Siebeck, 1992); Daniel Boyarin, *A Radical Jew: Paul and the Politics of Identity* (Berkeley, CA: University of California, 1994); James D. G. Dunn, 'Who Did Paul Think He Was? A Study of Jewish Christian Identity', *NTS* 45 (1999): 174–93; Jörg Frey, 'Paul's Jewish Identity', in *Jewish Identity in the Greco-Roman World*, eds Jörg Frey, Daniel R. Schwartz and Stephanie Gripentrog, (AGJU 71; Leiden: Brill, 2007), pp. 285–321; Caroline Johnson Hodge, 'Apostle to the Gentiles: Constructions of Paul's Identity', *BI* 13 (2005): 270–88; William S. Campbell, 'Religion, Identity and Ethnicity: The Contribution of Paul the Apostle', *Journal of Beliefs and Values* 29 (2008): 139–50; idem, *Paul and the Creation of Christian Identity* (London: T&T Clark, 2006).

Christ (Gal. 2.15). In Philippians, Paul famously states that he was 'circumcised on the eighth day, a member of the people of Israel, of the tribe of Benjamin, a Hebrew born of Hebrews; as to the law, a Pharisee' (Phil. 3.5). Paul can even affirm that his own ethnography as Hebrew, Israelite and Abrahamic is equal to that of the super-apostles who visited Corinth (2 Cor. 11.22). In Romans he says that Israel are, 'my own people, my kindred according to the flesh' (Rom. 9.3) and of himself, 'I myself am an Israelite, a descendant of Abraham, a member of the tribe of Benjamin' (Rom. 11.1). Paul's conceptual framework including particularized notions of God as 'one', his perspective on intermediary figures, his view of the afterlife and eschaton, his sacred texts and their interpretation, his theopolitics and mission strategy, as well as his piety and gospel are all rooted in the Judaism of the Graeco-Roman world. It seems that he even submitted himself to synagogue discipline on at least one occasion (2 Cor. 11.24), he strove to remain in amicable relations with the Jerusalem church who were still within the orbit of Palestinian Judaism (Gal. 2.1-10; Rom. 15.25-31; 1 Cor. 16.1-3), and chided a predominantly gentile congregation for anti-Judaism in favour of the interlocking destiny of Jews and gentiles in salvation-history (Romans 1.16; 11.1-32; 15.8-9). Thus Paul identified his own genealogical and religious origins in Israel and in Judaism, he endeavoured to maintain affable links with the Jerusalem church and Jewish diaspora communities, and his own thought world was firmly rooted in Jewish texts and traditions. What is more, even in his post-Damascus state he continued to have a particular bond of solidarity with the Jewish nation witnessed in his eschatological expectations (Rom. 11.25-32), his prayer for Israel's salvation (Rom. 10.1), and heart-felt anguish to the point of wishing for vicarious self-anathematization on their account (Rom. 9.3).

Nevertheless, much of the cerebral furniture in Paul's mind had been significantly rearranged since his conversion to the point where several of Paul's ideological fixtures were now clearly at odds with his Jewish contemporaries. A good example is that of circumcision, as Paul no longer required this of gentile converts to Jesus-faith. Circumcision was the distinguishing mark of the Jewish male, ordinarily the rite of entry into the commonwealth of Israel for male proselytes, and linked to the Mosaic legislation.[36] Paul, however, dissolved the category of Jewish adherent (i.e., 'God-fearers') and accepted uncircumcised persons as full and committed members of the Pauline assemblies and demanded their acceptance even in mixed Jewish/gentile Christian settings (Gal. 2.1-14).[37] In which case, Paul has replaced an ethnocentric nomism[38] (e.g., Gal. 2.11-21) with a messianic

---

36. Cf. Bird, *Crossing over Sea and Land*, pp. 17–43.

37. In a strange feat of irony, the teachers in Galatia aver that Paul usually preached circumcision but being fickle or expedient he misinformed them by omitting their obligation to be circumcised (Gal. 1.10; 5.11). In turn Paul alleges that the teachers are themselves fickle and false when they omit the obligation to obey the whole Torah (Gal. 5.3; 6.13).

38. Cf. Bird, *Saving Righteousness*, p. 117, and Bruce Longenecker (*Eschatology and the Covenant: A Comparison of 4 Ezra and Romans 9–11* (Sheffield: Sheffield Academic Press, 1991), pp. 278–9), developed a parallel concept of 'ethnocentric covenantalism'.

pneumatology (e.g., Gal. 4.6-7; Rom. 8.14-17)! Paul strikes hard and fast against the soteric invalidity of circumcision (Gal. 5.2, 6; Rom. 4.11; 1 Cor. 7.19; cf. Acts 15.1, 5). Even more potently he contends that membership in the people of God is no longer defined by circumcision but by an inward transformation through faith in the Messiah and reception of the Holy Spirit (Gal. 3.26-29; 6.15; Rom. 8.9-17). The obedience of the uncircumcised can be 'imputed' (λογίζομαι) as 'circumcision' (Rom. 2.26; cf. Phil. 3.3; 1 Cor. 7.19). The apostle explicitly redefines being a Ἰουδαῖος as something that is not φανερός ('outward') but κρυπτός ('hidden') in Rom. 2.28-29 (cf. Rom. 9.6-9); thus implying a redefinition of the designation so as to include those who are not circumcised (i.e., those who have neither ethnic descent from Israel nor possess the chief emblem of Israel's covenant identity). The value and privilege of circumcision and ethnic Jewish descent are not denied, but they are of little benefit in the face of disobedience to God and rejection of his Son (Rom. 2.25; 3.1-20; 9.1-29).

The designations 'Israel' and 'Israelite' were evidently positive for Paul as they denoted continuity with God's purposes and plan first announced to the Patriarchs and fulfilled in the economy of God's action in Jesus Christ. The terms relate to God's electing purposes and can transcend ethnic categories. Indeed, Paul's 'Israel of God' (Gal. 6.16) is to some degree analogous to Philo's 'Israel who sees God' which is a philosophical rather than ethnic category for the Alexandrian philosopher (Philo, *Migr. Abr.* 113-14; *Conf. Ling.* 56; *Rer. Div. Her.* 78).[39] Paul envisages salvation for the renewed Israel comprising of believing Jews and gentiles centred on Christ (Rom. 9.4-8; cf. Rom. 3.30; 4.10-12; Eph. 2.11-22) and the whole or part of national Israel in the eschatological future (Rom. 11.26). What separated Paul from other more 'liberal' approaches to circumcision and gentiles (e.g., Ananias in *Ant.* 20.34-42 or the allegorizers in Philo, *Migr.* 89-94) was three things: (1) the soteriological singularity of God's eschatological deliverance wrought in Jesus' death, resurrection and exaltation (e.g., Gal. 2.21; Rom. 8.3); (2) the experience of the Spirit being poured upon the uncircumcised (e.g., Gal. 3.2-5, 14; 4.6; Rom. 8.4-17); and (3) the salvation-historical priority of the Abrahamic promise over the Mosaic covenant (e.g., Gal. 3.6-14, 29; Rom. 4.10-11).[40]

Further to this theological transformation, Paul's explication of his own identity points in a direction away from the key nodes of Jewish identity. Obviously the question of who was a Jew/Judean in antiquity is a complex one.[41] Yet if we define Judaism in terms of ethnicity and shared custom[42] it is

---

39.   Cf. Ellen Birnbaum, *The Place of Judaism in Philo's Thought: Israel, Jews, and Proselytes* (Providence: Brown University Press, 1996), pp. 11–12.

40.   Terence Donaldson, *Paul and the Gentiles: Remapping the Apostle's Conviction World* (Minneapolis, MN: Fortress, 1997), pp. 215–48.

41.   I deal with the translation of Ἰουδαῖος further in Bird, *Crossing Over Sea and Land*, pp. 13–16.

42.   John Barclay, *Jews in the Mediterranean Diaspora: from Alexander to Trajan (323 BCE–117 CE)* (Edinburgh: T&T Clark, 1996), p. 405.

evident that Paul relativized the former and denied the efficacy of the latter in view of the saving event of God executed in Jesus Christ. Several features of Paul's construal of his identity suggest that being ἐν Χριστῷ does not negate his Jewish origins, but it does transcend it and even relativize it in relation to a new Christ-given and Spirit-endowed anthropology. That new identity is continuous with his Israelite ancestry, but also consciously distinct from it. For instance, in Phil. 3.7-8 Paul can consider his nationally inherited Jewish privileges as ζημία ('loss') and σκύβαλον ('filth') when *compared to* Christ. It is evident from 1 Cor. 9.20-23 that he considered 'becoming' (γίνομαι) a Jew (i.e., living like a Jew) just as much a compromise as becoming one 'without law' (ἄνομος) or 'weak' (ἀσθενής) for the sake of his missionary call to herald the gospel.[43] The exhortation in Gal. 3.28 with its οὐκ ... οὐδέ construction, which frames the binary pairing of Jew/Greek, Slave/Free and Male/Female, is not a negation of the ontological and cultural existence of the respective tags (e.g., believers do not suddenly cease to be Greek-speaking male freedmen), as much as it stipulates their transformation into a shared meta-identity defined by being ἐν Χριστῷ Ἰησοῦ. What is negated is the effectiveness of these tags to become vehicles of separation and superiority. The emphasis in Gal. 3.28-29 (and Gal. 2.19-21; 5.6; 6.15; 1 Cor. 7.18-19; 12.13; Col. 3.11) is not the obliteration of different human identities, but the *inclusion* and *transformation* of multiple identities under a single meta-identity marked by Christ and the new creation. But that can only be true if the existing identities,

---

43.   Cf. Richard Hays (*First Corinthians* (Int.; Louisville, KY: John Knox, 1997), p. 153): 'Since Paul was in fact a Jew, this formulation shows how radically he conceives the claim that in Christ he is ... in a position transcending all cultural allegiances.'; Wolfgang Schrage (*Der erste Brief an die Korinther* (Neukirchen-Vluyn: Neukirchener Verlag, 1991–9), 2.340): 'Paulus wird nicht einfach Jude oder Heide, sondern *wie* ein Jude und *wie* ein Heide, ihnen vergleichbar. Er läßt sich auf sie ein, wird in bestimmter Weise mit ihnen solidarisch. Das erweist gerade das Ἰουδαίοις ὡς Ἰουδαῖος. Denn wie kann Paulus, der geborene Jude (vgl. Gal 2,15 ἡμεῖς φύσει Ἰουδαῖοι), erst ein Jude *werden*? Nicht zufällig fehlt ein μὴ ὢν Ἰουδαῖος in Analogie zu den beiden folgenden Beispielen. Aber kann er nicht nur etwas werden, was er in bestimmter Weise nicht mehr ist? In der Tat. Weil es in Christus weder Juden noch Griechen gibt (Gal 3,28; vgl. zu 12,13), *ist* Paulus auch als geborener Jude nicht mehr einfach Jude, sonder wird es, "um Juden zu gewinnen".' Dunn ('Who Did Paul Think He Was?', p. 182): 'Paul speaks as one who does not acknowledge "Jew" as his own given identity, or as an identity inalienable from his person ... Instead, the term "Jew" is being treated almost as a role which one might assume or discard.' In contrast, Nanos ('Paul and Judaism') states that 'I understand Paul to be expressing *a rhetorical strategy*, not a change of halakhic behaviour ... I propose that "becoming like" signifies "arguing from the premises" of each.' But I wonder if Nanos has simply exchanged a legal duplicity for a philosophical one (see also Schrage (*Der erste Brief*, p. 342): 'Aber V20b ist auch nicht einfach eine Tautologie oder eine bloß rhetorische Wiederholung von V20a. Eher wird es sich um eine Explikation und Steigerung handeln. Explikation insofern, als das Gesetz den Juden zum Juden macht und das Sein ὑπὸ νόμου für Paulus das ist, was den Juden von Christen unterscheidet. Steigerung aber insofern, als Paulus erklärt, selbst unter den Nomos getreten zu sein, um die Gesetzesleute zu gewinnen. Wie ungewöhnlich und alles andere als selbstverständlich das ist, zeigt die konzessive Partizipialbestimmung μὴ ὢν αὐτὸς ὑπὸ νόμον. Christliches Leben wird nicht mehr durch die Tora konstituiert und determiniert.'

which are a means of distinction and status, are themselves negated in value and lessened in their ability to cause differentiation.[44] When this formulation is combined with Paul's remarks in 1 Cor. 10.32 that divides persons into Jews, Greeks and the church of God (cf. 1 Cor. 1.18-24), it seems hard to avoid the conclusion that Paul conceived of Christ-believers as a τρίτον γένος or *tertium genus* (Clement of Alexandria, *Strom.* 6.5.41.6; Aristides, *Apol.* 2.2), a third race.[45]

Does this mean that Paul is not a Jew? By no means! Paul is a Jew, but by his own admission he is an 'in-Christ' Jew. His Jewishness is retained but subsumed beneath and subordinated to being in-Christ. Yet can we say with Markus Barth that, 'Sein Leben war eines guten Juden Leben: ein Kampf für das Recht des Nächsten.'[46] Paul himself could have conceivably said so, but I doubt whether that would have been reciprocal from all Jews or from all Jewish Christians who may have regarded him as an apostate or schismatic.[47] Is Paul, then, in Judaism any longer? Broadly speaking it would seem no. His unique concoction of christology, eschatology and the transformation of identity could not be accommodated within a common Judaism. Paul consistently characterizes Judaism as 'pharisaic' Judaism and regarded this as fundamentally incompatible with the gospel (Gal. 1.13-14; Phil. 3.6-8).[48]

44. Bird, *Colossians and Philemon*, pp. 102–6. See also Nanos, *Irony of Galatians*, p. 99; Mark Seifrid, 'For the Jew first: Paul's Nota Bene for his Gentile Readers', in *To the Jew First: The Case for Jewish Evangelism in Scripture and History* (Grand Rapids, MI: Kregel, 2008), pp. 26–7, 37. Cf. Pauline Nigh Hogan, *'No Longer Male and Female': Interpreting Galatians 3:28 in Early Christianity* (LNTS 380; London: T&T Clark, 2008).

45. Cf. E. P. Sanders (*Paul, the Law, and the Jewish People* (Philadelphia, PA: Fortress, 1983), p. 178): 'Paul's view of the church, supported by his practice, against his own conscious intention was substantially that it was a third entity, not just because it was composed of both Jew and Greek, but also because it was in important ways neither Jewish nor Greek.'

46. Barth, 'Der gute Jude Paulus', p. 132. Nanos ('Paul and Judaism') characterizes the consensus of Pauline scholarship as supposing: 'He [Paul] may have thought of himself as a "good Jew", but no other practicing Jews would have.'

47. Paul's experience of a synagogue punishment (2 Cor. 11.24), having his mission hindered by Jewish groups (1 Thess. 2.16), praying for deliverance from Jews in Jerusalem (Rom. 15.31), accusations of antinomianism (Rom. 3.8; Acts 21.21) and antagonism from Jewish Christians (Gal. 6.17; Phil. 1.7) do not bode well for Paul being considered a 'good Jew' by others. That said, Paul did have a cohort of Jewish Christian supporters and we can safely assume that not all Jews would have been automatically hostile to him (e.g., Acts 28.17-24). See John M. G. Barclay, 'Paul among Diaspora Jews: Anomaly or Apostate?', *JSNT* 60 (1995): 89–120; Stanley E. Porter, 'Was Paul a Good Jew? Fundamental Issues in a Current Debate', in *Christian-Jewish Relations Through the Centuries*, eds S. E. Porter and B. W. R. Pearson (JSNTSup 192; Sheffield: Sheffield Academic Press, 2000), pp. 148–74; J. Ross Wagner, *Heralds of the Good News: Isaiah and Paul in Concern in the Letter to the Romans* (Leiden: Brill, 2003), p. 4; Bird and Sprinkle, 'Jewish Interpretation', pp. 355–6.

48. In this instance Paul seems at one with Josephus who also regards pharisaism as the default position of the Jewish masses (*Ant.* 13.288, 297-98; 18.15). Roland Deines ('The Pharisees Between "Judaisms" and "Common Judaism"', in *Justification and Variegated Nomism: The Complexities of Second Temple Judaism*, eds D. A. Carson, Peter T. O'Brien and Mark A. Seifrid (Grand Rapids, MI: Baker, 2001), p. 503) calls Pharisaism, 'the fundamental and most influential religious movement within Palestinian Judaism'. Dunn ('Who Did Paul

And herein lies the crux: it is precisely the question of Christ and Judaism – the crucified and risen Lord in relation to the emblems, ethos and ethnicity of the Jewish people – which perplexed the early Christian interpreters, and it became a matter of contention in their own communities. The focal point of debate revolved around how the God-given instruments of Torah and Christ related to each other. Should one interpret God's Messiah in light of God's Torah or interpret God's Torah in light of God's Messiah?[49] The resulting question, then, is what takes priority: christology or covenant?

3.2. Christology and covenant

For Paul, it seems that what had been a Torah-centred religion in the context of Israel's Sinaitic covenant has become a Christ-centred religion in the context of the new covenant that is the fulfilment of the Abrahamic promises. Thus Paul, paradoxically, strove to demonstrate tangible links between the Jesus movement and Israel's religious antiquity (principally through scripture), yet he also intended to provide an ideological legitimation for the separation of his gentile converts from the synagogue and their freedom from certain Torah observances. While precise elements of continuity and discontinuity between the Sinaitic covenant and the new covenant are many and debatable, I intend here to focus on two key texts from Paul that engage this subject, 2 Cor. 3.6-13 and Rom. 10.4-5, as indicative of the macro-structure of Paul's covenantal thinking.[50]

In 2 Corinthians 3, Paul provides a further defence of his apostolate by reference to the superiority of the ministry of the new covenant over that of the old covenant. God has made he and others sufficiently capable to serve in the dispensation of the new covenant that is defined not by γράμμα ('letter')[51] but by πνεῦμα ('Spirit'). Immediately, he adds an explanatory remark in v. 7, τὸ γὰρ γράμμα ἀποκτέννει, τὸ δὲ πνεῦμα ζῳοποιεῖ ('for the letter kills but the Spirit quickens'), echoing a thought that he will develop further in Romans (7.5-7; 8.2).[52] Paul's subsequent argument beginning in

Think He Was?', p. 185) thinks that Paul regarded Judaism as too much identified with Maccabean views of circumcision and food laws.

49.   J. L. Martyn, *Galatians: A New Translation with Introduction and Commentary* (AB; New York: Doubleday, 1997), p. 124.

50.   Markus Barth ('Der gute Jude Paulus', in *Richte unsere Füsse auf den Weg des Friedens* (FS Helmut Gollwitzer; München, 1979), pp. 112–14) cites these same two texts and argues that those who take them to imply that Paul regarded the Law/covenant as obsolete, cancelled, annulled or replaced have 'verachtet und verurteilt mit dem Gesetz die Juden' and consequently 'Mit dem Alten Bund und Testament fallen dann auch die Gottesverheissungen dahin betreffend Nachkommenschaft' (113).

51.   Here γράμμα refers to the ten commandments given the reference to 'tablets of stone' in v. 3.

52.   Augustine regarded the Epistle to the Romans as a commentary on 2 Cor. 3.6. See his *De Spiritu et Littera* (c. 412 CE).

vv. 7-11 uses a series of *qal wāḥômer* (*minori ad maius*) comparisons, built around the imagery of Exodus 32–34, to the effect that if the ministry of death and condemnation (Sinai covenant) was glorious, how much more so is the ministries of Spirit and righteousness (new covenant). He asserts that the glory of Moses' face was gradually set aside (καταργέω)[53] and the new service (διακονία) has surpassed (ὑπερβάλλω) the older one in glory. The doxological inferiority of the old ministry compared to the new ministry is restated further in vv. 10-11, emphasizing the even more glorious and permanent nature of the new dispensation.

In vv. 7, 11 and 13-14 it is clear that Paul reasons that the transitory nature of the glory that reflected from Moses' face is indicative of the transitory nature of the Mosaic legislation which is replaced with something yet more glorious and more permanent. In v. 7 it is the glory of Moses' face that was καταργέω, while in v. 11 it is that which came *through glory* that was being καταργέω, that is, the old covenant. The substantive participles designate a dispensation and its temporal status as τὸ καταργούμενον (old covenant) and τὸ μένον (new covenant). Hence, there is a switch from the cessation of the mosaic glory in v. 7 to the supersession of the mosaic service in v. 11. The fading/inoperability of the mosaic glory becomes a metonym for the limitation/ineffectiveness of the mosaic covenant.[54] The same pattern emerges in vv. 13-14. Moses wore a veil to prevent the Israelites from gazing εἰς τὸ τέλος τοῦ καταργουμένου ('the end that was being set aside'). The neuter or masculine substantive participle τοῦ καταργουμένου relates back not to the feminine δόξα ('glory') but to either κάλυμμα ('veil') or the ἀτενίζειν ('to stare'). In effect, Israel's error was its mesmerizing fixation on a face that symbolized a ministry that was already on the way out. In v. 14, Paul applies the analogy to his own time and he contends that the hardening of the Israelites' minds means that the same veil which covered Moses' face now covers Israel when they read the old covenant and so fail to understand its transitory nature. They have mistaken that which is preparatory for that which is permanent. That veil is only ἐν Χριστῷ καταργεῖται ('in Christ is taken away'). The net purpose undertaken in vv. 6-14, then, is to show that the καταργέω of Moses' δόξα ('glory') is symbolic for the καταργέω of the παλαιᾶς διαθήκης ('old covenant') and the γράμμα ('letter').

Several key implications emerge from analysis of 2 Cor. 3.6-18 for Paul and Judaism. (1) The socio-rhetorical function of this passage must be related to Paul's own social context. The intruding super-apostles (2 Cor. 11.5; 12.11) who have come to Corinth with letters of recommendation are ministers of this letter that kills. That is not to say that the intruders

53.   Cf. BDAG, 525–6; *TDNT* 1.452–54; *EDNT* 2.267–8; Scott J. Hafemann, *Paul, Moses, and the History of Israel* (Peabody, MA: Hendrickson, 1995), pp. 301–9.

54.   Hafemann, *Paul*, pp. 329–30.

55.   Cf. recently N. H. Taylor, 'Apostolic Identity and the Conflicts in Corinth and Galatia', in *Paul and His Opponents*, ed. Stanley E. Porter (PAST 2; Leiden: Brill, 2005), pp. 115–22.

are proselytizers as per Paul's opponents in Galatia – indeed they probably have a more sapiential and sophistic form of discourse[55] – but all the same, when postured polemically against them, Paul does feel the need to make a stark contrast between Jewish and Jesus-believing communities in order to buttress his own authority in opposition to these visitors. Rejection of these visitors necessitates Paul constructing a paradigm of how the old covenant relates to the new and providing an ideological justification for the separation of Christ-believing communities from the synagogues.[56] (2) Paul asserts the negative soteriological effect of the 'letter' and 'old covenant'. The 'letter' (i.e., Torah) kills and the old service is associated with death and condemnation. In contrast, the new service brought about by the Spirit brings righteousness and life. The glory of the new also eclipses the glory of the old. The hope that the righteous would share in God's glory at the eschaton was widespread in post-biblical Judaism and Paul attributes its realization to the new epoch of salvation-history.[57] The hope for transformation and glorification is brought by the Lord and Spirit thus showing that the new covenant brings in the new creation (2 Cor. 3.18). This is why Paul does not minister καθάπερ Μωϋσῆς ἐτίθει κάλυμμα ἐπὶ τὸ πρόσωπον αὐτοῦ (like Moses who put a veil over his face (2 Cor. 3.13)), but in a different order of service associated with hope, life, freedom, righteousness, transformation and glory.[58] (3) Paul implies the renewal of the old covenant with the advent of the new covenant. The precise meaning and application of the words τέλος (v. 13) and καταργέω (vv. 7, 11, 13, 14) are of course disputed. What is clear, however, is that Paul regards the old covenant as comparatively inglorious, transitory and ineffective next to the new covenant. The focus in vv. 6-14 is ultimately on the discontinuity between the two covenants. Otfried Hofius correctly suggests that already in v. 6 it is assumed that the new covenant relates antithetically to the old covenant even if 'old covenant' does not appear until v. 14.[59] The new covenant is the eschatological deed of God executed in Jesus Christ, mediated through the Spirit and enacted by the apostolic ministers. Yet it is impossible to excise all elements of continuity. What is brought forward is precisely a new covenant with the same God who made the first one. The new covenant is the eschatological fulfilment of the hopes expressed in Isaiah (49.8 (LXX)), Ezekiel (16.60, 62; 37.23, 26), Jeremiah (31.31-34) for the *renewal* of the old covenant and Spirit-enacted obedience of the Torah.[60] (4) The internal logic of Paul's covenant theology is that the position of Jews under the Torah is implied to be a dire

56.   Watson, *Paul, Judaism, and the Gentiles*, pp. 156–9.

57.   Peter Stuhlmacher, 'Erwägugen zum ontologischen Charakter der καινὴ κτίσις bei Paulus', *EvTh* 27 (1967): 1–35.

58.   Hafemann, *Paul*, pp. 352–3.

59.   Otfried Hofius, 'Gesetz und Evangelium nach 2. Korinther 3', in *Paulusstudien* (WUNT 51; Tübingen: Mohr/Siebeck, 1994), p. 75.

60.   Cf. Hermann Lichtenberger and Stefan Schreiner, 'Der neue Bund in jüdischer Überlieferung', *Theologische Quartalschrift* 176.4 (1996): 272–90.

condition. In vv. 14-15, the synagogues in which the Torah is read continues to exacerbate the problem of Moses' original audience. As Francis Watson states: 'There, each Sabbath, Moses is read and heard without any awareness that, beneath the surface of the veil, the glory has departed.'[61] What is more, a metaphorical veil covers their hearts and impairs their understanding of the very words before them. What is needed then, by those of the synagogue, is to turn to the Lord and have Christ remove the veil for them. That way, they will participate in the freedom bequeathed by the Spirit and so enter into the transforming glory of the new creation that has no reason to be veiled (vv. 17-18). It is probable that Χριστός as the remover of the veil in v. 14 is to be identified with the κύριος of v. 16, meaning that turning (ἐπιστρέφω) to the Lord is essentially conversion to Christ (see 2 Cor. 4.3-4).[62] In other words, the noetic liberation of Israel and their doxological transformation occurs through Jesus the Messiah.

An additional key text of Paul's covenant theology is Rom. 10.4: τέλος γὰρ νόμου Χριστὸς εἰς δικαιοσύνην παντὶ τῷ πιστεύοντι ('Christ is the end/ goal/terminus of the Torah/Covenant so that their might be righteousness for everyone who believes'). Obviously a central issue is the meaning of τέλος in context.[63] The larger and immediate contexts provide crucial evidence of how Paul conceived salvation in relation to Judaism. Paul writes this epistle to a predominantly gentile church (aware that it will also find its way into the hands of Jewish Christians) in order to garner support for his future mission to Spain, to return to Jerusalem with the gentile churches of Rome behind him, to defend himself against allegations of being antinomian or even anti-Israel, and to engage in some preventative pastoral care of a cluster of congregations that he suspects could fracture over ethnic lines or over *halakhic* issues.

In this apostolic manifesto of the Pauline gospel, Rom. 1.18-32 exhibits a fairly standard Jewish polemic against pagan religion and immorality typical of Isa. 44.9-20 and Wisd. 13.1-19. Paul converges here with what is often called an 'ethical monotheism' of Judaism.[64] The difference is that Paul will soon say that God's wrath against the nations is also against his Jewish interlocutor as well (Rom. 3.5). In 2.1–3.20, Paul endeavours to hold together two paradoxical axioms: God's faithfulness to Israel and God's impartiality in judgement. In Rom. 3.1-3, the apostle affirms the ὠφέλεια ('advantage')

---

61.   Watson, *Paul, Judaism, and the Gentiles*, p. 159.

62.   Cf. Richard H. Bell, *The Irrevocable Call of God* (WUNT 184; Tübingen: Mohr/ Siebeck, 2005), pp. 238–43.

63.   In Pauline usage τέλος ordinarily denotes cessation (2 Cor. 2.13; 1 Cor. 15.24), a gradual closure (1 Cor. 10.11), goal or result (Rom. 6.21, 22; 2 Cor. 11.15; Phil. 3.19), or can be used adverbially (1 Thess. 2.16; 1 Cor. 1.8; 2 Cor. 3.13). It is striking, however, that Rom. 10.4 occurs in a context filled with athletic imagery in 9.30-33 so a translation of 'goal' may be the meaning most contextually appropriate.

64.   Cf. Jacob Neusner, *The Emergence of Judaism* (Louisville, KY: Westminster John Knox, 2004), pp. 74–5, who lists four tenets of ethical monotheism: (1) Creation, Torah as the plan; (2) The perfection of creation and justice; (3) God's will and humanity's will in conflict; and (4) Restoration of perfection. And also Donaldson, *Judaism and the Gentiles*, pp. 493–8.

of circumcision with circumcision functioning as a metonym for the mosaic covenant and Israelite election. What is more, there is no denying the πίστις τοῦ θεοῦ ('faithfulness of God') towards Israel either. These pillars of Judaism are not denied by Paul, but transposed in light of the revelation in the gospel so that the advantage of Israelite identity and the purpose of mosaic covenant are realized in the manifesting of the Messiah through Israel and first to Israel in order to confirm God's promises to Abraham (Rom. 1.16; 9.1-6; 15.8-9). Yet Paul proceeds to undermine a genuine covenantal nomism by arguing, much in line with the Jewish tradition, that mere possession of the Torah (e.g., *m.'Abot.* 1.17; Jas. 1.22-25; 1QS 3.4-12) and physical lineage from Israel (e.g., Mt. 3.9/Lk. 3.8) does not ensure vindication at an eschatological judgement. When such a judgement is made without any προσωπολημψία ('favouritism') there is no διαστολή ('difference') between Jews and gentiles in judgement according to deeds, because all have sinned (Rom. 2.11; 3.20, 22-23; 5.12; 10.12). Indeed, Paul brings further shame on his imaginary interlocutor because an impartial judgement will show that (Jesus-believing?) gentiles are righteous according to deeds and they are reckoned as inward Jews as well (Rom. 2.13-16, 25-29).[65]

The *exornatio* of Rom. 3.21-26 provides further evidence for matters of continuity and discontinuity. In the new eschatological event (νυνὶ δὲ, 'but now'), the δικαιοσύνη θεοῦ ('righteousness of God') is being revealed χωρὶς νόμου ('apart from Torah') while simultaneously μαρτυρουμένη ὑπὸ τοῦ νόμου καὶ τῶν προφητῶν ('being testified by the Law and the prophets'). The Torah, as manifesto for the mosaic economy, is nullified as a means of salvation and signifier of election. As Paul says elsewhere, it was a temporary administration of God's grace to govern God's people and to reveal sin until the anointed deliverer came (Rom. 4.13-15; 5.20; Gal. 3.15–4.7). Justification is to be found διὰ/ἐκ πίστεως Ἰησοῦ Χριστοῦ ('through/from faith of Christ') and not in ἔργα νόμου ('works of Law'). The human response of faith to the God-in-Christ event replaces the human response of failed obedience to the mosaic covenant as the locus of God's saving action. The upshot of this is that there is righteousness, redemption and propitiatory sacrifice for everyone who was formerly condemned by the Torah and the scope of God's saving power has been expanded beyond the confines of ethnic Israel (Rom. 3.28-30). Still, continuity remains in effect, as God's saving work in the new age is proleptically anticipated and predicted in Israel's sacred traditions (e.g., Hab. 2.4; Gen. 15.6) and Paul can also say that faith upholds the Torah (Rom. 3.31; cf. 8.4).[66]

The employment of the Abrahamic and Adamic stories in Rom. 4.1–5.21 exemplifies the stated principle of Rom. 3.21-31. First, Abraham was righteous by faith and not by works; he was righteous as a gentile not as a Jew. Thus, all boasting in effort or ethnicity is excluded. Circumcision was a

---

65.   Cf. Bird, *Saving Righteousness*, pp. 155–78.
66.   Cf. Moo, *Romans*, pp. 222–3.

seal of righteousness not a means to it (Rom. 4.10-12). This story is applicable to Paul's readers as Abraham had faith in the power of God to bring life to Sarah's dead womb in the same way that Jews and gentiles look to Jesus as the one whom God raised from the dead (Rom. 4.23-24). Second, Romans 5 is somewhat of a bridging section that recapitulates motifs from Rom. 1.18–4.25 while looking ahead to Romans 6.1–8.17. In Rom. 5.1-11, Paul provides a *conplexio* of his thesis and begins to admix some exhortatory remarks as well. Third, the Adam/Christ typology in Rom. 5.12-21 provides an exposition of the Adamic condition of humanity that is aggravated rather than remedied by the coming of the Torah. The solution lay in the advent of the second Adam who, by one righteous act, overturned the one transgression of the first Adam and is able to vivify, justify and reconcile sinful humanity. The grace of God in Jesus Christ does what the grace of the Torah and nation of Israel could not do. The problem was not in God's call of Israel, but the nexus of Law, Sin and Flesh which rendered the Torah ineffective in dealing with sin. This is explained more fully in Rom. 6.1–8.30 which could be regarded as a commentary on 1 Cor. 15.56-57: 'The sting of death is sin, and the power of sin is the law. But thanks be to God, who gives us the victory through our Lord Jesus Christ.'

I am convinced by Thomas Tobin that Rom. 8.1-39 needs to be integrated more closely with Romans 9–11.[67] The link between them is threefold. (1) If divine redemption has arrived with the eschatological advent of the Messiah and the Spirit with the concomitant influx of gentiles, then why does this inclusive salvation remain so elusive for Israel? (2) How does one have assurance in God's eschatological purposes if the elect nation itself has rejected the offer of the gospel? (3) Who then is 'Israel' if ethnic Israelites have rejected the message? Underlying all of this is the practical matter of how do gentile believers relate to unbelieving Jews and the apologetic matter of how does the present circumstance of Israel and God's promises to the nation relate to Paul's gospel? The 'Israel Question' dominates Romans 9–11 and Paul addresses this in three phases: (1) Israel in the past (9.6-29); (2) Israel in the present (9.30–10.21); and (3) Israel in the future (11.1-36).[68]

The concern of 9.30–10.21 is to explain Israel's rejection of the righteousness of God that has come to all. In regards to 9.30–10.4 we should note that the ideas expressed in 9.30-33 are essentially restated anew in 10.1-4.[69] The parallel includes:

---

67. Thomas H. Tobin, *Paul's Rhetoric in Its Contexts: The Argument of Romans* (Peabody, MA: Hendrickson, 2004), pp. 251–72.

68. Ibid., p. 321.

69. Ibid., pp. 309–11, 341–2.

A	(30) Τί οὖν ἐροῦμεν; ὅτι <u>ἔθνη</u>	(1-2) Ἀδελφοί, ἡ μὲν εὐδοκία τῆς ἐμῆς καρδίας καὶ ἡ δέησις πρὸς τὸν θεὸν ὑπὲρ αὐτῶν εἰς σωτηρίαν. μαρτυρῶ γὰρ <u>αὐτοῖς</u> ὅτι ζῆλον θεοῦ ἔχουσιν ἀλλ᾽ οὐ κατ᾽ ἐπίγνωσιν·
B	τὰ μὴ <u>διώκοντα</u> δικαιοσύνην κατέλαβεν δικαιοσύνην, δικαιοσύνην δὲ τὴν ἐκ πίστεως,	(3) ἀγνοοῦντες γὰρ τὴν τοῦ θεοῦ δικαιοσύνην καὶ τὴν *ἰδίαν δικαιοσύνην* <u>ζητοῦντες</u> στῆσαι,
C	(31) Ἰσραὴλ δὲ διώκων *νόμον δικαιοσύνης* εἰς *νόμον* οὐκ ἔφθασεν	τῇ δικαιοσύνῃ τοῦ θεοῦ <u>οὐχ</u> ὑπετάγησαν
D	(32) διὰ τί; ὅτι οὐκ *ἐκ πίστεως* ἀλλ᾽ ὡς *ἐξ ἔργων*·	(4) *τέλος* γὰρ <u>νόμου</u> Χριστός εἰς δικαιοσύνην παντὶ τῷ πιστεύοντι
E	προσέκοψαν τῷ λίθῳ τοῦ προσκόμματος, (33) καθὼς γέγραπται· ἰδοὺ τίθημι ἐν Σιὼν λίθον προσκόμματος καὶ πέτραν σκανδάλου, καὶ ὁ πιστεύων ἐπ᾽ αὐτῷ οὐ καταισχυνθήσεται	(5-6) Μωϋσῆς γὰρ γράφει τὴν δικαιοσύνην τὴν ἐκ τοῦ νόμου ὅτι ὁ ποιήσας αὐτὰ ἄνθρωπος ζήσεται ἐν αὐτοῖς ἡ δὲ ἐκ πίστεως δικαιοσύνη οὕτως λέγει· μὴ εἴπῃς ἐν τῇ καρδίᾳ σου· τίς ἀναβήσεται εἰς τὸν οὐρανόν τοῦτ᾽ ἔστιν Χριστὸν καταγαγεῖν·

(A) Paul juxtaposes the response of the nations (9.30) and Israel (10.1-2) to God's righteousness.

(B) The contrast is twofold: first, between gentiles who did not seek righteousness with an Israel that did seek righteousness; second, between the gentiles who received a righteousness from faith whereas Israel sought to establish their own righteousness (9.30; 10.3).

(C) Despite Israel's efforts she did not attain a righteousness from Law (9.31) and as such she did not submit to the righteousness of God (10.3).

(D) The operating assumption of Paul is that righteousness is from faith and not from works (9.32), and the reason is that Christ is the τέλος of the Law so that righteousness would come to everyone who believes (10.4). In parallel, ἐκ πίστεως seems to be a metonym for Χριστός, and righteousness by means of ἐξ ἔργων has ended with the culmination of the νόμος.

(E) This argument is validated with scriptural citations including a conflation of Isa. 8.14, 28.16 (9.32-33) about Israel's stumbling and then again by Lev. 18.5, Dt. 9.4, 30.12-14 concerning the inability of persons to satisfy the Law in contrast to the efficacious descent of God's saving word (10.5-6).

What does this have to do with the meaning of τέλος γὰρ νόμου Χριστός? Matters about the discontinuity between the dispensations of Christ and Torah permeate Romans (3.21; 5.21; 6.14-15; 7.1-6) and the disjunction between the two reaches a climax here. In this immediate setting, Israel's stumbling in the wake of Christ consists of its failure to know that Christ is the *end* of the Law itself and that scripture points in the direction of a righteousness for Jews and gentiles. Righteousness is not the exclusive property of Israel because the Torah itself cannot properly be a source of righteousness. Rather, it is the righteousness of God, revealed in Christ, apprehended by faith, which provides righteousness for all. Yet continuity is not fully obviated as Paul endeavours to show the conformity of his message to Israel's scripture (esp. from Deuteronomy and Leviticus) and the parallels between 10.3-4 and 3.20-23 qualify the antithesis as forecast in Israel's sacred traditions. We can conclude that the Law is no more because its *goal* has been attained and, therefore, its operation has *terminated*. This means, as Paul goes on to argue, that salvation is located in the word of faith about Christ and not in the covenantal structures of the mosaic economy (10.6-14).

3.3. *Church and synagogue*

Paul's articulation of the Christ/Torah antithesis and his concomitant defence of gentile believers as gentiles emerge out of a particular social location. Paul's missionary career appears to have included periods of missionary activity oriented to Jews in Damascus/Arabia (Gal. 1.17; 5.11), Jews and gentiles in diasporan synagogues while connected with the Antioch church (Gal. 1.21), and focused *almost* exclusively on gentiles in his later Aegean mission (e.g., 1 Thess. 1.10). What is more, all of Paul's disputes over circumcision and Jewish observances in relation to gentiles can be situated within intra-diasporan Jewish debates over *halakah* for gentiles. Still, it appears that Paul soon began establishing Christ-believing assemblies that were separate from Judaism and included some persons who had never been part of the Jewish synagogues. As Wayne Meeks states: 'Socially the Pauline groups were never a sect of Judaism. They organized their lives independently from the Jewish associations of the cities where they were founded, and apparently, so far as the evidence reveals, they had little or no interaction with Jews.'[70] I hesitate in following Meeks on the degree of interaction between Jews and Christians (I think this was far more dynamic and varied depending on the individual contexts in Galatia, Corinth, Philippi, Thessalonica, Ephesus and Colossae), yet his central point of independence from Judaism at its formation probably holds true.

Paul's ecclesiology is a form of sectarianism that is built on a mixture of *socio-religious partitioning* and *theological reconfiguration* in relation to Jews and Judaism. The make-up of the Pauline churches undoubtedly

---

70. Wayne Meeks, 'Breaking Away: Three New Testament Pictures of Christianity's Separation from Jewish Communities', in *'To See Ourselves as Others see Us': Christians, Jews, and 'Others' in Late Antiquity*, eds J. Neusner and E. S. Frerich (Chico, CA: Scholars, 1985), p. 106; cf. Barclay (*Jews in the Mediterranean Diaspora*, p. 386): 'In social reality Paul's churches were distinct from the synagogues, and their predominantly Gentile members unattached to the Jewish community.'

included gentiles and Jews (e.g., Corinth: 1 Cor. 1.14; Acts 18.1-17). Yet if one of Paul's central convictions was that the 'dividing wall' between Jew and gentile had been broken down in Christ, then, as a matter of course, he was committed to providing an ideological defence of his thesis in order to defend the ethnic diversity of the churches under his apostolate. The ideological texture of Galatians and parts of Romans is that of a religious leader justifying separation from Judaism.[71] Paul's manner of *deviant labelling* (e.g., Phil. 3.2; Gal. 5.12) relates to those who endeavoured to bring his converts under the aegis of Torah as determinative for their identity and salvation. Similarly, his *reinterpretation* of Israel's sacred traditions (e.g., 2 Cor. 3.6-18; Gal. 3.10-29; 4.22-31; Rom. 4.1-25; 9.1-29) locates divine election through a route other than Jewish ethnicity and postulates reconciliation as occurring through Christ. This Pauline sectarianism should not be construed as entailing *denunciation* of Israel or Judaism; on the contrary, Paul is genuinely affirming of his parental religion, and he operates in terms of a promise/fulfilment framework and remains fixated not on Israel's destruction, but her deliverance.

Paul, then, marks a transition from a renewal movement within Judaism to the establishment of a sect on the fringes of Judaism. These communities are not *versus Judaism* but are para-Judaism in the social and theological sense. The 'parting of the ways' between Christianity and Judaism was a complex matter and differed through the centuries, in various geographical locales and in different socio-historical contexts of the ancient world. Nonetheless, it is hard to avoid the conclusion that Paul greatly contributed to that parting.[72]

4. Conclusion: Salvation from Judaism to Jesus

This study has provided a summary of the different ways in which Paul's perception of the soteriology of Judaism has been expressed in scholarship and to what extent Paul's own soteriological matrix is continuous with Judaism. Regardless of whether one places Paul within or exterior to Judaism, all commentators recognize that he had some point of contention with the way that salvation for gentiles was expressed by his Jewish and Jewish Christian contemporaries. That led us to explore the socio-religious location of Paul and his communities in relation to Judaism. We saw, first, that Paul's own identity is umbilically related to Judaism (even retaining its Israelite element) but is transcended and subsumed by being 'in Christ'. Second, it is evident from 2 Cor. 3.6-18 and Rom. 9.30–10.4 that Paul emphasized the discontinuity between the epochs of Christ and Torah/Moses in order to provide an ideological justification for maintaining the ethnic integrity of his

---

71. Watson, *Paul, Judaism, and the Gentiles*, pp. 51–6.
72. Cf. Barclay (*Jews in the Mediterranean Diaspora*, p. 395): 'Thus, mostly unwittingly, Paul fostered the fateful division between Christianity and Judaism.'; Frey ('Paul's Jewish Identity', p. 321): 'Even though Paul relentlessly worked for the unity of Jewish and Gentile Christians, it may well be the case that he actually contributed more to the later split between the increasingly Gentile church and Jewish Christianity.'

gentile converts as gentiles who worship the Jewish God through Jesus Christ, but wholly apart from proselytism. Yet the discontinuity is qualified and not absolute as Paul sees his Christ-faith as an extension of Judaism's scriptural heritage. Third, the Pauline communities eventually became separate from the institution of the synagogues. Though Paul himself seems to have engaged in some limited or spasmodic evangelistic activity towards Jews and pursued unity with Jewish Christians, he established predominantly gentile Christ-believing communities that never had been part of the synagogue.

What can we conclude about salvation in 'Paul's Judaism'? For a start, Paul teaches that salvation comes *from* Judaism in terms of its point of origin because Christ himself came from Israel and to Israel. In Pauline language, gentiles have been grafted into a Jewish olive tree and they receive the patriarchal promises only because Christ served (and continues to serve) the circumcision (Rom. 11.17-24; 15.8-9). Salvation will always be 'for' Israel as well since the messianic age gains currency from the efficacy of Israel's covenant promises. Still, there is no denying the tensions between himself and his Jew/Jewish Christian contemporaries when it comes to the means of 'salvation'. Paul knows of several soteric schemes in Judaism such as 'ethical monotheism' (Rom 1.18-32), 'covenantal nomism' (Romans 2–3; 9–11), an 'ethnocentric nomism' (Galatians), 'sapiential nomism' (1 Cor 1.10–3.23) and 'apocalyptic mysticism' (Colossians). Against all of these, salvation comes *from* Judaism in an antithetical sense because: (1) the Torah has served to antagonize rather than solve the Adamic condition of humanity in its state of alienation from God and one should not impose a deadly and defunct force upon his gentile converts; (2) because the majority of Israel including its leaders have vigorously opposed the message of the gospel; and (3) the Torah's temporal and ethnographic character did not lend itself to being the mechanism by which God achieved his purpose of extending salvation to the nations.

I want to stress to the point of calling anathemas down upon myself like Paul that such an antithesis should not be presented so as to evacuate Judaism, Israel and the Torah of its genuinely salvific role in salvation-history, nor to deny the irrevocable call that God has for Israel. Yet Paul's point of contention was not simply that Judaism needs to let the gentiles into a Christ-religion while the Jews themselves continue on under the Mosaic religion, nor is it that the eschatological sands had simply shifted and Israel was yet to catch up: it is far more problematic than that – the end had come in Christ and not in Torah. Furthermore, when Torah's role in salvation-history is viewed retrospectively through the lens of faith it is seen as oppressive, ineffectual and temporary.

Finally, it was formerly and famously said by E. P. Sanders: 'In short, this is what Paul finds wrong in Judaism: it is not Christianity.'[73] Similarly, Lloyd Gaston said: 'This is what Paul finds wrong with other Jews: that they do not

---

73. Sanders, *Paul and Palestinian Judaism*, p. 552.

share his revelation in Damascus.'[74] More recently, Mark Nanos has wryly written: 'this is what Paul would find wrong in Paulinism: *it is not Judaism*'.[75] But I say unto you: *this is what Paul finds wrong with Judaism, what the Torah could not do due to its exacerbation of the sin-flesh nexus and its limited role in salvation-history, God did by sending his son in the likeness of a human being and by bestowing his Spirit as a foretaste of the new creation by making Jews and gentile co-heirs of Abraham through Christ.* Consequently, for Paul, salvation is of Judaism only in so far as Judaism is of Jesus Christ.

74.   Gaston, *Paul and Torah*, p. 140
75.   Nanos, 'Paul and Judaism'.

Chapter 2

COVENANTAL THEOLOGY AND PARTICIPATION IN CHRIST:
PAULINE PERSPECTIVES ON TRANSFORMATION

William S. Campbell

1. Introduction: Aspects of an Ongoing Debate

In this essay I wish to emphasize aspects of commonality and continuity in Paul's understanding of covenant rather than those of opposition and discontinuity. In particular, I wish to situate my proposals in relation to recent discussion of this issue in interaction with some similar studies.[1]

The problem in discussing Paul's view of covenant is that there are so few explicit references to it in his letters;[2] moreover, all of these references are not general or absolute statements but entirely contextual, so that what they mean is determined not so much by the words Paul uses but by the context in which he has situated them. The interpretation of these contextual statements may also be further complicated by Paul's citation of scripture, within or in very close association to them. It seems to be a pattern that wherever Paul does cite scripture or use illustrations, this opens up an inviting space for commentators to fill with meaning in accord with their own presuppositions.[3]

1.   Cf. Thomas R. Blanton, IV, *Constructing a New Covenant* (Tübingen: Mohr/ Siebeck, 2007); Michael Bachmann, *Antijudaismus im Galaterbrief? Exegetische Studien zu einem polemischen Schreiben und der Theologie der Apostels Paulus* (Göttingen: Vandenhoeck/Ruprecht, 1999), pp. 127–58. ET *Antijudaism in Galatians?* by Robert Brawley (Grand Rapids, MI: Eerdmans, 2009); Paul B. Duff, 'Glory in the Ministry of Death: Gentile Condemnation and Letters of Recommendation', *Novum Testamentum*, 46 (2004), pp. 313–37. Cf. also '"Transformed from Glory to Glory": Paul's Appeal to the Experience of His Readers in 2 Corinthians 3.18', *JBL* 127 (2008), pp. 759–80; Robert Brawley, 'Contextuality, Intertextuality, and the Hendiadic Relationship of Promise and Law in Galatians, *Zeitschrift für die Neutestamentliche Wissenschaft*', 93 (2002): 99– 119.

2.   There are only eight references in Paul's undisputed letters: 1 Cor. 11.25; 2 Cor. 3.6, 14; Gal. 3.15, 17; 4.24; and Rom. 9.4, 11.27.

3.   Cf. James Crossley, 'Mark 7.1-23: Revisiting the Question of "All Foods Clean"', in *Torah in the New Testament*, Michael Tait and Peter Oakes (eds) (New York, NY: T&T Clark, 2009), pp. 8–20, 9.

This is sometimes done by putting together obscure and oblique references related to covenant in order to make a cumulative argument. But numerous instances of weak (apparently supportive) evidence are not as good as one clear witness, particularly when dealing with Paul's theologizing in differing contexts. Thus putting together very brief references involving scriptural citations in 2 Corinthians[4] with an allegorical passage from Galatians does not produce one convincing and coherent theology of covenant in Paul, although it is on these passages in particular that the latter may primarily have to be based. It is probably on account of issues such as those noted above that scholars come to diametrically opposed interpretations of the same passage from Paul.[5]

We will begin our discussion with a brief glance at the understanding of covenant in Galatians.[6] I cannot find evidence for J. Louis Martyn's claim that there is a sharp antithesis between two covenants in Paul.[7] I prefer Brawley's proposal that Paul denies such an antithesis, and attributes the division of two covenants to his interlocutors.[8] I likewise am persuaded that the problem of Law is not ethnocentricity; Michael Bachmann convincingly argues that the allegory of the two women in Galatians is not determined by ethnicity.[9] Brawley, in my opinion, rightly emphasizes the diatribe style of Gal. 3.19-21 in which the false premise of an imaginary interlocutor is rejected.[10] The false thesis proposed is that the Law is against the promises, but the solution of Paul is to synthesize Law and promise into one holistic hendiadic act of God.[11] Viewed from this perspective, Law and promise are not antithetic but ultimately complement one another in the ongoing story of how the monotheistic God blesses all the nations.[12]

4.   A basic issue in 2 Corinthians concerns the period of time to which Paul intends his comments to refer – is it to the time contemporaneous with the Moses reference or is it to Paul's own time? It is significant that interpreters frequently feel it necessary to introduce here the idea that Paul is thinking beyond the immediate context, i.e. to the whole of the old economy in general rather than in relation only to a more limited context. E. Nathan at several points draws attention to this tendency in his paper 'Paul Between Coherence and Contingency: Taking a Closer Look at Paul's Language in 2 Cor. 3', Pauline Theology in the Making Seminar, SBL Annual Meeting , New Orleans, 2009, pp. 1–8.

5.   Cf., for example, Mark Nanos's discussion of J. Louis Martyn's *Galatians: A New Translation with Introduction and Commentary* (AB 33; New York: Doubleday, 1997) in his article 'How Inter-Christian Approaches to Paul's Rhetoric Can Perpetuate Negative Evaluations of Jewishness – Although Proposing To avoid That Outcome', *Biblical Interpretation*, 13, no. 3 (2005): 255–69 (259–66).

6.   We will consider this theme particularly in the light of Robert Brawley's discussion of, and interaction with, the views of J. Louis Martyn (*Galatians*), and Michael Bachmann (*Antijudaism*).

7.   Martyn, *Galatians*, pp. 337–70. See Brawley's careful critique of this claim, 'Contextuality', pp. 109–19.

8.   Ibid., p. 110.

9.   Bachmann, *Antijudaism*, pp. 85–100; similarly Brawley, 'Contextuality', pp. 112–16.

10.   'Contextuality', pp. 109–10.

11.   Ibid., pp. 108–9.

12.   Brawley, 'Contextuality', p. 108. Bachmann argues that the relationship between promise and Law can be described from several different perspectives, and the function

Only with the greatest difficulty and extreme ingenuity can the παιδαγωγός be viewed as a negative image, as does H. D. Betz. Paul's image of the Law as παιδαγωγός is certainly not pejorative, otherwise the use of this image in a manner different from its normal use is inexplicable and self-defeating in terms of clear communication.[13]

Brawley is also convincing in his demonstration that in the citation of Isaiah 54.1 by Paul, the promise makes two Jerusalems into one, rather than setting up two parallel but differing and enduring entities. Jerusalem assumes two identities in Isaiah, a Jerusalem in captivity and a Jerusalem of hope in a promise, but the children of Jerusalem in captivity are also the ones who become the children of a free Jerusalem. Paul does not align his interlocutors with Hagar and his Christian readers with Sarah. But, significantly, his Christian readers may occupy either position.[14] I fully agree that the antithesis in the Jerusalem imagery in Galatians is not between gentile Christians and Jews but between slavery and freedom, options that actually pertain to the Galatian gentiles. Thus although rectification is ἐκ πίστεως and not by Law, yet it is also not *against* Law inasmuch as Paul synthesizes the Abrahamic and Sinaitic covenants.[15] Rather, in Christ the function of Law changes so that the Law is fulfilled as the fruit of being led by the Spirit.

It is evident that in recent as in former discussion of Paul, we have two major and conflicting images of the apostle which may be summarized as follows. Is the gospel which Paul preaches to be viewed in antithesis to the religion of Israel and/or to the Judaism contemporary with the apostle? Or is the gospel to be viewed not so much in antithesis to, as in comparison with, Moses and the era before Christ, in terms of 'how much more than' rather than in antithesis to? It is my contention that when the relevant texts are carefully and contextually considered, there is much more evidence of commonality and comparison between the Testaments, of greater glory revealed in Christ by the ongoing action of God, rather than of stark contrast between 'then' and 'now'. This perspective is most helpful in our attempt to understand why Paul has selected for discussion texts such as Exodus 34.29-35 in 2 Corinthians 3, and points also to Paul's own method of theologizing, to his role as an interpreter of texts, and to the continuity in the interpretative tradition which this implies.[16] That there is an element of comparison present

---

of the Law changes from its role as παιδαγωγός or disciplinarian in that it eventuates in Christ, having served its role in the divine purpose.

13.   Contra Hans Dieter Betz, *Galatians: A Commentary on Paul's Letter to the Churches in Galatia* (Hermeneia; Philadelphia, PA: Fortress, 1979), pp. 149, 163–73. Cf. Brawley, 'Contextuality', pp. 106–8.

14.   'Contextuality', pp. 114–18.

15.   Following Brawley, 'Contextuality', pp. 117–18.

16.   This is well illustrated in Thomas Blanton's careful demonstration that the common element in Jeremiah 31, Ezekiel 36 and Exodus 34 is the theme of covenantal renewal. 'Recent Research on 2 Cor. 3: Implications for the New Perspective', paper read in the Pauline Theology in the Making Seminar at the SBL Annual Meeting, New Orleans, 2009, p. 4.

in much of Pauline theologizing must not be denied. But this is genuine comparison implying some commonality in order for comparison to be valid and meaningful;[17] this differs greatly from the contrast of opposites and antitheses which we often encounter in any discussion of covenant.[18] As Blanton argues, if Paul cites in 2 Corinthians 3 traditions from Exodus 34, the paradigmatic example of covenant renewal in the Hebrew Bible, as well as other crucial texts dealing with covenant renewal such as Jeremiah 31 and Ezekiel 36, and speaks of himself as 'minister of the new covenant',[19] it is most likely that contrary to Sanders,[20] Paul has not transcended covenantal categories, but would seem rather to have relied on covenantal conceptions. But the question then arises as to what extent the theology that Paul creatively devises from these scriptural texts may itself be characterized as covenantal.

2. Commonality or Contrast? The Comparison between the Glory in the Ministry of Death and in Paul's Ministry of the Spirit

As already stated, one of the most fundamental texts in relation to covenant is 2 Corinthians 3. As E. P. Sanders has noted, Paul's argument is not simply expressed in black and white contrasts between the Old and New Testaments but also formulated as 'degrees of whiteness'.[21] A similar insight to this is developed by Paul B. Duff.[22] He notes that the *qal wahomer* type of analogy is basic to Paul's discussion – an argument from the lesser to the greater, or the light to the heavy – built on the premise that if X is true, then Y is also true but to a greater extent. This type of argument assumes X and Y's commonality. So important is this commonality between X and Y that an opposition (implied

---

17. Meaningful comparison implies commonality, whereas contrasting entities need have nothing at all in common. If in fact a covenant existed that was indeed completely new, it would serve only as a negative counterpart using the former covenant in negative self-definition, but bearing no intrinsic relation to it. The use of the terminology of the OT and NT in itself implies a relation, however that is to be defined. As D. Moo asserts, 'To break the link between old and new covenant is not to liberate the gospel but to destroy it for the gospel is nothing if it is not the continuation and fulfilment of all that God intended for and through his chosen people,' *Romans*, p. 535.

18. As for example in Heikki Räisänen, 'Galatians 2.16 and Paul's Break with Judaism', *NTS* 31 (1985): 543–53.

19. 'Recent Research on 2 Cor. 3', pp. 4–5.

20. *Paul and Palestinian Judaism* (Minneapolis, MN: Fortress, 1977), p. 514.

21. *Paul, the Law and the Jewish People* (Philadelphia, PA: Fortress, 1983), pp. 137–41. As Blanton notes ('Recent Research on 2 Cor. 3', p. 1), Sanders maintained his position on covenant in his second book on Paul (cf. pp. 207–10, esp. p. 210, n. 1). However, it is worth noting that Sanders does not make any mention of 2 Cor. 3 in relation to his subsequent discussion of covenant nomism in the latter publication.

22. In his article on 2 Cor. 3.6-18, Duff recognizes the problem in viewing the ministry (διακονία) of Moses as simultaneously accompanied by glory – i.e. the divine presence – and as also a ministry of Mosaic Law upon gentiles as a result of their not having kept the Law (as some Jews at Paul's time may have thought, even if not all shared this view) (pp. 320–6).

or otherwise) between the protasis and the apodosis would actually subvert the argument. Thus for the argument to succeed, both the protasis and the apodosis must share some commonality, and the protasis itself must be true as the starting point for the whole argument. If Paul compares the glory of the ministry of 'death' with the glory of his own ministry of the Spirit, then he is in fact acknowledging *commonality* in divine action, not merely contrasting or condemning this ministry in light of his own. Thus Duff paraphrases 2 Cor. 3.9 as follows: 'If Moses' ministry was glorious since it brought the Torah [i.e. 'the oracles of God', Rom.3.2] to humanity in general but more specifically to the Jews [although it also brought condemnation to the gentiles because they did not embrace it], how much more glorious is [Paul's] ministry which now brings reconciliation to the gentiles [without their having to follow the Torah]!' As Duff concludes, read in this way, 'the argument of 2 Cor. 3.7-11 truly functions as an argument from the lesser to the greater rather than an argument contrasting opposites'.[23]

I have sought to demonstrate elsewhere[24] that comparison, as already noted above, is a basic element in Paul's theologizing but one which is frequently misunderstood as a denigration of Judaism. In particular, Paul's listing of his Jewish credentials in Philippians chapter 3 is understood as a clear statement that these cherished Jewish credentials are to be regarded as loss, ζημία, or even as σκύβαλα,[25] refuse, something of little or no value to be quickly discarded. But this reading misinterprets the element of comparison present in the text. Paul is not making an absolute statement on the value or lack of value of Jewishness per se. Rather, he is evaluating in comparison to knowing Christ (Phil. 3.8). He would count everything as loss from this perspective. It is not just Jewish flesh or boasting that he includes but boasting in anything, gentile or Jewish, that is, πάντα, all things.[26] The problem is that because Paul uses his cherished Jewish attributes as examples, his statements in the comparison in Philippians 3 can be, and are, read almost universally as a denigration of Judaism. But Paul's rhetoric is concerned to emphasize to his gentile converts that *whatever* values you hold dear, these are as nothing compared with knowing Christ. Thus it is by means of the example of his own cherished Jewish attributes that Paul encourages his gentile converts to adopt a critical stance towards their own *gentile cultural values* and the

23. 'Glory in the Ministry of Death', p. 326.

24. '"I Rate All Things as Loss": Paul's Puzzling Accounting System: Judaism as Loss or The Re-Evaluation of All Things in Christ', *Celebrating Paul: Festschrift in Honour of J. A. Fitzmyer and J. Murphy-O'Connor*, ed. Peter Spitaler, CBQ Monograph Series (Washington, DC: Catholic Biblical Association of America, 2011); Duff, 'Glory in the Ministry of Death', p. 326.

25. In his use of σκύβαλα Paul does not intend to 'trash' his Jewish attributes but merely to revalue everything in comparison with Christ. It is not the entity itself that is changed but only Paul's evaluation of it. Food scraps for dogs probably has the correct nuance in view of the fact that Paul is speaking rhetorically here, cf. Marcus Bockmuehl, *The Epistle to the Philippians* (London: Black, 1997), pp. 207–8.

26. Dunn points out that after his conversion, Paul revalues all things. *The New Perspective on Paul*, rev. edn (Grand Rapids, MI: Eerdmans, 2008), pp. 481–6.

relation of these to life in Christ. This is achieved in this instance not by the denigration of Judaism, but rather by means of Paul as exemplar. Read from this perspective, Paul himself did not lose his Jewishness nor was he forced to reject it; rather, he was caused to revalue his Judaism and to express it in a new way.[27]

This interpretation is also valid for two similar passages, that is, 1 Cor. 7.19 and Gal. 6.15 respectively. In both of these Paul claims that circumcision is nothing (ἡ περιτομὴ οὐδέν ἐστιν; οὔτε γὰρ περιτομή τί ἐστιν) and this would seem to support the traditional critique of Judaism anticipated from Paul. But what is missed in interpreting these texts is that Paul not only asserts that circumcision is nothing, but goes on to state exactly the same about uncircumcision. In fact, rather than dealing with each as a separate entity, he ties the two tightly together so that *they should not be viewed in isolation but precisely in their relationship to one another and both together in comparison to being in Christ*.[28] Thus if we take Paul's meaning as indicating that living in the circumcision[29] is of the same negative value as being in a state of uncircumcision,[30] we might conclude that Paul is simply counter-cultural, equally critical of both Jewish and gentile society. But Paul does not mean these statements to be taken as absolutes – as ontological reality. Rather, the element of comparison present in the text is to be taken into account – it is in fact central here, and what Paul is actually saying is that 'compared with being in Christ, these significant and valued entities such as circumcision/ uncircumcision are as nothing'.

Thus he does not think that to be circumcised or uncircumcised is a matter of indifference.[31] Paul is not indifferent to certain things and concerned about others. Rather, he is indifferent to everything in the world in the same way. All is revalued in Christ.[32] Far from being indifferent to these things, these forms of living, in circumcision or in the foreskin, are still significant factors for Paul, though they have now all been radically re-evaluated in comparison with

27.   Cf. Alan Segal, *Paul, the Convert: The Apostolate and Apostasy of Saul the Pharisee* (New Haven, CT, London: Yale University Press, 1990), p. 70.

28.   If, in fact, we separate what Paul joins together in one construction, hermeneutically we are misreading Paul and forcing him to be responsible for statements he would actually never have made. Similarly, blessing and curse are two interrelated aspects of response to divine will and hermeneutically curse ought not to be seriously considered in isolation but only in its intrinsic relation to blessing. Cf. Michael Fishbane, *Text and Texture* (New York: Schocken, 1979), p. 61.

29.   Cf. Peter Tomson, 'Gamaliel's Counsel and the Apologetic Stance of Luke/Acts', in Joseph Verheyden (ed.), *The Unity of Luke/Acts* (Leuven: Peeters, 1999), pp. 585–604 (603).

30.   Cf. Ulrich Heckel, 'Das Bild der Heiden und die Identität der Christen bei Paulus', in Rolf Feldmeier and Ulrich Heckel (eds), *Die Heiden: Juden, Christen und das Problem des Fremden* (Tübingen: Mohr Siebeck, 1994), pp. 269–96 (273–4).

31.   Contra Niko Huttunen on 'Greco-Roman Philosophy and Paul's Teaching on the Law', in Lars Aejmelaeus and Antti Mustakallio (eds), *The Nordic Paul: Finnish Approaches to Pauline Theology* (London, New York: T&T Clark, 2008).

32.   See my unpublished paper '"As Having and as not Having": Paul and Indifferent Things in 1 Corinthians 7.17-32a.', SNTS Annual General Meeting, Aberdeen, 2006.

being in Christ. Hence these are not statements of ultimate value concerning circumcision/uncircumcision, but only comparative evaluations. Thus I might assert that health, wealth, home and family are of no significance compared with being in Christ, but that would not mean that I do not attribute great and lasting value to these in and by themselves.

When we parallel this form of argument with the similar argumentation Paul uses in Romans 5.8-10, 15-17 and Rom. 11.11-16, we can see how Paul relates the differing periods of salvation history. This is achieved in both instances by a *qal wahomer* form of argument which we have already noted in 2 Corinthians 3:[33] 'But God shows his love for us in that while we were yet sinners Christ died for us. Since, therefore, we are now justified by his blood, *much more* shall we be saved by him from the wrath of God. For if while we were enemies we were reconciled to God by the death of his Son, *much more*, now that we are reconciled, shall we be saved by his life' (Rom. 5.8-10). Similarly in Rom. 5.15-17: 'For if many died through one man's trespass, *much more* have the grace of God and the free gift in the grace of that one man Jesus Christ abounded for many ... If, because of one man's trespass, death reigned through that one man, *much more* will those who receive the abundance of grace and the free gift of righteousness reign in life through the one man, Jesus Christ.' So also in Rom. 11.12: 'For if their trespass means riches for the gentiles, how *much more* will their full inclusion mean!' Utilizing the same form of argument in vv. 13-15, Paul continues, 'Now I am speaking to you gentiles. Inasmuch then as I am an apostle to the gentiles, I magnify my ministry in order to make my fellow Jews jealous and thus save some of them. For if their rejection means the reconciliation of the world, what will their acceptance mean but life from the dead?' Here again in Romans, as already in 2 Corinthians, we find that Paul explains the effects and outcome of the Christ-event in terms of commonality, but with the emphasis from the lesser to the greater. We understand this to refer not to a presumed superiority of Christianity over Judaism, an anachronism in Paul's day, or even to the nullification of Israel's covenant.[34] The reference is rather

---

33. We are not here conflating the contents of the two letters but rather noting a parallel form of argument which itself is not determined by the differing contexts of the two epistles.

34. As Duff maintains, 'I suggest that what is veiled is not the nullification of Israel's covenant but rather that Moses has prevented Israel (past and present) from recognizing the deity's plan for the justification of all humanity, including the gentiles. In other words, it is the Torah's condemnation of those who do not keep the Law that is transitory, not Israel's covenant,' 'Transformed "From Glory to Glory": Paul's Appeal to the Experience of His Readers in 2 Corinthians 3.18', *JBL* 127 (2008): 759–80 (776), following his previous article 'Glory', pp. 327–8. According to Duff, the Corinthians 'see in themselves [i.e., as in a mirror] "the glory of the Lord" as they are transformed into "the same image", that is, into the image of the risen Christ', 'Transformed', pp. 773–4. This emphasis on transformation makes the meaning of 'τέλος' here (2 Cor. 3.13) as goal rather than termination all the more likely. As I have argued for in the case of Rom. 10.4, 'Christ the End of the Law: Rom. 10.4', in *Paul's Gospel in an Intercultural Context: Jew and Gentile in the Letter to the Romans* (Bern, Frankfurt, New York: Peter Lang, 1992), pp. 60–7; cf. also Robert Badenas, *Christ the End of the Law: Romans 10.4 in Pauline Perspective* (Sheffield: JSOT Press, 1985).

to the *extension* of the promises to the gentiles,[35] as Paul notes in passing in Rom. 9.24. In 2 Corinthians 3, whilst the argument is much more intricate, progress can be made if we stress the following aspects: Paul is addressing a gentile community, and therefore any reflections on Jews or Judaism are at the most, purely incidental.[36] Paul only employs the idea of the Corinthians' transformation to argue for the legitimacy of his own ministry.[37] He does not need written letters of commendation because he has the evidence of the Spirit in the formation of the Corinthians' community as evidence of the validity and effectiveness of his ministry (διακονία).

Whilst being generally in agreement with Duff's careful exegesis of this passage, we would not wish to perceive the comparison so much in terms of the *ministries* of Moses and of Paul. The comparison is more focused on the *glory of the divine presence* in the narrative of Exodus chapters 33–34 and on that same *divine activity and glory* in the proclamation of the gospel to gentiles. The glory of God had to be veiled lest the Israelites would be destroyed by that glory, but that same glory is now freely manifested to gentiles through Paul's ministry. The 'how much more' (πολλῷ μᾶλλον) of Paul's comparison should therefore not be read as an absolute statement or generalized as a comparison between the covenants. The glory of God present in Moses' activity meant death for gentiles, but the same glory of God now present in the extension of the promises to gentiles is so much greater, because it is through the Spirit a way to life (rather than death) for them.[38] We conclude, moreover, that *in Paul the different forms of divine activity and presence are not contrasted but compared, the glory of the new aeon in Christ being the greater (in extent) to which the lesser (in extent), but common, glory of God in the ministry of Moses is related*. In the working out of the divine purpose in both, the glory of God, that is, the presence of God, is operative and effective, but in differing ways. In qualitative terms it is the same glory of the same God but now through Christ extending to the world.

3. *Gentiles Share in the Blessings of the Promises but not in the Covenant*

It has become commonplace to note that the covenant is not a frequently used concept in the Pauline letters. Of course it has to be recognized that the covenant theme as such may occur at points where the term διαθήκη is absent.[39] Whether we can make much of this infrequency is a difficult

---

35.   Cf. Käsemann, *Romans*, p. 47.

36.   But see also the comments in note 86 below.

37.   Cf. Duff, 'Glory', pp. 765–8.

38.   As Duff states, 'the Corinthians , like virtually all gentiles, were under the sentence of death according to the Torah (brought by Moses). Paul points out that through his ministry (ἡ διακονία τῆς δικαιοσύνης) they have received the possibility of reconciliation with God and the commutation of that death sentence,' 'Transformed', p. 779.

39.   Cf. 'The Concept of Covenant in Paul', in Stanley E. Porter and Jacqueline C. R. de Roo (eds), *The Concept of the Covenant in the Second Temple Period* (Atlanta, GA: SBL, 2003), pp. 269–85.

issue. Did Paul really believe in a new covenant replacing or succeeding the old? Did he, as some scholars such as Lloyd Gaston[40] and John Gager maintain, actually believe in two covenants, one for Jews alongside another for gentiles?[41] It is more appropriate in my opinion to speak of a renewed rather than of a new covenant. The covenant with Israel is renewed through the action of God in Christ. Thus the covenant with Israel is renewed and the promises to the patriarchs are actualized so that gentiles can now share in the blessings brought through the Christ. The significance of the coming of Christ is formulated by Paul in Rom. 15.8 as having primarily the purpose of being a servant to the circumcised[42] in order to confirm the promises given to the patriarchs, and then only secondarily that 'the gentiles might glorify God for his mercy'. The actualization of the promises[43] in Christ means, according to Paul in this passage, that gentiles now have access to the promises (cf. Rom. 5.2, 'through him we have obtained access to this grace …'). But he does not state that this access is to the covenant – that is, that they are now *within the covenant*.[44] Rather, in baptism they participate in Christ (Gal. 3.26-29) , that is, all of their life is lived 'in Christ'[45] and by virtue of this relationship, they share through him in the blessings of the covenant promises.[46] In other words, whilst the covenant in the New Testament in relation to the inclusion of gentiles is necessarily a christological category, it cannot be used ecclesiologically.[47] If Beker is correct in his claim that there is a basic coherence in Paul's thought in Galatians and Romans despite the differing contextualization,[48] then it may be feasible to attempt an outline of Paul's understanding of the adoption of gentiles. It is only by virtue of being in Christ that gentiles are related to Abraham. They are not 'in Christ' in the same sense as they are 'in Abraham', but Christ is the firstborn of many brothers (Rom. 8.29). Gentiles in Christ

---

40. *Paul and the Torah* (Vancouver: University of British Columbia Press, 1987), esp. pp. 15–34.

41. *Reinventing Paul* (Oxford: Oxford University Press, 2000).

42. Cf. Bernd Schaller, '"Christus, der Diener der Beschneidung … auf ihn werden die Völker hoffen": Zu Charakter und Funktion der Schriftzitate in Röm. 15.7-13', in Dieter Sänger and Matthias Konradt (eds), *Das Gesetz im frühen Judentum und im Neuen Testament* (Göttingen: Vandenhoeck & Ruprecht, 2006), pp. 261–85.

43. I use this terminology to avoid any conception of an over-realised eschatology as suggested by fulfilment. Cf. J. Christiaan Beker, *Paul the Apostle: The Triumph of God in Life and Thought* (Edinburgh: T&T Clark, 1980), pp. 355–60; also Rolf Rendtorff, 'Ein gemeinsamer Bund für Juden und Christen? Auf der Suche nach einer neuen Bestimmung der christlich Identität', *KuI* 1 (1994): 3–20, 16–19.

44. Cf. Frank Crüsemann, *Kanon und Sozialgeschichte: Beiträge zum Alten Testament* (Gütersloh: Ch.Kaiser/Gütersloher Verlag, 2003), p. 294.

45. Cf. James D. G. Dunn, *The Theology of Paul* (Grand Rapids, MI: Eerdmans, 1998), pp. 399–402.

46. Since gentiles participate in the Lord's Supper as, e.g., in 1 Corinthians 11 where new covenant theology is used, it might seem inevitable that they are included within the covenant. This is, however, not the case as is well stated by Crüsemann, *Kanon*, pp. 297–9.

47. Cf. Crüsemann who states that 'Bund ist somit im Neuen Testament keine ekklesiologische, sondern eine christologische Kategorie', *Kanon*, p. 304.

48. Beker, *Paul*, p. 108.

become his siblings as sons of God (Gal. 3.26) and thus 'joint heirs with Christ' (Rom. 8.17). As Paul claims, 'And if you belong to Christ, then you are Abraham's descendants, heirs according to promise' (Gal. 3.29).[49] From this we conclude that: (a) gentiles are not within the covenant; (b) they do not have a covenant of their own; (c) there is no replacement of the old by the new covenant.[50]

The clearest point in Paul's argument in Romans in this respect is where he states in 11.16, 'if you, a wild olive shoot were grafted in to share the richness of the olive tree ...'. The gentiles only *share* in the blessings of God with Israel.[51] They are not designated as having a covenant of their own, in which case if they could go direct to God apart from the Jews, there would be no need to share with Israel. But gentiles do not have covenant association without Israel – 'for Paul there can be no church of gentile Christians alone'.[52] If anything is emphasized throughout Romans 11, it is that Jews and gentiles are intertwined in their destinies, the one without the other cannot find their full salvation – hence the incompleteness of salvation so long as the 'rest' of the Jews remains (Rom. 11.23). In short, since they have no covenant of their own the destiny of gentiles in Christ is necessarily intertwined with that of Israel.

A pointer to Paul's view of gentile status in relation to the promises is that he never designates Christ-following gentiles as Israel. In the past I have argued that gentile Christ-followers share in the covenant with Jews,[53] but despite this they are not designated as Israel – they remain as a community of gentiles in Christ, a satellite gathering or congregation alongside of

---

49. Cf. Caroline Hohnson Hodge, *If Sons Then Heirs: A Study of Kinship and Ethnicity in the Letters of Paul* (Oxford: Oxford University Press, 2007), pp. 103–6. I did not find that Hodge sufficiently differentiated the views of Paul on this issue in Galatians and Romans; e.g., in Galatians Christ is the one seed (σπέρμα) whereas in Rom. 4.16 all of Abraham's seed is mentioned, both Jews and gentiles. Also it is unclear how and in what sense it can be argued that being in Christ means being a part of Israel (p. 106). In my view being in Christ cannot be viewed as an ethnic category (pp. 132–5).

50. Similarly see Crüsemann's claim, 'Im Tod Jesu wäre damit nach dieser Deutung das realisiert, was einige alttestamentliche Texte als eschatologische Hoffnung formulieren ... dass aus dem Bund mit Israel schliesslich das Heil für die Völker erwächst, ohne dass diese einen eigenen Bund bekommen oder einfach in den Israelbund einbezogen werden,' *Kanon*, p. 299.

51. Note that in the case of Ishmael, although he is blessed, the covenant is only with Isaac; 'by framing the distinction between ברית and blessing, P contrasts the status of Abraham and Sarah, and Isaac and Ishmael', David A. Bernat, *Sign of the Covenant: Circumcision in the Priestly Tradition* (Atlanta, GA: SBL, 2009), p. 40; cf. also pp. 33–4.

52. Cf. Ernst Käsemann, *Commentary on Romans* (London: SCM, 1980), p. 309.

53. This implies the concept of gentile participation in an extended covenant rather than their participation in the covenant promises through Christ. For a good discussion of how the messianic promises should be understood, cf. Erich Zenger, 'Vom christlichen Umgang mit messianischen Texten der hebräischen Bibel', in Ekkehard W. Stegemann (ed.), *Messias-Vorstellungen bei Juden und Christen* (Stuttgart: Kohlhammer, 1993), pp. 129–45 (144–5).

Israel.[54] I still maintain the latter view, but recognize now that in the interests of consistency, if one claims that gentiles share in Israel's covenant, the consequence of this is that it must also be recognized that as equal members of the covenant, the title 'Israel' cannot then be withheld from them, as Paul appears to do. The arguments that gentiles do not become Israel are exegetically very strong despite much concentrated effort to dismiss these. James D. G. Dunn is consistent in his argument that if the covenant is opened up in Christ for gentiles, then they too become part of Israel, but I do not find a basis for such an inclusion in Paul.[55] The ending of Galatians chapter 6 clearly speaks of two entities, and not one, as indicated by the connecting καί, 'Peace and mercy be upon all who walk by this rule, and upon the Israel of God' (v. 16). Thus we have *another group* indicated in addition to those who follow the pattern of life in Christ affirmed in v. 15. It seems that Israel and the church remain two distinct entities.[56] When read in context, Gal. 6.15-16 gives no solid basis for designating the church of Jews and gentiles as new Israel, with the resultant potential for the displacement of Israel from the covenant.[57]

Romans 9–11 is also clear on this issue. The key point here is Romans chapter 9 in which Paul draws a distinction between Abraham's descendants and Abraham's seed. Although Israel κατὰ σάρκα is mentioned (in a neutral sense) in 9.3, neither here nor elsewhere in Paul do we find a reference to *Israel* κατὰ πνεύμα. In my opinion, the dichotomy of two Israels is a later development often anachronistically read back into Paul. The term 'Israel' is here limited to those who are children of promise (τὰ τέκνα τῆς ἐπαγγελίας,

---

54. Cf. Tomson, 'Gamaliel's Counsel and the Apologetic Stance of Luke/Acts', esp. pp. 601–4. Tomson, in a very careful argument, shows how Gamaliel's stance is open in relation to the emergent Christian group and the word βουλή in Acts 5.38 can be equivalent both to 'gathering' and to 'dissent', depending on whether the initiative is taken to be centripetal or centrifugal. Thus for Gamaliel, this gathering or 'initiative', as Tomson translates, may or may not be of God. Thus ἐκκλησία should not be viewed as having an anti-Jewish connotation, an alternative to Judaism, but as an assembly, 'in the sense of the local assembly of free citizens meeting in the theatre'. Cf. Dieter Georgi, 'The Early Church: Internal Jewish Migration or New Religion?', *HTR*, 1 (1995): 35–68 (41).

55. Cf. Dunn's comment, 'A Christianity which does not understand itself in some proper sense as "Israel" forfeits its claim to the scriptures of Israel,' *The Theology of Paul* (Grand Rapids, MI: Eerdmans, 1998), p. 508, cf. also pp. 509–13. In a similar vein, but arguing unconvincingly in my view on the basis of multiple identities, Johnson Hodge claims, 'Being in Christ means being a part of Israel' (p. 106) and that 'being in Christ is an ethnic designation' (p. 132); cf. also pp. 117–35.

56. In one sense it is possible to conceive of the ἐκκλησία τοῦ θεοῦ as one entity distinct from Jews and Greeks as in 1 Cor. 10.32, but this is not typical of Paul's general pattern. Although both Jews and gentiles share the same calling – see Paul's use of καλεῖν in Rom. 9.7 and 9.26 – this does not constitute an argument that they must live in the same pattern or share one common identity; rather, they maintain differing subgroup identities. Cf. my *Paul and the Creation of Christian Identity*, pp. 130–1.

57. Cf. Bachmann's comment, '... the Pauline terminology for Israel beyond Gal. 6.16 almost excludes the possibility that "the Israel of God" in this passage means the church made up of Jews and gentiles' (*Antijudaism*, p. 112).

9.8). Continuity with Abraham is not to be maintained or secured at the physical level only. Abraham's descendants should also share his faith. In light of this, Rom. 9.8 could be translated as: 'For it is not those of fleshly descent alone, but those of fleshly descent and of promise who are Abraham's seed.'[58] At this stage in his argument *Paul is not offering a general principle that any group of any descent could constitute the covenant people* as seems to be suggested by the RSV translation, 'This means that it is not the children of the flesh who are the children of God, but the children of the promise are reckoned as descendants.' In Paul's terms, the children of promise is here a subgroup *within* those of fleshly descent from Abraham, and at this point in chapter 9 he does not yet (prior to 9.24) include any beyond this group. It is not warranted to simply generalize this subgroup to refer to gentiles who at this stage in Paul's argument are not directly in focus. Paul bases his argument on the fact that the scripture says, ἐν Ἰσαὰκ κληθήσεταί σοι σπέρμα (9.7), thus recognizing a narrowing in the scope of the promise within the progeny of Abraham to only those whose descent is through Isaac and then Jacob. But this represents a limitation within the scope of the promise, not a transfer to others outside it, and certainly not to gentiles who do not come onto the scene until 9.24, and only then by analogy with the northern kingdom.[59] Paul is not here setting out a general principle that faith alone secures entry to the covenant promises, but only arguing the case for selection *within the descendants of Abraham*.

Of course this is only a section of a longer argument which goes on to speak of the inclusion of gentiles also in 9.24, and, when Paul comes to this, he will argue for an extension of covenant *promises* to include the gentiles. The pattern is this: first Paul establishes that not all those of fleshly descent are children of promise and then he argues that the God who had freedom to select from within the descendants of Abraham has the freedom to select gentiles also. But nowhere does he claim or assert that God has the freedom not to select any from within Israel – to do so would be to deny his own word of promise to Abraham and through him to the nations. The covenant with Israel is firm because even divine freedom is limited by divine commitment. As D. Harink has argued, 'God in his apocalyptic action cannot be unfaithful to his creative and elective action.'[60]

Moreover, the unity of Israel as a people is not sacrificed despite the wedge Paul appears to drive within his own people at 9.6b. A similar distinction appears at 11.23: 'and even the others, if they do not persist in their unbelief, will be grafted in …' But in his concluding verses of chapter 11, the unity

---

58. For a good discussion of Paul's differing statements in Galatians and Romans, see Beker, *Paul*, pp. 95–108.

59. Cf. my 'Divergent Images of Paul and His Mission', in Cristina Grenholm and Daniel Patte (eds), *Reading Israel in Romans: Legitimacy and Plausibility of Divergent Interpretations* (Harrisburg, PA: Trinity Press International, 1999), pp. 187–211, 198–200.

60. *Paul Among the Postliberals: Pauline Theology Beyond Christendom and Modernity* (Grand Rapids, MI: Brazos Press, 2003), p. 179, n. 34.

of Israel, 'all Israel', reappears. From this terminology, it seems that despite Paul's suggestive usage, Israel cannot be precisely limited only to those descendants of Abraham who share his faith.[61] The contrary view might prove enticing and convenient to Christian theologians since it would make feasible a definition of Israel which omits entirely to discuss those descendants who do not share their forefather's faith, and also leaps (too) easily from believing Israelites to gentile Christ-followers.

It is significant that Ernst Käsemann notes a similar point in relation to Rom. 4.11-12: 'His [Abraham's] example shows that everything depends only on faith. Becoming a proselyte is not a prior condition of this. In fact, then, Judaism is robbed of both Abraham and circumcision ...' Käsemann, however, in view of this problem goes on to add: 'This roughness is softened in v. 12. As often, Paul hastens to qualify an exaggerated statement. An ongoing relation of the patriarch to Judaism is now acknowledged. In fact the apostle is concerned to be able to call Abraham also the father of the circumcision, since any other course would take the promise away from Israel and contest its salvation history.'[62]

By thus making Abraham the forefather of all believers, 'the children of God' are in fact limited to this association – in theory they might be comprised only of Christ-followers of gentile origin with no connection with Abraham except through faith in Christ. This is not the route Paul followed in Romans. He is not content to salvage some remnant from the people of Israel and to sacrifice the rest. In this regard he sticks with the historical particularity of his own people Israel, and cannot be content even though at least some of them have found the new faith in Christ and shared it also with gentiles. A distinction remains in Paul's thought between Israel, whether or not it is faithful Israel or 'the rest', and those gentile Christ-followers who though not being Abraham's physical descendants become his lineage by virtue of Christ.[63] Thus Paul does not argue for a single family of Abraham's descendants but for a plurality of families.[64]

Having argued that the church of Jews and gentiles is not, in Paul's view, Israel, we need to clarify what are the implications of this for our understanding of covenant in Paul. It is very significant that in

61.   Pamela Eisenbaum points out that the exceptions to 'all Israel' are not those with exceptional sins whether in terms of quality or quantity (which is basically a Christian conception), but those who have chosen to opt out of being part of Israel: *Paul Was Not a Christian: The Original Message of a Misunderstood Apostle* (New York, NY: HarperCollins, 2009), p. 95. Cf. similarly Terence L. Donaldson, *Jews and Anti-Judaism in the New Testament: Decision Points and Interpretations* (London: SPCK, and Waco, TX: Baylor University Press, 2010), p. 119.

62.   *Commentary on Romans*, p. 116.

63.   Cf. Paula Fredriksen: 'Interpreters routinely slip from seeing the eschatological inclusion of the gentiles as meaning eschatological conversion. This is a category error. Saved gentiles are not Jews,' 'Judaism, the Circumcision of Gentiles, and Apocalyptic Hope', *JTH* 42 (1991), pp. 532–64, 547.

64.   This is well argued by Beker, *Paul*, pp. 96–9, 103; cf. esp. 'The Faithfulness of God and the Priority of Israel', pp. 13–16.

1 Thessalonians 1.9-12, Paul states to his gentile community that in their labour and toil for them, he and his co-workers 'exhorted each one … and encouraged and charged you to lead a life worthy of God, *who calls you into his own kingdom and glory*'. Here we do not have a reference to gentiles coming into the covenant but only into the kingdom and glory. It would seem that the gentile Christ-communities have access to the kingdom, that is, to 'this grace in which we stand' (Rom. 5.2), but not into the covenant.[65] As Paul states in 2 Cor. 7.1 (in a passage following on from a reference to gentile Christ-followers as a 'temple of the living God' (6.14b)), 'Since we have these promises …' We note he does not say, 'since we are in the covenant or in Israel'. The most significant description of gentile association with God is that they are 'in Christ' since all the promises of God find their affirmation in him (2 Cor. 1.20). But previously they were 'alienated from the commonwealth of Israel and the covenants of promise' (Eph. 2.12).[66] It would appear therefore that it is only in and through Christ that gentiles have the opportunity to share in the blessings of God also enjoyed by Jews in Christ. We can express it this way. Gentiles are blessed when the promises to the patriarchs are confirmed to Israel in the renewed covenant and thus actualized for all.[67] But they do not thereby join the covenant with Israel, else the distinction between Israel and the nations, so basic to Paul's own thinking, would be obliterated.[68]

As noted above, we prefer to use the terminology 'renewed' covenant rather than 'new' covenant since the latter might suggest a complete replacement of the former covenant or a new covenant specifically for the

65. Although there is a reference to the new covenant in 1 Corinthians 11 in relation to the Lord's Supper, this does not imply that gentiles are within the covenant. Cf. Crüsemann who states, 'Die Zueignung wie sie sich im Abendmahl gemäss dem Becherwort vollzieht, realisiert die Wirkung des Todes Jesu, also Sündenvergebung in Gestalt Tora-orientierter Herzenserneuerung bzw. als Sühne für die Vielen auch ausserhalb Israels. Sie realisiert sie für die Mahlteilnehmer in ihrer Gemeinschaft untereinander und mit Jesus bzw. mit Gott; das kann aber in keiner Weise als Eintritt in einen Bund bezeichnet werden,' *Kanon*, p. 299.

66. Stephen Fowl, 'Learning to Be a Gentile', in Andrew T. Lincoln and Angus Paddison (eds), *Christology and Scripture: Interdisciplinary Perspectives* (London/New York, NY: T&T Clark, 2007), pp. 22–40 (26–8).

67. Cf. Crüsemann's claim, 'Was also exegetisch im Alten Testament an einer Reihe von Texten zu beobachten ist, ist die Rede von einem Bund Gottes mit Israel, der Heilsfolgen für die Völker hat bzw. für sie eine eschatologische Nähe zu Gott eröffnet,' *Kanon*, p. 293.

68. Cf. J. C. Beker's comment, 'Paul never loses sight of the fact that Jews and gentiles are two distinct peoples who even in Christ cannot be fused into one general category of *homo universalis*,' 'The Faithfulness of God and the Priority of Israel in Paul's Letter to the Romans', in George W. E. Nickelsburg and George W. MacRae (eds), *Christians Among Jews and Gentiles: Essays in Honor of Krister Stendahl on His Sixty-fifth Birthday* (Philadelphia, PA: Fortress, 1986), pp. 10–16 (13). Similarly B. Schaller, who notes, 'dass die in ihm vorhandene terminologische Unterscheidung zwischen λαὸς αὐτοῦ und ἔθνη für die paulinische Israeltheologie geradezu grundsätzlich prägend ist. "Volk Gottes" ist und bleibt bei Paulus spezifische Bezeichnung Israels und damit der Juden,' 'Christus, der Diener der Beschneidung', p. 275.

church.[69] The differing covenants are thus seen as differing expressions of the ongoing faithfulness of God. The covenant remains a specifically Israelite entity, as Paul notes, 'to them belong the covenants' (Rom. 9.4). Paul does not take over the categories of covenant theology and apply them to Christians. If we are to speak of Paul's covenantal theology, it must be in terms of Paul affirming Israel's covenant, and of doing so in terms which Israel could recognize.[70] The renewed covenant is thus the 'old' covenant in a new light.[71] What is changed is the expansion of the blessings to gentiles as well as Jews, hence Paul's 'how much more' emphases. This is possibly one reason why Paul uses covenant terminology so sparsely in his letters to gentiles.[72] 'In Christ' language is rightly predominant. Gentiles in Christ are related to the covenant *only through Christ*. They do not become part of the covenant because its identity-forming dimension is specifically directed to Israelites, whereas for gentiles their identity is shaped by their location in Christ as gentiles and the pattern of life that appropriately flows from this through the work of the Spirit[73] (cf. Gal. 3.14, 'that in Christ Jesus the blessing of Abraham might come upon the gentiles'). The fact that Paul is a minister of the renewed covenant (2 Cor. 3.6) does not mean that he is anti-covenantal or that there is a new covenant with the church. What Paul conceives is a re-ratification of the former covenant with himself as the primary agent in administering this.[74] The covenant is renewed with Israel through Christ and though gentiles are not within the covenant, they are included in the promises now confirmed and as such share in a Jewish symbolic universe. Hence Paul must relate gentiles in Christ to the God of Israel and he does this through the Scriptures of Israel.[75]

69　Cf. Porter, *Covenant*, p. 306. Contra Ernst Käsemann, 'The Righteousness of God in Paul', *New Testament Questions of Today* (London: SCM Press, 1969), pp. 168–82 (180).

70.　Cf. Porter's comment, 'And in his single most important letter [Romans] the only covenant in view is the covenant(s) with Israel', *Covenant*, p. 306. Similarly Crüsemann, *Kanon*, p. 294.

71.　Cf. W. D. Davies, 'Paul and the People of Israel', *Jewish and Pauline Studies* (Philadelphia, PA: Fortress Press, 1984), pp. 123–52 (129).

72.　As noted by Nathan (see note 4 above) who demonstrates that in 2 Corinthians a good case can be made for both covenant and new creation categories in Paul's thought. Nathan rightly opposes any schematic conception of Paul's theologizing such as may be implied by covenantal theology. However, whilst recognizing the strength of this stance, I consider that my view of gentile association with Israel is capable of accommodating Paul's 'in Christ' contextualization.

73.　Thus everything in gentile culture has to be revalued and thus judged – as Paul states, 'Test everything, hold fast to what is good, abstain from every form of evil' (1 Thess. 5.21).

74.　As Blanton maintains, 'Only one covenant is envisaged in 2 Corinthians 3; one established, broken, and thus re-established. Paul depicts himself as the primary agent in administering this re-established covenant,' 'Recent Research on 2 Cor. 3', pp. 5–6.

75.　Cf. my *Paul and the Creation of Christian Identity*, pp. 57–61, and Kathy Ehrensperger, 'Paul and the Authority of Scripture: A Feminist Perspective', in Christopher D. Stanley and Stanley E. Porter (eds), *As It is Written: Studying Paul's Use of Scripture* (Atlanta, GA: SBL, 2008), pp. 281–308 (304–8). The significance of the Scriptures for the gentiles does not depend on their inclusion in Israel (contra Dunn, n. 55 above).

4. *Continuity and Transformation in Christ*

Although the renewed covenant is the 'old' covenant in a new perspective, it has nevertheless implications for the relationship of Jews and gentiles in Christ and thus, as noted above, for their ongoing identities. The covenant is not transformed but confirmed in Christ and it is this actualization that is the basis for the transformation of 'all things'. A crucial test of our understanding of Paul is whether we view him as seeking to obliterate or simply transform the previous value systems/hierarchies of his communities. Does he radically demand the obliteration of all identity distinctions such as gender and ethnic affiliation? If Gal. 3.28 is taken to mean that the Jew/gentile, male/female and slave/free distinctions are obliterated, it is hard to understand why married couples should remain married, especially to an unbelieving partner. As I have argued in my book on *Paul and the Creation of Christian Identity*, Paul does not seek to remove entirely all previous cultural affiliations and status, but decisively to transform Jews as Jews and gentiles as gentiles. Unlike some who stress new creation terminology in what might be termed a radical way, Paul recognizes that he starts from the given ('as you were when called'), recognizes it as a starting point in a process of change, and seeks to transform this given.[76] There is a parallel between new covenant and new creation terminology in Paul.[77] Just as the covenant is not annulled or obliterated so too the good creation that God has made is neither destroyed nor rejected. Like the covenant, creation is renewed in Christ. Käsemann rightly notes the link between covenant and creation[78] but, unfortunately in my view, posits an opposition between them much in the same way as he does with Abraham and Moses in terms of prototype and antitype.[79] As noted in the Introduction to this essay, I am not convinced that radical antitheses between past and present provide a good understanding of Paul's view of the world after the advent of Christ.

I recognize the strength of Sanders' assertion that 'the heart of Paul's thought is not one that ratifies and agrees to a covenant offered by God, and

---

76. As Segal claims, 'No convert forgets everything previously known. Rather, the convert changes a few key concepts, revaluing everything else accordingly. Old doctrines often remain intact but are completely changed in significance through the imposition of a new structure,' *Paul the Convert*, p. 75.

77. Cf. Käsemann's comment, 'For the apostle knows no God who can be isolated from his creation', *Romans*, p. 270. Cf. also pp. 93, 308–11 and 317; also '"The Righteousness of God" in Paul', *New Testament Questions of Today*, pp. 168–82 (178). Cf. Karl Kertelge's criticism that Käsemann and some of his followers put Israel at the margins of God's activity by overstressing divine creative action, which, though always present in Paul, is never at the centre of his thought, *Rechtfertigung bei Paulus* (Münster: Aschendorff, 1967), p. 308; similarly my *Paul and the Creation of Christian Identity*, pp. 136–9.

78. Käsemann notes that Judaism had already linked the traditions of creation and exodus, and of the fall and Israel's guilt, 'Paul presupposes this tradition', *Romans*, p. 46.

79. Cf. 'Paul and Israel', *New Testament Questions*, p. 185. Käsemann claims Paul did not speak of a *renewed* covenant as did the Jewish Christians before him, but of a *new* covenant. Moses is for him the antitype, not, like Abraham, the prototype of Christ the fulfiller of the promise (p. 185).

remaining in it on the condition of proper behaviour; but that one dies with Christ, obtaining new life and the initial transformation which leads to the resurrection and ultimate transformation, that one is a member of the body of Christ and one Spirit with him, and that one remains so unless one breaks the participatory union by forming another'.[80] Nevertheless, the renewal of the covenant with Israel need not require, as I have argued above, that Paul's understanding of gentile Christ-followers' obligations through the gospel must be explicitly identical with those of Jews in Christ. Thus Sanders' important insight need not be sacrificed despite his overall rejection of covenant in Paul. But to pose an opposition between covenantal theology and participation in Christ is not in my view an adequate or sufficiently comprehensive interpretation of Paul. Covenantal theology and participation in Christ, rather than being in opposition as proposed by Sanders, are complementary and demonstrate simultaneously both continuity and transformation. Were it not for the renewal of the covenant through Christ, there would be no good news either for Jews or gentiles, since being in Christ is an outcome of the actualized covenant. So we do not oppose in any way the continuing use of the term new covenant, provided it is understood in the sense of renewal as we believe to have been the case in earliest Christianity.[81] It should be kept in mind that the concept of 'new creation' is itself a Jewish one.[82] The promise of a new covenant in Jer. 31.31 does not imply an end to Israel's relationship with God or a new covenant with an entity other than Israel, but a re-ratified covenant with Israel. However, it is understandable that when the church became increasingly gentile and self-definition of the church over against Israel developed, the term new covenant developed overtones absent from earliest Christianity.[83]

It seems more appropriate in Pauline terms to view the renewal of the covenant as inalienably linked to the renewal of creation. The covenant is thereby not dissolved in the new creation but retains its nature and function within the purpose of God. The blessings of the covenant expand and extend now not only to gentiles in Christ but to the whole of creation (Rom. 8.18-25).[84] But as Blanton asserts, 'neither Paul's language of "cosmic reconciliation" nor that of "new creation" transcends covenantal categories. On closer inspection both logically presuppose a prior covenantal theology.'[85]

80. *Paul and Palestinian Judaism*, p. 514.
81. Cf. Crüsemann, *Kanon*, pp. 296–8.
82. Imported knowledge requires a social base – a plausibility structure – otherwise the knowledge becomes meaningless because it has been separated from the authenticating community. Cf. *Paul and the Creation of Christian Identity*, p. 143.
83. Cf. Crüsemann, *Kanon*, p. 296.
84. Cf. Käsemann's comment on 9.24-29: 'In place of the earlier restriction, we now have extension', *Romans*, p. 273.
85. Blanton, 'Recent Research on 2 Cor. 3', p. 12. As Beker has pointed out, 'Paul's interpretative achievement is that he combines particularity and universality ... he struggles to transform the apocalyptic language in which he lived and thought, so that it can correspond to the new event in his life, God's action in Christ for the sake of the liberation of the creation,' *Paul*, pp. 351–2.

We agree that covenantal categories are essential for a full understanding of Paul, whether in relation to Jews or to gentiles in Christ, but the question remains – what kind of covenantal categories are we dealing with? Though Paul does still think in terms of covenant both in respect of Judaism, and therefore also of himself, he is not obligated to include believing gentiles within the covenant. Thus their gentile context outside the covenant is foundational to his theologizing.[86] The problems of the world are neither covenant nor creation but the power of sin which affects everything.[87] The goal of transformation is the overcoming of sin and as such does not imply a denial either of particular identity or socio-cultural reality. It is a world affirming transformation not world denying as such. Again as Wayne Meeks notes, Paul is not counter-cultural despite his radical critiques of the Greco-Roman world in which he lived and worked.[88] Evidence of Paul's inclusive ethic is that the differing expressions of the living out of the life in Christ by Jews and gentiles are recognized as equally valid despite continuing to be different (e.g., Rom. 14.1–15.13).[89]

86.   It should be noted that some of Paul's forms of argument on behalf of his gentile communities may not be due to his own choice of language, or the normal categories of gentile Christ-following groups, but are expressly formulated in relation to the theses of his opponents, who may have been demanding full gentile incorporation into Israel and the covenant. Thus, although Paul may be defending the rights of gentiles who are not within the covenant category, he may nevertheless feel obligated to discuss the status of gentiles in relation to the covenantal presuppositions of his opponents. This factor is all the more accentuated because Paul does share some premises with his opponents since he is not, despite scholarly arguments to the contrary, advocating a new religion, but rather a differentiated understanding of Jewishness after the advent of Christ. As Blanton has argued, 'the fact that Paul is able to creatively modify certain of these structural elements in an effort to legitimate his position over against that of his missionary rivals in Corinth serves only to reinforce this conclusion: in-house disputes over the proper way to understand and actualize inherited theological structures engender, not a separate, self-generated classificatory category [i.e., a third race] but subsets within the prior category by which the terms of the debate had been set. In this case, the prior category is defined by the taxononomic construct, "covenantal nomism",' 'Recent Research on 2 Cor. 3', pp. 12–13.

87.   The argument in Romans 1–3 is not to prove that Jews and gentiles are both sinners but rather that they all, whether Jew or gentile, live in a world dominated by the power of sin. Cf. Kathy Ehrensperger, 'Reading Romans in the Face of the "Other": Levinas, the Jewish Philosopher, Meets Paul, the Jewish Apostle', in David Odell-Scott (ed.), *Reading Romans with Contemporary Philosophers and Theologians* (London, New York, NY: T&T Clark International, 2007), pp. 115–54 (133–6).

88.   *Christ Is the Question*, Louisville, KY: Westminster/John Knox Press, 2006, pp. 83–100.

89.   'Biblical revelation is the manifestation of God's empathy, God's caring for all creatures in their difference. These differences are an essential part of their commonality, of God's communion with human beings and our communion with one another. Biblical identity means solidarity with all other creatures, the respect for their otherness included. Their otherness is an essential part of their integrity, their independent and equal worth, and only in respecting that do we retain and maintain our own integrity and identity,' Georgi, 'The Early Church: Internal Jewish Migration or New Religion?', p. 68. Similarly, see my article on Ephesians, 'Unity and Diversity in the Church: Transformed Identities and the

We must not impose on Paul the sectarian mentality of sections of modern Christianity. He does not fear to discuss hopefully the future of those Jews who fail to recognize the Christ he proclaims, nor to debate with them in a shared use of common scriptural traditions the validity of his gospel. His hope is a hope that embraces even those who now reject his proclamation, but he refuses to accept *what is* as the ultimate reality which for him is Christ crucified and resurrected, the hope of the world. Thus Paul does not hold to a dualistic understanding of the world, but sees Christ as the supreme victor whose death and resurrection will eventually transform the whole created order. In this present time, he views his communities as proleptically participating through Christ in the coming kingdom in which all things will be completely transformed. Yet these same communities in the present time are still only in the process of being transformed (cf.μεταμορφούμεθα, 2 Cor. 3.18) by the word of the cross and through the example of Paul as he in turn imitates Christ as the pattern of life. They are called to be saints and Paul seeks to transform their identity by all possible means so that Christ is formed in them through their living together as a community in Christ.[90]

As Paula Fredriksen argues, 'through Christ in the Spirit these gentiles are no longer common ... but holy ... and thus suitable to be brought close to holiness'.[91] The key issue for gentiles in Christ is their change in status from profane to holy. This is clearly demonstrated by Paul's use of holiness language in places such as Rom. 12.1 ff.: 'present your bodies as a living sacrifice which is your appropriate worship'; and similarly 2 Corinthians 7.1: 'Since we have these promises, beloved, let us cleanse ourselves from every defilement of body and of spirit, making holiness perfect in the fear of God.'

Without becoming part of the covenant or adhering to Jewish ritual laws but having 'turned away from idols to the true and living God' (1 Thess. 1.9) these gentiles in Christ are now under God's sovereignty and thus in the sphere of holiness. To be in this sphere requires the holiness of the entire community and is thus the identity-forming agenda of that community.[92]

Holiness for Jews as distinct from gentiles in Christ has a different starting point. They still have the Law as an identity-determining factor and they retain their Jewish identity. But one aspect is different: they are now required

Peace of Christ in Ephesians', *Transformation: An International Journal of Holistic Mission Studies*, no. 1 (2008): 15–31. Cf. also Fowl: 'As Ephesians makes clear, however, although becoming a Christian does not require the erasure of one's ethnic or cultural past, it also requires the remembering of that past as a gentile past. It demands an understanding of one's past and present in relation to Israel and the God of Israel,' 'Learning To Be a Gentile', p. 39.

90.   Cf. chapter 10, 'Paul's Theology of Transformation', in *Paul and the Creation of Christian Identity*, pp. 158–73.

91.   Paula Fredriksen, 'Paul, Purity, and *Ekklesia* of the Gentiles', in Jack Pastor and Menahem Mor (eds), *The Beginnings of Christianity: A Collection of Articles* (Jerusalem: Yad Ben-Zvi Press, 2005), pp. 205–17, 213.

92.   Cf. K. Ehrensperger, '"nothing is profane" and "everything is indeed pure": Hospitality and Paul's Discussion of κοινός and καθαρος in Romans 14.14 and 14.20', short paper presented at the SNTS General Meeting, Vienna, 2009.

to recognize gentiles in Christ as equally holy despite their holiness not being determined by the Law. In Paul's view it is in and through this recognition that Israel fulfils her destiny to be a light to the gentiles.

Gentiles in Christ, on the other hand, can never relinquish their indebtedness to Abraham and thus to Israel; they have no separate covenant in which to boast over against Israel, but must humbly acknowledge that in the divine wisdom and mystery, salvation is 'to the Jew first' and also to the gentile, so that the salvation of the one without the other cannot be complete.

Chapter 3

PAUL'S COVENANTAL THEOLOGY IN 2 CORINTHIANS 2.14–7.4

Thomas R. Blanton, IV

In *Paul and Palestinian Judaism: A Comparison of Patterns of Religion*, E. P. Sanders argued that Paul's theological formulations should not be characterized as a form of covenantal nomism, but instead transcended covenantal categories altogether.[1] In Sanders' view, although Paul could speak of the community established after the death of Jesus as participating in a 'new covenant', this language is subsumed within the broader and more theologically germane category of new creation. The universal scope of Paul's soteriology is viewed as incompatible with the more limited purview of covenantal nomism, which is predicated on the election of Israel. Although Sanders drew the key phrase, 'new covenant', from 2 Cor. 3, he did not ground his views on a close investigation of that important text.[2]

This paper argues that covenantal conceptions are central theological categories in 2 Cor. 2.14–7.4[3] for the following reasons: 1) the biblical traditions on which Paul relies are related to the covenant renewal theologoumenon; 2) the claims advanced by a rival group of missionaries, who themselves advocated a form of the covenant renewal theologoumenon, has influenced

---

1.   *Paul and Palestinian Judaism: A Comparison of Patterns of Religion* (Minneapolis, MN: Fortress, 1977), pp. 513–14. Sanders maintains this position in *Paul, the Law, and the Jewish People* (Minneapolis, MN: Fortress, 1983), pp. 207–10 (see esp. n. 1, p. 210), and in his more recent article, 'Covenantal Nomism Revisited', *JSQ* 16 (2009): 23–55 (esp. 54–5).

2.   Sanders does, however, briefly discuss 2 Cor. 3 in *Paul, the Law, and the Jewish People*, pp. 137–41.

3.   Although I favour the hypothesis that canonical Second Corinthians is composed of five originally distinct letters (letter #1: 2 Cor. 1.1–2.13; 7.5-16; 13.11-13; letter #2: 2.14–6.13; 7.1-4; letter #3: 8.1-24; letter #4: 9.1-15; letter #5: 10.1–13.10; in addition to a fragment of a Pauline letter or a post-Pauline insertion: 6.14–7.1), the conclusions reached in this study do not depend on this view. For overviews of the partition theories, see Margaret Thrall, *The Second Epistle to the Corinthians* (2 vols, ICC; Edinburgh: T&T Clark, 1994, 2000), 1.1-49; Reimund Bieringer, 'Teilungshypothesen zum 2. Korintherbrief. Ein Forschungsüberblick', in Reimund Bieringer and Jan Lambrecht, *Studies on 2 Corinthians* (BETL 112; Leuven: Leuven University Press, 1994), pp. 67–105; Hans Dieter Betz, *2 Corinthians 8 and 9. A Commentary on Two Administrative Letters of the Apostle Paul* (Hermeneia; Philadelphia, PA: Fortress Press, 1985), pp. 3–36.

the format in which Paul's own theological arguments are advanced; and 3) the resultant theological pattern that Paul employs in 2 Cor. 2–7 is adequately characterized by the phrase 'covenantal nomism'. In addition, the paper falsifies Sanders' contention that the universalistic language of 'new creation' transcends the more limited purview of the covenant with Israel.[4] Second Temple Judaism already knew of a 'creational pattern of Torah observance', according to which the terms of YHWH's covenant with Israel were retrojected onto the story of creation, thus universalizing the terms of the covenant. Paul's universalistic and creational language in 2 Cor. 2–7 assumes the same 'creational pattern', which itself is both covenantal and nomistic.

From the outset, I would like to make clear a methodological consideration that will orient this study. Unlike studies that seek to reconstruct a synthetic 'Pauline theology' by privileging certain statements in Romans, and to a lesser extent, Galatians, and then reading Paul's other letters in light of those, I view Paul as operating in a manner analogous to that of a Greco-Roman orator, who first identifies his audience and then constructs an argument that is calculated to win the most favourable hearing by adapting his arguments to the particular characteristics and capacities of the addressees. (In Greco-Roman rhetorical theory, this procedure falls under the heading εὕρεσις or *inventio*.)[5] Paul was well aware of this oratorical convention, and he employed it as a missionary strategy (1 Cor. 9.19-23).[6] The extent to which this may have affected fundamental elements of his own theologizing can only be determined by a careful consideration of each of Paul's letters, viewed in terms of its own internal logic and arrangement. The present study approaches 2 Cor. 2.14–7.4 from this standpoint.

The terms of Paul's argument in 2 Cor. 2.14–7.4 were set by a dispute, evident also in 2 Cor. 10–13, in which he engaged the claims of rival missionaries who styled themselves 'ministers of righteousness' (2 Cor. 11.15), 'apostles of Christ' (11.13), 'ministers of Christ' (11.23) and, some have

---

4.   Sanders writes, '[A]lthough Paul uses the term "new covenant" to describe the community established by Christ's death, here doubtless following traditional Christian terminology (I Cor. 11.25; II Cor. 3.6), he can also speak of "new creation" (II Cor. 5.17; Gal. 6.15). What Christ has done is not … contrasted with what Moses did, but with what Adam did. Adam did not establish a covenant, but his transgression did determine the entire fate of mankind; and so has Christ's act determined the fate of the world. Here again we see the covenantal categories transcended' (*Paul and Palestinian Judaism*, p. 514).

5.   See Heinrich Lausberg, *Handbook of Literary Rhetoric: A Foundation for Literary Study* (Leiden, Boston, Köln: Brill, 1998; trans. by M. T. Bliss, A. Jansen and D. E. Orton of *Handbuch der literarischen Rhetorik. Eine Grundlegung der Literaturwissenschaft* (München: Max Hueber, 1973 (1960)), pp. 119–208; Malcolm Heath, 'Invention', in Stanley E. Porter, ed., *Handbook of Classical Rhetoric in the Hellenistic Period: 330 B.C.–A.D. 400* (Boston, MA, and Leiden: Brill, 2001), pp. 89–119.

6.   As argued extensively by Mark Nanos in his article in this volume, 'Paul's Relationship to Torah in Light of his Strategy "to Become Everything to Everyone" (1 Corinthians 9.19-22)'.

argued, 'ministers of the new covenant' (cp. 3.6).[7] This group preached a version of the gospel (11.4) that was at odds in some important respects with Paul's own. This paper builds on arguments that I have advanced elsewhere to the effect that these missionaries espoused a version of the covenant renewal theologoumenon, such as that evident in Jeremiah 32, Ezekiel 36, Jubilees, the Qumran *Community Rule* and the Epistle to the Hebrews.[8] The main points of the covenant renewal theologoumenon may be summarized as follows:

1) It is stated or implied that YHWH's people failed to obey the stipulations of the covenant, bringing upon them the curses attendant on breaking the covenant, including exile (cf. Deut. 28.47-68; Jer. 31.32; Ezek. 36.24, 28; Jub. 1.22-23; Heb. 8.7-9).

2) In response to the failure of the people to keep the terms of the covenant, a renewal of the covenant, or 'new covenant', is envisioned (Jer. 31.31; cp. 1QS iv.22; Heb. 8.8).

3) The ratification of the new covenant entails the forgiveness of prior transgressions against the covenant's terms (Jer. 31.34) or alternatively, the removal of impurity contracted as the result of the violation of covenantal stipulations (Ezek. 36.25; Jub. 1.23; 1QS iv.20-21).

4) In order to forestall the possibility that the renewed covenant might, like the former one, be broken, YHWH is described as providing the spirit to his people so as to endow them with the capacity to follow the Law perfectly (Ezek. 36.27; Jub. 1.23-24; 1QS iv.22-23; Heb. 8.10-11; 10.16).

5) Because the spirit transforms the people's minds so that they become perfectly obedient to the Torah, the new covenant remains in effect in perpetuity (Jub. 1.23b; 1QS iv.23-24; Heb. 9.15; 13.20).

Each of these points is reflected in Paul's 'Letter of Reconciliation' in 2 Cor. 2.14–7.4. Paul's (gentile) converts are viewed as culpable for violating covenantal stipulations (5.19-21; cp. #1); Paul refers to himself as a 'minister of the new covenant' (3.6; cp. #2); the possibility of forgiveness of prior covenantal transgressions is extended (5.19–6.2; cp. #3); and the transformation brought about by the spirit takes a central role (3.6, 8, 17-18; cp. #4). Due to the fact that it could be broken, the former covenant is viewed as temporally limited in scope (in Paul's treatment, its glory fades, 3.7, 11),

7.   So, tentatively, Annie Jaubert, *La notion d'alliance dans le judaïsme aux abords de l'ère chrétienne* (Patristica Sorboniensia 6; Paris: Éditions du Seuil, 1963), pp. 447–8; Mathias Rissi, *Studien zum zweiten Korintherbrief: Der alte Bund–Der Prediger–Der Tod* (ATANT 56; Zürich: Zwingli Verlag, 1969), pp. 23–4; Jerome Murphy-O'Connor, 'A Ministry Beyond the Letter (2 Cor. 3.1-6)', in Lorenzo De Lorenzi, ed., *Paolo Ministro del nuovo Testamento (2 Co 2,14–4,6)* (Serie Monographica di 'Benedictina': Sezione Biblico Ecumenica 9; Rome, 1987), pp. 105–57, esp. pp. 116–17.

8.   'Spirit and Covenant Renewal: A Theologoumenon of Paul's Opponents in Second Corinthians', *JBL*; *Constructing a New Covenant: Discursive Strategies in the Damascus Document and Second Corinthians* (WUNT 2.233; Tübingen: Mohr Siebeck, 2007), pp. 140–54, 203–4, 237. The list below is drawn from the former article.

whereas the new covenant is viewed as remaining in perpetuity (3.11; cp. #5). Each of these themes in 2 Cor. 2.14–7.4 corresponds with themes present in the covenant renewal theologoumenon, and all five of the themes of the theologoumenon are present in this section of Second Corinthians.

In the context of a dispute with his missionary rivals over issues involving letters of recommendation, Paul cites the central new covenant oracle of Jer. 31.31-34 in 2 Cor. 3.2-4 and alludes to Ezekiel's version of the covenant renewal theologoumenon (Ezek. 36.24-28) in the same passage. The letter that is described as 'written in your hearts' is generally recognized as an allusion to Jer. 31.33. The reference to the 'spirit of the living God' which writes 'not on stone tablets but on tablets of fleshly hearts' alludes to Ezek. 36.26-27.

Jeremiah 31 and Ezekiel 36 are not the only narratives of covenant renewal to which Paul alludes. The Moses narrative from Exodus 34 that Paul creatively reinterprets in 2 Cor. 3.7-18 was itself a story of covenant renewal. As Moses brought the tablets of the Law down from Mount Sinai, the people were in the act of breaking the first commandment by casting an image of YHWH in the form of a golden calf, necessitating a renewed covenant and a second giving of the Law. When he cites traditions from Exod. 34 in 2 Cor. 3, Paul cites the paradigmatic example of covenant renewal in the Hebrew Bible. The references to Jer. 31, Ezek. 36 and Exod. 34 indicate that covenantal categories, and in particular covenant renewal, form the background of Paul's thought in 2 Cor. 2.14–7.4.

The facts that the scriptural texts that Paul quotes or alludes to deal with the theme of covenant renewal, and that Paul even speaks of himself as a 'minister of the new covenant' in 2 Cor. 3.6, call into question Sanders' contention that Paul's theology transcends covenantal categories. In terms of the scriptural traditions from which he borrowed, he would seem rather to have relied on covenantal conceptions. This observation must, however, be tested by asking to what extent the theology that Paul creatively devises as the result of his interaction with these scriptural texts may also be characterized as covenantal. For this reason, we now turn to an examination of the theological structure of 2 Cor. 2–7.

The theological structure of Paul's 'Letter of Reconciliation' in 2 Cor. 2.14–7.4 involves five main points: 1) Paul's ministry 2) imparts the spirit 3) which brings about transformation and 4) effects reconciliation between God and humans. A positive response to this ministry results in 5) future resurrection, eternal glory and acquittal before God at the final judgment – in a word, σωτηρία, 'salvation'. This theological structure mirrors elements of the covenant renewal theologoumenon, and may be characterized as covenantal nomism according to Sanders' definition.[9] We now turn to examine this theological structure in more detail.

9.   Sanders defines covenantal nomism as follows: '(1) God has chosen Israel and (2) given the law. The law implies both (3) God's promise to maintain the election and (4) the requirement to obey. (5) God rewards obedience and punishes transgression. (6) The law provides for means of atonement, and atonement results in (7) maintenance or

Paul describes himself as a 'minister of the new covenant' in 2 Cor. 3.6, only a few lines after citing Jer. 31.33 and alluding to Ezek. 36.26-27. By citing Jer. 31 and alluding to Ezek. 36, Paul intimates that his ministry of the new covenant should be understood as a fulfilment of the act of covenant renewal envisioned in these prophetic texts.[10] The new covenant is therefore not to be seen as discontinuous with the former one. Rather, in keeping with the covenant renewal theologoumenon, it is portrayed as a reratification of the former covenant. This construal stands in tension with the two-covenant formulation of Gal. 4.21-31. Only one covenant is envisioned in 2 Cor. 3; one established, broken and then re-established. Paul depicts himself as the primary agent in administering this re-established covenant.[11]

In keeping with the tenets of the covenant renewal theologoumenon, Paul connects his new covenant ministry with the imparting of the Spirit. Paul's ministry is connected with the Spirit of the living God in 3.3, 3.6, and in his notice that he serves in a 'ministry of the Spirit' in 3.8. The function of the Spirit is specified in 3.18: it is responsible for transforming individuals gradually into 'the same image' as that of Christ. In an important caveat, Paul indicates in 3.16-17 that, although the Spirit is responsible for the glorification of those who 'turn to the Lord', it does not entail the necessity of adhering to all of the precepts of the Law of Moses: 'where the spirit of the Lord is, is freedom' with respect to the Law (i.e., the Spirit obviates the necessity of obedience to all of the precepts of the Law; cf. Gal. 2.4; 5.1).[12]

Does the 'freedom' that Paul espouses here indicate that the phrase 'covenantal nomism' does not apply to his theology? Paul's statements in 1 Cor. 5.13; 9.8-9; 10.6-11 and 14.21 impute to precepts of the Torah an authoritative status even for his gentile converts. In each of these passages, Paul legitimates by recourse to biblical texts practices that he enjoins his gentile converts to observe.[13] This mode of argumentation is rightly characterized

---

re-establishment of the covenantal relationship. (8) All those who are maintained in the covenant by obedience, atonement and God's mercy belong to the group which will be saved' (*Paul and Palestinian Judaism*, p. 422).

10. Similarly, Scott Hafemann argues in *Paul, Moses, and the History of Israel: The Letter/Spirit Contrast and the Argument from Scripture in 2 Corinthians 3* (WUNT 81; Tübingen: Mohr Siebeck, 1995), p. 139, that Paul portrayed 'his ministry as a fulfillment of the eschatological new age of the Spirit pictured in Ezekiel 11.19 and 36.26f'.

11. Paul's argument here assumes, rather than denies, the election of Israel (contra Sanders, *Paul, the Law, and the Jewish People*, p. 207).

12. Commentators interpret the 'freedom' mentioned in 3.13 either as a reference to 1) freedom from the Law; 2) freedom from the noetic effects of the 'veil' referred to in vv. 14-15; 3) a reference to or synonym for the παρρησία of 3.12, or a combination of these. The references to freedom/slavery in Gal. 2.4 and 5.1 argue strongly in favour of the view that 2 Cor. 3.17 refers to freedom from the obligation of fulfilling all of the stipulations of the Law.

13. Sanders notes such instances, but concludes that 'Paul's instruction still could not actually function as law ... There are only a few instances in which the motive or rationale behind an instruction is said to be that God commanded it ... More typically, however, Paul,

as halakhic.[14] Even more to the point, Paul takes the Torah's prohibition of idolatry as a foundational element of his ministry to the gentiles (e.g., 1 Thess. 1.9; 2 Cor. 6.14–7.1).[15] This indicates that the 'freedom' that Paul envisions is not absolute. This 'freedom' is only relative to what Paul construes as the more coercive standard of his missionary rivals, who likely, in accordance with the tenets of the covenant renewal *theologoumenon*, advocated a more thoroughgoing gentile adoption of the precepts of the Torah. According to Paul, this amounts to an attempt to 'enslave' the Corinthians (2 Cor. 11.20). In its practical aspect, we have in 2 Cor. 2–7 not an either/or debate over whether gentile converts should or should not follow the precepts of the Torah, but a more nuanced debate over which and how many of the precepts of the Torah applied to the gentiles under the conditions of the new covenant. This is a dispute about the practical application and actualization of covenantal nomism for gentiles, not an attempt to step outside of that category.

Turning again to our discussion of themes of transformation, we may point out that it recurs in 5.17, where Paul uses the category of 'new creation' as the guiding metaphor. Here, the one who is 'in Christ'[16] is described as a new creation: 'The old things have passed away. Look! The new has come!' The metaphor of new creation parallels other metaphors of transformation used in 2 Cor. 3–5 (i.e., transformation by degrees of glory in 3.18;[17] the

in dealing with concrete problems, offers an assortment of arguments (some, to be sure, based on scripture) without citing a commandment *qua* commandment to settle the issue' (*Paul, the Law, and the Jewish People*, pp. 106–7). This argument wrongly treats form and function as identical. The function of Law is to serve as a (prescriptive and/or proscriptive) norm for behaviour. This function may be, and in most cases is, achieved in the absence of a formal citation of the statute pertaining to a given act.

14. As demonstrated by Peter J. Tomson, *Paul and the Jewish Law: Halakha in the Letters of the Apostle to the Gentiles* (CRINT 3.1; Assen/Maastricht: Van Gorcum and Minneapolis, MN: Fortress, 1990). Sanders denies that Paul's arguments may be classified as *halakhah* on the grounds that they do not correspond with the formal characteristics of the (third–fifth century) halakhic midrashim (*Paul, the Law, and the Jewish People*, pp. 95, 106–7 and nn. 43, 47). The issue of literary genre must, however, be taken into consideration: Paul writes not compendia of legal rulings, but epistles which address specific issues that had arisen in particular communities.

15. In light of this, I now view my earlier statements to the effect that Paul preached a 'law-free gospel' as insufficiently nuanced (cf. *Constructing a New Covenant*, pp. 188, 226; 'Spirit and Covenant Renewal'). For a critique of the characterization of Paul's preaching as 'law-free', see Mark Nanos, 'The Myth of the "Law-Free" Paul Standing between Christians and Jews', in *Studies in Christian-Jewish Relations*, 4.1.4 (2009), pp. 1–21 (accessible online at http://escholarship.bc.edu/scjr/vol4/iss1/4/).

16. That is, one who has been incorporated into the body of Christ (i.e., the ἐκκλησία) through baptism (Gal. 3.27-28; Rom. 6.3-4) and/or one in whom the spirit of Christ dwells (Rom. 8.9-10). For a discussion, see James Dunn, *The Theology of Paul the Apostle* (Grand Rapids, MI, and Cambridge: Eerdmans, 1998), pp. 390–412.

17. On the passage, see Jan Lambrecht, 'Transformation in 2 Cor. 3.18', in Bieringer and Lambrecht, *Studies on 2 Corinthians*, pp. 295–307. This statement is clarified by 2 Cor. 4.4, which refers to the 'the enlightenment of the gospel of the glory of Christ, who is an image of God' (εἰκὼν τοῦ θεοῦ), while 4.6 speaks of 'the enlightenment of the knowledge

renewal of the 'inner human being' in 4.16;[18] and the hope of receiving the 'clothing' of a heavenly body in 5.2-4). These metaphors refer to acts of transformation accomplished through the agency of the Spirit.

Contrary to Sanders' view that Paul's covenantal theology is subordinated to his new creation language, the theme of new creation here does not supersede or negate the covenantal category. Rather, it depends on and presupposes it. Transformation (i.e., new creation) is accomplished through the agency of the Spirit, a Spirit construed in Ezekiel 36 as YHWH's means of guaranteeing successful renewal of the covenant. By citing this prophetic text, Paul implicitly endorses this position. This is confirmed by 3.6, in which Paul connects the spirit with covenant: 'a covenant not of the letter, but of the Spirit'. The function of the Spirit is not construed as independent of the covenantal category; its presence serves the instrumental role of generating a people divinely enabled to maintain covenant fidelity (cf. points 4 and 5 of the covenant renewal theologoumenon). Since the Spirit is deployed by the God of Israel specifically for the purpose of covenant renewal, and 'new creation' is the result of the transformation effected by that Spirit, new creation is contingent on new covenant.

The metaphor of transformation employed in 5.17 is immediately connected with reconciliation in the following verse. 'All of this', writes Paul, is the work of 'God who has reconciled himself to us through Christ' by entrusting Paul with the 'ministry of reconciliation'.[19] In 5.19 as in 5.17, Paul applies cosmological language to an anthropological issue: 'God was, through Christ, reconciling the world (κόσμος) to himself.' God reconciles the world (i.e., human beings) to himself by not counting their covenantal transgressions against them and by commissioning Paul as the mediator of the message of reconciliation. This reconciliation is made possible through the sacrificial death of Christ (5.21). The theology espoused here is both covenantal and nomistic: the use of the terms 'transgression' and 'sin' in these passages assumes a legal standard whereby transgressions could be defined and therefore identified,[20] and the reference to Christ as a sacrifice for sin assumes an established mechanism for the maintenance of covenantal

---

of the glory of God in the face of Jesus Christ'. Moyer Hubbard points out the important parallels between 3.18, 4.4 and 4.6 (*New Creation in Paul's Letters and Thought* (Cambridge: Cambridge University Press, 2002), p. 158).

18. See Hans-Dieter Betz, 'The Concept of the "Inner Human Being" (ὁ ἔσω ἄνθρωπος) in the Anthropology of Paul', *NTS* 46 (2000): 315–41.

19. 'All of this' (τὰ δὲ πάντα) refers to Christ's sacrificial death and the concomitant life of service that this entails for believers in vv. 14-17; so Thrall, *Second Corinthians*, 1.429. Furnish's argument that τὰ πάντα refers to 'all things' (i.e., the universe) is less likely (*II Corinthians* (AB; New York, NY, and London: Doubleday, 1984), p. 316).

20. Note that 'sin' denotes rebellion against covenantal stipulations; see Moshe Weinfeld, 'The Covenant of Grant in the Old Testament and in the Ancient Near East', *JAOS* 90.2 (1970): 189; idem, *Deuteronomy and the Deuteronomic School* (Oxford: Clarendon Press, 1972), p. 138, n. 1.

relationship despite occasional breeches of covenantal stipulations.[21] Finally, the state of justification that this sacrifice produces assumes a legal standard for the conviction or acquittal of the wrongdoer.

Although at first glance it may appear that Paul has transcended the covenantal category in that the covenant was established between God and Israel, whereas the reconciliation that Paul envisions is described as cosmic in scope, a closer inspection reveals that this universal scope was already a standard feature of the covenantal nomism of Second Temple Judaism. Texts of this period declare that God has a covenant lawsuit (ריב) with all humanity, since gentiles in particular were viewed as guilty of violating the first commandment (e.g., Jer. 25.31; CD 1.2).[22] The universal reconciliation that Paul envisions does not presuppose a prior or more germane covenant than the covenant between God and Israel. 'The gentiles' needed reconciliation with God because they had transgressed the stipulations set forth in God's covenant with Israel.

Paul universalizes the need to follow the stipulations of God's covenant with Israel, that is, the stipulations of the Torah, in a manner familiar from other early Jewish texts such as 4 Ezra,[23] 2 Baruch[24] and *Pesiqta de-Rav Kahana*. There is a tendency in these texts to retroject some or all of the stipulations of the Torah onto the story of creation. The ideological legitimation of Sabbath observance presented in the biblical priestly writer's account of the creation of the world in seven days is an early example of this phenomenon (Gen. 1.1–2.3).[25] A similar tendency is evidenced in rabbinic literature, as noted by Friedrich Avemarie, whose analysis of *Pesiqta de-Rav*

21.   This aspect of Paul's theology involves an important element of Sanders' definition of covenantal nomism; cf. n. 9, point #7 above. Sanders states, 'If there is atonement, there is also election and, of course, the law, which defines transgression and atonement. That is, if you have atonement you have covenantal nomism' ('Covenantal Nomism Revisited', p. 35).

22.   CD 1.2: ריב לו עם כל בשר; 'He [i.e., YHWH] has a covenant lawsuit with all flesh'; Jer. 25.31: ריב ליהוה בגוים; 'YHWH has a covenant lawsuit with the nations.' The view that gentiles were culpable for violating the stipulations of the Torah was fairly widespread in Second Temple Judaism; see Paul J. Duff, 'Glory in the Ministry of Death: Gentile Condemnation and Letters of Recommendation in 2 Cor. 3.6-18', *NovT* 46.4 (2004), pp. 313–37; Blanton, *Constructing a New Covenant*, pp. 41–3.

23.   IV Ezra 7.21-22, 24: 'For God strictly commanded those who came into the world, when they came, what they should do to live, and what they should do to avoid punishment. Nevertheless, they were not obedient ... They scorned his Law, and denied his covenants, and they have been unfaithful to his statutes and have not performed his works' (trans. of Bruce Metzger in *OTP* 1.537).

24.   2 Baruch 48.39-40 states that 'the Judge will come and not hesitate. For each of the inhabitants of the earth knew when he acted unrighteously, and they did not know my Law because of their pride' (trans. of A. F. J. Klijn in *OTP* 1.637).

25.   Genesis 2.1-4: 'Thus the heavens and the earth were finished, and all their multitude. And on the seventh day God finished the work that he had done, and he rested on the seventh day from all the work that he had done. So God blessed the seventh day and hallowed it, because on it God rested from all the work that he had done in creation' (NRSV).

Kahana 12.1 is apropos:[26] 'The human body and its natural environment are fashioned in accordance with the Torah, which implies that conformity to its prescriptions and prohibitions is the creational purpose of mankind. Although it is probably presupposed that this purpose can be realized only within Israel, the purpose itself is described as an anthropological constant independent of Israel's election.'[27] Avemarie refers to this tendency to retroject the terms of the covenant (i.e., the Torah) onto creation itself as a 'creational pattern of Torah observance'.

Paul's use of universalistic language does not, as Sanders argued, transcend covenantal categories. As was the case with his 'new creation' language, the universalistic language depends on these categories. Paul assumes a 'creational pattern of Torah observance' in 2 Cor. 2.14–7.4. This explains how he is able to assert that gentiles could be held guilty of 'transgressions' (5.19). As Paul is well aware, 'Where there is no law, there is no transgression' (Rom. 4.15). In this case, the Law is viewed as present from the time of creation.[28] This also explains why imagery from the creation story in Genesis is evoked in 2 Cor. 4.6 and 'new creation' language is used in 5.17. The problematic creational pattern, according to which gentiles were universally held guilty of covenantal transgressions, needed to be corrected by a 'new creation' in which gentiles were transformed into beings no longer guilty of transgression.

The function of new creation therefore parallels the function of regeneration by the Spirit under the conditions of the new covenant. In both cases, even (or perhaps especially) gentiles are held guilty of covenantal transgressions. Paul ascribes culpability not only to Israelites, who received the Law, but also to gentiles, for whom the Law, inscribed in the very fabric of nature, was always implicitly present. As we have seen, the 'new creation' is accomplished by the Spirit, the very agency that is designated as the means of effecting covenant renewal in 2 Cor. 2–7. 'New creation' is only accomplished when former covenantal transgressions are forgiven (5.19) on the basis of the sacrifice of Christ (which itself serves a restorative function within the covenantal economy; 5.21), and individuals are transformed by this Spirit whose purpose

---

26. *Pesiqta de-Rav Kahana* 12.1: 'The first man was obligated to six commandments … But you at Sinai have been obligated to 613 commandments: 248 prescriptions and 365 prohibitions. The 248 prescriptions correspond to the 248 limbs which are part of a man. And the 365 prohibitions correspond to the days of the solar year. Each day says to the man, I beg you, do not do this transgression on me!' Another important text is *Sifre Deuteronomy* 41: 'Behold, it says, *And the Lord God took the man and put him in the garden of Eden to work it* (לעבדה) *and to keep it* (לשמרה, Gen. 2.15). But what (can) working (have been) and what (can) keeping (have been) then? *To work it*, this refers to the study, and *to keep it*, this refers to the performance of the commandments.' The translations of both passages are those of Friedrich Avemarie, 'Tension Between God's Command and Israel's Obedience as Reflected in the Early Rabbinic Literature', in John Barclay and Simon Gathercole, eds, *Divine and Human Agency in Paul and his Cultural Environment* (London: T&T Clark, 2007), pp. 50–70 (59).

27. 'Tension Between God's Command and Israel's Obedience', p. 59.

28. Paul makes a similar assumption in Rom. 1.18-32. Contrast Gal. 3.19, in which the Law was not 'added' until the time of Moses.

is covenant renewal. Rather than transcending covenantal categories, Paul's 'new creation' theology in 2 Cor. 2–7 assumes them.

The last elements of Paul's theology that I will consider are his views on Christ as sacrifice and the final judgement. Paul adheres to the terms of the covenant renewal theologoumenon, albeit in Christianized form, as Christ appears as the sacrifice by which the new covenant is ratified (5.18-19).[29] Paul's sacrificial theology coheres with Sanders' definition of covenantal nomism (cf. n. 9, point #7). On that day in which all will be judged for their deeds, 'whether good or bad', at the judgement seat of Christ (5.10), those who have been reconciled to God through Paul's preaching will be declared righteous by God (cf. 5.21), since their transgression will not be counted against them (5.19). Here we see elements of covenantal nomism determining Paul's own theological formulations: Christ appears as a sacrifice for sins, this sacrifice (in accordance with Sanders' definition) 'maintains or re-establishes the covenantal relationship', by mediating forgiveness of former covenantal transgressions, resulting in 'righteousness', a state in which the individual is held to be acquitted of any covenantal transgression. This divine acquittal results in eternal life in a heavenly abode, an outcome also envisioned in other early Jewish texts (e.g., Dan. 12.3; *Jos. Asen.* 8.9; 22.13; *2 Bar.* 51.7-12; *L.A.B.* 19.12-13; *T. Mos.* 10.9-10).

In conclusion, Paul's theology in 2 Cor. 2–7, influenced by the covenant renewal theologoumenon and the 'creational pattern of Torah observance', follows the 'pattern' of covenantal nomism as Sanders defines it. Neither Paul's language of 'cosmic' reconciliation nor that of 'new creation' transcends covenantal categories. On closer inspection, both logically presuppose a prior covenantal theology.[30]

The fact that Paul creatively modifies some of the elements of the covenant renewal theologoumenon (most notably, in his contention that the presence of the Spirit effects a state of relative 'freedom' with respect to the Torah,

29.   Paul also connects the new covenant with Jesus' death, interpreted in sacrificial terms, in his citation of the Eucharistic formula in 1 Cor. 11.25 (cf. Joseph A. Fitzmyer, *First Corinthians: A New Translation with Introduction and Commentary* (AB 32; New Haven, CT, and London: Yale University Press, 2008), p. 443).

30.   In his contribution to this volume, William Campbell argues that in Paul's view, gentiles do not enter a covenant, but instead inherit the promises or blessings associated with YHWH's covenants with Israel. However, in Paul's view, gentile inheritance of promises or blessings such as being called into God's kingdom and glory (1 Thess. 2.12) or of becoming children of God (Gal. 3.26; 2 Cor. 6.18; Rom. 8.29) are contingent on the performance of practical obligations: one must not murder, steal, or engage in idolatry or illicit sexual relationships (e.g., Gal. 5.19-21; 1 Cor. 5.11; 6.9-10; Rom. 1.23-32; 2.21-22). In other words, one must adhere to certain stipulations outlined in the Torah (cp. Exod. 20.3-5a, 13-15; Deut. 5.7-9a, 17-19). Inasmuch as Paul construes the relationship between YHWH and gentile converts as one marked by mutual obligation, he viewed the two parties as existing in a covenantal relationship. Paul's statement in 2 Cor. 3.6 would seem strange if he did not think that he was the mediator of a covenant. I agree with Campbell, however, that Paul does not construe his gentile converts as becoming incorporated into the entity, 'Israel'. (On Paul's careful distinction between gentile converts and 'Israel', see Michael Bachmann's essay in this volume.)

rather than a divinely empowered ability to adhere perfectly to all of its precepts) does not alter this conclusion. In terms of the logic of classification, it is the presence and quantity of structures for which analogies can be found that determines the placement of a given entity within a taxonomic system.[31] The theological structures that Paul employs in 2 Cor. 2–7 find their analogies in Jewish systems that are themselves to be characterized as iterations of covenantal nomism: the covenant renewal theologoumenon, the 'creational pattern of Torah observance', and other structures such as final judgement on the basis of deeds. These structures occur in sufficient quantity to mark Paul's discourse in 2 Cor. 2.14–7.4 as a species of covenantal nomism. The fact that Paul creatively modifies certain of these structural elements in an effort to legitimate his position over against that of his missionary rivals in Corinth serves only to reinforce this conclusion: in-house disputes over the proper way to understand and actualize inherited theological structures engender, not separate, self-generated classificatory categories, but subsets within the prior category by which the terms of the debate had been set. In this case, the prior category is defined by the taxonomic construct, 'covenantal nomism'. Since according to Sanders' model, covenantal nomism is coterminous with Judaism, the implication is clear: Paul's theology in 2 Cor. 2–7 is to be classified as a subset within the broader category, Judaism.

31.　　Here I rely on Jonathan Z. Smith, who advocates a polythetic mode of classification in his essay, 'Fences and Neighbors: Some Contours of Early Judaism', repr. in J. Z. Smith, *Imagining Religion: From Jonestown to Babylon* (Chicago, IL, and London: University of Chicago Press, 1982), pp. 1–18. Smith states: 'In this new mode, a class is defined as consisting of a set of properties, each individual member of the class to possess 'a large (but unspecified) number' of these properties, with each property to be possessed by a 'large number' of individuals in the class, but no single property to be possessed by every member of the class' (p. 4).

Chapter 4

PAUL, ISRAEL AND THE GENTILES:
HERMENEUTICAL AND EXEGETICAL NOTES[*]

Michael Bachmann

1. On the Hermeneutical Situation

The present hermeneutical situation, in my judgement, unquestionably calls for a note of caution with regard to the subject area mentioned in the main title. In order to clarify this for oneself and for others, more than a hasty glance at more recent publications that are concerned with this area is required. Naturally they are not easy to overview. But some information on three spheres might suffice to gain an impression of the situation. Accordingly, I distinguish the recent discussions of some philosophers (see i) from Protestant and Catholic discourses (see ii and iii).

(i) Concerning the philosophical considerations, the publications of Alain Badiou (born 1937), Paris, Giorgio Agamben (born 1942), Venice, and Slavoj Žižek (born 1949), Ljubljana, should briefly be discussed. These publications,[1]

[*]   The paper presented in Leuven has been prepared nearly simultaneously with two further publications, and the content of this paper touches these two in several points, i.e.: M. Bachmann, 'Neue Zugänge zu Paulus – und ihre ökumenische Relevanz', in Cath(M) 63, 2009: 241–61; idem, 'Bemerkungen zur Auslegung zweier Genitivverbindungen des Galaterbriefs: "Werke des Gesetzes" (Gal 2,16 u.ö.) und "Israel Gottes" (Gal 6,16)', in idem/B. Kollmann (eds), *Umstrittener Galaterbrief. Studien zur Situierung und Theologie des Paulus-Schreibens* (BThSt 106), Neukirchen-Vluyn, 2009, pp. 95–118. There will be no special references given to these publications in the following. They and also other of my essays are now reprinted in M. Bachmann, *Von Paulus zur Apokalypse – und weiter. Exegetische und rezeptionsgeschichtliche Studien zum Neuen Testament* (samt englischsprachigen *summaries*) (NTOA 91), Göttingen, 2011. Many thanks to Thomas R. Blanton, IV, who kindly proofread the English of this essay. This chapter breaks with the volume style at the author's request.

[1]   Of these, this paper refers to the following books (in German translations): A. Badiou, *Paulus. Die Begründung des Universalismus*, München, 2002 (published again with different page numbers): Zürich/Berlin, 2009; translated by H. Jatho); G. Agamben, *Die Zeit, die bleibt. Ein Kommentar zum Römerbrief* (edition suhrkamp 2453), Frankfurt am Main, 2006 (translated by G. Giuriato); S. Žižek, *Das fragile Absolute. Warum es sich lohnt, das christliche Erbe zu verteidigen*, Berlin, 2000 (translated by N. G. Schneider (and J. Hagestedt)); idem, *Die gnadenlose Liebe* (stw 1545), Frankfurt am Main, 2001 (translated by N. G. Schneider).

which R. Spinnler put together in December 2008 in the weekly newspaper *Die Zeit*,[2] were at least partially written by areligious or atheist thinkers,[3] and it applies without exception to these authors that one has to attribute to them 'the complete unfamiliarity ... with more recent historical-critical and biblical-scientific discourses' (to pick up and to generalize a comment of E. W. Stegemann that refers only to Agamben).[4] Though these facts do not exclude interesting theses, this (bipartite) state of affairs at the same time is significant under hermeneutical points of view: The specific position of each philosopher, shaped not least by the Enlightenment, leave little room for the integration of other perceptions which would perhaps have enabled them to better judge the validity of their individually expressed interpretations.

At any rate, one can possibly escape in this manner from what A. Badiou denotes as a 'centuries-lasting obscurantism' and as 'churchly patois'.[5] His statements indicate, at least, that Paul can be of considerable relevance for people outside of the church. According to Spinnler's judgement, the 'discontent with political neoliberalism' and additionally 'with the cultural postmodernism era' play a significant role.[6] Badiou, who regards the apostle as a 'figure of uppermost importance',[7] so emphasizes a factor of our paradoxical political and social situation. This situation can be approximately described: In spite of the 'global market' (or the 'generalised circulation') 'one increases everywhere the rules and regulations preventing the circulation of people', for instance of 'foreign persons'.[8] In contrast, Paul stresses the phenomenon that Badiou already emphasizes in the subtitle of his book, *The Foundation of Universalism*, a phenomenon for which statements like Gal. 3.28 (and also Rom. 2.10; 1 Cor. 7.19) are offered as evidence.[9] It is remarkable how Badiou establishes Paul's relation to Judaism. He claims 'that there is nothing in the scriptures of Paul that even slightly resembles any anti-semitic statement'.[10] This seems to be noticed quite freshly!

G. Agamben criticizes the conception of Badiou (inter alia) because of the formulation of the spiritual, not fleshly, circumcision, as mentioned in Rom. 2.28-29, and because of a congruent Pauline differentiation with respect to the term 'Ἰουδαῖος'. From this, according to Agamben, 'the difference' may become obvious, 'that the Pauline procedure departs from modern

---

2.   R. Spinnler, 'Ein Sieg über das Siegen. Radikal im Denken, extrem in der Hoffnung: Warum der Apostel Paulus aktueller ist denn je und sich selbst die wichtigsten Philosophen der Gegegenwart für ihn begeistern', in *Die Zeit*, 17.12.2008, no. 52: 54–5. Cf. below n. 16.

3.   On this see only Badiou, *Paulus* (see n. 1), pp. 7–8, and Žižek, *Liebe* (see n. 1), p. 10.

4.   E. W. Stegemann, 'Die befristete Zeit. Der Philosoph Giorgio Agamben über den Römerbrief des Paulus', in *Neue Zürcher Zeitung*, 1.3.2007, no. 50: 55.

5.   Badiou, *Paulus* (see n. 1), p. 55.

6.   Spinnler, 'Sieg' (see n. 2), p. 54.

7.   Badiou, *Paulus* (see n. 1), p. 7.

8.   Quotations: Badiou, *Paulus*, pp. 20–1.

9.   On this see only Badiou, *Paulus*, pp. 20.46.

10.   Badiou, *Paulus*, p. 187.

universalism'.[11] But Agamben is close to the Frenchman insofar as he rejects all churchly and Jewish attempts to display 'Paul as founder of a new religion' and so to 'delete the Judaism of Paul or at least to extenuate it'.[12] In essence the Italian here, too, wants to point out what he primarily focuses on, mentioned also in the book's title, which alludes to 1 Cor. 7.29 (ff.), *The time that remains*,[13] that is, 'the structure of the messianic time', 'an aporia' which concerns 'the special connection of reminiscence and hope, past and presence, abundance and emptiness, origin and fulfilment'.[14] In as much as he emphasizes (like W. D. Davies and afterwards J. Taubes) 'the fundamentally Jewish messianic character of the Pauline faith',[15] this is also unquestionably a noteworthy attempt!

S. Žižek[16] has a similar but slightly different emphasis. One of his book titles reflecting the subject matter offers a clear hint: *The Fragile Absolute*. The author thinks that he can identify in Jesus, in early Christianity, and especially in Paul, a disruption of that (gentile) conception which 'experiences today an artificial renaissance ... in the multiplicity of the New Age approximations to nature and society'.[17] This disruption, according to Žižek, occurs with an antique conception which claims that 'the pagan cosmos, the divine hierarchical order of the cosmic principles that, if one applies them to society, results in the picture of a corresponding building in which each member resides in her/his position'.[18] With reference to Luke 14.26 and 1 Cor. 13 and with an allusion – again – to Gal. 3.28, Žižek formulates:[19] 'It is love itself that instructs us to separate from our organic environment, or, to speak with Paul: "For a Christian there are neither men nor women, neither

---

11.   Agamben, *Zeit* (see n. 1), p. 64.

12.   Agamben, *Zeit*, p. 12. Cf. further K. Wengst, '*Freut euch, ihr Völker, mit Gottes Volk!' Israel und die Völker als Thema des Paulus – ein Gang durch den Römerbrief*, Stuttgart, 2008, esp. p. 62 together with n. 278.

13.   On this see Agamben, *Zeit* (see n. 1), p. 16.

14.   Quotations: Agamben, *Zeit*, p. 11.

15.   Agamben, *Zeit*, p. 12. Agamben in this context (pp. 12–13) refers to the following publications: W. D. Davies, *Paul and Rabbinic Judaism. Some Rabbinic Elements in Pauline Theology*, 2nd edn (with additional notes), London, 1955 (1st edn: 1948); J. Taubes, *Die politische Theologie des Paulus. Vorträge, gehalten an der Forschungsstätte der evangelischen Studiengemeinschaft in Heidelberg, 23–27. Feb. 1987*, ed. A. and J. Assmann, München, 1993 (3rd edn: 2003).

16.   On (inter alia) him, see Th. R. Flynn, 'Das Ereignis lesen: Žižek liest Badiou über den Heiligen Paulus', in E. M. Voigt/H. J. Silverman (eds), *Über Žižek. Perspektiven und Kritiken*, Wien, 2004, pp. 191–209 (together with notes); D. Finkelde, *Politische Eschatologie nach Paulus. Badiou – Žižek – Agamben – Santner*, Wien, 2007, pp. 41–73 (including notes); A. Kotsko, *Žižek and Theology*, London/New York (NY), 2008; H. Löhr, 'Paulus unter den Philosophen. Eine Besinnung auf den Zweck paulinischer Theologie', in GlLern 23, 2008: 150–63. Concerning Badiou, the following paper has also recently been published: L. L. Welborn, '"Extraction from the Mortal Site": Badiou on the Resurrection in Paul', in NTS 55, 2009: 295–314.

17.   Žižek, *Absolute* (see n. 1), p. 130.

18.   Žižek, *Absolute*, p. 129.

19.   Žižek, *Absolute*, p. 131. Cf. 134: 1 Cor. 12.24.

Jews nor Greeks."' Again a philosophical view commands a certain respect, as was the case before with the 'universalism' and the 'Jewish messianic character of the Pauline faith'!

However, Žižek considers this disruption with gentile cosmological thought and the emphasis on love with regard to the apostle also as 'the suspension of the law's vicious circle and of its law-breaking desire'.[20] The Slovenian further considers Rom. 10.4 in terms of the thesis of the ending of the Law.[21] The philosophical interpretations mentioned here seem to be untouched by the most recent exegetical debates – and apparently really are – but they are finally incorporated into a centuries-long tradition of the reception of Paul, as this example of the Law shows quite plainly. Beyond that, it is therefore not precluded that something like 'churchly patois' may reoccur unintentionally from time to time, as is the case with the modern interpreters of the apostle discussed here.

(ii) That 'wing' of the more recent exegesis of Paul, consisting mostly of Protestant exegetes, which J. D. G. Dunn has, with some justification, and doubtlessly very effectively for the public, named 'The New Perspective on Paul' in 1982–3,[22] is largely characterized by the conviction that certain aspects of the history of the reception of Paul must be (partly) overcome if the apostle's statements are to appear unobscured. Consequently, traditions of biblical interpretation are scrutinized, especially those connected with the name of the reformer Martin Luther, but also with something like 'the' Lutheranism and the exegesis proceeding from it. This 'Gemengelage' (K. Haacker), especially the coexistence of a 'Lutheran and [a] New Perspective on Paul' – which is, by the way, the main title of a multiple-author work that I published in 2005[23] – entails not only quite fresh new approaches, but also remarkable hermeneutical problems. What initially concerns these new approaches, to designate two items as constituting something like a consensus still seems to me to be basically correct. Ch. Strecker already formulated them a decade ago as follows: '1) The quintessence of the Pauline doctrine of justification here is not ... the question of the salvation of the individual, but the question of the soteriological status of the Gentiles'; it 'is, in other words, primarily about the inclusion of the Gentiles into the salvation of God's people ... 2) The apostle's doctrine of justification will no longer be read as an attack against an alleged "righteousness by works" or "legalistic" Judaism'; in this respect room is made for 'a more just and appropriate characterisation of

20.   Žižek, *Absolute*, p. 180. Cf. pp. 127–8 (Rom. 7) and 183.
21.   On this, see only Žižek, *Liebe* (see n. 1), pp. 168.173.
22.   J. D. G. Dunn, 'The New Perspective on Paul', in idem, *The New Perspective on Paul: Collected Essays* (WUNT 185), Tübingen, 2005 (first: 1983), pp. 89–110. The paper is based on a lecture from 4 November 1982 in Manchester (Manson Memorial Lecture). Cf. further M. Bachmann, 'J. D. G. Dunn und die Neue Paulusperspektive', in ThZ 63, 2007: 25–43.
23.   This is where K. Haacker uses just this expression: K. H., 'Verdienste und Grenzen der "neuen Perspektive" der Paulus-Auslegung', in M. Bachmann (ed. [in cooperation with J. Woyke]), *Lutherische und Neue Paulusperspektive. Beiträge zu einem Schlüsselproblem der gegenwärtigen exegetischen Diskussion* (WUNT 182), Tübingen, 2005, pp. 1–15, 3.

ancient Jewish religiosity'.[24] Nevertheless, complications of a hermeneutical nature are already abundantly connected with these two items. Even if one, similar to Strecker, briefly outlines the list for this 'wing' of the exegesis of Paul, naming only the prominent New Testament scholars Krister Stendahl, Ed Parish Sanders, Heikki Raisänen, J. D. G. Dunn, Nicholas Thomas Wright and Lloyd Gaston (thereby placing the chronological beginning of this research approach in the early 1960s of the last century[25]) – especially if one does not include non-Anglo-Saxon exegetes like Klaus Haacker, Mogens Müller and myself[26] – at least three problems would occur, as follows.

Firstly, subtleties and differences of conceptions within this 'wing' already recede with such a 'Gemengelage' and this excessively strains and clouds the more recent exegetical conversation. E. P. Sanders, for instance, had already attested in the Fourth Book of Ezra something like works righteousness[27] – and concerning myself, in 1994, with reference to Wisdom 6.18b, I addressed similar traits in the broader area of early Judaism.[28] Furthermore, as should briefly be mentioned, the Pauline estimation of the relationship of the Christian community to Judaism is evaluated quite differently, for instance, by E. P. Sanders and J. D. G. Dunn – and differently again by K. Stendahl and L. Gaston.[29] As formulated by Strecker, 'a thesis of discontinuity towards Judaism' (Sanders) and one of 'continuity towards Judaism' (Dunn) are placed side by side.[30] The neglect of these subtleties and differences is not necessarily imposed by, but may indeed be suggested by the pithy formulation,

24. Ch. Strecker, 'Paulus aus einer "neuen Perspektive". Der Paradigmenwechsel in der jüngeren Paulusforschung', KuI 11, 1996: 3–18, 4 (St., however, partly uses italics here).

25. K. Stendahl, 'The Apostle Paul and the Introspective Conscience of the West', in HThR 56, 1963: 199–215; the essay (republished, inter alia, in idem, *Paul among Jews and Gentiles and Other Essays*, Philadelphia, PA, 1976, pp. 78–96; a German translation in idem, 'Paulus und das introspektive Gewissen des Westens', in KuI 11, 1996: 19–33) which was preceded by some other versions (on this, see M. Bachmann, *Sünder oder Übertreter. Studien zur Argumentation in Gal 2,15ff.* [WUNT 59], Tübingen, 1992, p. 3 together with nn. 13–14, and F. W. Horn, 'Juden und Heiden. Aspekte der Verhältnisbestimmung in den paulinischen Briefen. Ein Gespräch mit Krister Stendahl', in Bachmann (ed.), *Lutherische ... Paulusperspektive* [see n. 23], pp. 17–39, 17–18). Cf. K. Stendahl, *Das Vermächtnis des Paulus. Eine neue Sicht auf den Römerbrief*, Zürich, 2001 (English: 1995).

26. For K. Haacker, see only his study referred to above, n. 23, and for myself, correspondingly, see only, above, n. 22. Furthermore, the following essays should be mentioned here: M. Müller, 'Jesus und das Gesetz. Eine Skizze im Licht der Rezeptionen', KuD 50, 2004: 208–25; idem, 'Aufhören oder Vollendung des Gesetzes? Eine Antwort an Friedrich Beißer', in KuD 53, 2005: 308–9.

27. On this, see E. P. Sanders, *Paulus und das palästinische Judentum. Ein Vergleich zweier Religionsstrukturen* (StUNT 17), Göttingen, 1985 (English: 1977), p. 384.

28. On this, see M. Bachmann, 'Jüdischer Bundesnomismus und paulinisches Gesetzesverständnis, das Fußbodenmosaik von Bet Alfa und das Textsegment Gal 3,15-29', in, idem, *Antijudaismus im Galaterbrief? Exegetische Studien zu einem polemischen Schreiben und zur Theologie des Apostels Paulus* (NTOA 40), Freiburg (Schweiz)/Göttingen, 1999 (first: 1994, English: 2009 [on this, see, below, n. 50]), pp. 57–77/80, (58–)9.

29. On this, see only Horn, 'Juden' (see n. 25), pp. 31–4 together with n. 48.

30. Quotations: Strecker, 'Paradigmenwechsel' (see n. 24), pp. 8 and 11.

'*The* New Perspective on Paul'. But perhaps with the criticism of Sanders 'forming a portrait of Early Judaism that it too homogeneous',[31] the question of what is right and wrong in the new approach is still not decisively brought forward.[32]

Secondly, the roughly outlined situation about 'The New Perspective on Paul' seems to entail a further form of malfunction. With the focusing on certain 'masterminds' like Sanders and Dunn – the more so in the case that one of these exegetes has recently given his opinion on an appointed complex of problems – the dissent in this 'wing', which cannot be denied, is often considered as simply settled. So, for instance, J. Schröter tries to make use of the critical response of J. G. D. Dunn to my interpretation of the syntagma ἔργα νόμου,[33] a syntagma that I, as might be known, unlike the English exegete, do not simultaneously relate to regulations *and* practices, but exclusively to something like halakhot, and the Berlin scholar proceeds this way, even though I argumentatively rejected Dunn's criticism.[34] [35] Similarly, occasionally a certain completion of the discussion about the new approach portrayed here is assumed, so that a new 'Post-"New Perspective" Perspective' is proclaimed.[36]

Thirdly, the 'Gemengelage' around 'The New Perspective on Paul' naturally provokes, as mentioned above, heavy replies, since a '(not always fairly sketched) "negative-foil"'[37] plays a role here, namely the 'Lutheran

31.   So St. Schreiber, 'Paulus und die Tradition. Zur Hermeneutik der "Rechtfertigung" in neuer Perspektive', in ThRv 105, 2009: 91–102, p. 95 (together with n. 20) – who, however, here only gives a report!

32.   On this, see Schreiber, 'Hermeneutik', p. 95, where he indicates this immediately: 'Nonetheless Sanders' result is important because it points to the possibility of finding in covenantal nomism a structural and factual basis connecting ancient Jews of different groups in spite of dividing lines.'

33.   J. Schröter, 'Die Universalisierung des Gesetzes im Galaterbrief. Ein Beitrag zum Gesetzesverständnis des Paulus', in, idem, *Von Jesus zum Neuen Testament. Studien zur urchristlichen Theologiegeschichte und zur Entstehung des neutestamentlichen Kanons* (WUNT 204), Tübingen, 2007, pp. 171–201 (first [in another version]: 2000), p. 177 (together with) n. 19. (Similarly, for instance, P. M. Sprinkle, *Law and Life. The Interpretation of Leviticus 18:5 in Early Judaism and in Paul* [WUNT II/241], Tübingen, 2008, pp. 156–8 [together with] n. 17.) Cf. (on this) already M. Bachmann, 'Zur Entstehung (und zur Überwindung) des christlichen Antijudaismus', in ZNT 10 (5th year), 2002: 44–52, p. 48 together with nn. 39–40 (esp. n. 39), furthermore, below, what has to be said in the text after n. 87.

34.   On this, see esp. J. D. G. Dunn, 'The Dialogue Progresses', in Bachmann (ed.), *Lutherische ... Paulusperspektive* (see n. 23), pp. 389–430. 398–401.

35.   On this, see esp. M. Bachmann, 'Vorwort', in idem (ed.), *Lutherische ... Paulusperspektive* (see n. 23), pp. VII–XIII, XI–XII. Cf., furthermore, for instance, idem, 'Dunn' (see n. 22), pp. 36–41.

36.   On this, cf. only the essay B. Byrne, 'Interpreting Romans in a Post-"New Perspective" Perspective', in HThR 49, 2001: 227–41. Cf. also M. Zetterholm, *Approaches to Paul: A Student's Guide to Recent Scholarship*, Minneapolis, MN, 2009, pp. 127–63 ('Beyond the New Perspective') and pp. 195–224 ('Breaking Boundaries').

37.   J. Frey, 'Das Judentum des Paulus', in O. Wischmeyer (ed.), *Paulus. Leben – Umwelt – Werke – Briefe* (UTB 2767), Tübingen/Basel, 2006, pp. 5–43, 36.

Perspective on Paul', or more precisely the '"Lutheran" Perspective on Paul'. In this process, as a matter of course, confessional or theological identities or principles will be handled delicately – which is why in the meantime systematic theologians (such as F. Beißer and W. Härle) chimed into the conversation.[38]

(iii) Conversely, a 'de-Lutherisation of Pauline theology'[39] could seem thoroughly attractive to Catholic exegetes – to the extent that the not insignificant influence of the Bultmann school, interpreting Paul in a 'Lutheran way', in this area does not tend to prevent this. Also a (more) positive estimation of Judaism and of the Mosaic Law, as seems to be provided by Paul, is suitable in the decades after Vatican II, especially after the passing of the declaration *Nostra aetate*. However, as much as the Holocaust has not insignificantly influenced the previously characterized hermeneutical positions – and this undoubtedly often in a quite adequate manner, adequate to a time of cooperation of *Jewish*-Christian groups (of very significant extent) and of additionally joining Gentile-Christians – as little does contemporary Catholicism and contemporary Catholic exegesis, concerning Paul and Judaism – also the Mosaic Law – reveal a homogeneous picture. Therefore, the reference to the intensity of the discussions about the recently published declaration by the 'Gesprächskreis "Juden und Christen"' at the 'Zentralkommitee' of German Catholics (adopted on 11 February 2009), might suffice; the 'No to missionizing of Jews …' is here especially justified with reference to statements of Paul.[40]

38.   On this, see only F. Beißer, 'Was heißt bei Paulus "Jesus Christus ist das Ende des Gesetzes"?', in KuD 51, 2005: 52–4 (critically on this, Müller, 'Vollendung' [see n. 26], and M. Bachmann, 'Christus, "das Ende des Gesetzes des Dekalogs und des Liebesgebots"?', ThZ 63, 2007: 171–4), and W. Härle, 'Paulus und Luther. Ein kritischer Blick auf die "New Perspective"', in ZThK 103, 2006: 326–39. Cf. incidentally esp. V. Stolle, *Luther und Paulus. Die exegetischen und hermeneutischen Grundlagen der lutherischen Rechtfertigungslehre im Paulinismus Luthers* (Arbeiten zur Bibel und ihrer Geschichte 10), Leipzig, 2002 (and, furthermore, idem, 'Nomos zwischen Tora und Lex. Der paulinische Gesetzesbegriff und seine Interpretation durch Luther in der zweiten Disputation gegen die Antinomer vom 12. Januar 1538', in Bachmann (ed.), *Lutherische … Paulusperspektive* [see n. 23], pp. 41–67), also M. Dreher, 'Luther als Paulus-Interpret bei Adolf Schlatter und Wilhelm Heitmüller. Ein forschungsgeschichtlicher Beitrag zur "New Perspective on Paul"', in Luther 79, 2008: 109–20/25 (cf. on this moreover M. Bachmann, 'Keil oder Mikroskop. Zur jüngeren Diskussion um den Ausdruck "'Werke' des Gesetzes"', in idem (ed.), *Lutherische … Paulusperspektive* [see n. 23], pp. 69–134, 76 together with n. 31).

39.   On this, see M. Theobald, *Der Römerbrief* (EdF 294), Darmstadt, 2000, pp. 317–20 (cf. Schreiber, Hermeneutik [see n. 31], esp. pp. 101–2). Quotation: Theobald, *Römerbrief*, p. 318 – following H.-J. Schoeps.

40.   The declaration was published on 9.3.2009, and this, precisely, with the following title: *Nein zur Judenmission – Ja zum Dialog zwischen Juden und Christen*. It is referred here to Paul not without accentuation (see pp. 13–16, 21–22). Concerning the controversy caused by the declaration I only point here to three readers' letters to the *Frankfurter Allgemeine Zeitung* (actually of Th. Söding [23.4.2009, No. 94: 35], of W. Trutwin (2.5.2009, No. 101: 39) and of H. Thomas [28.5.2009, No. 122: 36]). A similar disagreement is also flaring up these days in Protestantism (as articles and readers' letters in issues 7 and 8 of the journal *Zeitzeichen* [vol. 10, 2009] exhibit).

The look at the realms of discourse which have been marked out by some recent philosophers, by Protestant exegetes (as well as systematic theologians, dogmatics) and by Catholic theologians reveals easily how difficult the contemporary hermeneutical situation is, not least since 'different perceptions are governed partly by particular focal points of research and partly by traditions and interests that are brought to bear',[41] and since, moreover, truncated formulations inadequate to the complex data are used. Nonetheless, in my opinion, if one takes all three realms into consideration, the impression evolves that in the attempt to question the simple updating of habits of interpretation – not to simply take up 'churchly patois'– something like an 'innovative potential'[42] has become noticeable in the last decades. However, one cannot proceed from this 'potential' as if an extensive consensus has been achieved; that is not even the case within the 'wing' of that which could be characterized by the pithy formulation, 'The New Perspective on Paul'.

Rather, it seems to be reasonable and necessary to follow up on some of the impulses previously alluded to (see 2). This should now be conducted in two attempts, as the questions of the Pauline point of view of Judaism and Law as well as of a possible universalism took the centre stage. With the example of 'Israel' terminology one must try to capture the Pauline view of Judaism in more detail (see 2.1). Using the examples of the apostle's statements on the topic of the Law, the question of 'freedom from the Law' in Pauline contexts should briefly be considered and furthermore – and above all – the expression 'works of the Law', that is consistently encountered with a negative connotation throughout the Pauline corpus, should be taken into account, if it could have something to do with the inclusion of non-Jews in the community of salvation (see 2.2). With all due caution according to our conversational setting it should be suitable if the questions concerning hermeneutics, dealing with the meaning of the exegetical results for the present, are only taken up again later (see 3).

2. On the Exegetical Detail

2.1. On the Terminology of 'Israel'

Naturally the concept with which Paul genuinely or apparently quite instantaneously addresses, 'Jewish' issues plays a central role concerning our topic. Hardly a statement of the apostle has become of such importance after the Shoah as the statement of Rom. 11.1:[43] 'Has God rejected his people?

---

41.   So Haacker, 'Verdienste' (see n. 23), p. 5.
42.   This is the expression of Schreiber, 'Hermeneutik' (see n. 31), p. 101.
43.   The following title points to this rather unambiguously: R. Rendtorff, *Hat denn Gott sein Volk verstoßen? Die evangelische Kirche und das Judentum seit 1945. Ein Kommentar* (ACJD 18), München, 1989.

By no means! For I [i.e., Paul] too am an Israelite myself, a descendant of Abraham, from the tribe of Benjamin.' In the widely Gentile-Christian church of the last centuries it had become self-evident not only to use 'the language of Canaan' but – in a certain deviation from this Pauline formulation – at the same time to consider oneself to be 'Israel' and thereby to think about real Jews no more, or only barely. In German Protestantism, for instance, one has sung and still sings since the mid-seventeenth century (Matthäus Apelles von Löwenstern (1594–1648), 1644 (Evangelisches Gesangbuch 502.1)):

> Nun preiset alle Gottes Barmherzigkeit!
> Lob ihn mit Schalle, werteste *Christenheit*!
> Er lässt *dich* freundlich zu sich laden,
> freue *dich*, Israel, seiner Gnaden,
> freue *dich*, Israel, seiner Gnaden.

Something like that has a tradition, or, more precisely, has a long tradition. One already encounters it in the second century with Justin Martyr. In his *Dialogue with the Jew Trypho* the I-narrator, a Gentile-Christian philosopher, says (11.5):

> The true, spiritual Israel, and the descendants [γένος] of Judah, Jacob, Isaac, and Abraham, who though [!] in uncircumcision was approved of and blessed by God on account of his faith, and was called the father of many nations, are we, who have been led to God through this crucified Christ ...'[44]

This formulation amounts to something like disinheritance or rather disappropriation of Judaism,[45] and especially this has coined the self-conception of western Christianity – unfortunately coined. Therefore one can comprehend well to some extent both: (i) that particularly after the Holocaust one has tried to strictly distinguish the statements about Israel of Paul, who was writing in a Christianity that significantly still mainly consisted of born Jews, from the later reception – one might now like to think of the corresponding publications of G. Schrenk and of P. Richardson for instance, but one could also integrate two of my studies;[46] (ii) that furthermore it

---

44. So the translation by Ph. Haeuser (in *Justinus, Dialog mit dem Juden Thryphon*, übers. v. Ph. H. [first: 1917], ed. by K. Greschat and M. Tilly, Wiesbaden, 2005, p. 56). Here by means of square brackets I have tried to introduce some emphases. In the German hymn above, the italics are mine.

45. On this, see only P. Richardson, *Israel in the Apostolic Church* (SNTS MS, 10), Cambridge, 1969, pp. 9–14.

46. G. Schrenk, 'Was bedeutet "Israel Gottes"?', in Jud. 5, 1949: 81–94; idem, 'Der Segenswunsch nach der Kampfepistel', in Jud. 6, 1950: 170–90; Richardson, *Israel* (see n. 45); M. Bachmann, 'Kirche und Israel Gottes. Zur Bedeutung und ekklesiologischen Relevanz des Segenswortes am Schluß des Galaterbriefs', in idem, *Antijudaismus* (see n. 28), pp. 159–89; idem, '*Verus Israel*: Ein Vorschlag zu einer "mengentheoretischen" Neubeschreibung der betreffenden paulinischen Terminologie', in NTS 48, 2002: 500–12.

does not lack pronouncements of exegetes taken seriously, who interpret in terms of the tradition just concisely outlined – as for instance N. A. Dahl and W. Kraus.[47] The 'traditionalists' are sometimes determined by a further custom of interpretation, which expresses itself in a more or less anti-Judaic understanding of Galatians and in the thesis of a new, more Jew-friendly theological level reached by Paul with the letter of Romans.[48] As well as one can at least understand the continuing customs of interpretation on the field of Pauline statements on Judaism in principle, as little one can comprehend the neglect of counter-arguments (which meanwhile, fortunately, also result in positive effects, as with S. Schewe, with W. S. Campbell and with S. G. Eastman[49]).

To refute again the thesis of the alleged anti-Judaism of Galatians, which I opposed not least with an anthology published in 1999 (which

47. N.A. Dahl, 'Zur Auslegung von Gal. 6.16', in Jud. 6, 1950: 161–70; W. Kraus, *Das Volk Gottes. Zur Grundlegung der Ekklesiologie bei Paulus* (WUNT 85), Tübingen, 1996, esp. pp. 251–2. Further secondary literature to such a view (which seems to be shared also by D. Sänger, 'Review of G. Harvey, *The True Israel. Uses of the Names Jew, Hebrew and Israel in Ancient Jewish and Early Christian Literature* [AGJU 35], Leiden et al. 1996', in ThLZ 123, 1998: 737–40, p. 740) and to others opposed to it at Bachmann, 'Kirche' (see n. 46), esp. pp. 159–64.

48. A prominent representative of such a conception is U. Schnelle (cf., for instance, idem, 'Paulus und das Gesetz. Biographisches und Konstruktives', in E.-M. Becker/P. Pilhofer (eds), *Biographie und Persönlichkeit des Paulus* [WUNT 187], Tübingen, 2005, pp. 245–70, esp. 262–70). Cf. on this question also M. Bachmann, 'Die andere Frau. Synchrone und diachrone Beobachtungen zu Gal 4.21–5.1', in: idem, *Antijudaismus* (see n. 28), pp. 127–58 (first [in another version]: 1998), esp. pp. 157–8 together with n. 103.

49. Susan Grove Eastman expressed her opinion in this way (on 7.8.2009) on the Vienna meeting of the Studiorum Novi Testamenti Societas in the seminar on 'Pauline Theology in Galatians and Romans' (see now S. G. E., 'Israel and the Mercy of God: A reading of Galatians 6.16 and Romans 9-11', in NTS 56, 2010: 367–95). Somewhat earlier: S. Schewe, *Die Galater zurückgewinnen. Paulinische Strategien in Gal 5 und 6* (FRLANT 208), Göttingen, 2005, pp. 199–200 n. 51; W. S. Campbell, *Paul and the Creation of Christian Identity* (Library of New Testament Studies 322), London/New York (NY), 2006, pp. 46–53; cf., furthermore, R. Penna, 'L'évolution de l'attitude de Paul envers les Juifs', in A. Vanhoye (ed.), *L'apôtre Paul. Personalité, style et conception du ministère* (BEThL 73), Leuven, 1986, pp. 390–421, 407–8; moreover S. C. Keesmaat, 'Paul and his Story. Exodus and Tradition in Galatians', in C. A. Evans/J. A. Sanders (eds), *Early Christian Interpretation of the Scriptures of Israel. Investigations and Proposals* (JSNT.S 148), Sheffield, 1997, pp. 301–33, 314 and 323 n. 74 (here: a reference to B. R. Gaventa); M. Neubrand, *Israel, die Völker und die Kirche. Eine exegetische Studie zu Apg 15* (SBB 55), Stuttgart, 2006, p. 164 together with n. 163 (against W. Kraus), and D. J. Downs, *The Offering of the Gentiles. Paul's Collection for Jerusalem in Its Chronological, Cultural, and Cultic Contexts* (WUNT II/248), Tübingen, 2008, p. 5 (together with n. 17). A just published book on this theme fits in here very well, i.e., M. J. Vlach, *The Church as a Replacement of Israel: An Analysis of Supersessionism* (Edition Israelogie 2), Frankfurt am Main et al., 2009, esp. pp. 105–9, 172–5 (174: 'not … enough evidence to go with a non-ethnic sense of Israel', and this in Gal. 6.16); similarly also P. T. Gadenz, *Called from the Jews and from the Gentiles. Pauline Ecclesiology in Romans 9–11* (WUNT II/267), Tübingen, 2009, (pp. 75–8 together with n. 234 and) p. 82.

is now also available in English[50]), must not and cannot be omitted here. My 'Vorschlag zu einer "mengentheoretischen" Neubeschreibung der ... paulinischen Terminologie' concerning Judaism, however, may meanwhile be concisely depicted by three tableaus,[51] before the exceptional position of the concept 'Israel' will be illustrated with regards to Gal. 6.16, especially with due consideration of the formulation encountered there: '... peace be upon them, and mercy, and upon the Israel of God'. I would like to distance myself especially from more recent statements of M. Wolter.[52]

To begin with the first tableau:

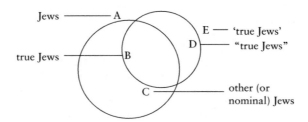

Here one has distinguished the set A, the set of the Jews, from the set E, the set of the Christians (which is in Paul's time even smaller, as it is noted here for the sake of clarity). At the term *Jews*, nominal Jews (i.e., *merely* nominal Jews), C, are distinguished from true Jews, B, and the term *true Jews*, which was suggested by Justin (besides Dial 11.5 compare, e.g., Dial 116.3; 135.3) especially for non-Jews, moreover is visualized twice, once with double quotation marks for Gentile-Christians, D, and once with single quotation marks for Jewish- *and* Gentile-Christians, E.

50.   Bachmann, *Antijudaismus* (see n. 28). English, American translation (by R. L. Brawley): M. B., *Anti-Judaism in Galatians? Exegetical Studies on a Polemical Letter and on Paul's Theology*, Grand Rapids (MI), 2009.

51.   Bachmann, '*Israel*' (see n. 46), here 503.507.510 the corresponding tableaus (however, in German language). Cf. Gadenz, *Ecclesiology* (see n. 49), (p. 75 n. 234 and) p. 148.

52.   M. Wolter, 'Von der Entmachtung des Buchstabens durch seine Attribute. Eine Spurensuche, ausgehend von Röm 2,29', in H. Assel/H.-Ch. Askani (eds), *Sprachgewinn. Festschrift für Günter Bader* (Arbeiten zur historischen und systematischen Theologie 11), Berlin/Münster, 2008, pp. 149–61. Cf. A. Du Toit, '*Paulus Oecumenicus*: Interculturality in the Shaping of Paul's Theology', in NTS 55, 2009: 121–43, esp. pp. 141–2.

The second tableau is more complex:

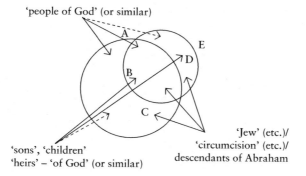

It indicates that in his vocabulary concerning Judaism, Paul, at least to a large extent, knows in addition to a literal understanding also something like a transferred application (i.e., so to speak, particularly also for the subset D). This is unquestionably the case with the word Ἰουδαῖος (see Rom. 2.28-29), also with the circumcision terminology and the conceptualization of descent from Abraham (see Rom. 2.26, 29; 4.17-18). In a weakened manner it is in particular valid for the 'sons', 'children' and 'heirs' of God (see Rom. 8.14-21), though, however, even with Gal. 4.1-5 '[a] candid characterization of all Jews – ... also the ones belonging to the subset C – as heirs of God (or also as his sons or children) is ... not' simple to state.[53] Things are somewhat different with the expression 'people of God', more exact: with 'my [i.e., God's] people' (Rom. 9.25, 26), respectively with 'his [i.e., God's] people' (Rom. 11.1, 2; 15.10; 2 Cor. 6.16); because here, despite Rom. 9.25-26, a clear reference to non-Jews is not at all given, and so Paul says in Rom. 15.10 with regard to Deut. 32.42 that the nations should rejoice with his, that is, with God's people – with the Jews. When the apostle goes back to the Old Testament here and also in his five other 'people of God' instances, it fits in a certain sense with the fact that Paul does not, seen from a traditional-historical point of view, break ranks too with the other terms of this tableau.[54]

53.   Bachmann, '*Israel*' (see n. 46), p. 506.
54.   On this see ibid., p. 510.

Hence, the third tableau might be easier to understand:

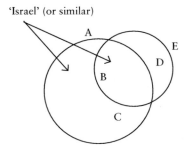

'Israel' (or similar)

On the one hand, the apostle proceeds similarly with the Israel terminology, but even a little bit more radically than in the case of the 'people of God' expression.[55] With his three instances of the gentilic (or 'gentilium') Ἰσραηλίτης (Rom. 9.4; 11.1; 2 Cor. 11.22) – of which one has already been cited – and at least with all 15 Pauline occurrences of the 'ethnicon' Ἰσραήλ *beyond* Gal. 6.16c (Rom. 9.6a, 6b, 27a, 27b, 31; 10.19, 21; 11.2, 7, 25, 26; 1 Cor. 10.18; 2 Cor. 3.7, 13; Phil. 3.5; compare Rom. 10.1 *v.l.*; Eph. 2.12) the word family is used in a way just not referring to something like the subset D, just not to non-Jews. It therefore seems to be unsurprising that a contextual overlapping is given with λαός (Rom. 9.25, 26) and with ὁ λαὸς αὐτοῦ (Rom. 11.1, 2; compare further Rom. 10.21). *On the other hand*, over 20 years ago P.J. Tomson described the tradition-historical peculiarity of this term with good reasons as follows: It is 'the cherished, *inner*-Jewish name of the Covenant People'.[56] So far solely the expression of Gal. 6.16c, ὁ Ἰσραὴλ τοῦ θεοῦ, not attested in the Greek literature before Paul, has as a precaution not been accounted for in the third tableau. But this example, which belongs to something like a word of blessing, could optimally match the other results. There Paul, so we just had to notice, with the concept 'Israel' refers consistently to real Jews, just as is customary in the tradition, and he thereby proceeds similarly to his usage of his expression, used reasonably synonymously, 'his' or rather 'my people', which in addition interestingly offers in each case a pronoun referring to God.

One is all the more astounded when recently reading M. Wolter's thesis, that in this syntagma the genitive attribute τοῦ θεοῦ should, as for instance with the expression ἡ ἐκκλησία τοῦ θεοῦ of Gal. 1.13, be comprehended as 'a semantic innovation'.[57] It should be 'probable that Paul intended to undertake a semantic redefinition of the Israel concept here': 'The supplement

55.   On this see Bachmann, '*Israel*', pp. 507–10. Cf. Bachmann, 'Kirche' (see n. 46), pp. 172–5.

56.   P. J. Tomson, 'The Names Israel and Jew in Ancient Judaism and in the New Testament', in Bijdr. 47, 1986: 120–40.268–89, 288 (italics: M. B.).

57.   Wolter, 'Entmachtung' (see n 52), pp. 155–7 (quotation: p. 155).

τοῦ θεοῦ enables an Israel concept to be defined whose extension is a group that is located beyond Judaism.'[58] In no case am I to dispute a considerable relevance of an attributive genitive! But already not taking account of Jewish-Christians, for instance of a Jewish-Christian like the author of the letter – Paul (merely see Gal. 2.15-16; 3.28; 4.26; 5.6; 6.15; compare e.g., Rom. 11.1) – in Wolter's thesis cannot convince. This could also be in view by A. Du Toit, who leaves it open whether with the ὁ Ἰσραὴλ τοῦ θεοῦ in Gal. 6.16c the church simply replaces Israel or 'that "Israel" now included Israelite as well as non-Israelite believers'. Nevertheless, the South African scholar speaks of a 're-definition of Israel' in Gal. 6.16 and thereof, that Wolter 'aptly describes it as a "semantic reclassification of the Israel concept"'.[59] However, the thesis of the Protestant New Testament scholar from Bonn barely fits the diachronic and synchronic data to be considered – beyond this it also does not really take into account the contemporary situation of scholarly discussion.

Concerning the claimed 'semantic innovation', something like that will not have begun only with Paul or elsewhere in early Christianity, but rather before that. Wolter has to note this[60] for the 'church of God' at least with Neh. 13.1 (2 Esdr. 23.1: ἐκκλησία θεοῦ; compare e.g., Philo, Ebr. 213; compare in addition e.g., Deut. 23.2 [ἐκκλησία κυρίου]; Judg. 20.2 [ἡ ἐκκλησία τοῦ λαοῦ τοῦ θεοῦ]; 2 Chron. 6.3 [ἡ πᾶσα ἐκκλησία Ἰσραήλ]; Sir. 24.2 [ἐκκλησία ὑψίστου]; Thr. 1.10 [ἐκκλησία σου]; 1QM 4.10 [קהל אל]), even though he tries to minimize the continuity. For he advocates the hypothesis 'that the word ἐκκλησία, as distinct from the use of language in the Septuagint ... suddenly and exclusively in early Christianity was employed as a *group-expresssion*'.[61] Already with regard to Judg. 20.2; 2 Chron. 6.3; Sir. 24.2 and Thr. 1.10 one rather should agree with H. Merklein: 'Particularly instructive is the syntagma ἡ ἐκκλησία (τοῦ) θεοῦ or κυρίου (קהל יהוה), in which ἐκκλησία (קהל) always has a meaning that goes beyond the concrete gathering, tending at least towards the direction of a group-expression', 'particularly because ... the connection of the syntagma with "Israel" (qua God's people) distinctly emerges'.[62]

Accordingly, relevant tradition-historical data can be given for the expression of ὁ Ἰσραὴλ τοῦ θεοῦ, probably first occurring in Gal. 6.16. For

---

58.   Quotation: Wolter, 'Entmachtung', p. 158. (Wolter's estimation [p. 158 n. 23], that apart from himself only H. D. Betz 'points to the analogy (of Gal 6.16) to the expression ἐκκλησία τοῦ θεοῦ (of Gal 1.13)', could incidentally be corrected, for instance, by a glance at Bachmann, 'Kirche' [see n. 46], pp. 185–9, not insignificantly.)

59.   Quotations: Du Toit, *'Paulus Oecumenicus'* (see n. 52), pp. (141–)2, 142 and 142 n. 108. Cf., furthermore, for instance R. Senk, *Das 'Israel Gottes'. Die Frage nach dem Volk Gottes im Neuen Testament* (Reformatorische Paperbacks 24), 2nd, revised edn, Hamburg, 2006, pp. 20–1, and G. Jossa, *Jews or Christians? The Followers of Jesus in Search of their own Identity* (WUNT 2002), Tübingen, 2006 (Italian: 2004), p. 99 (together with) n. 145.

60.   Wolter, 'Entmachtung' (see n. 52), p. 156.

61.   Ibid.

62.   H. Merklein, 'Die Ekklesia Gottes. Der Kirchenbegriff bei Paulus und in Jerusalem', in idem, *Studien zu Jesus und Paulus* (WUNT 43), Tübingen, 1987 (first: 1979), pp. 296–318, 309–10 (quotations: 309). Similarly: Du Toit, *'Paulus Oecumenicus'* (see n. 52), pp. 134–8, esp. 137–8.

instance, a remarkable phrase of the 18th benediction of the Palestinian version of the Shmone Esre, 'Place your freedom upon Israel, your people [עַל יִשְׂרָאֵל עַמְּךָ], upon your city and upon your inheritance',[63] prompts (e.g.) U. Kellermann to the statement: 'Potentially Paul's wish of blessing in Gal. 6.16 depends on the tefilla'.[64] Furthermore, definitely four real or at least possible points of contact deserve to be mentioned here: (i) The Jewish formulation of prayer is also a kind of closing remark; (ii) it refers to 'peace' – in the (later) Babylonian version it even says: 'Peace, benevolence and blessing, grace and community loyalty and mercy'; (iii) as it seems, more than one group of addressees is mentioned; (iv) the affiliation of Israel with God is expressed, namely according to the form of the prayer, with a second person suffix.[65] Next to the statement of the Shmone Esre other parallels can be indicated (not at least also 1 En. 1.8). At the end of Ps. 124 (125) one can find the words εἰρήνη ἐπὶ τὸν Ἰσραήλ (v. 5), and, earlier, v. 2. speaks of ὁ λαὸς αὐτοῦ (i.e., of the κύριος). One can encounter the same closing remark also in Ps. 127 (128) – namely in v. 6 – and the attention of God for his people is also addressed here within the preceding context (see especially vv. 1, 5; compare v. 4). One is doubtlessly closer to the literary genre of a letter with the interesting and important (Qumran) document 4QMMT, ending with the following words (C31-32; compare C27): 'for your own welfare and for the welfare of Israel' (לטוב לך ולישראל).[66] Considerably later originated the letter papMur 42,[67] probably written in the ending phase of the Bar Kokhba rebellion. The 'closing greetings' (which are merely followed by the signatures [lines 8–13][68]) of this writing, which concerns economic matters, are (line 7): 'Best wishes to you and to all Beth-Israel.' Thereby interestingly the word שלום is used,[69] and just as in 4QMMT C31-32 the blessing is addressed to two groups connected linguistically by 'and' – and the gentiles mentioned in line 5 obviously are not

---

63. Translation and the Hebrew phrase according to U. Kellermann, *Das Achtzehn-Bitten-Gebet. Jüdischer Glaube in neutestamentlicher Zeit. Ein Kommentar*, Neukirchen-Vluyn, 2007, p. 191 (where it is partly given in italics) – whose rendering of the text is used also in the following.

64. Kellermann, *Achtzehn-Bitten-Gebet* (see n. 63), p. 196 (cf. 192). Incidentally this has been taken into consideration already several times (on this see only Bachmann, 'Kirche' [see n. 46], 159.163.183).

65. On this cf. Bachmann, 'Kirche' (see n. 46), 178–84. On the following pieces of evidence (or 'evidence') see esp. 182–3.

66. So E. Qimron/J. Strugnell, *Qumran Cave 4. Vol. V: Miqṣat Maʿaśe Ha-Torah* (DJD X), Oxford, 1994, (p. 62 and p. 63).

67. Rendered (and commentated) by D. Pardee, *Handbook of Ancient Hebrew Letters* (SBL.SBibSt 15), Chico (CA), 1982, pp. 122–8 (text: 123; translation: 124; dating: 127–8). Cf. K. Beyer, *Die aramäischen Texte vom Toten Meer samt den Inschriften aus Palästina, dem Testament Levis aus der Kairoer Genisa, den Fastenrolle und den alten, talmudischen Zitaten. Ergänzungsband*, Göttingen, 1994, pp. 218–19, and J. Kottsieper, 'Hebräische, transjordanische und aramäische Briefe', in TUAT.NF 3 (2006): 357–83, pp. 381–2.

68. Quotations: Pardee, *Handbook* (see n. 67), p. 127.

69. Ibid., pp. (123–)4, and Beyer, *Texte* (see n. 67), p. 218. Cf. Kottsieper, 'Briefe' (see n. 67), p. 382: 'Be (in) peace and the whole house of Israel (too)'.

regarded as belonging to (one of) them. If we look back at the early Jewish formulations compiled in this passage – and compiled by me also earlier – it should be obvious that the formulation ὁ Ἰσραὴλ τοῦ θεοῦ from Gal. 6.16c is at most only an 'innovation' insofar as the second person singular suffix or the pronouns σοῦ and αὐτοῦ now became, so to speak, a τοῦ θεοῦ (which furthermore has a series of substantive 'precursors', for example, in the expression of ἡ ἐκκλησία τοῦ λαοῦ τοῦ θεοῦ in Judg. 20.2). Apart from that, the passages just listed are so closely related with the Pauline word at the end of Galatians, that a real 'semantic innovation' here seems nearly excluded.

Let's return to Paul and thereby to synchrony! Before we talk about the context of Gal. 6.16c in this respect, two other moments of the Pauline conceptualization of Israel should be addressed.

(i) The formulation Ἰσραὴλ κατὰ σάρκα in 1 Cor. 10.18 belongs to those instances that in Paul's view deal at least initially with the past (see especially Rom. 9.27; 2 Cor. 3.7, 13) or with the recent past, or rather with the present (see Rom. 9.4; 11.1; 1 Cor. 10.18; Phil. 3.5).[70] Wolter, according to whom 'empirical Judaism' is meant here,[71] seems to share this view. However, 'a group that is located beyond Judaism' – to cite Wolter's formulation anew[72] – cannot be taken into consideration as a 'semantic complement', despite the 'typology' operative here in First Corinthians. According to W. Schrage, the passage (see especially 1 Cor. 10.7, 9, 14, 19, 22) probably forces the following interpretation: 'not Israel as a whole is "Israel according to the flesh" but the idol worshipping [Israel] of vv. 6-10' – and for this reason also the view should be rejected that the passage 'indirectly reveals the reclamation of the term "Israel" for the church'.[73]

(ii) As one might assume due to the 'typology' of 1 Cor. 10, invariably or nearly invariably a future dimension appears fairly obviously with the Pauline usage of Ἰσραηλίτης and Ἰσραήλ (see only Rom. 9.4-5; 11.25-26). It is still especially remarkable that thereby the relation of this quantity particularly to the non-Jews, to the gentiles, is discussed. This occurs most impressively in Rom. 11.25-26 (namely with a succession of (a partly 'hardened') Ἰσραήλ, of ἔθνη and of [πᾶς] Ἰσραήλ), but also elsewhere in Rom. 9-11, furthermore in 2 Cor. 3 (and also in 2 Cor. 11; compare also Rom. 15.8-12, especially v. 10 [Deut. 32.43]!). With this the conclusion recommends itself, that the apostle deals with the term Ἰσραήλ in a different way than with the word ἐκκλησία. In both cases he considers also the non-Jews. But with (ἡ) ἐκκλησία (τοῦ θεοῦ) he leaves out (and this not only in Gal. 1.22) such formulations

---

70. On this see only Bachmann, 'Kirche' (see n. 46), pp. 172–3.
71. Wolter, 'Entmachtung' (see n. 52), p. 158.
72. Cf. above (at) n. 58.
73. Quotations: W. Schrage, *Der erste Brief an die Korinther 2: 1Kor 6,12–11,16* (EKK VI/2), (Solothurn and) Düsseldorf/Neukirchen-Vluyn, 1995, p. 443 and p. 442. Cf. idem, '"Israel nach dem Fleisch" (1Kor 10,18)', in H.-G. Geyer et al. (eds), *'Wenn nicht jetzt, wann dann?' Aufsätze für Hans-Joachim Kraus zum 65. Geburtstag*, Neukirchen-Vluyn, 1983, pp. 143–51, esp. 144–50. Similarly W. S. Campbell in his theses, given in preparation of the Leuven meeting.

under the semantic characteristics mentioned above,[74] which like τοῦ λαοῦ τοῦ θεοῦ (Judg. 20.2) or Ἰσραήλ (2 Chron. 6.3) were linguistically able to exclude non-Jews or non-Jewish Christians from this community.[75] However, with the use of Ἰσραήλ he particularly respects the idea that God united himself and still is united with this people (see especially Rom. 9.1-5; 11.1-2) and that Gentile-Christians, that is, non-Jews, owe their new status particularly to this phenomenon of 'Heilsgeschichte' (see especially Rom. 11.25-26; 15.8-12).[76]

The literary context of Gal. 6.16 now confirms the impression attained. At least two traits of this fairly polemical document must indeed – other than usual – not be withheld.[77] (i) The narrowing of the descent from Abraham through the *one* 'seed', Christ, in Gal. 3.16 does not at all prevent the apostle – as we already touched on – from referring back to and insisting in Gal. 4.1-7 (compare already Gal. 3.29!) that especially and firstly *Jews* fall in the category of κληρονόμος. (ii) The 'we' from Gal. 2.15-21 (more exactly: 2.15-17a) which refers to Jews (thus excluding other persons)[78] is taken up in Gal. 3.1-4.7, and it expresses the temporal and factual priority of Jews (Jewish-Christians) over non-Jews and over Gentile-Christians. These are addressed only at the completion of the three levels of argumentation – 3.1-14, 3.15-29 and 4.1-7 (3.14a; 3.26-29; 4.6a) – partly by a 'you', and they are also incorporated twice (3.14b; 4.6b) by an inclusive 'we'. Concerning Gal. 6.16 itself, already before the καὶ ἐπὶ τὸν Ἰσραὴλ τοῦ θεοῦ a blessing is enunciated for those who will live according to the guideline of v. 15 – 'neither circumcision nor uncircumcision, but new creation!'. The just quoted καί, the last of this verse, is regarded by W. Kraus as καί *explicativum*.[79] But this view has to be ruled out. Firstly, Paul nowhere else uses this kind of an epexegetical καί. Secondly, he addressed beforehand, as we have already seen, in Galatians the 'heilsgeschichtliche' connection of Jews (Jewish-Christians) and gentiles (Gentile-Christians). This guideline – prepared for also tradition-historically (see only Isa. 2.1-5; Tob. 14.5-7)[80] and occurring too in Rom 9–11 and Rom 15.8-12 – is thus obviously taken up. (One should not deviate from this exegetical estimation since Rom 4.11-12 suggests a similar succession as

74.   That is, (at) n. 60–1.

75.   Cf. E. W. Stegemann, 'Zwischen Juden und Heiden, aber "mehr" als Juden und Heiden? Neutestamentliche Anmerkungen zur Identitätsproblematik des frühen Christentums', in idem, *Paulus und die Welt. Aufsätze*, selected and ed. by Ch. Tuor and P. Wick, Zürich, 2005 (first: 1994), pp. 73–92, 76–8.

76.   On this cf. only Bachmann, 'Kirche' (see n. 46), pp. 173– 4 (together with n. 67) – and also, idem, 'Frau' (see n. 48), pp. 157–8 n. 103.

77.   On this in more detail, Bachmann, 'Kirche' (see n. 46), pp. 164–72. Cf. idem, 'Zur Argumentation von Gal 3.10-12', in NTS 53, 2007: 524–44, esp. pp. 535–6.

78.   On this question (which is frequently interpreted differently), see Bachmann, 'Frau' (see n. 48), pp. 146–7 together with n. 52; idem, 'Argumentation' (see n. 77), pp. 534–5 together with n. 42.

79.   Kraus, *Volk* (see n. 47), p. 251. On this and against it, see Bachmann, 'Kirche' (see n. 46), pp. 168–71.

80.   On this in more detail, for instance T. L. Donaldson, 'The "Curse of the Law" and the Inclusion of the Gentiles: Galatians 3.13-14', in NTS 32, 1986: 94–112, p. 99 (together with nn. 41–50).

answer to the question of v. 9, namely that the macarism [of vv. 8-9] goes out ἐπὶ τὴν ἀκροβυστίαν καὶ ἐπὶ τὴν περιτομήν.[81]) It is exactly at such a connection that Gal. 6.16c aims with its καί (which corresponds to the 'and' in Rom. 4.9). Thereby Paul clarifies at the end of his quite harsh letter to the Galatians, that his opinion against the circumcision of Gentile-Christians (Gal. 5.2-4; 6.12-13) is not at all an opinion against the 'heilsgeschichtliche' fixing of the gospel in Judaism (Gal. 4.4) and also not an opinion against promises of God addressing especially Jews (see only Gal. 3.28-29). The quantity ἡ ἐκκλησία τοῦ θεοῦ (Gal. 1.13-17; compare Rom. 16.16) that refers particularly to the Christ-event therefore does not dishonour what is expressed with the ceremonial expression ὁ Ἰσραὴλ τοῦ θεοῦ about God's past and future attention to the Jewish people. With the adoption of the traditional blessing, Paul obviously intends to protect his contemporary addressees at any rate from an anti-Judaic misunderstanding of his polemics.[82]

In summary, very differently than it has often been interpreted,[83] and very differently than especially M. Wolter again has recently interpreted, even Gal. 6.16 and particularly Gal. 6.16c conforms, if one takes a closer look, to the manner in which Paul otherwise defines the relation(ship) of the Christian community of Jews and non-Jews towards Judaism, for instance – but not exclusively – in Romans (compare [again] especially Rom. 1.16; 3.30; 4.9-12; 9–11; 15.8-12; further Gal. 3.1-4.7, especially 3.28). Ἰσραήλ refers to real Judaism, and the wish expressed in Gal. 6.16 is compatible with the formulation in Rom. 11.26-27 (compare Isa. 27.9; 59.20-21), according to which – however – 'all Israel will be saved' (Rom. 11.26a).

2.2. *On the Terminology of* νόμος

There have been written countless books and essays on the topic of the Law in Paul, on his usage of the term νόμος and also on the syntagma ἔργα νόμου,[84] and

---

81.   On this (and on the immediately following), see Bachmann, 'Kirche' (see n. 46), pp. 170–1.

82.   Cf. ibid., 188–9.

83.   Cf. once again Bachmann, 'Frau' (see n. 48), pp. 157–8 (together with) n. 103.

84.   To point for the moment generally at H. Räisänen, 'Gesetz III: Neues Testament', in RGG[4] 3 (2000): 848–50, esp. p. 850, may suffice here. For the 'works of the law' see the following bibliography: Bachmann, 'Keil' (see n. 38), esp. pp. 70–1 n. 5. There also R. K. Rapa, *The Meaning of 'Works of the Law' in Galatians and Romans* (Studies in Biblical Literature 31), New York (NY) et al., 2001, is mentioned, but the following monograph was published only later: J. C. R. de Roo, *Works of the Law at Qumran and in Paul* (New Testament Monographs 13), Sheffield, 2007 (on this see the review by R. Bergmeier, ThLZ 134, 2009: 313–14, esp. p. 314: 'utterly wrong', and on earlier studies of Mrs de Roo and on the book of Rapa cf., for instance, Bachmann, 'Keil' [see n. 38], pp. 123–4 together with n. 231; the estimation, which G. H. Visscher, *Romans 4 and the New Perspective on Paul. Faith Embraces the Promise* (Studies in Biblical Literature 122), New York, NY, 2009, esp. pp. 241–5, gives concerning the [problematic] theses of J. C. R. de Roo seems to me not really adequate [on the book of Visscher see my review, BZ NF 55, 2011: 295–8, esp. p. 298]).

still we seem to be fairly distant from a scientific consensus in this field – even in the area of the 'wing' which I introduced initially, citing J. D. G. Dunn, as 'The New Perspective on Paul'. The consensus is lacking even in spite of or because of the remarkable fact which F. W. Horn (not without good reasons) describes as follows: 'The exact definition of what should be understood by ἔργα νόμου, provided the so called *new perspective* with an issue in which all the problems that it originated converge in odd ways.'[85] That the circumstances prove to be thus complicated is due to the largely difficult hermeneutical situation that was addressed also at the beginning. For instance, our Western habits of comprehension concerning the Pauline terminology of Law are substantially co-determined by a reception of Paul shaped by Augustine and the Reformation, and further by the medieval *opus*-terminology – extending also to confession formulations (compare, for instance, Confessio Augustana [abbreviated: CA], here the articles IV and VI).[86] For the 'New Perspective on Paul', a dissent between J. D. G. Dunn and myself[87] has to be added. It has risen quite early. And seemingly rather inconspicuously on the background of 2000 years of ecclesiastical and theological history, however, it may be of some importance. Currently, as already mentioned,[88] this dissent is often 'cleared up' by agreeing with the famous New Testament scholar of Durham – who commented sooner on the subject area than I did, and who considered and, as I assume, still considers,[89] in contrast to me, the genitive connection ἔργα νόμου, not only as regulations, but as regulations *and* as deeds fulfilling (or neglecting) these regulations. A connection with Dunn is therefore doubtlessly an option for a 'more traditional' 'solution'.

In the following I would like to highlight my perception – as it may suggest in the 'introspective West'[90] and hopefully be reasonably tolerable – in a somewhat autobiographical manner (see i). After that, I briefly dwell on the comments of Paul that are apparently more or less critical of the Law (see ii), in order to enlarge then upon the expression ἔργα νόμου (see iii), and eventually to quickly address further plural phrases of the apostle that seem to be 'somehow' connected with the Law (see iv).

(i) Two decades ago I worked on my postdoctoral dissertation on Gal. 2.15-21, and so I had to deal with the syntagma ἔργα νόμου that occurs three

---

85.   Horn, 'Juden' (see n. 25), p. 29.

86.   On this see only W. Krötke, 'Gute Werke II: Dogmatisch', in RGG⁴ 3 (2000): 1344–5, and J. Freitag, 'Werke II: Systematisch-theologisch', in LThK³ 10 (2001): 1097–8, furthermore M. Bachmann, 'Rechtfertigung und Gesetzeswerke bei Paulus', in idem, *Antijudaismus* (see n. 28), pp. 1–31, 1–14 (cf. idem, 'Was für Praktiken? Zur jüngsten Diskussion um die ἔργα νόμου', in NTS 55, 2009: 35–54, pp. 51–4).

87.   On this dissent cf. M. Bachmann, 'Von den Schwierigkeiten des exegetischen Verstehens. Erwägungen am Beispiel der Interpretation des paulinischen Ausdrucks "'Werke' des Gesetzes"', in G. Gelardini (ed.), *Kontexte der Schrift I: Text, Ethik, Judentum und Christentum, Gesellschaft. Ekkehard W. Stegemann zum 60. Geburtstag*, Stuttgart, 2005, pp. 49–59, esp. 52–4, furthermore idem (M. B.), 'Dunn' (see n. 22), 37–41.

88.   That is, above (at) n. 33–6.

89.   On this, see only Dunn, 'Perspective' (see n. 22), p. 98; idem, 'The Dialogue Progresses' (see n. 34), pp. 399.401.

90.   Cf. above n. 25.

times in Gal. 2.16, but this expression remained difficult to me. Nonetheless, I read articles written by Dunn, and I became aware of and impressed by his formulations on 'identity' and 'boundary markers' concerning this matter.[91] Besides, I then came upon a short comment of D. Flusser from the year 1987 that adverted to (at least) one extra-Pauline parallel: 'For the expression "the works of the Law" in the DSS see E. Qimron and J. Strugnell, "An Unpublished Halachic Letter from Qumran", Biblical Archaeology Today ..., 1985, pp. 401 and 406, note 5'.[92] There I also found a more precise naming, or counting of the respective 'Qumran' fragments, 4Q394–399, and of the writing to be reconstructed from them, as both authors suggested, namely (4Q)MMT.[93] Incidentally, Dunn also alluded to it in 1988, pointing (inter alia) to 'an unpublished 4Q text' as evidence for 'deeds of the law' 'in the Dead Sea Scrolls'.[94] Via E. W. Stegemann in Basel, who brought in H. Lichtenberger, at that time in Münster, I relatively quickly and fortunately came by an 'unauthorised edition' of 4QMMT that emerged in December 1990 in Krakow,[95] and M. Hengel, Tübingen, kindly gave me copies of two transcriptions (including an appropriate translation suggestion of H. Stegemann) for the particularly important passage with the expression 'works of the law' – which can be found in that line, which then only according to the 1994 edition produced by Qimron and Strugnell,[96] is denoted as 4QMMT C27.[97] That summer, 1989, I therefore was conscious of two things: On the one hand, it was now possible to name a quite obvious parallel to the expression 'works of the law', a parallel independent of Paul, indeed decades before him, and it does not occur in Greek but in Hebrew – and exactly this analogy was assumed before,[98] yet had not been verified; but

91.   On this see only Dunn, 'Perspective' (see n. 22), pp. 100–1.
92.   D. Flusser, 'Paul's Jewish-Christian Opponents in the Didache', in Sh. Shaked (ed.), *Gilgul. Essays on Transformation, Revolution and Permanence in the History of Religion*, dedicated to R.J. Zwi Werblowsky (SHR 50), Leiden, 1987, pp. 71–90, 82 n. 20 (where it is partly given in italics).
93.   E. Qimron/J. Strugnell, 'An Unpublished Halakhic Letter from Qumran', in *Biblical Archaeology Today. Proceedings of the International Congress on Biblical Archaeology, Jerusalem, April 1984*, ed. by J. Aviram et al., Jerusalem, 1985, pp. 400–7, 400.
94.   J. G. D. Dunn, 'The Theology of Galatians', in idem, *Jesus, Paul, and the Law. Studies in Mark and Galatians*, London, 1990 (first: 1988), pp. 240–64, 244. In the register (p. 270) it is said: '4Q (unpublished)', whereas later in Dunn, *Essays* (see n. 22), p. 511, concerning this (1991 slightly reformulated) comment (see p. 170) in fact '4QMMT' is named.
95.   On this, see only Bachmann, 'Rechtfertigung' (see n. 86), p. 28 (together with) n. 149.
96.   Qimron/Strugnell, *DJD X* (see n. 66).
97.   On this, see only M. Bachmann, '4QMMT und Galaterbrief, התורה מעשי und ΕΡΓΑ ΝΟΜΟΥ', in idem, *Antijudaismus* (first: 1998) (see n. 28), pp. 33–56, 33 n. 1 and 40–1 together with n. 35.
98.   So at (H. L. Strack/)P. Billerbeck, *Kommentar zum Neuen Testament aus Talmud und Midrasch*, I–IV, München, 1926–8, it is said (III, p. 160): 'ἔργα νόμου should be rendered in Hebrew by חוֹרָה מַעֲשֵׂי' and correspondingly 'retranslations' of the New Testament (going back to F. Delitzsch) represent this expression, by the way several times also with the article, used in 4QMMT C27 (on this, see only Bachmann, '4QMMT' [see n. 97], pp. 47–8 (together with) nn. 78-9).

on the other hand, it seemed unclear with the analogous Hebrew expression, whether one should relate it to regulations or (also) to the action(s) realizing them (or rather disregarding them). Qimron and Strugnell (and then also the Krakow edition) translated, already in 1985, with 'precepts' or with 'precepts of the Torah'[99] and Dunn – whose just addressed article of 1988 does not offer a reference to Qimron and Strugnell – mentioned besides 'deeds of the law', also 'deeds/works', 'praxis', 'covenantal obligatons' and 'commandments'.[100] What gave me pause, was that sensational fact and the issue of the translation which is highly significant from the perspective of the history of theology. Here we only need to point to the meaning of 'good works' in the Middle Ages (and also of CA VI)! There possibly might lie an interesting angle of interpretation! I tried to trace the semantic problems meanwhile, primarily with the help of the Pauline contexts, thus essentially synchronically, then in addition, of course, also diachronically. In the postdoctoral dissertation of 1989, which was then published in 1992, I came to the conclusion that 'the commandments and prohibitions of the Torah' would be meant.[101] In principle, I've retained this proposition ever since, however altered slightly, inasmuch as I soon after – now still closer to the sociological impulse of Dunn – intended to represent the proximity of the Pauline expression to what the New Testament scholar of Durham had defined with 'identity' and 'boundary markers' of Judaism. My 'comprehension of the phrase ἔργα νόμου … according to which halakhot are meant here',[102] is not at all consistently taken up, as already mentioned; in fact some reject it rapidly – as it seems to me, all too rapidly – while others try to reject it, particularly O. Hofius.[103]

In light of the difficult hermeneutical situation with regard to this syntagma, which has become so important in the history of the church and is especially interwoven in the process of separation between Lutherans or Protestants and 'Catholics' (see again CA IV), I am admittedly still very glad that the thesis, initially surprising, in the meantime has won some attention.[104]

99.   Qimron/Strugnell, 'Letter' (see n. 93), p. 401. Cf. Bachmann, 'Rechtfertigung' (see n. 86), p. 29 together with n. 153.

100.   Dunn, 'Theology' (see n. 94), pp. 244–5.

101.   Bachmann, *Sünder* (see n. 25), pp. 91–100 (quotation: 100).

102.   Bachmann, '4QMMT' (see n. 97), 55. Cf. already idem, 'Rechtfertigung' (see n. 86), p. 14.

103.   On this, see only Bachmann, 'Praktiken' (see n. 86), pp. 37(-9). The detailed statement of the New Testament scholar of Tübingen is now referred to here according to his new collection of essays: O. Hofius, '"Werke des Gesetzes". Untersuchungen zu der paulinischen Rede von den ἔργα νόμου', in idem, *Exegetische Studien* (WUNT 223), Tübingen, 2008, pp. 49–88 (first: 2006). Cf. also pp. 89–94: idem, '"Werke des Gesetzes" – Zwei Nachträge'.

104.   On this, see only J.-N. Aletti, 'Où ent sont les études sur Saint Paul? Enjeux et proposition', in RSR 90, 2002: 329–52, pp. 344–5 together with n. 49, and Bachmann, 'Praktiken' (see n. 86), p. 37 together with n. 15 and pp. 39–41 together with n. 28 ; furthermore Wengst, *Israel* (see n. 12), p. 185 together with n. 168 (against Hofius), and M. Ebner, 'Die Rechtfertigungslehre des Paulus in soziologisch-sozialgeschichtlicher Perspektive', in N. Kleyboldt (ed.), *Paulus. Identität und Universalität des Evangeliums*, Münster, 2009, pp. 93–104, (94 and) 101.

A not insignificant number of – partly quite prominent – scholars agree with it or at least comment in the sense of the thesis. Some names should be named after all: Pierre Grelot, Miguel Pérez Fernandez, Romano Penna, Jean-Noël Aletti, Holger Sonntag, Johannes Woyke, Volker Stolle, Mogens Müller, Ulrich Wilckens, Klaus Wengst and Martin Ebner; the conception is also assented to with cautious words by Eduard Lohse and Jörg Frey.[105] By the way, I developed this semantic possibility in 1989, and this under quite favourable circumstances, but in principle it is significantly older, represented especially in a ZNW article written 1929 by E. Lohmeyer,[106] and it is by no means unknown to patristic exegesis.[107] If there should be something to this thesis, then the apostle's consistently negative connotation of ἔργα νόμου could possibly be understood like this: Paul refuses with the statements – given only in Galatians and Romans – the opinion that regulations like the requirement of circumcision are also valid for Gentile-Christians (compare, e.g., Gal. 2.3, 7; Rom. 3.30). Such halakhot were *by no means*, according to the apostle, meant for these people: Non-Jews, gentiles – with faith in Christ – ought to be included just as non-Jews in the community of salvation, which insofar then indeed would have a universal feature.

(ii) Under the 118 Pauline νόμος-references[108] occasional harsh formulations occur, and they occur also besides the eight appearances of ἔργα νόμου; one should, however, preferably not simply blend them all together in one pot with the ἔργα-νόμου formulations, which, as it might be, could be related to 'the inclusion of ... Gentiles'.[109] There are unquestionably several pots – as,

---

105. At the beginning of the discussion following this (Leuven) lecture, M. D. Nanos said that I could add him to the list of those scholars who understand the expression ἔργα νόμου in the sense of halakhot.

106. E. Lohmeyer, 'Gesetzeswerke', in ZNW 28, 1929: 177–207, afterwards in idem, *Probleme paulinischer Theologie*, Darmstadt (or Stuttgart), 1954, pp. 31–74, here esp. 64.

107. On this, see only M. Meiser, 'Vom Nutzen der patristischen Exegese für die neutestamentliche Schriftauslegung (am Beispiel des Galaterbriefes)', in D. C. Bienert/J. Jeska/ Th. Witulski (eds), *Paulus und die antike Welt. Beiträge zur zeit- und religionskundlichen Erforschung des paulinischen Christentums. Festgabe für Dietrich-Alex Koch zum 65. Geburtstag* (FRLANT 222), Göttingen, 2008, pp. 189–209, 202–3 (cf. idem [M. M.], *Galater* [Novum Testamentum Patristicum 9], Göttingen, 2007, 104–6); furthermore Bachmann, 'Keil' (see n. 38), p. 78 together with n. 32 and p. 85 together with n. 68. The paper of D. Langton read first at the Leuven meeting allows the assumption that Jews of the Middle Ages (for instance in the *Toledot Yeshu*) and of the early modern era (for instance Isaak Troki) did apply Paul's ἔργα νόμου phrases to the regulation(s) of circumcision and to dietary laws. Also Johannes Calvin takes this in consideration (so on Rom. 3.20 [Calvin-Studienausgabe 501, pp. 180–5, esp. 180–1] and on Gal 2.14-16 [Johannes Calvins Auslegung der Heiligen Schrift NR 17, pp. 37–9]; on this cf. Wengst, *Israel* [see n. 12], p. 186), and in the twentieth century at any rate D. Flusser approaches this thesis (on this, see Bachmann, 'Keil' [see n. 38], p. 88). Cf. below (at) n. 142.

108. So the counting by H. Hübner, 'νόμος', in EWNT II (1981): 1158–72, p. 1161.

109. I pick up this impressive phrase from T. L. Donaldson ('Inclusion ...' [see n. 80], p. 109).

for instance, one for phrases sounding positively.[110] In this pot one could place at any rate the remarks on νόμος and on the commandment of love (Rom. 13.9-10 [here also a hint to the ethical decalogue]; Gal. 5.13-14 [compare 5.23, further 5.6]; compare also 1 Cor. 9.21; Gal. 6.2, further Rom. 3.27cβ; 7.12, 14, 22 [compare v. 25]; 8.2a). As well, it does not otherwise lack references that reasonably fit into this pot: for instance Rom. 2.14 and 8.4,[111] and beyond that statements in which νόμος is referred to the 'Old Testament' or to the Pentateuch (especially 1 Cor. 9.8-9; 14.21, 34; Gal. 4.21b; compare, e.g., Rom. 3.19, 21b; 7.1). The phrases in Rom. 7.23 and 8.2 about the 'law of sin (and of death)' are certainly not simply positive; that the expression ἕτερος νόμος in 7.23a encounters, causes one after all to think about putting them into a different pot. With certain formulations one should arguably be cautious in considering them as merely *negative* in regard to the Law, for instance, where the cooperation of Law and sin – better, of sin and Law – is involved (e.g., Rom. 5.13-14; 7.1[ff.]; 1 Cor. 15.56) because, to loosely paraphrase Rom. 7.7-14 (compare 3.20; Gal. 3.10), the mirror is naturally not responsible for my wrinkles, even though it makes me conscious of them. This cooperation of Law and sin, of sin and Law is now – according to Paul – considerably affected by the Christ-event, that, according to Gal. 2.(15-)17, leads even Jews to the confession of their being sinners and that according to Rom. 3.(21-)23 generally forces the sentence 'all have sinned ...' Who for this reason requires 'justification' through Christ and engages it, may not require it from the Law, so particularly Gal. 5.4. Inasmuch as the Christ-event definitely connects Law and sin, the apostle gives statements which are willingly understood in exegesis as criticism of the Law and as expressions of (complete) 'freedom from the law' (compare Rom. 7.3).[112] This, however, is at odds with the results accumulated here, and in detail more questions unfold. At least three contexts of this field should be touched upon: the Pauline formulation (occurring in Rom. 6.14, 15; 1 Cor. 9.20; Gal. 3.23; 4.4, 5, 21a) ὑπὸ νόμον (see γ); the involvement of angels in the legislation according to Gal. 3.19-20 (see β); the phrase τέλος ... νόμου Χριστός (see α) in Rom. 10.4. In my opinion *none* of these contexts is a matter of radical criticism of Law, and

110. On this, see, for instance, the paper just published by H. Giesen, 'Befreiung des Gesetzes aus der Sklaverei als Ermöglichung der Gesetzeserfüllung (Röm 8,1-4)', in BZ NF 53, 2009: 179–211 – which, as it seems to me, points in the correct direction.

111. I think (on this, see only Bachmann, *Sünder* [see n. 25, pp. 57–8.62–3], that in Gal. 2.21b a syllogism is indicated, i.e., (1) 'If justification [comes] through the law, then Christ died for nothing'; (2) Christ, indeed, did not die for nothing (on this, see only Gal. 1.4; 2.20d); (3) Justification does not come through the law. So it seems to me to be correct when Sanders says, 'that Paul's thought ran from solution to plight' (Sanders, *Religionsstrukturen* [see n. 27], p. 451; cf. 457).

112. Two examples may suffice: Hübner, 'νόμος' (see n. 107), p. 1168 ('principal freedom from the law'), and Räisänen, 'Gesetz III' (see n. 84), p. 848 ('freedom from the law'). On this question see the monograph of W. Coppins, *The Interpretation of Freedom in the Letters of Paul. With Special Reference to the 'German' Tradition* (WUNT II/261), Tübingen, 2009, esp. pp. 34–40, 107–8, 114–15, 120–1, 175–9; and cf., furthermore, Wengst, *Israel* (see n. 12), pp. 90–1.100–11 (together with n. 20), moreover pp. 97(–8) n. 100; P. Frederiksen, 'Judaizing the Nations: The Ritual Demands of Paul's Gospel', in NTS 56, 2010: 232–52, esp. pp. 234, 252.

insofar it is here not really a question of 'freedom from the law'. It is in fact decisive throughout that the Christ-event (for instance according to 1 Cor. 15.3b[-5]) suggests the following: Even the Law, the Mosaic Torah, is de facto not capable of giving 'life' and of imparting 'justification' (compare especially Gal. 3.21c-22).

(α) Hence, in Rom. 10.4, to begin with this item, the Christ-event is unquestionably emphasized. However, in the light of the syntagma 'law of God' in Rom. 7.22 (compare again especially Rom. 13.9-10) the expression disputed here will hardly be translated with 'end/ending of the law'. Additionally, the formulation and vocabulary of Rom. 10.4 with τέλος barely causes one to think firstly of 'end/ending of the law', but the formulation, as K. Haacker with reference, inter alia, to 1 Tim. 1.5 has – as I think – convincingly reasoned, rather refers to teleology.[113] Christ therefore should here be somehow understood as the goal of the law.[114]

(β) The contemporary still dominating perception of Gal. 3.19-20 can be briefly and clearly described with Hübner as follows: 'The nomos derives from demonic angelic powers.'[115] A significant role here befits a special interpretation, which has been on the market with the commentary on Galatians by H. Schlier since 1949 (and which he already mentions in a letter to R. Bultmann in 1939 [19-08-1939]).[116] Schlier claims the presence of imaginations of 'early-gnostic' provenience, and this suggests that v. 20, according to this exegete, seems to mean that the one, the mediator ('The figure of a μεσίτης') exists 'not … amongst One', 'but that God is One'; therefore 'the peculiar idea of a multiplicity in God' should be assumed, whereby one seems to have reached the gnosis and thereby also negative deities.[117] This all seems very far-fetched to me:[118] We encounter angels within the legislation for instance in Acts 7.53 and in Heb. 2.2 (compare, for example, Josephus, *Ant.* 15.136; further Deut. 33.2LXX; Ps. 68.18) and there they underline the impact of the legislation. In Gal. 3.19 the speech is not even explicitly from a

113. K. Haacker, *Der Brief des Paulus an die Römer* (ThHK 6), 2nd, corrected edn, Leipzig, 2002, pp. 206–9, esp. 208.

114. Cf. idem, '"Ende des Gesetzes" und kein Ende? Zur Diskussion über τέλος νόμου in Röm 10,4', in K. Wengst/G. Saß (eds [in cooperation with K. Kriener/R. Stuhlmann]), *Ja und nein. Christliche Theologie im Angesicht Israels. Festschrift zum 70. Geburtstag von Wolfgang Schrage*, Neukirchen-Vluyn, 1998, pp. 127–38, esp. 134, furthermore Theobald, *Römerbrief* (see n. 39), pp. 215–19 (bibliography). Cf. R. Bergmeier, 'Vom Tun der Tora', in Bachmann, *Lutherische … Paulusperspektive* (see n. 23), pp. 161–81, 176–7, and Wengst, *Israel* (see n. 12), pp. 331–2.

115. H. Hübner, *Das Gesetz bei Paulus. Ein Beitrag zum Werden der paulinischen Theologie* (FRLANT 119), 3rd edn, Göttingen, 1982, p. 32. Cf. idem, 'νόμος' (see n. 107), pp. 1168–9, furthermore Räisänen, 'Gesetz III' (see n. 84), p. 848.

116. On this see R. von Bendemann, *Heinrich Schlier. Eine kritische Analyse seiner Interpretation paulinischer Theologie* (BEvTh 115), Göttingen, 1995, p. 91 n. 338.

117. H. Schlier, *Der Brief an die Galater* (KEK 7; 10th edn), Göttingen, 1949, pp. 116–17 (quotations: 116).

118. On this in more detail the essay: M. Bachmann, 'Ermittlungen zum Mittler: Gal 3,20 und der Charakter des mosaischen Gesetzes', in idem, *Antijudaismus* (see n. 28), pp. 81–126.

multitude of angels (different for instance: Ps. 68.18), whereas, on the other hand, earlier in v. 16 a multitude was talked about, yet, with regard to the *many* (Jewish) *descendants* of Abraham; there the *one* descendant, Christ, was opposed to them. Furthermore, because with the 'one' God of v. 20b, the Shema' Yisrael in Deut. 6.4 is alluded to, the outcome is that the '*one*' God causes the Christ-event as well as the Law, and as the Christ-event according to v. 8 (compare generally vv. 6-9) is valid for 'all nations', the God of the Law (or of the legislation) simultaneously is the God of the whole world. A tableau developed by me in (1997 and) 1999[119] might clarify this issue:

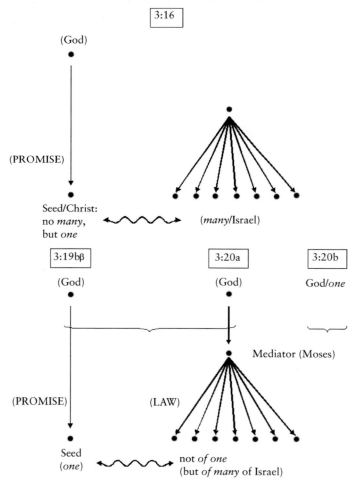

119. Bachmann, 'Charakter' (see n. 118), pp. 119 and 122 (cf. already M. Bachmann, 'Ermittlungen zum Mittler', in Amt und Gemeinde (ed. by the bishop of the Protestant Church A. B. in Austria) 48, 1997: 78–85, esp. p. 84). The (English) tableau offered now immediately goes back to: Bachmann, *Anti-Judaism* (see n. 50), pp. 79 and 81.

However, the irrealis in the conditional clause in the irrealis in Gal. 3.21b implies that the Law *cannot* make alive; however, by contrast, the Christ-event can (compare v. 22).

(γ) Insofar as, according to Gal. 4.4-5, Christ is γενόμενον ὑπὸ νόμον, ἵνα τοὺς ὑπὸ νόμον ἐξαγοράσῃ, he has redeemed those who according to 3.23 have been up to that point just 'under the law'. It would be precarious – so 4.21 – to equate Gentile-Christians with them. Conversely, the Jewish-Christian Paul says in 1 Cor. 9.20 that he, ὡς ὑπὸ νόμον, was able to meet with other Jews, however, without himself still being ὑπὸ νόμον. Notwithstanding, so v. 21, he is not ἄνομος, rather ἔννομος Χριστοῦ.

In short, the term νόμος usually is not really used negatively by Paul. But the Christ-event allows one to comprehend the conviction that the Law itself could give 'life' (compare again Gal. 3.21c-22) as an illusion. On the other hand, the Christ-event (that somehow deals with Jesus' love [see Gal. 2.20]) causes Christians – this at least is the apostle's conviction! – to lovingly meet the Torah (see again Gal. 5.13-14[120]).

(iii) The syntagma ἔργα νόμου which has become so meaningful and which now should move over to the centre of this paper,[121] occurs only eight times in Paul, namely in Rom. 3.20, 28 and in Gal. 2.16a, 16b, 16c; 3.2, 5, 10. Thereby seven times it says ἐξ ἔργων νόμου (compare Rom. 9.32 *v.l.*) and only in Rom. 3.28 χωρὶς ἔργων νόμου. My thesis, namely that prescriptions, and not individual actions,[122] are consistently meant, draws synchronically inter alia upon items which E. Lohmeyer had already observed.[123] Nowhere in these passages is a personal involvement of a possible agent indicated by a personal pronoun, and, moreover, a qualifying adjective is missing consistently which could describe an action, for instance, as 'good' or 'bad'. In addition, a certain parallelism of ἔργα νόμου with νόμος has to be noticed (see only Rom. 3.10, 21, 27, 31; Gal. 2.[19 and] 21). Further, the familiar *crux interpretum* in Gal. 3.10 then becomes irrelevant, when in v. 10a actions in fulfilment of the Torah are not addressed, and similarly the reference in Rom. 3.20b to v. 20a which is signalled by γάρ becomes completely clear, as soon as the formulation introducing the verse does not concern actions according to requirements of the Torah, but just regulations of the Torah. They are possibly also in view in the expression (ὁ) νόμος (τῶν) ἔργων suggested by Rom. 3.27b (compare Eph. 2.15), and in Rom. 2.15 the singular τὸ ἔργον τοῦ νόμου probably relates to something like a sum total of the prescriptions of the Mosaic Law.

Naturally, to this, in my opinion, very formidable set of synchronic arguments surveyed, a considerable number of not insignificant diachronic

---

120. On this cf., for instance, Bachmann, *Sünder* (see n. 25), 115–20, esp. pp. 118–20.
121. On this I generally point to some of my studies (which will be mentioned in the following passages only exceptionally): Bachmann, 'Rechtfertigung' (see n. 86); idem, '4QMMT' (see n. 97); idem, 'Vorwort' (see n. 35); idem, 'Keil' (see n. 38); idem, 'Praktiken' (see n. 86).
122. On this, see above (at) nn. 34–5.87–9.
123. On this, see Lohmeyer, *Probleme* (see n. 106), pp. 34, 59, 62–4, 68, 71.

findings can and must be added: inter alia Exod. 18.20; Apc 2.26; TestLev. 19.1-2 – and now 4QMMT C27. This should be the more so as the expression encountered here, מקצת מעשי התורה, at least formally complies closely with the Pauline ἐξ ἔργων νόμου (insofar as מקצת [precisely: מקצתם] in Dan. 1.5LXX is reflected by ἐκ). Moreover, that (Aramaic-)Hebraic formulation finds its counterpart in 4QMMT B1 (compare B2: 'works') and C30 in the expression מקצת דברינו, and thereby it deals (just against the background of Exod. 34.28; Deut. 1.1; 4.13; 10.4) unquestionably with the specific halakhot itemized in this writing, which are estimated as obligatory within the radius of the addressor and the persons around him, thus potentially on the part of the 'teacher of righteousness' and on the part of the ('Qumran') community. Three aspects in the document 4QMMT, which might be particularly illuminating for the Pauline usage of the syntagma ἔργα νόμου, should be mentioned: As then with the apostle (Rom. 4.3 [compare v. 9]; Gal. 3.6) also for instance in 4QMMT C28, questions concerning the Torah are dealt with; like Paul, 4QMMT C31 alludes, to say it thus, to Gen. 15.6 (compare especially Ps. 106.31; 1 Macc. 2.52); not otherwise than with Paul (see especially Gal. 3.10 (compare v. 12) and Rom. 10.5, with reference to Lev. 18.5) a verb relating to the doing, עשה (compare further for instance TestLev. 19.2), is encountered in 4QMMT C31 within the context of the phrase 'works of the law'.

So the thesis of the ἔργα νόμου as halakhot imposes itself massively. Taking a closer look, one recognizes that in 4QMMT something like the 'we-group' gathered around the author (for instance B1; C7) hopes to get a 'you-group' (for instance B68; C8; compare, for instance, C26.28: you singular, further C27.31-32) that sides with the 'we-group' concerning the rendered halakhot (see especially C30), whereas obvious reservation exists towards a 'they-group'. Therefore one has to take into account seriously the option 'boundary markers' (Dunn) also with regard to the Pauline syntagma. For this reason in a pre-Pauline early Christian tradition, as it can be assumed behind Gal. 2.16, potentially inner-Jewish 'boundary markers' come into consideration,[124] not other than in 4QMMT. The apostle himself, within the context of his references to ἔργα νόμου deals, however, with the prescription of circumcision (compare to this in Romans [besides Rom. 2.14; 3.29; 4.16-18], the juxtaposition of περιτομή [Rom. 2.25, 26, 27, 28, 29; 3.1, 30, further 4.9-12]and ἀκροβυστία [Rom. 2.25, 26, 27; 3.30, further 4.9-12], and in Galatians the statements in Gal. 2.3, 7-8 [also in vv. 6, 9-10], further in 5.2-3; 6.12-15 [as well as in 3.28], and also with dietary laws [see Gal. 2.11-14]). In this respect, I think that the reason for connoting the 'works of the law' negatively is that regulations such as the prescription of circumcision shall not be imposed on gentiles and Gentile-Christians. That is, their inclusion in the community of salvation does not entail the acceptance of such halakhot by non-Jews, and

124. On this see esp. Ch. Burchard, 'Nicht aus Werken des Gesetzes gerecht, sondern aus Glauben an Jesus Christus – seit wann?', in idem, *Studien zur Theologie, Sprache und Umwelt des Neuen Testaments* (WUNT 107), ed. by D. Sänger, Tübingen, 1998 (first: 1996), pp. 230–40, esp. 235.

therefore does not request their conversion to Judaism. The only condition indeed is Christ, or rather faith in Christ (see merely Gal. 2.16).

So a reasonable abundance of indications have been presented to take up Dunn's formulation 'boundary markers', and to think of the Pauline ἔργα νόμου more precisely as something like halakhot, and thereby primarily to think of those halakhot that in particular in the first century of the common era could be regarded as differentiating between Jews and non-Jews. In light of this I am wondering a little, to put it bluntly, that Dunn up to now, as it seems to me, has not taken this small, but hardly unimportant step beyond his earlier statements – given for instance in 1988 – relating to this topic.[125] This also includes the 'method' mentioned above which I regard as (self-)immunization, that is, the 'method' of referring again to Dunn's, and at times also to Hofius', refutation of my thesis. This is generally done without reference to the (since that time) growing group of exegetes that, like me, points to halakhot![126] Those scholars' rejection of my position sounds like *Roma locuta, causa finita* (Augustine, *Sermones* 131.10). Such an approach astonishes me all the more, as the reason given by Dunn by no means convinced me, nor does it convince me, as I have published more or less succinctly – and recently I argumentatively countered as well Hofius' respective paper (or rather his respective papers).

Concerning my answer to Hofius,[127] that offers further material besides the points just presented, the echo regarding the ἔργα νόμου is exclusively positive until now. Two confirmations have especially pleased me. A scholar in New Testament and Judaism writes: 'Concerning the philological line of reason ... I can hardly contradict you', and a not unimportant Old Testament scholar adds to his very friendly vote an additional argument: 'Maybe, concerning the Hebrew Old Testament, in your favour, Lev. 18.3, 4 still should be referred to. Here "ma'se" means ... in Lev. 18.3 certainly as much as "customary practices, operational conventions" (in Egypt and Canaan), contextualised by "huqqot". In v. 3 and v. 4 "asa ma'se" and "asa mischpat" stand parallel.' These latter observations comply with Gal. 3.10-12 – and also with my NTS article on this, published in 2007[128]; for Gal. 3.12 refers to Lev. 18.5, a formulation that for its part includes vocabulary of the preceding verses.

With regard to Dunn, here I will solely refer to his criticism in the closing article of the anthology edited by me with the title *Lutherische und Neue Paulusperspektive* (WUNT 182). Two aspects of my reasoning are not clear to Dunn: the philological division of the ἔργα νόμου understood as halakhot

---

125. On this see above (at) nn. 87.94–100. Cf. esp. Dunn, 'The Dialogue Progresses' (see n. 34), pp. 397–401.

126. On this see above (at) nn. 33–5; furthermore also (at) n. 103.

127. That is (as already mentioned) Bachmann, 'Praktiken' (see n. 86), here esp. pp. 38–51. Cf. furthermore, once again, Wengst, *Israel* (see n. 12), p. 187 n. 168.

128. Bachmann, 'Argumentation' (see n. 77), esp. pp. 527–8.537–9. Concerning the criticism of Dunn I only point, once again, to: Bachmann, 'Keil' (see n. 38); idem, 'Vorwort' (see n. 35), pp. XI–XII; idem, 'Dunn' (see n. 22), pp. 437–41.

from ἔργα in terms of actions (see α); the theological impact of the distinction (see β).[129] Let's begin with the semiological item in the narrower sense – after having recorded beforehand two further similarities between Dunn and me, here not addressed up to now, but fairly remarkable, namely that, on the one hand, a close connection between the formulations ἐξ/χωρὶς ἔργων νόμου and (short of νόμου) ἐξ/χωρὶς ἔργων (in Rom. 4.2, 6; 9.12, 32; 11.6) exists and that, on the other hand, in Paul in any case, 'on some occasions "works" can be seen as referring primarily to regulations, prescriptions'.[130]

(α) That with ἔργα νόμου for instance in Gal. 3.10a, prescriptions are in view, can be seen with some probability from the counterparts, that this plural expression finds in v. 10b in τὰ γεγραμμένα ἐν τῷ βιβλίῳ τοῦ νόμου and also in the following pronoun αὐτά (compare v. 12), and the Hebrew vocabulary of Lev. 18.3ff., that has just been mentioned, confirms this result, especially as Gal. 3.12 (compare Rom. 10.5) ties in with it. Just as in Lev. 18, also in Gal. 3.10-12 the action has to be distinguished from the instructions which have to be obeyed. And it would be a fallacy disproved by countless examples – among them the 'stone of stumbling' from 1 Pet. 2.8 (compare Isa. 8.14), of course not belonging to the field of mineralogy – to want to claim from the *nomens regens* of a genitive connection a necessarily closely connected meaning of the syntagma.[131] If Dunn says that the 'spectrum of meaning'[132] is in this case 'a continuum',[133] it clouds the mind, for the spectrum embraces here for ἔργα (νόμου), with 'actions' and with 'regulations of the Torah', two different meanings which have to be semiologically distinguished – as a test of polysemy might indicate without question.[134] To put it pointedly, one had

129. Dunn, 'The Dialogue Progresses' (see n. 34), pp. 399–401.

130. Ibid., pp. 399–400 (cf. 403–4) and 401 (quotation). On this, see already Bachmann, 'Vorwort' (see n. 35), p. XI, and cf. esp. idem, 'Rechtfertigung' (see n. 86), pp. 3–4 together with nn. 8–9, and idem, 'Keil' (see n. 38), pp. 99–100 n. 120 and 101–2 n. 127; moreover pp. 106–7 together with n. 148. Cf. Wengst, *Israel* (see n. 12), p. 206 (together with n. 217).

131. On this, see only Bachmann, 'Keil' (see n. 38), pp. 95.100–2.132–43 (cf. idem, 'Vorwort' [see n. 35], pp. XI–XII), and idem, 'Praktiken' (see n. 86), p. 43 together with n. 40, where I refer to Th. Schippan, *Einführung in die Semasiologie*, 2nd, revised edn, Leipzig, 1975, pp. 93–113 and 126–31, esp. 108–9.

132. J. D. G. Dunn, 'Noch einmal "Works of the Law": The Dialogue Continues', in idem, *Essays* (first: 2002) (see n. 27), pp. 407–22, p. 414.

133. Dunn, 'The Dialogue Progresses' (see n. 34), p. 400.

134. On this, see only Bachmann, 'Keil' (see n. 38), pp. 93–4 (cf. idem, 'Vorwort' [see n.35], p. XI). S. Grindheim, 'Review of: Bachmann, *Lutherische … Paulusperspektive*' (see n. 26), in Bulletin for Biblical Research 18, 2008: 336–8, p. 337, comments on the test of polysemy in the following way: 'Bachmann's argument is not convincing.' But the reason given for this estimation is simply incorrect. He explains his counter-example, 'The promise belongs to the law (Torah) but not to the law (Sinai covenant),' declaring, 'But, in this example, "law" is not polysemous.' However, just what he denies is accurate: 'law' is used here in two different meanings, i.e., for the complex Pentateuch ('Torah') *and* for statements or facts, which in a much more specific way refer to Sinai ('Sinai covenant'). Therefore the first meaning is clearly distinguished from the second one. Similarly, a person who refers to the Baltic Sea by the word 'puddle' can and should distinguish from it a 'puddle' which has arisen on his sailboat, situated just in that sea.

better not mistake green *traffic lights* for a *pedestrian*, who crosses the street according to the signal (and the reversed case, to stick with this example, would be even worse).

(β) This leads to Dunn's claim that my differentiation is irrelevant.[135] The contrary is the case![136] (And the *tohuwabohu* in the discussion we addressed at the beginning is probably to be ascribed to the factor of this [seemingly] unclear point, complicating the hermeneutical situation!) Two items seem to be of special importance with regard to the so-called Pauline doctrine of justification. *On the one hand*, when the syntagma ἔργα νόμου at least primarily deals with something like Jewish ritual instructions, it is more comprehensible than usual why Paul, as we have already seen in (ii), can talk so positively of the νόμος as in Rom. 13.8-11, and why he, moreover, as we will forthwith regard briefly in (iv), uses other plural phrases like τὰ δικαιώματα τοῦ νόμου (Rom. 2.26) in an unrestrainedly positive sense. With this differentiation and with the negative connotation of ἔργα νόμου it becomes clear what the corresponding phrases of the particularly 'prominent' Pauline 'sentences on justification' (Rom. 3.20, 28; Gal. 2.16; 3.2, 5) are getting at: 'Justification' does not presuppose for gentiles or Gentile-Christians the acceptance of Jewish 'boundary markers', as if they were also valid for non-Jews. Inclusion in the community of salvation does not run through the detour of a halakhically regulated inclusion into Judaism, but is in this respect universally possible. The Pauline doctrine of justification is easy to distinguish from 'Lutheran' interpretations, which for instance turn against attempts to earn 'justification' for example through 'a monk's vow of renunciation' or through donation(s).[137] *On the other hand*, the positive aspect of the 'doctrine of justification' just mentioned remains completely unmodified with the new comprehension of ἔργα νόμου:[138] Christ or rather faith in Christ imparts 'justification' (see once again Gal. 2.16-17), in fact also with regard to non-Jews. However, now – and *only* now! – a fairly symmetric relation can be discerned for the questions of Gal. 3.2, 5, when there ἔργα νόμου and ἀκοὴ πίστεως as theoretically conceivable sources of salvation for the origin of the spirit are juxtaposed,[139] and this in such a way that v. 5 can arouse the impression that ὁ ... ἐπιχορηγῶν ... τὸ πνεῦμα καὶ ἐνεργῶν δυνάμεις might somehow deal with *both* of those dimensions. With the 'Lutheran' view a rather crooked alternative would be presented in the verses of Gal. 3.2, 5: The human action belonging, so to speak, to the horizontal would be juxtaposed by ἐξ ἀκοῆ πίστεως to the 'vertical'. It would then be about, as it seems, a rivalry between human works and Godly donation. This is by no means the case with the thesis that I defend here! For this reason our argumentation results in a bipartite *corollary*. At the end

---

135. Dunn, 'The Dialogue Progresses' (see n. 34), pp. 400–1.
136. On this see already Bachmann, 'Vorwort' (see n. 35), pp. XI–XII.
137. On this, see, for instance, Bachmann, 'Rechtfertigung (see n. 86), pp. 5–10.
138. On this, see Bachmann, 'Praktiken' (see n. 86), pp. 53–4.
139. On this, see, for instance, Bachmann, 'Rechtfertigung' (see n 86), p. 25.

of his article picked up here, Dunn poses two questions (and these problems have considerably influenced ecclesiastical history and its fights over many centuries[140]) the question of how one can distinguish what, for instance, the phrase 'living by the spirit' in Gal. 5.16 may mean from the ἔργα νόμου, and the other question of why in view of the negative connotation of the 'works of the law', nevertheless, for example, Rom. 2.6 (or 2.6-13; compare 2 Cor. 5.10) talks about a judgement 'according to each one's deeds'.[141] These grave questions now are *not* posed *anymore*! For the 'works of the law', according to my thesis, are not about actions but precisely about regulations, at least primarily about something that was denoted as 'ceremonial commandments' in the Middle Ages;[142] in any case, they specifically pertain to such regulations as those that are regarded as Jewish 'boundary markers'. Apparently they have only little to do with the ethical behaviour of Christians and with the 'judgement according to works' (obviously) combined with ethics. Not a trace of irrelevance, unlike Dunn claims!

(iv) We already had to note that Paul is indeed able to speak positively of the νόμος and that he, for example, makes a totally positive use of the snytagma τὰ δικαιώματα τοῦ νόμου. When he nowhere uses the plural νόμοι, then this is naturally conditioned by the singular talk of the νόμος (with regard to the Torah) which was carried out fairly consistently in the scriptures of the Septuagint.[143] All the more the juxtaposition of ἔργα νόμου and of other plural expressions referring to prescriptions seems very conspicuous, this all the more so because these have *positive* connotations – different than ἔργα νόμου. Obviously it has to do with the fact that the apostle felt compelled to speak of such 'individual commandments', with which particularly the Christian life should harmonize.[144] The congruous terminology, which often is barely noticed – even though it finds a certain analogy in the 'ethical commandments' of the Middle Ages – should be itemized here. It deals, if one confines oneself just to plural formations, besides τὰ δικαιώματα τοῦ νόμου (Rom. 2.26), with τὰ τοῦ νόμου (Rom. 2.17) and with ἐντολαὶ θεοῦ (1 Cor. 7.19).[145]

140. On this, see only W. Krötke, 'Gute Werke II' (see n. 86), pp. 1344-5, and Freitag, 'Werke II' (see n. 86). Cf., for instance, Bachmann, 'Rechtfertigung' (see n. 86), pp. 1–2, and idem, 'Praktiken' (see n. 86), pp. 53(–4).

141. On this, see Dunn, 'The Dialogue Progresses' (see n. 34), p. 430.

142. On this, see only Bachmann, 'Keil' (see n. 38), pp. 76–7 n. 31, and M. Tiwald, *Hebräer von Hebräern. Paulus auf dem Hintergrund frühjüdischer Argumentation und biblischer Interpretation* (Herders Biblische Studien 52), Freiburg et al., 2008, pp. 302–64, esp. 359–60 (cf. also my review of this book: BZ NF 53, 2009: 286–9, esp. p. 289). Cf. above (at) n. 107.

143. On this, see, for instance, Hübner, 'νόμος' (see n. 108), p. 1163 ('It is conspicuous ... that LXX translates plur. *tôrôt* nearly exclusively with the sing. *v.*; for this the plur. νόμοι is to be found only rarely, for instance 2Esr. 19.13 for the laws of Sinai').

144. On this, see esp. Bachmann, 'Keil' (see n. 38), pp. 108–12.

145. It may be pointed here, at any rate, on the singular phrases, somewhat corresponding, i.e., on τὸ δικαίωμα τοῦ θεοῦ (Rom. 1.32), on τὸ δικαίωμα τοῦ νόμου (Rom. 8.4), also on τὸ ἔργον τοῦ νόμου (Rom. 2.15).

In summary, very differently than is often understood, Paul speaks overall quite positively of the νόμος, of the Mosaic Law (compare, however, Rom. 7.23; 8.2). Admittedly, in view of the cooperation of sin and Law, cautious formulations develop. Ultimately it is the Christ-event that indicates the sin of all men and women. Throughout negatively connoted, at any rate, is the expression ἔργα νόμου that for synchronic as well as diachronic reasons alludes to halakhot and not yet to their fulfilment. The syntagma in Rom. 3 and in Gal. 2–3 is used in such a polemical manner since Jewish 'boundary markers' are thought of here which, according to Paul, non-Jews should not assess as compulsory – and should not perform – in view of the justifying Christ-event. The inclusion of gentiles within the community of salvation, therefore, is not to be understood as ethnic inclusion in Judaism: The God of the Jews, as the apostle argues, is at the same time the one who through Christ or by faith in Christ can universally become approachable. Such a comprehension, which relates ἔργα νόμου to halakhot, also allows us better to understand the Pauline statements on ethics and on the 'judgement according to works'.

3. On the Theological and Ecumenical Relevance

In my opinion the suggestions of the New Perspective on Paul, and there especially also the sociological impulse that above all is connected with the name J. D. G. Dunn, promote exegesis, theology and ecumenical movement in a fairly considerable way. On the other side, the 'churchly patois' and reasons of the history of theology and church – and also some peculiarities of the exegetical dialogue – result in a very difficult hermeneutical situation, which makes it anything but easy to quickly proceed here. But I consider significant steps as possible – especially when grave reasons that argue for something like a certain new evaluation of the Pauline syntagmas ὁ Ἰσραὴλ τοῦ θεοῦ (Gal. 6.16) and ἔργα νόμου (Rom. 3.20 inter alia) are not rejected without thinking. In what follows, I will bring up four points (and the information should not suppress that philosophical works on and about Paul as well as the approaches gained by them can in my opinion be regarded as an encouragement).

(i) Paul does not consider the 'church (of God)' as an anti-Judaic reality; because it arises in Judaism and out of Judaism, it is, according to the apostle, something like a universalization of the Jewish people – at any rate a more universal quantity, that for this reason is not tied to Jewish 'boundary markers', not tied to ἔργα νόμου. Beyond these regulations, there remains the ethical impulse of the Mosaic Law obtained with the Christ-event and with the brotherly love connected with it, at least in principle.

(ii) Correspondingly, Paul clings in the letters of Galatians and Romans to a hope for 'Israel' – he seems, however, to imagine the 'salvation of all Israel' not as salvation without Christ.[146] The apostle applies that vocabulary

---

146. Similarly the opinion of R. Bergmeier, phrased in a reader's letter in issue 8 of *Zeitzeichen* 10, 2009, here p. 59. Cf., moreover, K. Haacker, 'Umkehr zu Israel und

related to Jewish issues, which in the tradition prior to Paul is used also in a figurative sense for non-Jews, in the same way. However, he uses the word Ἰσραήλ – and this also might not least be owed to traditional history – exclusively with regard to real Judaism, corresponding also Ἰσραηλίτης. Thus, a disinheritance or expropriation of Judaism does not (yet) take place!

(iii) Should an exegetical development occur, as optimistically may be presumed, just in those directions that were in view in (i) and (ii), this would then be, in my opinion, a reason for hope for the theologies of the Christian churches and for ecumenical cooperation. Besides the 'big ecumenical movement' of Jews and Christians, I think of the relation between Lutherans/Protestants and Catholics, further of the broad field of Protestant, or rather evangelical, groups. The area of the discussion about Christian ethics and about eschatology can then be separated very strictly from the discourse about the 'works of the law'. In particular, one should considerably get beyond the *Gemeinsame Erklärung zur Rechtfertigungslehre* (1999) and its supplementary documents.

(iv) The ethic ultimately determined by the Torah and the Christ-event provides, in my opinion, an important contribution[147] for the globalized and yet still strangely torn world, at any rate when Christians and Jews, Jews and

"Heimholung ins Judentum". Schritte zur Versöhnung zwischen Christen und Juden', in idem, *Versöhnung mit Israel. Exegetische Beiträge* (Veröffentlichungen der Kirchlichen Hochschule Wuppertal 5), Neukirchen-Vluyn, 2002 (first: 2000), pp. 191–208, esp. 205–6.

147.   In my opinion (on this cf. what has been said above in the text at the end of passage II), the conclusion of F. W. Horn, 'Die Darstellung und Begründung der Ethik des Apostels Paulus in der *new perspective*', in idem/R. Zimmermann (eds), *Jenseits von Indikativ und Imperativ. Kontexte und Normen neutestamentlicher Ethik I* (WUNT 238), Tübingen, 2009, pp. 213–31, esp. 230–1, definitively is too negative. For, that it seems to be successful 'to tie Paul to the Old Testament-Jewish tradition' (p. 231), is – regarding the history of theology – a considerable step forward (cf. pp. 225–6), and this does not exclude, and this shall not exclude in my evaluation, that in Paul and elsewhere in ancient Christianity (also beyond this stratum) 'connections to Greek-Hellenistic ethics' develop (p. 231), all the less because the ethnic boundaries of Judaism indeed were crossed programmatically. On this, see only M. Bachmann, 'Auseinandersetzungen um Verhaltensregeln im frühen Christentum als Indizien eines Ringens um Identität und Universalisierung der Religionsgemeinschaft', in J. Rüpke (ed. [in cooperation with F. Fabricius]), *Religionsgeschichte in räumlicher Perspektive. Abschlussbericht zum Schwerpunktprogramm 1080 der Deutschen Forschungsgemeinschaft 'Römische Reichsreligion und Provinzialreligion'*, Tübingen, 2007, pp. 213–22, 218(-20) (cf. idem [M. B.], 'Zur Rezeptions- und Traditionsgeschichte des paulinischen Ausdrucks ἔργα νόμου: Notizen im Blick auf Verhaltensregeln im frühen Christentum als einer "Gruppenreligion"', in J. Rüpke [ed.], *Gruppenreligionen im römischen Reich. Sozialformen, Grenzziehungen und Leistungen* [Studien und Texte zu Antike und Christentum 43], Tübingen, 2007, pp. 69–86, esp. 72–82). Incidentally, the questions put by O. Hofius (and J. Frey) (on this see Horn, 'Ethik' [pp. 225–]226) I did answer in the meantime (see, once again, Bachmann, 'Praktiken' [see n. 86]). The impression that the controversy about the expression ἔργα νόμου could be 'overviewed in its individual ramifications still only with great difficulties' (Horn, 'Ethik', p. 226), is – as already has been touched on (see above esp. [at] nn. 85–6.136) – just a consequence of the difficult hermeneutical situation, and this impression can be overcome, as this paper should display.

Christians do not contort this asset. In addition, the formidable relativization of 'boundary markers' seems to be not unimportant – the relativization at which Paul aims with the negative connotation of ἔργα νόμου. This relativization, that already played a significant role in the coexistence of Jews and 'God-fearers' at the time of the apostle and even earlier,[148] should also be of relevance for life in the present and the future, not at least as a paradigm considerable for other contexts. Differences in religion, culture, property, habitus, and so on, should – this maxim one probably has to recover from the Pauline literature – be perceived and definitely not disclaimed, also not wantonly be levelled. But such 'boundary markers' should, compared to some tendencies that are currently encountered in many places, also have to be extensively relativized.[149] 'Works of the law', according to the apostle, namely are not what 'justifies'!

148. On this, see, for instance, B. Wander, 'Gottesfürchtige und Proselyten', in J. Zangenberg (ed.), *Neues Testament und antike Kultur 3: Weltauffassung – Kult – Ethos*, Neukirchen-Vluyn, 2005, pp. 50–2, esp. 52. In this context the following passage is of great interest: Josephus, Ant. 20.34-53. Here we learn that in the first half of the first century CE, Jews were of different opinions regarding a non-Jew, i.e., (king) Izates (II.) of Adiabene: 'if the demand of circumcision, here (in § 42, 43 and 46) called ἔργον, should be obligatory for this man or if he still χωρὶς τῆς περιτομῆς could give reference to' the 'God of the Jews (§ 41)' (M. Bachmann, 'Neutestamentliche Hinweise auf halakhische Regelungen', in N. Ciola/G. Pulcinelli [eds], *Nuovo Testamento: Teologie in dialogo culturale. Scritti in onore di Romano Penna nel suo 70° compleanno* [SRivBiB 50], Bologna, 2008, pp. 449–62, 453).

149. On this, see M. Bachmann, 'Die Botschaft für alle und der Antijudaismus: Nachdenken über Paulus und die Folgen', in M. Hofheinz/G. Plasger (eds), *Ernstfall Frieden. Biblisch-theologische Perspektiven*, Wuppertal, 2002, pp. 57–74, esp. 73–4. Cf. idem (M. B.), 'Biblische Didaktik ohne historische Rechenschaft? Einige Notizen und das Beispiel der (paulinischen) Rechtfertigungsbotschaft', in idem/J. Woyke (eds), *Erstaunlich lebendig und bestürzend verständlich? Studien und Impulse zur Bibeldidaktik*, Neukirchen-Vluyn, 2009, pp. 1–25, esp. 20–1.

Chapter 5

PAUL'S RELATIONSHIP TO TORAH IN LIGHT OF HIS STRATEGY 'TO BECOME EVERYTHING TO EVERYONE' (1 CORINTHIANS 9.19-23)[1]

Mark D. Nanos

For though I am free with respect to all, I have made myself a slave to all, so that I might win more of them. To the Jews I became as a Jew, in order to win Jews. To those under the law I became as one under the law (though I myself am not under the law) so that I might win those under the law. To those outside the law I became as one outside the law (though I am not free from God's law but am under Christ's law) so that I might win those outside the law. To the weak I became weak, so that I might win the weak. I have become all things to all people, that I might by all means save some. I do it all for the sake of the gospel, so that I may share in its blessings.[2]

After Paul's turn to Christ, what was his relationship to Torah? The traditional and almost undisputed answer is that he renounced Torah-observance for disciples of Christ – except to imitate Jewish behaviour to evangelize among Jews. Yet to me it seems more logical that a Jew, such as Paul claims to be (2 Cor. 11.22; Phil. 3.5-6), who is seeking to convince

---

1.   I am grateful for comments from the conference attendees, and pre-conference reviews by Joel Willitts, Loren Rosson, Gerald McDermott and Mark Given, as well as responses to variations delivered at the 2009 Society of Biblical Literature International (Rome) and Annual (New Orleans) meetings.

2.   NRSV translation. Lit.: 'For being a free one from everyone, I enslaved myself to everyone, so that I might gain [κερδήσω] the many. And I became [ἐγενόμην] to the Jews/ Judeans [τοῖς Ἰουδαίοις] as/like a Jew/Judean [ὡς Ἰουδαῖος], in order to gain Jews/Judeans; to the ones under law/convention [τοῖς ὑπὸ νόμον] as/like under law/convention [ὡς ὑπὸ νόμον], not being myself under law/convention, so that I might gain the ones under law/ convention; to the ones lawless [ἀνόμοις] as lawless [ὡς ἄνομος], not being lawless of God but lawful/in-law [ἔννομος] of Christ, so that I might gain the ones lawless; I became to the ones weak/impaired [as/like] weak/impaired [ἐγενόμην τοῖς ἀσθενέσιν ἀσθενής], in order that I might gain the ones weak/impaired. To everyone I become [γέγονα] everything, so that by all means I might save some. Now I do everything because of the good news, so that I might have become [γένωμαι] a joint-sharer [συγκοινωνὸς] of it.' It is also useful to note that the context that v. 23 ties back to its set in v. 18: 'What therefore is my payment/reward? That proclaiming the good news without charge I might offer good news for which [I have] not made full use of my authority/power/rights in/with/by way of the good news.'

fellow Jews as well as gentiles to turn to Jesus as the one representing the ideals and promises of Torah, would uphold the quintessential basis of that message, that is, he would observe Torah (cf. Rom. 1.1-5; 3; 9.32–11.36; 15.8-9; 1 Cor. 15.1-28; Gal. 3.19; 5.14).[3] Moreover, Paul's rhetoric makes sense when approached from this perspective. Paul's arguments assume that his statements about Torah as well as criticism of some of his fellow Jews, which arise in letters full of appeal to the authority of Torah to support his positions, will be perceived to represent the views of a movement faithful to the Mosaic covenant, albeit maintaining some interpretations that are in rivalry with the interpretations of other Jewish groups. Moreover, these arguments seem to be targeted at gentiles (i.e., members of the nations other than Israel) who understand themselves to be participating in Judaism (i.e., Jewish communal life) by becoming Christ-followers, although remaining non-Jews.[4] For example, why would the non-Jews in Galatia want to become proselytes, and how would Paul expect his argument to be persuasive when declaring that proselyte conversion (circumcision) would thereafter oblige non-Jewish Christ-believers to keep the whole Torah (Gal. 5.3), if they do not know him, a circumcised Jewish Christ-believer, to exemplify that obligation as logically concomitant?[5]

Based on these and other similar examples, it is probable that Paul approached his audience with this assumption if he imagined his arguments would be convincing. I find no reason to believe that the recipients of Paul's letters, who knew him personally, or knew others who did (in the case of Rome), would interpret his language in terms of later 'Paulinism', a construction of Paul that operates around the proposition that the role

---

3.   How much sense would it make for Paul to proclaim Jesus to demonstrate the righteous ideals of Torah and to be its goal in order to convince Jews or non-Jews to turn to Jesus as Messiah/Christ if at the same time Paul either degraded Torah as ineffective or less than divine or even worthless, as many propose (e.g., when interpreting Romans 2; 3; 7; Galatians 3; 4; Phil. 3), or obsolete, as most do (e.g., when interpreting Rom. 10; Gal. 3), and to thus eschew any obligation to keep it as holy, and for Jews (which he claims to remain and represent the aspirations of), a responsibility to uphold in covenant faithfulness? Cf. H. L. Ellison, 'Paul and the Law – "All Things to All Men"', in *Apostolic History and the Gospel: Biblical and Historical Essays Presented to F. F. Bruce on his 60th Birthday*, eds W. Ward Gasque and Ralph P. Martin (Grand Rapids, MI: Eerdmans, 1970), pp. 195–202; Jacob Jervell, *The Unknown Paul: Essays on Luke–Acts and Early Christian History* (Minneapolis, MN: Augsburg, 1984).

4.   Full bibliography is available at www.marknanos.com. Recent summary discussions include Mark D. Nanos, 'The Myth of the "Law-Free" Paul Standing Between Christians and Jews', *Studies in Christian–Jewish Relations* 4 (2009): 1–21 <http://escholarship.bc.edu/scjr/vol4/iss1/4/>; idem, 'Paul and Judaism: Why Not Paul's Judaism?', in *Paul Unbound: Other Perspectives on the Apostle* (ed. Mark Douglas Given; Peabody, MA: Hendrickson, 2009), pp. 117–60.

5.   Mark D. Nanos, *The Irony of Galatians: Paul's Letter in First-Century Context* (Minneapolis, MN: Fortress Press, 2002), offers a sustained exegetical argument in this direction.

of Torah to express covenant faithfulness had ended for Christians – often applied to everyone else too – whether Jew or non-Jew.[6]

First Corinthians 9.19-23, however, is widely perceived to support the traditional conceptualization of Paulinism (i.e., privileging of gentileness, freedom from Torah and Jewish identity) and to counter any challenges mounted against it, such as I propose, irrespective of the specific arguments made regarding the particulars of the other letters.[7] That interpretation is predicated on his audiences knowing that Paul did not observe Torah when among non-Jews, such as themselves. Just as importantly, it proceeds as if the meaning of this passage is self-evident for the later interpreter, without the hesitation one might expect in view of several suspect lexical and exegetical moves required to make that case, and the ethical compromises it must embrace as central to the character of Paul, and thus Christian ideology. For the Paul who is celebrated here for his passion to win for Christ everyone in everything he does adopts a highly questionable way of life. That Paul is deceitful and hypocritical in terms of the principles of choosing righteousness and suffering over expedience, which he otherwise teaches emphatically, and according to which standard he condemns others (e.g., Peter at Antioch in Gal. 2.11-21).[8] He subverts his own teaching in this letter of his 'rule for all the assemblies', which includes the principle that a circumcised one is to 'remain in the state' of circumcision in which he was in 'when called', not to mention the ultimate priority of 'keeping the commandments of God' regardless of in which state it is that one remains (1 Cor. 7.17-24). He misleads anyone responding positively to his message into a religious affiliation that represents convictions and lifestyles that are other than he or she supposed, including important propositions that are absolutely contrary to critical convictions that he or she believes to be central

6.   This perception is evident even at the level of popular culture: 'Paulinism' is 'the teachings of the apostle Paul, who believed that people should be emancipated from Jewish law and allowed to follow the faith and spirit of Christ', according to <http://www.thefreedictionary.com/Paulinism>, accessed on 25 May 2009.

7.   The raising of objections based on this text has not only been my frequent experience when speaking or delivering papers, but is also a topic in discussions of my work, even among those sharing my view of a more Jewish Paul: Caroline Johnson Hodge, *If Sons, Then Heirs: A Study of Kinship and Ethnicity in the Letters of Paul* (New York, NY: Oxford University Press, 2007), pp. 122–5; Alan F. Segal, 'Paul's Religious Experience in the Eyes of Jewish Scholars', in *Israel's God and Rebecca's Children: Christology and Community in Early Judaism and Christianity: Essays in Honor of Larry W. Hurtado and Alan F. Segal* (ed. David B. Capes et al.; Waco, TX: Baylor University Press, 2007), p. 341 (321–43). I have briefly engaged this text when discussing the idol food context of the players, issues and instructions of 1 Cor. 8–10: Mark D. Nanos, 'The Polytheist Identity of the "Weak," And Paul's Strategy to "Gain" Them: A New Reading of 1 Corinthians 8.1–11.1', in *Paul: Jew, Greek, and Roman* (ed. Stanley E. Porter; Pauline Studies 5; Leiden and Boston, MA: Brill, 2008), pp. 209–10 (179–210); idem, 'Paul and Judaism'.

8.   Cf. Peter Richardson, 'Pauline Inconsistency: 1 Corinthians 9.19-23 and Galatians 2.11-14', *New Testament Studies* 26 (1979): 347–62.

to the proper worship of God (or gods).[9] It follows that he or she thereafter will be committed to adopting this same strategy of misleading others to win them to the gospel.

In addition to such serious moral compromises, the prevailing reading almost certainly involves Paul in an ineffective bait and switch strategy. While his disguising of his convictions is based on compromising truthfulness for expedience as he moves among different groups to successfully gain a hearing among each, this inconsistency will almost certainly result in failure, giving truth to the life he lives. For each party will ultimately learn of his absolutely contrary behaviour when among other parties subscribing to opposite propositional truths, whether by directly witnessing his flip-flopping, or by way of rumours.

Nevertheless, the prevailing readings have a long and powerful legacy. Peter Richardson perceptively observes that 'rarely' is there 'a passage that is as pregnant with implications – particularly for understanding his [Paul's] behavior – as 1 Corinthians 9.19-23'.[10] Heikki Räisänen presents those implications in starkly simple terms with which Richardson's analysis also agrees: '1 Cor. 9.20 f. is absolutely incompatible with the theory of an observant Paul.'[11]

Already in the fourth century, Chrysostom sought to defend Paul from charges of inconsistency by non-Christian critics who developed the negative logical inferences of the Christian interpretation to demonstrate Paul's indifference to Torah as a central ideology that made him suspect. An anonymous apologetic work arguably preserving Porphyry's criticisms includes the accusations that it is neither reasonable, nor clear headed, nor healthy, nor independent, nor will it be effective, but corrupt and confused for Paul to claim to be free in 1 Cor. 9.19 and call circumcision 'mutilation' in Phil. 3.2[12] while also circumcising Timothy in Acts 16.3;[13] moreover,

---

9.   John M. G. Barclay, '"Do We Undermine the Law?": A Study of Romans 14.1–15.6', in *Paul and the Mosaic Law* (ed. James D. G. Dunn; rev. edn; Grand Rapids, MI, and Cambridge: Eerdmans, 2001), p. 308 (287–308), cleverly compares Paul's theology with 'a Trojan horse which threatens the integrity of those who sought to live according to the law'. The relevance of this comment is accentuated by the discussion below of Odysseus as *polytropos*.

10.   Richardson, 'Pauline Inconsistency', p. 347. The impact of this essay on Lloyd Gaston's interpretation of Paul is telling. The only comment I find for Gaston on this passage is Lloyd Gaston, *Paul and the Torah* (Vancouver: University of British Columbia Press, 1987), pp. 78–9, where he states that if Richardson is right, then 'perhaps he [Paul] did not' keep the commandments.

11.   Heikki Räisänen, *Paul and the Law* (Philadelphia, PA: Fortress Press, 1986), p. 75, n. 171; cf. pp. 73–6.

12.   I have challenged this long-standing interpretation, and argued that Paul's reference to 'mutilation' is likely to some 'pagan' phenomenon rather than circumcision, in Mark D. Nanos, 'Paul's Reversal of Jews Calling Gentiles "Dogs" (Philippians 3.2): 1600 Years of an Ideological Tale Wagging an Exegetical Dog?', *BibInt* 17 (2009): 448–82.

13.   Macarius Magnes, *Apocritus* 3.30. See also, e.g., Julian, *Against the Galileans*, 106a-c, including Paul as responsible for Christians disregarding Torah and circumcision.

But anyone saying [both] 'I am a Jew' and 'I am a Roman' is neither, even if he would like to be.

The man who hypocritically pretends to be what he is not makes himself a liar in everything that he does. He disguises himself in a mask. He cheats those who are entitled to hear the truth. He assaults the soul's comprehension by various tactics, and like any charlatan he wins the gullible over to his side.

Whoever accepts such principles as a guide for living cannot but be regarded as an enemy of the worse kind – the kind who brings others to submission by lying to them, who reaches out to make captives of everyone within earshot with his deceitful ways. And if, therefore, this Paul is a Jew one minute and the next a Roman, [or a student] of the [Jewish] law now, but at another time [an enemy of the law] – if, in short, Paul can be an enemy to each whenever he likes by burglarizing each, then clearly he nullifies the usefulness of each [tradition] for he limits their worthwhile distinctions with his flattery.

We may conclude that [Paul] is a liar. He is the adopted brother of everything false, so that it is useless for him to declaim, 'I speak the truth in Christ, I do not lie' [Rom. 9.1]; for a man who one day uses the law as his rule and the next day uses the gospel is either a knave or a fool in what he does in the sight of others and even when hidden away by himself.[14]

The Christian apologist does not offer a satisfactory reply to the charges, including the duplicity, but simply seeks to justify this behaviour.[15] Chrysostom also did not deny these problems, the criticisms of which he was acutely aware, but rather legitimated Paul's behaviour as faithful to Jesus:

Therefore Paul, in imitating his master, should not be blamed if at one time he was as a Jew, and at another as one not under the Law; or if once he was keeping the Law, but at another time he was overlooking it … once offering sacrifices and shaving his head, and again anathematizing those who did such things; at one time circumcising, at another casting out circumcision.[16]

Elaborating an argument already made briefly by the author of the *Apocriticus*, Chrysostom also excused Paul's inconsistent and morally suspect behaviour by appeal to a popular Greco-Roman topos of Paul's time, that of the physician who misleads a patient for the good of the patient, not that of the doctor.[17] The physician is expected to treat each patient differently

14.   Macarius Magnes, *Apocritus* 3.31 (transl. R. Joseph Hoffmann, *Porphyry's Against the Christians: The Literary Remains* (New York, NY: Prometheus Books, 1994), pp. 60–1).

15.   3.37 responding to 3.30, and 3.38 responding to 3.3: T. W. Crafer, *The Apocriticus of Macarius Magnes* (Translations of Christian Literature Series 1: Greek Texts; London: Society for Promoting Christian Knowledge, and New York, NY: Macmillan Company, 1919), pp. 101–3.

16.   *Laud. Paul.* 5.6 (SC 300.240), cited in Margaret M. Mitchell, '"A Variable and Many-sorted Man": John Chrysostom's Treatment of Pauline Inconsistency', *Journal of Early Christian Studies* 6.1 (1998): 107 (93–111).

17.   On the physician topos, see Philo, *Unchangeable*, 65–7; *Joseph*, 32–4, 74–9; Stanley K. Stowers, 'Paul on the Use and Abuse of Reason', in David L. Balch, Everett Ferguson and Wayne A. Meeks (eds), *Greeks, Romans, and Christians: Essays in Honor of Abraham J. Malherbe* (Minneapolis, MN: Fortress Press, 1990), pp. 253–86 (274–5);

according to the needs of each, including changing treatments as the patient's level of illness or return to health progresses. This 'condescending' behaviour extends to lying to the patient, or play-acting. That conduct is justified by the physician's overriding concern for the advantage of the patient, not of the doctor's own self. Thus Chrysostom explains: 'as a physician rather, as a teacher, as a father, the one to the sick, the other to the disciple, the third to the son, condescends for his correction, not for his hurt; so likewise did he'.[18] Chrysostom does not simply analogize the behaviour of the doctor to Paul's rhetorical adaptability, but also to Paul's conduct: Paul 'was variable and many-sorted not only in what he did, but also in what he said'.[19] And what Paul did was based on indifference to Torah: 'Therefore at one time he exalts the Law and at another he destroys it.'[20]

In addition to failing to answer the criticisms, the topos does not actually correspond to Paul's language in 9.19-23, for it is based on becoming a physician to a patient, et al., whereas to correspond to Paul's language it would have to call for conduct like a patient to patients, student to students, and child to children. To the degree that Chrysostom understands Paul to be free of Torah and adopt variability in his behaviour as well as his speech, his argument represents a variation on the focus of the traditional argument, but no serious challenge to it.[21] I do not see how it successfully explains this passage, or defends Paul of the charges made.

Clarence E. Glad, *Paul and Philodemus: Adaptability in Epicurean and Early Christian Psychagogy* (Supplements to Novum Testamentum 81; Leiden and New York, NY: E.J. Brill, 1995), pp. 21–2, 35–40, 53–98; Mitchell, '"A Variable and Many-sorted Man"', pp. 102–3; idem, 'Pauline Accommodation and "Condescension" (συγκατάβασις): 1 Cor. 9.19-23 and the History of Influence', in *Paul Beyond the Judaism/Hellenism Divide* (ed. Troels Engberg-Pedersen; Louisville, KY: Westminster John Knox Press, 2001), pp. 201–5 (197–214).

18.   Homily XXII.6, in Philip Schaff (ed.), *A Select Library of the Nicene and Post-Nicene Fathers of the Christian Church*. First Series. Vol. XII. *Saint Chrysostom: Homilies on the Epistles of Paul to the Corinthians* (Grand Rapids, MI: Eerdmans, 1978), p. 129 (PG 61.185); and see Hom. in Gen. 2.3 (PG 53.29); Hom. in Gal. 2.11; 3 (PG 51.374); Hom. in 1 Cor. 12.1 (PG 61.96); Hom. in 1 Cor. 12.3-4 (PG 61.184–5); Hom. in 2 Cor. 4.13; 2.2 (PG 51.283); *Laud. Paul.* 5.7 (SC 300.242–4); Hom. in Eph. 6.3 (PG 62.46); Hom. in Tit. 3.1-2 (PG 6.677–8). Jesus provides Chrysostom with the precedent for this variation, for he both praised and rebuked Peter at various times (Mitchell, 'Pauline Accommodation', pp. 208–14). In Homily XX.8 on 1 Corinthians 8.7, he explains that the knowledgeable are approaching the impaired incorrectly: 'they gained no ground by their refusing to condescend. For this was not the way to bring them in, but in some other way persuading them by word and by teaching' (Schaff (ed.), *Nicene and Post-Nicene Fathers*. First Series. Vol. XII. *Chrysostom: Corinthians*, p. 115 (emphasis added)).

19.   *Laud. Paul.* 5.6 (SC 300.242), from Mitchell, '"A Variable and Many-sorted Man"', p. 111, n. 74.

20.   *Laud. Paul.* 5.6 (SC 300.242), from ibid., p. 108.

21.   Augustine argued that Paul observed Torah because that was expected of the first generation of Jewish Christians, as long as they did not observe it for salvation (an early witness to the assumption of Jewish motives for Torah-observance as works-righteousness) (Augustine, *Letter* 40.4, 6, in Joseph W. Trigg, 'Augustine/Jerome, *Correspondence*', in *Biblical Interpretation* (ed. Michael Glazier; Message of the Fathers of the Church 9; Wilmington, DE: 1988), pp. 264–5 (250–95). But he also argued that they did so only in

In contemporary scholarship, the need for such apologies based on the prevailing interpretation of this passage continues unabated. Consider this example from Gordon Fee:

> ... when he [Paul] was among Jews he was kosher; when he was among Gentiles he was non-kosher – precisely because, as with circumcision, neither mattered to God (cf. 7.19; 8.8). But such conduct tends to matter a great deal to the religious – on either side! – so that inconsistency in such matters ranks among the greatest of evils. Paul's policy quite transcended petty consistency – and 'religion' itself ... How can Paul determine to 'become *like* a Jew'? The obvious answer is, in matters that have to do with Jewish religious peculiarities that Paul as a Christian had long ago given up as essential to a right relationship with God.[22]

order 'to show them [the Jews] what he thought he would need to be shown if he were still unconverted' (Augustine, *Letter* 40.6, in Trigg, 'Augustine/Jerome, *Correspondence*', p. 266). In other words, Augustine denied that Paul was merely pretending, but his explanation was actually still based on pretence, yet ostensibly legitimate because of justifiable motives, namely, empathy. Augustine nevertheless sought to challenge the idea that Paul behaved like a Jew 'out of any intention to mislead. Obviously the person who looks after sick people has to think like a sick person himself. I do not mean that he pretends to be sick, but he has to put himself in the place of the sick person in order to understand fully what he should be doing to help the sick person' (Augustine, *Letter* 40.4, in idem, 'Augustine/Jerome, *Correspondence*', p. 264). Augustine was so concerned with the topos of the physician's lie being adopted, as it had been by Chrysostom, and before him Origen (Origen, *Hom. in Jer.* 20.3 (PG 13.476)), that he wrote a treatise at about this time, *On Lying*, in which he challenged all lying, especially for the sake of religion, which effectively ended the perpetuation of the medicinal lie tradition in Western ethics (idem, 'Augustine/Jerome, *Correspondence*', p. 252).

It is interesting to observe that Jerome strongly disagreed with Augustine, revealing his ideologically based disgust of the notion that Paul or any Christian would observe Torah for any reason other than pretence, and maintaining not only that Paul pretended to Jewish behaviour to gain Jews (Jerome, *Letter* 104.17, in idem, 'Augustine/Jerome, *Correspondence*', p. 289, and see Jerome, *Letter* 104.13 (285)), but also that Augustine's explanation actually supported behavioural pretence, regardless of the different motives for which Augustine argued, which Jerome also denied (Jerome, *Letter* 104.17, in idem, 'Augustine/Jerome, *Correspondence*', pp. 289–90).

22.   Gordon D. Fee, *The First Epistle to the Corinthians* (New International Commentary on the New Testament; Grand Rapids, MI: W. B. Eerdmans Pub. Co., 1987), pp. 427–8 (emphasis his). Here we witness how this text is used not only to indicate that Paul was no longer a Jew in a religious behavioural sense, but that such identity and concomitant behaviour was regarded now by Paul to be irrelevant to God; hence, that judgement is applied to everyone. Anyone who might criticize Paul on the basis that it ought to be relevant is simply being 'religious', which is negatively valued, and not what Paul – on Fee's model of Pauline religion – is understood to represent. Rather, Paul is engaged in something superior; Fee is too, presumably, since no hermeneutical distance from this interpretation is expressed. Moreover, we learn that being religiously Jewish would also entail by definition participation in peculiarities that are not essential to a right relationship with God, including the concern for petty consistency. Yet Fee's assessment involves a logical double standard. For this Jewish behaviour seeks to be consistent with observing the covenant obligations of Torah, which had originated from God according to the Jewish tradition (but Fee's argument presumes that this is not so for Paul), and been articulated in the very Scriptures from which Paul drew his authority to speak of Jesus as Christ and to instruct his assemblies in the (peculiar)

The apologies offered continue to seek to legitimate the infraction by denial of the problem or appeal to supposed superior values and noble motives rather than attempting to actually eliminate the problem, which would, it seems, be accomplished by the exegetical approach to this passage that I seek to demonstrate, but that comes at the cost of eliminating the brush strokes supplied by this passage in the prevailing composite portrait of a Torah-indifferent Paul.

The virtually lone exception (of which I am aware) that proves the rule is stated by Wilfred Knox, who argues, against the consensus, that Paul did not 'deny that the Jewish nation itself was still bound to the observance of the Law; indeed he himself kept it with all the rigour of a Pharisee'. For his claim to be a Pharisee to be meaningful, 'it is clear that S. Paul continued throughout his life to practise Judaism, and that he expected Jewish converts to do so'. Yet one passage stands in the way:

> ... *the only objection* that can be brought against this view is the language of 1 Cor. *ix.21*, where S. Paul seems to imply that when dealing with Gentiles *he behaved* as if not bound by the Law ... On the other hand *this interpretation* of the passage *is impossible*. S. Paul could not both behave as a Jew when dealing with Jews and as free from the Law when dealing with Gentiles, since apart from the *moral dishonesty* of pretending to observe the Law when in Jewish society and neglecting it in Gentile society, it *would be impossible for him to conceal* from Jews whom he hoped to convert the fact that he disregarded the Law when not in Jewish company.[23]

behaviour that is consistent with God's will for them, which they are therefore to consistently observe.

Many other examples of this kind of reasoning to seek to resolve this matter could be provided. For example, Donald A. Hagner, 'Paul as a Jewish Believer – According to his Letters', in *Jewish Believers in Jesus: The Early Centuries* (eds Oskar Skarsaune and Reidar Hvalvik; Peabody, MA: Hendrickson Publishers, 2007), p. 113 (97–120), explains that 'Paul regards himself as no longer under the law' since he 'obeys it now and then. Paul thus feels free to identify with the Gentiles and not to remain an observant Jew. Incidentally, how remarkable it is that the Jew Paul can speak of himself as an outsider: "To the Jews I became as a Jew"!' This implies a 'break with Judaism', and 'it is clear, furthermore, that observing or not observing the law is an unimportant issue before God. The position taken by Paul is one of complete expedience: he will or will not observe the law only in relation to its usefulness in the proclamation of the gospel.' Also Paul W. Gooch, 'The Ethics of Accommodation: A Study in Paul', *TynBul* 29 (1978): 111–12 (93–117).

23. Wilfred L. Knox, *St. Paul and the Church of Jerusalem* (Cambridge: The University Press, 1925), p. 103 (emphasis mine). Knox's solution is that Paul 'means that in dealing with those outside the Law, he *behaves* as if he were free from the Law ... not in the sense of refusing to recognize any divine Law, but as in fact obeying the Jewish Law in Christ, or *in a Christian sense*, as something which he is *more or less* bound to observe, but which others [i.e., gentiles (?)] are not. The rhetorical tone of the passage obscures the facts' (emphasis mine). In other words, Knox derives the opposite implication from the text: Paul was sincere and consistent when behaving jewishly among Jews, albeit 'more or less' and adjusted to 'a Christian sense', thus the mimicry of lifestyles was when modifying his Jewish behaviour among non-Jews. It is unclear why this is not, inversely, still moral dishonesty, or how his Law behaviour among Jews could be concealed from gentiles. Moreover, Knox undermines his solution, which already equivocated on Paul's level of Torah observance, when he states: 'S. Paul is *not entirely consistent* with his own teaching, since he here

It is difficult not to wonder if this interpretive conundrum does not result from an a priori driving the exegesis of this passage. For those who look to Paul's life and teaching for guidance, the deeply troubling nature of the problems it creates require excusing or defending Paul, the hero of many disguises, and thereby, Christianity. But those defences come up short on explanatory power for anyone else. In response, some Christians will develop hermeneutical distance: Paul was like that, yes, but in this behaviour he should not serve as a model. For some others, the prevailing interpretation of this passage can be central to criticizing Paul and Christianity, for it provides legitimacy to, if not also cause for, dismissing him as immoral and incompetent.[24] This passage clearly stands in the way of improving relations between Christians and Jews – make that between Christians and non-Christians in general – because it undermines truthfulness as a core value, an essential element for the complete trust required in mutually respectful relationships. Is the prevailing interpretation of this passage really so clear, and is it so necessary that these many problems must be qualified or legitimated, go unrecognized or ignored, or left open to demonstrating the moral bankruptcy of Paul?

---

denies that he is bound to keep the Law, whereas in vii.18 he regards obedience to it as a duty ... It is, however, not surprising that his language is inconsistent. He was clear that it was necessary for Jewish Christians to continue to obey the Law; whether this was merely a matter of expediency, or a matter of principle, *he would hardly trouble to consider*. It must be noticed that on his own principles, if he obeyed the Law at all, *he was bound to obey it as a Pharisee ... Anything less was really worthless*' (p. 122, n. 54; emphasis mine). However, if Paul would not 'trouble to consider' whether obeying was motivated by expediency or principle, and if he sometimes obeyed it 'more or less', he can hardly be observing Torah as a Pharisee.

Knox has raised an insightful objection, but in addition to compromising his own alternative with an inconsistent and non-Pharisaic portrayal of a more or less observant Paul, he has merely reversed which sensibilities to privilege, and thus failed to offer a satisfactory solution to the charges of inconsistency and moral dishonesty. And he has not explained how the strategy could have succeeded. Ellison, 'Paul', also objects, and insists that Paul observed Torah, but does not explain the proposition; and Jervell, *Unknown Paul*, comments that 1 Cor. 9.19-21 makes it 'obvious that Paul lived as a pious Jew', although no argument is made, and it is clearly not obvious to the overwhelming majority of interpreters. Others objecting are listed in footnotes below.

24.   In addition to the kinds of 'pagan' criticisms already discussed, see Jewish criticisms by Hyam Maccoby, *The Mythmaker: Paul and the Invention of Christianity* (New York, NY: Harper & Row, 1986), pp. 151–7, 166–7; David Klinghoffer, *Why the Jews Rejected Jesus: The Turning Point in Western History* (New York, NY: Doubleday, 2005), pp. 106–10; and Amy-Jill Levine, *The Misunderstood Jew: The Church and the Scandal of the Jewish Jesus* (New York, NY: HarperSanFranscisco, 2006), pp. 75–86. The history of this line of Jewish critique is discussed by Nancy Fuchs-Kreimer, 'The "Essential Heresy": Paul's View of the Law According to Jewish Writers: 1886–1986' (PhD dissertation, Temple University, 1990), pp. 63–82. See also the examples discussed in Daniel R. Langton, 'The Myth of the "Traditional View of Paul" and the Role of the Apostle in Modern Jewish-Christian Polemics', *JSNT* 28.1 (2005): 69–104; Stefan Meißner, *Die Heimholung des Ketzers: Studien zur jüdischen Auseinandersetzung mit Paulus* (WUNT 2.87; Tübingen: Mohr Siebeck, 1996).

For a Jewish interpreter of Paul and Christian–Jewish relations critic, this interpretive tradition is intriguing, including the way the problems that it generates are handled by Pauline scholars, while at the same time the obstacles these represent to advancing Christian–Jewish relations are troubling. Have my working hypotheses that Paul was probably Torah-observant, and his movement best approached as Judaism, been mistaken? Are the roots of Christianity far more discontinuous with Judaism, as sustained in the prevailing readings of Paul, than I have supposed?

The fact that this text is embedded in the rhetorical aims of a particular letter, combined with the fact that it deals specifically with how Paul seeks to win those who do not believe in Christ, makes it an unlikely text to turn to for ultimate proof that Paul was not Torah-observant, or that he upheld a Torah-free lifestyle to be the ideal for Christ-believing Jews. More importantly, I propose that this text has been misinterpreted.

This passage does not and cannot by itself demonstrate that Paul was or had to be Torah-observant, and that is not my objective in this study. Rather, I seek to show that it does not support the claim that he *cannot* observe Torah as an expression of covenant fidelity; for example, that he only practised circumcision, dietary regulations and calendrical celebrations such as Sabbath when judged expedient for the purpose of gaining a hearing among Jews, and then only as matters of indifference (*adiaphora*). The interpretation proposed not only challenges such conclusions, but also opens up for consideration other interesting matters relevant to Pauline studies, including several of concern to this book. Moreover, although I am not a Christian, I believe it offers many solutions to the ethical problems that must, or at least I would think should, vex any Christian beholden to the prevailing interpretation of this serpent-like guile at the very heart of Paulinism, and thus Christianity itself.

First, I will focus on the topic of Paul's behaviour as presented in prevailing views, and develop analytical categories to assess this matter. In the case of the consensus reading, Paul is describing his tactics in terms of 'conduct' or 'lifestyle adaptability'. I will offer a different way to read Paul's language, suggesting instead that Paul was describing his 'rhetorical adaptability'. Then I will discuss examples from Acts 17 and Antisthenes' Odysseus that support my case. Throughout this essay, I note some of the problems that arise from the prevailing views, and how my reading avoids, solves or problematizes them further, at the same time raising a few challenges of its own, certainly for anyone ideologically bound to the traditional 'law-free' Paul.

1. The Prevailing Interpretations

Central to the traditional and still prevailing readings is the proposition that Paul adapts his *behavioural conduct* to the different audiences he seeks to gain to Christ, as can be clearly seen in the citations already presented. Paul is understood to be describing his *lifestyle* in terms of Torah or Jewishness as variable depending upon the social context in which he is operating. But it is specifically Jewish behaviour that is primarily regarded to be compromised by Paul, for he is no longer Torah-observant, and therefore implicitly more aligned with non-Jewish behaviour in principle, and thus involved in mimicking Jews more so than gentiles, whom he rather represents, because 'gentileness' is the default setting for Pauline Christianity. Richardson states the prevailing view concisely:

> In 1 Corinthians 9 Paul describes his motivation for his *conduct*; the basic principle is that he adjusts his *conduct* to fit the immediate circumstances as long as this adjustment will help to win some to Jesus. This statement is found within a treatment of the problem of eating meat offered to idols (1 Cor. 8.1ff.) in which he suggests that it is *acceptable to eat* such meat …[25]

> The accusations in Acts 21 against Paul *are probably true*; he counsels certain kinds of non-observance of the customary practices of Judaism, even to the point of agreeing to suggestions that Jews might cease to circumcise their children.[26]

For Richardson, it is plain that it is eating behaviour that Paul has in mind, and that Paul's theological position represents gentile (Christian) norms.[27] The subject of dietary behaviour offers a good example to work around, since it represents a tangible expression of Torah-observance, or not, and one that involves different interpretations of certain elements from group to group, but one that nevertheless, however practised, bears witness to the importance of seeking to live according to Torah as Jews, or not. We will return to this issue.

---

25.   Richardson, 'Pauline Inconsistency', p. 347 (emphasis added); see also the interrelated essay by Gooch, 'Ethics of Accommodation', p. 97 (93–117), who states that 'the passage clearly deals with Paul's behavior and not simply his methodology in mission or instruction'. Mark Douglas Given, *Paul's True Rhetoric: Ambiguity, Cunning, and Deception in Greece and Rome* (Emory Studies in Early Christianity 7; Harrisburg, PA: Trinity Press International, 2001), pp. 106–7, interprets Paul's reference to ἐγενόμην ('I became') to mean 'temporarily assuming a different identity', and 'refers to concrete, observable changes' (p. 109). For a different view of Paul on idol food, that he instead teaches that no food known to be idol food can be eaten by Christ-believers or by Jews, implying also by himself as a Christ-believing Jew, as well as several other elements that challenge the consensus readings in these chapters, including the identity of the 'weak', whom I propose to be idolaters who are not Christ-believers, see Nanos, 'Polytheist Identity', pp. 179–210; in agreement that Paul does not permit eating idol food per se, see also Peter J. Tomson, *Paul and the Jewish Law: Halakha in the Letters of the Apostle to the Gentiles* (CRINT; Assen and Minneapolis, MN: Van Gorcum and Fortress Press, 1990); Alex T. Cheung, *Idol Food in Corinth: Jewish Background and Pauline Legacy* (JSNTSup 176; Sheffield: Sheffield Academic Press, 1999); John Fotopoulos, *Food Offered to Idols in Roman Corinth: A Social-rhetorical Reconsideration of 1 Corinthians 8.1–11.1* (WUNT 2.151; Tübingen: Mohr Siebeck, 2003).
26.   Richardson, 'Pauline Inconsistency', p. 361.
27.   Peter Richardson, 'Early Christian Sources of an Accommodation Ethic – From Jesus to Paul', *TynBul* 29 (1978): 118–42.

Interpreters representing the New Perspective basically adopt the current consensus view that Paul was writing about adapting his behavioural *conduct* such as dietary practices to match that of the various audiences he addressed, with a Pauline Christianity-based propositional bias towards gentleness, that is, toward norms that are not derived from an interpretation of Torah, but rather from its non-applicability for Christians, Jewish or gentile.[28] E. P. Sanders explains that,

> Paul is obviously attempting to formulate <u>how he can live</u> *outside* the law when evangelizing gentiles and living among them, yet remain *within* the law of Christ and thus of God. He is attempting to formulate that possibility, yet the passage does not say how he can manage both. The truth is that he has no clear way of defining his own situation theoretically. <u>When among Gentiles he does not observe the Jewish law</u>: that is clear in Gal. 2.11-14 ... Christians, of whom Paul is here the example, are not *under* the law, but they are not thereby lawless toward God.[29]

Sanders interprets 'became like' to mean 'lived according to the law in order to win Jews', and not according to it to win gentiles.[30] He challenges the idea that this can be 'a literal description of Paul's life and work', because it would not work for Paul to observe Law when he goes to a synagogue and then not when he was with gentiles *'in the same church'*.[31] For Sanders, this language is 'hyperbolic', and the exception, when Paul practices Judaism, is only when Paul goes to Jerusalem: Paul lived like a Jew in Jerusalem, where that was expected in order not to give offence, but 'in all probability, when he entered each city, he went to Gentiles, he preached to them with some success, and he lived like a Gentile'.[32] In other words, Paul's lifestyle as far as Torah

---

28.   See Nanos, 'Myth of the "Law-Free" Paul', for a summary investigation of Paul's arguments about dietary matters challenging this consensus, and for more detail, see my *The Mystery of Romans: The Jewish Context of Paul's Letter* (Minneapolis, MN: Fortress Press, 1996), pp. 85–238; idem, *Irony of Galatians*; idem, 'What Was at Stake in Peter's "Eating with Gentiles" at Antioch?', in *The Galatians Debate: Contemporary Issues in Rhetorical and Historical Interpretation* (ed. Mark D. Nanos; Peabody, MA: Hendrickson, 2002), pp. 282–318; 'Polytheist Identity'.

29.   E. P. Sanders, *Paul, the Law, and the Jewish People* (Philadelphia, PA: Fortress Press, 1985), p. 100 (italic emphasis his; underline emphasis mine). I challenge this reading of the Antioch Incident in Nanos, 'What Was at Stake?'.

30.   Sanders, *Paul, the Law*, p. 185.

31.   Ibid. (emphasis his).

32.   Ibid., p. 186. The comments on this passage by New Perspectives critics are brief, and generally do not address the problems which this interpretation raises. James D. G. Dunn, *The Theology of Paul the Apostle* (Grand Rapids, MI: Eerdmans, 1997), pp. 576–8, observes: 'His freedom as an apostle was freedom to adapt policy and practice to particular situations, even when that meant running counter to all precedent, and to both scriptural and dominical authorization' (p. 577); idem, 'Who Did Paul Think He Was? A Study of Jewish-Christian Identity', *NTS* 45 (1999): 174–93. Tom Wright, *Paul for Everyone: 1 Corinthians* (London: SPCK, 2003), p. 115, makes it plain that Paul could not describe himself becoming a Jew to Jews 'if he regarded Christianity as simply a sub-branch of Judaism; it is a new thing, a fulfilment, no longer bound by ethnic or geographical identity'. Paul was 'prepared to observe customs and key commands of the law, presumably meaning

was concerned was like that of a gentile, and this was the direct result of having changed his convictions about Torah. Paul lived like a non-Jew when he worked in the diaspora among non-Jews, which represented virtually all of his time, but he mimicked Jewish behaviour on the few occasions he was in Jerusalem.

There are some minority interpretive approaches which are of interest for this discussion. But given the limits of this paper, and the fact that in the end these also lead to the same primary conclusions – that Paul no longer practised Torah as a matter of covenant faithfulness, adopted a Torah-free lifestyle to the degree that he could do so in the diaspora where he lived mainly among non-Jews, and that he varied his lifestyle to mimic Jewish and other groups of people, perhaps to a lesser degree, or in a supposedly less benign fashion, or with a different focus, or with more empathy or more admirable motives than are emphasized in the prevailing portrayals – they will not be presented here.[33] The few that point in the direction of my proposal will be discussed below.[34]

by this that he would keep the Sabbaths and the food-laws' in order to win Jews to the gospel, with the caveat that Paul's 'justification … didn't depend on these observances' (p. 116). At the same time, Wright understands Paul to also become like non-Jews 'without regard for the regulations of the Jewish law' in order to win them (p. 116). Richard B. Hays, *First Corinthians* (Interpretation; Louisville, KY: John Knox Press, 1997), pp. 153–4, views Paul as 'free from the Law': 'This sentence [9.21] states clearly what is abundantly apparent from many other bits of evidence: Paul not only resisted the imposition of Jewish Law on Gentiles but also himself adopted a casual attitude about Law observance (kosher laws, etc.) when he was among Gentiles.'

Similar interpretations are mounted against the New Perspective, especially to accentuate Paul's discontinuity with Jewish observance and identity. Stephen Westerholm, *Perspectives Old and New on Paul: The 'Lutheran' Paul and his Critics* (Grand Rapids, MI: W.B. Eerdmans, 2004), p. 172, observes that, 'Paul himself did not scrupulously adhere to the law. In 1 Corinthians 9.20-21 he notes that he behaves differently ("as one outside the law") in the presence of Gentiles than he does among Jews; nonobservance of the "ritual" Torah must be meant.' D. A. Carson, 'Mystery and Fulfillment: Toward a More Comprehensive Paradigm of Paul's Understanding of the Old and the New', in *Justification and Variegated Nomism: Vol. 2: The Paradoxes of Paul* (ed. D. A. Carson et al.; Tübingen and Grand Rapids, MI: Mohr Siebeck and Baker Academic, 2004), p. 402 (393–436), adds, 'Perhaps the most startling passage is 1 Corinthians 9.19-23 … these [discontinuities] are of such a nature that Paul can think of himself, in this context, as not being a Jew …' See also David Carson, 'Pauline Inconsistency: Reflections on 1 Corinthians 9.19-23 and Galatians 2.11-14', *Churchman* 100 (1986): 6–45, esp. pp. 10–16, 37. Here we witness not only Paul discontinuous with Jewish behaviour, but also with Jewish identity: Paul is no longer a Jew; similarly, see also Gooch, 'Ethics of Accommodation', p. 96; Given, *True Rhetoric*, pp. 103–17; Hagner, 'Paul as a Jewish Believer', p. 113.

33.   They are discussed below when rhetorical adaptability is introduced.

34.   Knox, *St. Paul*; Ellison, 'Paul'; and Jervell, *Unknown Paul*, have already been noted.

2. Analytical Options for Interpreting Paul's Adaptability

The interpretations of Paul's language we have reviewed focus on Paul *adopting the lifestyle* of his audiences, *varying his conduct* to *imitate* or *mimic* the way that each of them *lives relative to Jewish halakhic practices* when he is among them. For analytical purposes I will refer to this as '*behavioural*' or '*lifestyle adaptability*'.[35]

Adapting one's lifestyle to fit into the social context of another does not necessitate adopting *the propositional values* of the one whose behaviour is imitated. One can pretend by mimicking behaviour in an outward fashion in order to appear to share the values of the other, and thus to gain access and trust which might otherwise not be gained except by deception, with the intention of advancing one's own self-interests at the eventual expense of the other.[36] If one adopts the lifestyles of groups with contrary rational (or divine) bases for their very different behaviour, such as Paul's language describes for the various referents, this by definition cannot represent adopting their propositional values.

Paul is interpreted to undertake this behaviour solely in order to win each person or group to the Christian gospel's propositional values, which he believes to be superior. For interpreters who subscribe to and by way of Paul promote that ideology, the justification of this deceptive tactic is apparently self-evident. As noted, the charges of inconsistency and moral dishonesty are treated as if benign, generally discussed without offering explanations sufficient to those who do not share this ideological perspective. In less generous terms, for example, expressed by those not inclined to defend Paul, or instead toward demonstrating his faults, he is portrayed to ape the behaviour of each in order to trick everyone into mistakenly believing that the message he proclaims does not subvert the rational basis or convictional value of living in the particular way that each lives.[37] In the case of non-Jews (idolaters or atheists), especially the lawless or weak, he appears to worship

---

35. I am drawing on the suggestions of Paul Gooch, but with some modifications, including different labels for the categories. Gooch describes this category as 'ethical accommodation', that which is 'concerned not with the truth or transmission of beliefs, but with *behavior*. It is practised whenever one *adapts his pattern of living to the lifestyles of various groups*, having his *actions* dictated by the situations and circumstances in which he finds himself' (Gooch, 'Ethics of Accommodation', p. 99 (emphasis mine)). Gooch places Paul in this category, and expresses the view that Paul has left Judaism and a Torah-defined way of life following his conversion to Christianity, in keeping with the prevailing views we have reviewed (p. 107).

I do not find 'ethical' helpful, since the behaviour being described as duplicity is arguably not ethical but unethical, and 'accommodation' has been used in ways that can confuse as much as clarify the issues, as his own discussion of the terminology demonstrates (Peter Richardson and Paul W. Gooch, 'Accommodation Ethics', *TynBul* 29 (1978): 89–93).

36. Cf. Josephus, *Ant.* 17.205.

37. Although not an example of imitating a person, treachery can be expressed in terms of becoming as if one preparing to kiss a friend, when intending instead to stab the person after close access is thereby gained; Josephus, *Ant.* 7.284.

their gods, or alternatively, to oppose any gods, when he believes in neither of these propositions. In the case of Jews, when Paul conducts himself like a Jew when among Jews, he is 'misleading' Jews into thinking that he is a Jew whose message upholds the propositional conviction that Torah-based behaviour is enjoined upon Jews by God, although he no longer shares that conviction. This policy obscures the fact that any Jews who valued Torah-observance enough for Paul to adopt it to gain their trust, would be, if they accepted his message, becoming members of a community characterized by the renunciation of Torah-faith, yet unbeknownst to them. It follows that if 'converted', they too will adopt this chameleon-like expedient behaviour thereafter on the same terms, that is, only in order to trick other Jews. That creates a spiral of duplicity, with long-range deleterious results for their psychological and spiritual as well as social well-being should they remain 'Christians' after finding out the truth.

In sharp contrast, one who adopts the lifestyle of another convinced of its superior value undertakes *'convictional adaptability'*.[38] I am not aware of any interpretation of this passage that understands Paul to be describing convictional adaptation, and since he includes parties who uphold opposite propositional values, it would make little sense to do so.[39] But that is literally

---

38.   Gooch, 'Ethics of Accommodation', p. 99, names this phenomenon 'theological accommodation', and describes it as surrendering 'some item or items of belief in order to be acceptable to some other party. What was formerly considered true is renounced and the other party's doctrine is substituted for it.' According to Gooch, this could stretch from compromises on small matters of doctrine to achieve harmony to conversion to the doctrinal system of the other. I prefer to call this category *convictional* adaptability, because it is not merely imitating or mimicking the behaviour of the target audience, but involves subscribing to their convictions for undertaking just such behaviour, and not other kinds.

39.   The exception to this would be cases of non-doctrinal practices among those who share the same core convictions, which is not what Paul is describing, but would apply to moving between different Jewish groups for a Jew, or between different Christian groups for a Christian. This falls under the category of lifestyle adaptability, but in the specific sense of locative adaptability (adapting to local custom variations that arise within a shared propositional set of overarching convictions).

Certainly the idea of respecting the customs of one's hosts is ancient, reflected, for example, independent of any idea of compromising Torah-based norms, in R. Meir's maxim (c. mid-second century CE), 'If you come into a city, do according to their customs' (*Gen. Rabba* on 18.8; *Exod. Rabba* on 34.38), and in Jesus' instruction in Lk. 10.7-8 to those he sent out throughout Israel to eat what was offered by their hosts (cf. David Jacob Rudolph, 'A Jew to the Jews: Jewish Contours of Pauline Flexibility in 1 Corinthians 9.19-23' (PhD dissertation: Selwyn College, University of Cambridge, 2006; forthcoming in revised version, Mohr Siebeck), pp. 138–43, 178–81, 185–7). Another parallel, although not about travelling, is Hillel's teaching about empathy and polite manners among one's peers: 'Do not appear naked [where others go clothed], and do not appear clothed [where others go naked], and do not appear standing [where others sit], and do not appear sitting [where others stand] and do not appear laughing [where others weep] and do not appear weeping [where others laugh], because Scripture states, "a time to weep, a time to laugh … a time to embrace, a time to refrain from embracing" (Eccl. 3.4-5)' (*t. Ber.* 2.21; trans. Neusner, *Tosefta* (p. 13); cf. *Let. Aris.* pp. 257, 267; *Sir.* 31.1-2; *Gen. Rab.* 48.14; *Exod. Rab.* 42.5; Rom. 12.9-18!). See also David Daube, *The New Testament and Rabbinic Judaism* (Peabody, MA: Hendrickson

what 'becoming like' (or, all the more, 'becoming') someone of a particular persuasion such as Paul describes would mean.[40] In keeping with the many references just annotated, few would suppose that when Jesus is reported to tell his disciples in Matt. 18.3 that they 'should cause themselves to become like children [γένησθε ὡς τὰ παιδία]', that this meant to conduct themselves childishly in general, for example, in the sense of playing with toys, or teasing each other, and so on, or to pretend to be children; rather, they are to take on an unassuming humility of character that eschews the quest for greatness among peers, a characteristic that he attributes to a child (I assume not just

Publishers, 1990; original London, 1956), pp. 336–51 ('Missionary Maxims in Paul'), for a discussion of similarities with the rabbinic missionary practice of accommodation, although not from the same point of view on Paul's language, and with no evidence that this teaching parallels the kind of moral matters at issue if Paul was refering to lifestyle adaptability. The behaviour enjoined is not against halakhic norms, but about living empathetically and politely in matters of halakhic indifference among fellow Jews.

In later Christian teaching, the case of Augustine's appeal to Ambrose's teaching on how to behave when attending a church other than one's own is instructive, albeit different than the case we are investigating, which would require a parallel concerning how a Christian should behave when in a pagan context, not another Christian one. In *Book I of Replies to Questions of Januarius (Letter 54)* 2.3, Augustine quoted Ambrose to uphold that one should seek to avoid giving offence on matters of 'custom' that were not of doctrinal significance, but instead reflected different local practices among Christians: '"When I visit Rome, I fast on Saturday; when I am here, I do not fast"' (trans. J. G. Cunningham, *Nicene and Post-Nicene Fathers, First Series*, Vol. 1, ed. Philip Schaff (Buffalo, NY: Christian Literature Publishing Co., 1887); see also 2.2; 5.5-6; in 1.1, it is made clear that this does not include adopting any Jewish practices). Note that this citation of Ambrose was later developed into the famous slogan, 'when in Rome, do as the Romans do', which no longer always expresses the same sentiment or limitations, but is just as likely to be appealed to as a warrant for escaping moral norms (a transitional development is witnessed in Justin Taylor, *Ductor Dubitantium, or the Rule of Conscience*, I.i.5 (1660): 'If you are at Rome, live in the Roman style; if you are elsewhere, live as they live there [*Si fueris Romae, Romano vivito more; / Si fueris alibi, vivito sicut ibi.*]'; cf. *The Oxford Dictionary of Quotations*, ed. Angela Partington, 4th edn (Oxford: Oxford University Press, 1992), 10.679).

40.   See, e.g., Gen. 34.15; Num. 23.10; Jud. 16.11; 17.11; Ruth 4.12; 2 Sam. 18.32; Sir. 18.23; Hos. 9.10; Matt. 10.25; 15.28; Gal. 4.12; Eph. 5.1. In Jdt. 12.13, γενηθῆναι ... ὡς is used differently, to describe how Judith is received and told that she can join those serving the king by becoming a concubine in a way normally filled by Assyrian women. This usage is not about duplicity from their point of view, but actually taking on the role of another (she does not use this to describe her strategic behaviour, although these terms could be used to describe her tactics as deceptive lifestyle adaptability). In the metaphorical sense of becoming like something or someone else in character qualities, destiny, etc., but not in terms of pretence, see LXX Ps. 31.9; 77.8; 87.5; 108.19; 118.83; 125.1; 128.6; Sir. 4.10; 32.8; Hos. 5.10; 7.16; 8.8; Amos 4.11; Micah 7.1; Isa. 1.9; 37.27; 48.18-19; 63.19; 64.6, 10; Jer. 4.17; 12.8; 14.8; 15.18; 20.9; 23.9, 14; 31.28; Lam. 1.1, 6; 2.5; Ezek. 16.31; 36.35; Dan. 4.33; Matt. 17.2; 18.3; Lk. 22.26; 1 Thess. 2.7; Rev. 6.12. Given, *Paul's True Rhetoric*, p. 109, cites a few of these examples against the interpretation of Glad that Paul has in view association with these various people, but Given does not acknowledge that these examples also work against his own interpretation (which is that of the majority), that this language signifies behavioural as well as rhetorical pretence intended to create misleading perceptions about Paul's own propositional values.

any child, either). It represents a call to undertake a particular change of behaviour, and to do so wholeheartedly.

A third option for describing Paul's behaviour is very different from either of the first two, focusing on his *argumentative* behaviour, which can be undertaken without suggesting any adaptation of the practical lifestyles of others. Such *'rhetorical adaptability'* consists of varying one's speech to different audiences: reasoning from their premises, but not imitating their conduct in other ways.[41] In fact, to uphold the ideals to which the argument calls the audience, it is far more likely that the propositionally driven differences between the speaker's lifestyle and that of his or her audience will be magnified.

This behaviour arises when one seeks to express views in vocabulary and by way of models and examples that are calculated to persuade.[42] One thus works from the audiences' premises or world-views, even though seeking to lead them to a conclusion that is based on another set of premises or world-views. Teachers normally seek to relate to students in this way. It is highly useful for making a persuasive argument in any context, especially in philosophical or religious debates, including recruitment and discipleship, as well as for apologetical purposes.[43] That is just how Socrates approached his

41.   Gooch, 'Ethics of Accommodation', p. 99, describes this as 'epistemological accommodation'. Note that however unclear the parallel with language may be, Philo, *QG* 4.69, is about rhetorical behaviour; cf. Rudolph, 'A Jew to the Jews', pp. 127–32. This must be distinguished from flattery and deceptive speech, which fall within the model of lifestyle adaptability as an extension of changed behaviour only at the surface level in order to mislead the other into mistakenly supposing that one upholds a certain view or course of action as a matter of conviction (cf. Josephus, *Ant.* 16.301-4, for flattery and deceptive speech as well as actions).

There is another model of adaptability that is compatible with rhetorical adaptability, but not precisely the same, and does not align with what Paul describes here. This could be described as 'hierarchical adaptability'. It applies to cases where someone of superior status – such as an employer among employees, rulers among the ruled, and so on, inclusive of social position in arrangements such as parents with children – seeks to relate on equal terms by not pulling rank. It does not include compromising moral behaviour, but rather is exemplified when a parent seeks to relate to a teenager on a fishing trip, becoming friends as far as possible apart from the role of parent/child. It is also relevant for how to gain the trust of others of inferior rank, or when among strangers. This kind of strategic adaptability for rulers is instructed in Sir. 32.1-2: 'If they make you master of the feast, do not exalt yourself; be among them as one of their number [γίνου ἐν αὐτοῖς ὡς εἷς ἐξ αὐτῶν]. Take care of them first and then sit down ...' (NRSV). Paul's examples of referents for his adaptability here do not indicate that rank is the topic, but rhetorical adaptability can include this element of adapting in terms of rank, to which Paul appeals elsewhere.

42.   Gooch, 'Ethics of Accommodation', p. 99. This is when 'two parties operate with conceptual frameworks some distance apart and where one wishes to communicate with the other. The message needs to be accommodated to the epistemological conditions of the hearer, else it will be lost in ambiguity and misunderstanding.'

43   Philo was troubled by the implications of anthropomorphisms in Scripture, in particular, that they could be exploited to argue that God had a body. He thus explained God's 'coming down' to meet people in their weak state in the various forms in terms of rhetorical adaptability: these expressed God's way of communicating with humans by

interlocutors, starting from their premises in a way calculated to lead them step by step to conclusions they had not foreseen and might otherwise be unwilling to accept. For example, in order to explain the relation between knowledge and action, Socrates begins by articulating common assumptions about pleasure (*Protagoras*, p. 352ff.). In order to win his interlocutor to a new understanding of *aretē* that conflicts with the conventional usage, Socrates works his argument beginning from the conventional usage (*Meno*).[44]

Moreover, this approach approximates much more closely the topos of physicians and patients, of teachers and students, of parents and children, but highlights a very different dynamic with far-reaching implications for modelling the case. For, regardless of how empathetically the instructor relates to the one he or she instructs, and regardless of the highest of motives at work, it is more likely that he or she will appeal to the *differences in their lifestyles* to exemplify or prove the value of the instruction being offered, rather than adopting the conduct of the student, which would often run contrary to the instructional objective.

I propose Paul's self-description here refers entirely to his evangelistic tactic of rhetorical adaptability, and did not include the adoption of conduct representing his various audiences' convictional propositions, but not his own.[45] He could undertake this argumentative tactic as a Jew faithfully

words and revelations within the confines of their human limitations; see Mitchell, 'Pauline Accommodation', pp. 205–8. Note also a pertinent rabbinic parallel in *Pesikta de-Rab Kahana* 12.24-25 (trans. William G. Braude and Israel J. Kapstein, pp. 223–4): 'Moreover, said R. Jose bar R. Hanina, the Divine Word spoke to each and every person according to his particular capacity.' Origen analogized God's condescension to that of philosophers toward youths just taking up the study, not bodily, but in terms of speech (Mitchell, 'Pauline Accommodation', p. 210).

44. Gooch, 'Ethics of Accommodation', p. 104.

45. The appeal to rhetorical adaptability is not entirely unprecedented, but as far as I am aware it has always been coupled with lifestyle adaptability, and almost always with Paul as Torah-free as a matter of principle. Aspects have been noted in Origen, Chrysostom and Augustine. Knox, *St. Paul*, has been discussed; see also Henry Chadwick, '"All Things to All Men" (1 Cor. IX.22)', *NTS* 1 (1954–5): p. 275 (261–75); idem, *The Enigma of St Paul* (London: University of London, The Athlone Press, 1969), p. 14; idem, 'St. Paul and Philo of Alexandria', in *History and Thought of the Early Church*, ed. Henry Chadwick (London: Variorum Reprints, 1982; Original: *BJRL* 48 (1965–6: pp. 297–8 (286–307)); Richard Norman Longenecker, *Paul, Apostle of Liberty* (New York, NY: Harper & Row, 1964), p. 244, addressing specifically pastoral rhetorical adaptability (pp. 230–44), but he does not discuss Torah-observance, and the message of the monograph turns around freedom from Torah (see pp. 153–5); Ellison, 'Paul', p. 200, without caveat for speaking to Jews as a Torah-observant Jew (!), although not explaining how this works for the other referents (pp. 195–202); Gooch, 'Ethics of Accommodation', pp. 94, 95, n. 57, 107, but see also pp. 1, 105, 114; Günther Bornkamm, 'The Missionary Stance of Paul in 1 Corinthians 9 and in Acts', in *Studies in Luke–Acts* (ed. Leander E. Keck and J. Louis Martyn; Philadelphia, PA: Fortress Press, 1980), p. 199, but see pp. 202–5 (194–207); Margaret Mary Mitchell, *Paul and the Rhetoric of Reconciliation: An Exegetical Investigation of the Language and Composition of 1 Corinthians* (Louisville, KY: Westminster/John Knox Press, 1992), p. 248, interprets Paul to call them 'to be accommodating of one another in all things, but especially in regard to meat-eating practices', although she says that in addition to 'Paul's *behavior*'

observing Torah, even when speaking to lawless Jews, Jews upholding different halakhic standards, and non-Jews of any stripe. Thus Paul's behaviour can be described as free of the duplicitous conduct which serves as the basis for the charges of moral dishonesty, inconsistency, and so on, that arise logically from the prevailing views.

3. *Paul's Rhetorical Adaptability*

In the midst of the discourse of chapters 8–10, in which 9.19-23 is embedded, Paul seeks to show his 'knowledgeable' addressees in Corinth how he exemplifies the behaviour to which he calls them.[46] The context for 9.20-

attention should also be paid 'to the *rhetorical strategy* in Paul's call for accommodation here in 1 Cor.' (emphasis hers); Glad, *Paul and Philodemus*, pp. 240, 273, 327, but see pp. 1, 258; Joop Smit, '*About the Idol Offerings': Rhetoric, Social Context, and Theology of Paul's Discourse in First Corinthians 8.1–11.1* (Contributions to Biblical Exegesis and Theology 27; Leuven and Sterling, VA: Peeters, 2000), pp. 64–5; Stephen C. Barton, '"All Things to All People": Paul and the Law in the Light of 1 Corinthians 9.19-23', in *Paul and the Mosaic Law* (ed. James D. G. Dunn; Grand Rapids, MI, and Cambridge: Eerdmans, 2001), p. 280, but see p. 285 (271–85); C. Johnson Hodge, '*If Sons, Then Heirs*', pp. 124–5; Rudolph, 'A Jew to the Jews', pp. 169–207, esp. pp. 185–8, and see pp. 130–2, maintains that Paul was Torah-observant, although his argument provides for some level of compromised behaviour for table-fellowship. Fee, *First Epistle to the Corinthians*, p. 428, n. 36; and pp. 432–3, and Given, *Paul's True Rhetoric*, pp. 105–17, specifically reject arguments in this direction.

46.   This approach to the purpose of chapter 9, to articulate how Paul embodies what he calls for the knowledgeable to do in chapter 8, rather than supposing it to be in the first instance a defence against charges brought against his apostleship by opponents, can be traced to at least Chrysostom, *Homily XXI*, in Schaff, ed., *Nicene and Post-Nicene Fathers. First Series. Vol. XII. Chrysostom: Corinthians*, pp. 118, 129. Wendell Willis, 'An Apostolic Apologia? The Form and Function of 1 Corinthians 9', *JSNT* 24 (1985): 33–48; Mitchell, *Paul* , pp. 243–50, for detailed discussions. Note that throughout the letter, epistolary terms that relate to a discourse on adaptability are also attested: '*symphoros* (benefit, advantage), *euschemon* (proper, good order), and *kalos* (good, useful; 5.12; 7.1, 8, 26, 35, 37, 38; cf. 10.23; 12.7)' (Clarence E. Glad, 'Paul and Adaptability', in *Paul in the Greco-Roman World: A Handbook* (ed. J. Paul Sampley; Harrisburg, PA: Trinity Press International, 2003), p. 31 (17–41)). See also Chadwick, 'All Things', p. 268; Harry P. Nasuti, 'The Woes of the Prophets and the Rights of the Apostle: The Internal Dynamics of 1 Corinthians 9', *CBQ* 50 (1988): 246–64; Barbara Hall, 'All Things to All People: A Study of 1 Corinthians 9.19-23', in *The Conversation Continues: Studies in Paul & John In Honor of J. Louis Martyn* (ed. Robert T. Fortna and Beverly R. Gaventa; Nashville, TN: Abingdon Press, 1990), pp. 141–2 (137–57); Dale B. Martin, *Slavery as Salvation: The Metaphor of Slavery in Pauline Christianity* (New Haven, CT: Yale University Press, 1990), p. 78; Peter David Gooch, *Dangerous Food: I Corinthians 8-10 in its Context* (SCJ 5; Waterloo: Wilfrid Laurier University Press, 1993), pp. 83–4; Anders Eriksson, *Traditions as Rhetorical Proof: Pauline Argumentation in 1 Corinthians* (CBNT 29; Stockholm: Almqvist & Wiksell International, 1998), pp. 148–53, 154–73; Victor Paul Furnish, *The Theology of the First Letter to the Corinthians* (New Testament Theology; Cambridge and New York, NY: Cambridge University Press, 1999), pp. 23–4; David E. Garland, 'The Dispute Over Food Sacrificed to Idols (1 Cor. 8.1–11.1)', *PrST* 30.2 (2003): 185–97 (173–97); Smit, '*About the Idol Offerings*', pp. 64–5, 84–5, 153–4; Cheung, *Idol Food*, pp. 115–17.

23 begins with the comments in vv. 16-19, and illustrates Paul's tactic for convincing those who do not believe in Christ of the gospel message. He explains that this expresses a specific choice that he makes to be 'enslaved' to all people without receiving payment for his proclamation of the gospel, even though theoretically free to choose to do otherwise, and therefore he expects to be rewarded.[47]

Earlier in the letter Paul explained how his approach to their instruction is limited by his audience's condition as 'fleshly' or immature, although he would prefer to inform them differently if 'spiritual' or mature (3.1). That this does not indicate that Paul behaved in a fleshly or immature manner beyond the way he adapted his speech to them is readily evident to commentators. That is also how teachers adapt their speech to students at various levels, how parents adapt their speech to children at various levels (even baby talking), and so on. But specifically in view is speech behaviour, how one relates to others discursively, not how one behaves in terms of conducting themselves like students, or children. The teacher or parent wants the students or children to recognize the very different behaviour of the teacher or parent; they seek to provoke emulation, not confirmation of an immature status quo (cf. 4.8-17). This matter can also involve the obvious concern to speak pleasantly and respectfully. It is perhaps in this vein that *Acts of Paul* 3.1 begins the story of Thecla by describing Paul as having 'sweetened them [ἐγλύκαινεν αὐτούς]' when declaring the gospel message to his travelling companions from loving intentions in contrast to their hypocritical treatment of Paul, entreating him as if they loved him, when they intended him harm.

In chapters 8–10, Paul's instructions to the knowledgeable to make lifestyle changes – in keeping with Christ-faith values, including learning to live in ways that take into consideration the best interests of others – actually exemplify Paul's rhetorical adaptability. Paul's 'becoming' can be explained by examining the way that he relates to the 'knowledgeable' at Corinth in this argument by becoming knowledgeable rhetorically:[48] although he disagrees with their thinking and approach, he tries to persuade them from their own premises. Paul does not eat like them (or how they propose to eat), or behave like them (or how they propose to behave), but his argument is based on their own premises (and proposals), at least at the start, in order to lead them to an entirely different set of conclusions that are in keeping with Scripture, and a different way of living than their own reasoning had led them to suppose followed from the renunciation

47. If confronting works-righteousness was as central to Paul as the traditional interpretations require, it is surprising that he is willing to admit to seeking to be rewarded for his choices and labour, as he does here, seemingly without caveat that the idea of earning something from God is anathema according to his most important theological teaching.

48. Cf. Richard Horsley, *Wisdom and Spiritual Transcendence at Corinth: Studies in First Corinthians* (Eugene, OR: Cascade Books, 2008) pp. 86–8 ('Gnosis in Corinth?').

of idols.[49] Notwithstanding that Paul was probably citing sayings of the knowledgeable in 8.1, 4, rather than declaring his own point of view, he moves on to state the contradictory proposition that *not everyone* knows what they suppose to be self-evident now in vv. 7ff. And in chapter 9, Paul illustrates his very different lifestyle, including his rhetorical adaptability, to demonstrate the lifestyle they should now imitate. Although Paul does not explicitly call the Corinthians to proclaim the gospel to their families and neighbours as much as to seek to live with respect for one another, he does call them to imitate his lifestyle in order to gain others in 10.31–11.1, and elsewhere throughout the letter (e.g., 7.16; 10.24, 27-30; 14.22-25).[50] This brings up an interesting topic.

I join those who understand Paul to be explicitly describing his evangelizing tactics in 9.19-23, and my interpretation of the identity of the 'weak' throughout these chapters as non-Christ-believing idolaters strengthens that case;[51] nevertheless, it would be surprising if Paul did not exemplify this rhetorical tactic in his pastoral approach to these Christ-believers.[52] In his

49.   One of the interesting things about this argument in 1 Corinthians 8–10 is that it was necessary for Paul to make it. It appears that when he taught among them he did not anticipate where their logic would lead, in the very unjewish direction of supposing that because of renouncing the reality of the gods to which idol rites were devoted they were thus free to eat idol food or even participate in idol rites. They probably reasoned that this demonstrated that they regarded idols as merely profane, and also maintained the relationships that complete avoidance of such rites and food or meals would compromise if not destroy, with deleterious results for themselves. If Paul had anticipated this line of reasoning, it would seem that this exchange would not arise, or he would approach it by appeal to his earlier teaching among them. As a Jew, he would reason and likely suppose any Christ-believer would thus reason that regardless of the proposition that these were not gods as non-Jews supposed, that these gods and the rites and thus food dedicated to them were nevertheless anathema for worshippers of the God of Israel as the only God. Thus even when Jews trivialized idols, they refrained from anything having to do with idolatry. As Paul represents the issue of marketplace food, the food is not designated idol food, but is rather assumed to be profane unless known to be otherwise (announcing this option implies that there was food available there that was not idolatrous; likewise, it could be available at the home to which one might be invited). Rabbinic material is replete with discussions of the difference between interaction with things sold or used by idolaters and those which are specifically set apart to idols, the latter forbidden, while the former are often permitted (cf. *m.Aboda Zara* 1.4-5; 2.3; 3.4; 4.3-6; 5.1; see Tomson, *Paul*, pp. 151–77, 208–20; Cheung, *Idol Food*, pp. 39–81, 152–64, 300–1; Smit, *'About the Idol Offerings'*, pp. 52–8, 65, passim; Magnus Zetterholm, 'Purity and Anger: Gentiles and Idolatry in Antioch', *Interdisciplinary Journal of Research on Religion* (2005): 15 (1–24); Rudolph, 'A Jew to the Jews', pp. 97–104; Nanos, 'Polytheist Identity', pp. 179–210.

50.   For more discussion of the specifically polytheist orientation of the letter's message, see Nanos, 'Polytheist Identity', esp. pp. 203–9.

51.   Ibid., pp. 189–97, 200–2.

52.   That Paul is approaching his addressees from their premises is evident throughout the letter, representing pastoral rather than evangelistic-oriented rhetorical adaptability. Chadwick, '"All Things"', pp. 268, 275; idem, *Enigma of Paul*, pp. 12, 14, notes that 1 Cor. 7.1-6 similarly begins by hypothetical agreement in principle that it is good for a man not to touch a woman, but moves to a different conclusion that the wife controls whether that is good or not for the husband; Longenecker, *Paul*, pp. 230–44; Gooch, 'Ethics of Accommodation',

argument throughout chapters 8 to 10, Paul does not become knowledgeable to the knowledgeable in the sense of lifestyle adaptability, but his rhetorical adaptation to the premises of the knowledgeable is based on empathy toward the weak as well as communicating this empathy to the knowledgeable. He calls the knowledgeable to change their lifestyle, to be sure, something he does not describe seeking among the recipients of his evangelistic tactics in 9.16-23. Paul also explains how he adapts his own lifestyle to accomplish various goals throughout chapter 9; but it is important to notice that he does not write that he mimics the behaviour of others. Quite the contrary, he claims to do many things very differently than others do, including other apostles, in order to succeed in ways that he believes would be compromised otherwise, or less effective, or less able to gain him reward.

When engaging in pastoral adaptability, Paul relates to the knowledgeable from their premises at the beginning of his argument. He reasons from first principles that there is only one God and thus that idols are nobodies (8.4-6), and therefore the food offered to them can be eaten as profane (8.8; 10.19, 23, 25-26). But he grants this line of argument only in theory – even undermining it in the way it is first stated, for he includes the caveat that '*there are* many gods and many lords' (8.5) – thereafter seeking to lead them to a very different conclusion. For he explains that there are those who believe in these idols who will be encouraged to continue to believe in them rather than coming to know what the knowledgeable know (vv. 7-13), and that there are such things as daemons represented by these idols (10.19-22). Thus they are not to eat any food known to be dedicated to idols, just as Jews, who do not believe idols represent gods nevertheless do not eat idol food as if profane, but flee from anything that is associated with idolatry or pay the price for not doing so (10.1-23). In the end, the only food that can be eaten is food that they do not know to be idol related, and even if they are guests and informed that certain food has been offered to idols previously, they are not to eat it (10.14-33).

Paul thus moves his addressees from non-Jewish premises, since they are not Jews, to very Jewish conclusions, since they are Christ-believers, which represents a Jewish (communal, philosophical, religious, moral, etc.) way of being in the world – even for non-Jews. Note that Paul leads these non-Jews to the same conclusions to which he would lead them if he was addressing Jews, arguing many of the same essential points (that God is One, that they must love their neighbour, that they cannot eat idol food if known to be

p. 114, observes that Paul does demonstrate epistemological accommodation in this letter: 'if they were to reflect on the very things that Paul reveals to them about himself, they would discover interesting examples of his accommodation towards them', and although he includes examples of ethical accommodation based on interpretations of passages with which I disagree, he also notes: 'he is willing to agree with the starting points of various groups in Corinth in order to move them from their extremes of liberty or asceticism or enthusiasm'. Cf. Gooch, *Dangerous Food*, pp. 83–4, 93; Smit, '*About the Idol Offerings*', pp. 64–5, 84, 153–4; Cheung, *Idol Food*, pp. 115–17.

such, that idols represent daemons, that Scripture teaches these things[53]), and incorporating allusions to Torah, as in the rhetorical question of 10.22: 'Or do we provoke the Lord to jealousy?' In this way, Paul has become like a non-Jew – rhetorically speaking, that is. If his addressees had been instead Jews, then I propose that we would have seen Paul appeal directly to Torah to discuss this matter, rather than begin with first principles or consideration of the other's sensibilities, or to the mere example of Israelites. We would have seen him instead becoming like a Jew, rhetorically, which would have been quite natural for him, since he was a Jew.

3.1. The issue of 'becoming like'

One of the interesting facets of the prevailing lifestyle adaptability viewpoint is that it is supposed to be a straightforward explanation of Paul's tactic of how he 'became as/like [ἐγενόμην...ὡς]' the other, or in the case of the 'weak', simply that he 'became' weak.[54] But 'becoming as' (and all the more 'becoming') someone from some group according to their relationship to Torah or Law are not lexical equivalents to the notions expressed by the prevailing lifestyle adaptability interpretation. For 'imitating', 'mimicking', 'pretending to be', 'aping', and so on, are actually descriptions of merely adopting the outward behavioural conduct of the other, but not at the propositional level that behaviour is designed to express. There are Greek words for describing such behaviour undertaken only at the surface level, including μιμέομαι (imitate, mimic, represent, portray), ὑποκρίνομαι (play a part; feign, pretend; hypocrisy), and δοκέω (seem, pretend, suppose, imagine, expect). In other words, the prevailing views are not based on what Paul has written, which does not describe a general case, but a specific one that revolves around the contrary behaviours to be expected among each of the referents named. Paul is not understood to have actually 'become like' each of them, which would instead literally be represented by the convictional adaptability model, although this logical problem does not seem to be generally recognized.[55]

---

53.   Cf. Deut. 32.17; Ps. 95.5 LXX; 106.37; Isa. 65.3, 11.

54.   Some variants do include the ὡς with this clause too, but even if omitted, this strikes me as another example of Paul's elliptical style and variation of language, probably an effort to be brief and get the readers'/hearers' attention, or simply variation. In other words, the missing ὡς is probably implied, although either way does not really affect my argument (note the poetic variation in Lam. 5.3; and the reverse case of what is dropped in Matt. 10.25). Note too that the verb ἐγενόμην is missing for two of the four referents, but the verb is understood to be implied.

55.   See, e.g., Philo, *Laws* 4.126. Pace Given, *Paul's True Rhetoric*, pp. 105–17. Although I appreciate the argument against interpretations that seek to protect Paul's integrity, on p. 111, after Given concludes that Paul's 'becoming like' signifies eating or otherwise behaving like each of the groups, Given's interpretation does not represent 'the realm of being' rather than 'that of seeming' anymore than do the viewpoints he criticizes (Glad in particular). On p. 112, Given uses 'appearing as' synonymously with 'becoming

For example, interpreters do not read Paul to mean he actually *became* 'under law', however defined (e.g., a proselyte),[56] or 'lawless', which if read as 'wicked' is even more difficult to imagine than that he *became* a Jew. And he could not actually 'become *weak*' on the prevailing interpretations of the 'weak', which suppose they are insecure about eating idol food as if such gods were thereby worshipped, or that he was overscrupulous when he resisted doing so, or did so under compulsion but with qualms about it.[57] To return briefly to the case of becoming like a Jew, taken literally, that would mean that Paul was not already a Jew, which he claims to have been, and still to be. Although many interpreters may work with the notion that Paul left behind Judaism and thus being a Jew in a religious sense, few claim that he left behind his ethnic identity as a Jew – albeit now defining him to be a 'Christian', however described or labelled – even if it is not unusual to see perplexed references to this conundrum, as already encountered. Thus interpreters actually read this to connote that Paul *behaved* like a Jew, referring to *playing at* or *mimicking* or *pretending to* Jewish behaviour, although not subscribing to the values of that Jewish behaviour as a matter

like'. At the same time, I do not think that Given's reading need be far from the one I propose, if dropping *acting* like but keeping *speaking* like, for on p. 117 he concludes that Paul shapes his 'insinuative rhetorical strategy similar to that imagined by Luke with respect to Jews and Gentiles'. Gooch, 'Ethics of Accommodation', pp. 104–5, also argues that, 'He [Paul] does not say he adopted the language of those within law or outside of it; he does not present himself as agreeing with the basic premises of Jew or the weak. Instead he claims that he has *become* as one of those he is trying to win: he has adopted, not terminology, but ways of behaving' (emphasis his). But Gooch is interpreting 'becoming' in a certain way, as 'behaving'. That 'becoming as' does not equate to ethical accommodation in behaviour as in mimicking others is not apparently noticed. Since Paul cannot become opposites at the propositional level, i.e., he cannot observe Torah as a matter of covenant conviction and also discard Torah as a covenantal behavioural norm because he is with a different audience, for Torah by definition involves a way of life that maintains different behaviour in the midst of the other nations to bear witness to God's righteousness. Paul can but only 'mimic' their behaviour in the way that Gooch, with the consensus, proposes, and thus Gooch is translating 'becoming' into 'mimicking' without an argument that this is what Paul must mean by it. There is no proof that Paul ever, e.g., ate like an idolater, or alternatively, that he ever ate contrary to Torah-defined dietary norms. I am proposing herein that what Paul is doing in 1 Cor. 8–10 is an example of the Socratic epistemology that Gooch identifies in 9.19-23 as Paul's tactic. Glad, *Paul*, pp. 259–60, reads this as 'Paul's willingness to *associate* with all' (emphasis added).

56.   Chrysostom, *Homily XXII.5*, in Schaff, ed., *Nicene and Post-Nicene Fathers, First Series*, Vol. *XII, Chrysostom: Corinthians*, p. 128.

57.   Anthony C. Thiselton, *The First Epistle to the Corinthians: A Commentary on the Greek Text* (NIGTC; Grand Rapids, MI, and Carlisle: W.B. Eerdmans and Paternoster Press, 2000), p. 705, recognizes the problem, but does not resolve it. In view of such problems, many interpreters alter the identity of the 'weak' here from representing those who are non-Christ-believers whom Paul seeks to win to Christ, to that of Christ-believers whom Paul seeks to win to a new way of expressing that faith (e.g., Wendell Lee Willis, *Idol Meat in Corinth: the Pauline Argument in 1 Corinthians 8 and 10* (SBL dissertation Series 68; Chico, CA: Scholars Press, 1985), p. 37; Richard B. Hays, *First Corinthians* (Interpretation; Louisville, KY: John Knox Press, 1997), p. 155).

of conviction, of faith, of loyalty to Torah. Similarly, when Paul describes in his own case being *'enslaved to'* everyone, interpreters do not suppose that Paul is an actual slave to the other, but he says he becomes one. It is not literal slavery, but signifies that he puts the concerns of the other above his own, that he serves them instead of himself. He is 'like' a slave, which connotes his empathetic concern for the other.

In short, when Paul writes *behaved like,* his denotation is read with the connotation of *mimicked the behaviour of,* because it defies logic that he *became* each of these contrary identities. In other words, short of postulating the unimaginable model of convictional adaptability, to actually coming over to another's way of life because one believes what the other believes, every interpreter has to fill out what Paul means by 'I became', or 'I caused myself to *become*', if the causative quality of the middle voice of this verb is emphasized.

Thus the prevailing interpretations of this passage are based on supposed connotations, but not denotation. And they have as central to their adoption of the lifestyle adaptability model the presupposition that Paul does not observe Torah, certainly not as a matter of covenant fidelity. As I have explained, and as the many problems that emerge not only from Christian interpreters but also from non-Christian critics of the prevailing lifestyle adaptability view (as well as the defences offered to those criticisms) make obvious, there is good reason to consider another model, that of rhetorical adaptability.

I propose that instead of 'behaving like' according to the model of lifestyle adaptability, this language signifies how Paul *reasons like* and *relates* his convictions *like,* how he *engages like,* how he rhetorically meets people where they are, according to their own world-views and premises. Paul *reasons* with, *relates* to, or *engages* Jews as/like (in the manner of) a Jew, and so on. In this rhetorical, discursive sense Paul could actually *become like* – or even *become – everything to everyone.*

As a consequence, as interesting as it is to imagine who each of the specific referents represent and why Paul chose these referents to exemplify his tactics – Jews, those under Law, the lawless, or the weak – or how any or all of these relate to Torah observance, or not, it is not necessary to do so on the interpretation I propose. Rhetorical adaptability can be undertaken by a Torah-observant Jew without the need to compromise those values by adopting outward behaviour like that of the target audience even if the audience does not similarly subscribe to Torah-defined behaviour. In fact, this difference in behaviour may be emphasized or minimized, depending upon the audience and circumstance. What Paul is describing requires knowing how to communicate effectively, and within the limits of his objectives, respectfully.

Importantly, we have an example of Paul engaging in rhetorical adaptability by his earliest known biographer in Acts 17, regardless of whether this case accurately describes an historical event. It not only illustrates rhetorical adaptability in principle, but also that the author presumed it would be a persuasive example for his audience.

3.2. An example of Paul's rhetorical adaptability from Acts 17

In Acts 17.17-31, Luke relates the story of Paul's proclamation of the One God and Christ in Athens. Paul does not start with a denial of the reality of the gods in which the philosophers and other elites gathered at the Areopagus believe, although he does eventually criticize the effort to make representations of the divine.[58] Like a philosopher *becoming like* as in *relating to* fellow philosophers, he begins by recognizing them to be 'very religious [δεισιδαιμονεστέρους]'.[59]

Paul argues from within their propositional world-view towards declaring that the idol they have designated 'To an Unknown God [Ἀγνώστῳ θεῷ]', need no longer remain unknown to them. He does not introduce a new god, which is a function of the judiciary meetings held at the Areopagus, but discloses the identity of the One true God in whom they should logically already believe.[60] Interestingly, Paul is described to say that which the Athenians worship is done 'without knowledge/ in ignorance [ἀγνοοῦντες]' (v. 23); he also refers to the 'times of ignorance [χρόνους τῆς ἀγνοίας]' that his gospel declaration proposes to bring to an end (v. 30). Paul draws on scriptural concepts throughout his speech, and could have offered many proof-texts for his argumentative points. But Paul does not cite any Scriptures. Rather, the only explicit citations he incorporates include the inscription to the unknown deity on the altar, and a line from 'some of your own poets': τοῦ γὰρ καὶ γένος ἐσμέν ('for we also are his offspring'; v. 28).[61]

---

58.   Concerning Cynic and Stoic critiques of statues to represent gods, see Dio Chrysostom, *Orations* 12.52; 31.15; Ps.-Heraclitus 4.2.5; Antisthenes, in Clement, *Protreptikos* 6.71.1; 7.75.3; Epictetus, *Dissertation* 1.6.23-29; 2.30.26; Diogenes Laertius, *Lives* 7.147; Seneca, *Epistulae morales* 41.1; Francis Gerald Downing, *God with Everything: The Divine in the Discourse of the First Christian Century* (The Social World of Biblical Antiquity, Second Series 2; Sheffield: Sheffield Phoenix Press, 2008), p. 27, n. 24 (20–42). See also Matthias Baltes, 'Mixed Monotheism? The Areopagos Speech of Paul', in *With Unperfumed Voice: Studies in Plutarch, in Greek Literature, Religion and Philosophy, and in the New Testament Background* (ed. Frederick E. Brenk; Stuttgart: Franz Steiner, 2007), pp. 470–94.

59.   This can be translated also as 'superstitious', and arguably the speech plays with this ambiguity throughout, but here likely in language that the audience would hear in positive terms, to be expected in an introduction, although recognized to have a negative twist by Luke's Christ-believing reader: see Hans Conzelmann, 'The Address of Paul on the Areopagus', in *Studies in Luke–Acts* (eds Leander E. Keck and J. Louis Martyn; Philadelphia, PA: Fortress Press, 1980), p. 220; Given, *Paul's True Rhetoric*, pp. 68–74, discusses the double, ironic language choices through this section.

60.   Lynn Allan Kauppi, *Foreign but Familiar Gods: Greco-Romans Read Religion in Acts* (Library of New Testament Studies 277; London and New York, NY: T&T Clark, 2006), pp. 83–93, discusses the possibility that Paul draws on an allusion to Aeschylus' *Eumenides* here. See also David W. J. Gill and Conrad H. Gempf, eds, *The Book of Acts in its Graeco-Roman Setting* (Book of Acts in its First Century Setting; Grand Rapids, MI, and Carlisle: Eerdmans and Paternoster Press, 1994), pp. 446–8.

61.   Apparently from the Cretan poet Epimenides, and Paul's usage perhaps draws on criticism of some Cretans pointing to a tomb for Zeus to undermine his immortality, so that

I submit that Luke's example represents the rhetorical strategy of 'I became [i.e., reasoned] to the idolaters as [in the manner of] an idolater.' Paul related his message to them – inclusive of challenges to their concepts, conclusions and behaviour – from within their own premises in order to gain them to Christ.

This example from Acts was similarly drawn upon to interpret 1 Cor. 9.19-23 by Origen and Chrysostom, *mutatis mutandis*, that is, granting that they were not seeking to make the overarching case that I propose for rhetorical in sharp contrast to lifestyle adaptability, and they interpreted Paul to be free of Torah as a matter of policy, indeed, to be free of Judaism. Nevertheless, Origen referred to the example in Acts 17.23, 28, to explain how Paul adapted his speech 'to the lawless' by becoming 'lawless': Paul 'did not use either prophetic or halakhic terms, but if he had a memory of some Greek learning from his preparatory instruction he *spoke* about it to the Athenians', and he did not uphold that Paul behaved lawlessly in doing so.[62] In addition, Origen provided examples for two of the other referents in terms of adaptability, one rhetorical and the other lifestyle: in rhetorical terms when he spoke to the weak as weak in 1 Cor. 7.6; and in lifestyle terms when he behaved as a Jew by circumcising Timothy because of the Jews (Acts 16.3), and taking the Nazarite vow (Acts 21).[63] Commenting on 9.21, Chrysostom notes that others before him had already made the point: 'But some say that he hints at his *discourse* with the Athenians from the inscription on the altar, and that so he saith, "to them that are without law, as without law".'[64] He concludes that in Athens, Paul 'was *speaking* to pagan Greeks, who believed in none of our sacred books, and *so he used arguments from their own beliefs to subdue them*'.[65]

An example of Paul's rhetorical adaptability in terms of becoming to Jews as a Jew is illustrated just prior to his arrival in Athens among the idolaters. In

Paul may be playing off a commonly known dispute about whether a statue undermines the reality of the deity to which it is built to point: Kirsopp Lake, '"Your Own Poets": Note XX', in *The Acts of the Apostles: Part 1, Vol. 5* (eds Kirsopp Lake and Henry Joel Cadbury; *The Beginnings of Christianity*; London: Macmillan and Co., Limited, 1920), pp. 246–51; F. F. Bruce, *The Acts of the Apostles: The Greek Text with Introduction and Commentary* (3rd revised and enlarged edn; Grand Rapids, MI, and Leicester: Eerdmans and Apollos, 1990), pp. 384–5.

62.   *Comm. in 1 Cor.* 3.43 (emphasis mine), ed. C. Jenkins, 'Origen on 1 Corinthians', *JTS* 9 (1907–8): 513 (231–47, 353–72, 500–14); cited by Mitchell, 'Pauline Accommodation', p. 208.

63.   Origen apparently did not provide an example of becoming under Law to those under Law, which he took to mean non-Jews who placed themselves under Law, but he was sure there were examples; from ibid., p. 306, n. 58, referring to SC 157.400–2.

64.   *Homily XXII.5*, in Schaff, ed., *Nicene and Post-Nicene Fathers, First Series, Vol. XII, Chrysostom: Corinthians*, p. 128 (emphasis mine).

65.   *Adv. Jud.* 5.3.2 (emphasis mine); translation from Paul W. Harkins, *Saint John Chrysostom: Discourses Against Judaizing Christians* (The Fathers of the Church: A New Translation 68; Washington, DC: Catholic University Press of America, 1979), p. 105; see also Chrysostom's comments on speaking to Jews differently, in *Adv. Jud.* 5.3.3.

Acts 17.1-3, Paul is described proceeding immediately to the synagogue upon his arrival in Thessalonica:

> After Paul and Silas had passed through Amphipolis and Apollonia, they came to Thessalonica, where there was a synagogue of the Jews. And Paul went in, as was his custom, and on three sabbath days *argued* with them *from the scriptures, explaining* and *proving* that it was necessary for the Messiah to suffer and to rise from the dead, and saying, 'This is the Messiah, Jesus whom I am proclaiming to you.' (NRSV, emphasis mine)

Such an argument would have made little to no sense to non-Jews, for example, among the philosophers at the Areopagus. He would have to describe why he appealed to Scripture as proof, what a messiah is or why that should be of concern to them, especially his suffering and rising from the dead. And that is just the point that Luke makes about the problems that emerge for Paul among the philosophers. For even though these Jewish premises are not the place from which Luke portrays Paul to begin his argument with the philosophers, as already discussed, these are nevertheless the kinds of topics to which his speech drives, even if Luke also describes the results encumbered by this propositional gap. The philosophers are puzzled by some of his premises, and elements of the conclusions to which he seeks to move them. Paul does not make as clear a case for the relevance of these matters as he can among Jews, because he (or Luke) is unaware of adequate analogies from their non-Jewish culture, or does not know how to prepare an argument that will effectively bridge the cultural divide between them.

Thus in two almost immediately concurrent examples, the author of Acts describes two cases of variability in terms of the rhetorical adaptability model. And note that in the synagogue example, Luke presents it to be 'his custom' to argue in this manner at Sabbath meetings (17.10-12 continues this pattern in Beroea, and in v. 17 it is implied that he argues thus in the synagogues of Athens, but it is not the way he is shown to argue in the marketplace with the philosophers; immediately after Athens, it is still the way Paul is presented to proceed in the synagogue of Corinth in 18.4-5, and throughout ch. 18 as he moves from place to place).[66]

Luke's example of rhetorical adaptability among philosophers seeking to win each other to their positions or schools is not the only example of the discussion or presentation of this model among Paul's contemporaries.[67]

---

66.   Cf. Jacob Jervell, *Luke and the People of God: A New Look at Luke–Acts* (Minneapolis, MN: Augsburg, 1972), pp. 41–74.

67.   Other examples, not discussed here for the sake of space, include at least the philosopher Aristobulus, and Philo, the latter overlapping with Paul, and exemplifying rhetorical adaptability while declaring commitment to Torah observance. In addition, *The Letter of Aristeas* expresses Jewish views of God and righteousness (including topics like dietary regulations) in Hellenistic philosophical terms argued from within Greek premises when among non-Jews in Egypt, including to the king and his representatives, which involved respectful analogies drawn to Egyptian practices and even worship (e.g., 16, where worship of Zeus and Jove is likened to worship of God, but under different names). Following the

3.3. Antisthenes on Odysseus as polytrope

The tactic Paul describes can be compared to that of Odysseus as interpreted by Antisthenes, a student of Socrates. The similarities are not exact, and there is a tendency in the discussions of Homer's passage on Odysseus to blur the lines between lifestyle and rhetorical adaptability just as arises in discussion of Paul's passage, where I am trying to draw a sharp line between these models for the sake of clarifying what I propose Paul meant. Moreover, the few interpreters discussing this parallel (of whom I am aware), conclude that Antisthenes' Odysseus model stands in contrast to Paul's message; but that is largely based on their view of Paul's language in the direction of the consensus lifestyle adaptability model, including that he was indifferent to Torah, if not opposed to it in principle.[68] From the perspective I propose, the dynamics are much more suggestive of similarity, although the frequent blending with figures such as that of the physician to patient (which is not the same as patient to patient), and discussions of motives rather than simply tactics, lead to an examination that must be carefully nuanced and critical of every example discussed.

The simplest way to interpret the opening line of the *Odyssey*, 'Tell me, Muse, of the *polytropic* man', is that he will wander on his journey home rather than taking a direct course.[69] However, by the fifth century BCE, the image of Odysseus had taken on the negative ethical connotation of 'often changing one's character, hence unstable, unprincipled, unscrupulous', a chameleon-like quality that moralists condemned among party politicians of the period.[70] After all, with Odysseus, the innovator of the Trojan horse and many other cunning disguises, it does not take much to get to a model

introductory arguments made to his scholarly brother, Philocrates, similar arguments are delivered in conversation with the king and his guests during the time when philosophical conversation normally took place according to symposium conventions, that is, following the shared meal with these non-Jews, which was served according to Jewish halakhic norms, albeit by the king's (non-Jewish) servants. The kind of Jewish men Eleazar, the High Priest in Jerusalem, is said to have selected to travel to Alexandria, is of interest: 'they had not only mastered the Jewish literature, but had made a serious study of that of the Greeks as well … they had a tremendous natural facility for the negotiations and questions arising from the Law, with the middle way as their commendable ideal; they forsook any uncouth and uncultured attitude of mind; in the same way they rose above conceit and contempt of other people, and instead engaged in discourse and listening to and answering each and every one, as is meet and right' (pp. 121–2; trans. Shutt).

68. For application to Paul, from which I learned much, albeit taken to different conclusions, see W. B. Stanford, *The Ulysses Theme: A Study in the Adaptability of a Traditional Hero* (Dallas, TX: Spring Publications, 1992), p. 91; Abraham J. Malherbe, *Paul and the Popular Philosophers* (Minneapolis, MN: Fortress Press, 1989), pp. 100, 118–19 (91–119); Glad, *Paul and Philodemus*, pp. 97–8, 251, 272–3; David Reis, 'Flip-Flop?: John Chrysostom's Polytropic Paul', *JGRChJ* 4 (2007): 17–23 (9–31) <http://jgrchj.net/volume4/JGRChJ4-1_Reis.pdf>, accessed 7 September 2007.

69. Porphyry's scholion on *Odysseus* 1.1, begins the epic with Homer's request: 'Tell me, Muse, of the man of many devices [πολύτροπον] …'

70. Stanford, *Ulysses Theme*, p. 99.

of lifestyle adaptability in the negative sense of duplicity and expedience over principle, and this had been the subject of philosophical discussion for some time.[71] Already Achilles had declared the moral depravity of the man who compromises his character for expedience: 'For hateful in my eyes as the gates of Hades is that man who hides one thing in his mind and says another' (*Iliad* 9.312-13; trans. Murray and Wyatt). Many Athenians found fault with Odysseus and Homer, especially in the context of the stricter ideals of morality and truth following from Pythagoras and Xenophanes versus the style of the Sophists, who were unscrupulous to achieve their ends, since this kind of model was used to justify political exploitation by those who relished self-aggrandizement and ambition over truth, and debased moral values along the way, just as they did the Athenian coinage, according to Thucydides.[72] Political victory became associated with the immoral expedience, to success at all costs, and thus, with Homer's trickster hero.[73] The Sophists, ironically, were also critical of Odysseus's character, including his clever use of language.[74]

Antisthenes countered this interpretive tradition with a controversial reading of Odysseus according to the model of rhetorical adaptability. It stands in stark contrast to the prevailing readings, which were based on the model of lifestyle adaptability:

> And what then? Are we perhaps to believe that Odysseus is wicked because he is called *polytropos*? Nevertheless, the poet has called him that at a point where he is thought wise (*sophos*). Perhaps, in fact, the word *tropos* is not applied to moral character (*ethos*), as much as to his skill in speaking (*logou khresis*)? One is called *eutropos* if one has a moral character that is 'turned' (*tetrammenon*) toward the good, and in discourse *tropoi* are called diverse styles (*hai poiai plaseis*). Homer has also adopted the word *tropos* with regard to the voice and variety of melodies, as in the case of the nightingale: '... changing (*troposa*) it over and over again, she pours forth her many-toned voice' (Odyssey 19.521). Therefore, if wise men are skilled in speaking and know how to express the same thought in many ways (*kata pollous tropous*), those who know many ways of expression concerning the same thing can rightly be called *polutropoi*. The wise men are therefore also excellent men (*hoi sophoi kai agathoi eisin*). For this reason Homer bestows upon Odysseus, as a wise man, the epithet *polutropos*: because he can speak with men in many ways. So it is also said that Pythagoras, having been invited to speak with children, used the language of children; in speaking with women, the language appropriate to women, in speaking with rulers, the language of rulers; in speaking with youths the language of youths. For it is a mark of wisdom to discover a form of wisdom appropriate to each person, and a mark of ignorance to use only one form (*monotropo*) of speech with dissimilar people. This is a specialty which also belongs to medicine, in a case that is well treated. For the care of the ill ought to be *polutropos*, because of various predispositions of the cured. *Tropos* is therefore that which changes, that which is variable in the human spirit. The multiplicity of the ways of speaking

71.   Ibid., pp. 95–9.
72.   Ibid., pp. 100–1.
73.   Ibid., p. 101.
74.   Ibid., pp. 95–6, 146.

(*polutropia logou*) and the <u>use of varied speech for various ears</u> becomes a single type (*monotropia*) of speech. For <u>one thing is appropriate for each person</u>. Thus, that which is <u>adapted to each person</u> reduces <u>variety of speech</u> to one thing – that which is <u>suitable</u> for each person. But that which is uniform and unadapted to different ears renders <u>a speech</u> (which is rejected by many) *polutropos*, because it has been rejected by them.[75]

Antisthenes begins his appeal by reference to the fact that the context of Homer's language usage calls for a challenge to the prevailing interpretation of it because of the logical inconsistency it creates between Odysseus' words and the moral character of Odysseus that Homer is otherwise seeking to communicate, which sets up a very close parallel to the problem under discussion about Paul's language. Antisthenes thus argued that this description of Odysseus exemplified rhetorical rather than lifestyle adaptability.[76]

He maintained that *polytropos* does not refer to Odysseus adapting his lifestyle in duplicitous ways, with the concomitant ethical problems of the lifestyle model, but to Odysseus as the example of the virtuous man who adapted his *figures of speech* ('*tropes*') to his various audiences ('*poly*') in order to persuade each of them in terms to which they could relate. Antisthenes linked Odysseus' adaptability to that which was exemplified and taught by the austere Pythagoras, famed for his commitment to moral fidelity and truth, but who nevertheless recommended rhetorical adaptation to one's various audiences: the right word for the right person at the right time is the way of the wise.[77] The concern to match different verbal styles of rhetorical presentation to suit different character types to enhance persuasion became a focus of rhetorical theorists seeking to match various speaking styles to different famous orators.[78]

Paul need not be a student of Homer to expect his readers to understand him to be describing the practice of rhetorical adaptability. He and his audiences were products of a Greco-Roman culture in which debates about adaptability were lively and included the topics of rhetorical versus lifestyle and the ethical consequences thereof, witnessed in the works of Philo, Plutarch, Maximus of Tyre, Philodemus, Horace, Dio Chrysostom, Epictetus and Lucian, among others.[79] Antisthenes and his Odysseus became

75. *Antisthenis Fragmenta* 51 (Fernanda Decleva Caizzi, ed. (Milan: Instituto Editoriale Cisalpino, 1966), p. 43); trans. Augusto Rostagni, 'A New Chapter in the History of Rhetoric and Sophistry', in *Rhetoric and Kairos: Essays in History, Theory, and Praxis* (eds Phillip Sipiora and James S. Baumlin; trans. Phillip Sipiora; Albany, NY: State University of New York Press, 2002), pp. 25–6 (underline emphasis mine) (23–48).
76. Cf. Stanford, *Ulysses Theme*, p. 99; Glad, *Paul and Philodemus*, p. 272.
77. Rostagni, 'New Chapter', pp. 30–1.
78. Nancy Baker Worman, *The Cast of Character: Style in Greek Literature* (1st edn; Austin, TX: University of Texas Press, 2002), p. 33.
79. Glad, 'Paul and Adaptability', pp. 21–2, 26, 28–9. Idem, *Paul and Philodemus*, p. 273, notes that 'By Paul's time versatility and charges of cunning focused both on behavior and speech; one could adapt both by conforming to different manners as well as being discriminating in speech. Discrimination in speech is already seen in Pythagoras' practice of teaching his disciples to speak to children in childlike terms, to women in womenlike terms.

the heroes and models for the Cynics and Stoics – or the heroes and models to oppose – including in the matter of rhetorical adaptability.[80] Diogenes Laertius writes that 'of all the Socratics Antisthenes alone is praised by Theopompus, who says he had consummate skill and could by means of agreeable discourse win over whomsoever he pleased' (6.14; trans. Hicks). Diogenes was famous for 'a wonderful gift of persuasion, so that he could vanquish anyone he liked in argument' (*Diog. Laertius* 6.75-76; Loeb). Crates became famous for *philanthro pia*, nicknamed '"the Door Opener" – the caller to whom all doors fly open – from his habit of entering every house and admonishing those within' (*Diog. Laertius* 6.86; Loeb). In an epigram echoing funerary epithets, Meleager expressed his cosmopolitan variability, bidding each in their own language: 'Be you Phoenician, *naidios*! Be you Syrian, I bid you *salam*! Be you Greek, *chaire*! – and you respond in kind' (*Anth. Gr.* 7.419.7-8).[81] Dio Chrysostom maintained that the philosopher must teach 'sometimes by persuasion and exhortation, at other times by abuse and reproach, [hoping] he may rescue some from folly ... taking them on one side on their own but also admonishing them together, whenever the opportunity arises, with gentle words at times, [and] at other [times] harsh' (*Or.* 77/78.35-38).[82]

Paul's competitive metaphors in verses 24-27, immediately following our passage, resemble those closely associated with Antisthenes and the Cynics, and there are many other similarities throughout the Corinthian correspondence, from word usage to concepts. The Pythagorean and Antisthenean traditions focused on finding the right word for each circumstance, and Paul is engaged in explaining the variable of the theoretical 'good' in terms of food and eating, adapted to variable factors and social circumstances. In fact, Abraham Malherbe goes so far as to suggest that Paul may have thought of himself within the Antisthenic model.[83] That Odysseus is portrayed as the wise man

Such concerns are also present in the moralists' focus on character portrayal. Because of this, and in light of the intricate connection between the philosopher's *schema* and *logos*, we should be careful not to focus solely on adaptation in behavior when explicating Paul's statements on adaptability.' See also Reis, 'Flip-Flop?', pp. 10–12.

80. Malherbe, *Paul and the Popular Philosophers*, pp. 35–48, 95–119, discusses the conflicting views of Odysseus among Cynics, whether he was the father of Cynicism or not, including the range from more rigorous to more moderate Cynic practices. The cloak is an issue: Odysseus wore it once, while Diogenes wore it all the time, etc. Thus Diogenes is upheld as the father by the more rigorous such as Ps.-Crates and Ps.-Diogenes. But rigorous Cynics rejected his adaptability of speech (pp. 109–12). Stoics celebrated Odysseus as an example of virtue and wisdom, as sensible, in control his passions, adaptable, courteous, and affable to everyone in his every word (cf. Cicero, *De Off.* 1.113–14).

81. Menahem Luz, 'Salam, Meleager!', *Studi italiani di filologia classica* 6 (1988): 222–31.

82. Citation from Reis, 'Flip-Flop?', p. 16.

83. Malherbe, *Paul and the Popular Philosophers*, pp. 118–19; cf. Hermann Funke in 'Antisthenes bei Paulus', *Hermes* 98 (1970): 459–71; William D. Desmond, *Cynics* (Ancient Philosophies; Berkeley, CA: University of California Press, 2008), pp. 106–7.

who plays the fool, which is how Paul also describes himself in this letter, may also suggest further comparisons at work.[84]

The tradition of interpreting Odysseus in terms of rhetorical rather than lifestyle adaptability represents a minority position, to be sure.[85] Moreover, whether it accurately characterizes Odysseus as Homer and the Homeric tradition intended remains an open question. But the tradition bears witness to a deep awareness of the moral problems which arose from the prevailing interpretations of the great-hearted sacker of cities as a morally compromised chameleon who expediently disguised his true convictions by mimicking the lifestyle of different people in order to gain victory when he might otherwise risk failure – and thus the place for challenging that interpretation in terms of rhetorical adaptability. Surprisingly, that stands in sharp contrast to the apparently unchallenged tradition of interpreting Paul's language in 1 Cor. 9.19-23 in terms of lifestyle adaptability, modified occasionally by the addition of rhetorical adaptability, even though it yields morally reprehensible results for Paul's character, significantly affects the interpretation of other texts, and plays a profound role in larger constructions of Paul, and thus Christianity.

I do not propose Odysseus to be a perfect analogy for Paul. But the tradition for reading Odysseus in terms of *rhetorical* adaptability is suggestive and parallels my own effort to read Paul here, *mutatis mutandis*. It certainly legitimates the direction of this challenge to the prevailing view, which proceeds to read Paul's language here as if self-evidently bearing witness to a variation of *lifestyle*, just as did the prevailing interpretation of Odysseus. Quite unlike the clever 'Nobody' of many disguises, I submit that Paul was easily recognizable as somebody Torah-observant and willing to suffer misunderstanding and much more to announce a controversial if not dangerous interpretation of his nation's ruler as the saviour of the world. At the same time, and in keeping with the universal aspirations of that message, like one enslaved to ply the wine-dark seas, Paul cleverly turned every phrase in every way he could to make it intelligible to everybody.

4. Conclusion

Since the earliest commentators on Paul, 1 Cor. 9.19-23 has been explained in terms of compromising his behaviour according to the model of lifestyle adaptability. Central to that interpretation is the overarching concept that Paul no longer expressed covenant faithfulness in terms of Torah observance, but rather taught indifference to and freedom from Torah (i.e., gentileness)

---

84. And Socrates is the classic rhetorical 'fool' in ironic terms; cf. L. L. Welborn, *Paul, the Fool of Christ: A Study of 1 Corinthians 1-4 in the Comic-Philosophic Tradition* (Early Christianity in Context; London and New York, NY: T&T Clark International, 2005), pp. 149–51, 158.

85. Stanford, *Ulysses Theme*; Luis E. Navia, *Antisthenes of Athens: Setting the World Aright* (Contributions in Philosophy 80; Westport, CT: Greenwood Press, 2001), pp. 39–52.

as the norm for those who believe in Christ, although he did intermittently pretend to Torah observance in order to evangelize among Jews. A few interpreters recognize rhetorical adaptability as at least a facet of the tactic Paul describes. They draw attention to Paul's motives as noble, and modify the degree to which he would adapt his conduct to facilitate association. Some have even objected to the prevailing view that Paul adopted a gentile ideological view of the value of Torah and its observance. However, these arguments have generally not been developed in detail and primarily appear designed to defend Paul from charges of moral dishonesty arising from the lifestyle model, to which they still fundamentally subscribe.

As demonstrated, 1 Cor. 9.19-23 can be understood very differently, with a working hypothesis that Paul was Torah-observant as a matter of covenant fidelity, and known to be halakhically faithful by the audience to which he addressed this text. When approached from this perspective, there is no reason to suppose that his addressees would imagine Paul's language signified lifestyle adaptability. Rather, it would immediately be recognized that Paul was explaining his evangelistic tactic of adapting rhetorically, a discursive strategy they had witnessed themselves, and one that is also evident in his pastoral approach to them in this letter. A similar interpretation of Paul's tactics can be demonstrated at points in Luke's interpretation of Paul, and it is mirrored in the interpretation of Odysseus by Antisthenes, which was developed among the Cynics and Stoics of Paul's time.

Reading this passage in terms of rhetorical adaptability yields a coherent and productive interpretation. It also significantly impacts on the interpretation of critical elements for overall constructions of Paul. It offers many other important benefits too. Reading Paul's text this way eliminates the charges against Paul, at least on the basis of this text, of moral dishonesty, hypocrisy, misrepresentation, trickery, inconsistency, subversion of principles for expedience, and practical shortsightedness, all of which ineluctably result from the traditional and still prevailing interpretations. A thorny obstacle to improving Christian–Jewish relations is thereby removed. At the same time, a different concern is raised. This passage could be used as a warrant and guideline for how to conduct the evangelizing of Jews in addition to other people.

I respectfully hope that, in view of the history of Christian pronouncements about and policies and actions toward Jews (and others), such adaptability will be hermeneutically qualified as unwarranted and unreasonable in evangelistic terms. Jews have had more than enough opportunity to be made aware of Christian propositional truths, including by coercion, and have suffered enough for them. Christianity is no longer Judaism, unlike the case was for Paul. Alternatively, inter-faith dialogue also involves learning the premises and cultural world-view of the other, but for very different reasons. It seeks to understand the other on their own terms, and to successfully explain one's own premises and world-view in cross-culturally intelligible terms in order to advance mutual respect and beneficial relationships going forward. These are goals to which one can hardly object.

Any historical–critical interpretation of this passage implicitly carries ideological freight. The results offered here come with a challenge to several long-standing elements central to the interpretation of Paul and thus Paulinism, including a challenge to important ideological elements in the constructions of Christianity and in its conceptualizations of Jews and Judaism as the 'other' by which to ostensibly define superior difference. At the same time, it eliminates elements central to ideological criticisms by non-Christians developed in reaction to these traditional Christian interpretations of Paul. Thus the implications have the potential to challenge Jewish (mis)perceptions of Christianity as much as Christian (mis)perceptions of Judaism where Paul's voice is concerned, and thereby to advance Christian–Jewish relations. This is perhaps a strange approach to that desirable outcome for a Jewish investigator to support, and should not be understood to express approval of Paul's objectives; nevertheless, I find this to be the most historically probable reading of his text and of the contribution it makes to understanding Paul.

In view of such desirable possibilities, is it wrong to hope that rosy-fingered dawn might rise on a different Pauline tradition in years to come, including new perspectives on Paul and the Jews?

Chapter 6

PAUL'S LETTERS AND THE RELATIONSHIP BETWEEN THE PEOPLE OF ISRAEL AND THE CHURCH TODAY

Philip A. Cunningham

1. Introduction: Actualizing Paul Today

In recent years, certain passages from Paul's letters have proven to be very significant for the Roman Catholic community's understanding of its relationship with the Jewish people and tradition. Most notably, his words provided a scriptural foundation for several points in *Nostra Aetate*, the Second Vatican Council's groundbreaking declaration on non-Christian religions, issued on 28 October 1965. For instance, the Council praised contemporary Judaism by quoting from the Letter to the Romans:

> The Church keeps ever in mind the words of the Apostle about his kinsmen: 'theirs are the sonship and the glory and the covenants and the law and the worship and the promises; theirs are the fathers and from them is the Christ according to the flesh' (Rom. 9.4-5) ...[1]

This important affirmation contains within it a hidden methodological move. Since the Greek text permits a rendering in either the present or past tenses, translators – and in this case, the Council fathers – must decide whether to construe the passage as, 'theirs *are*' or 'theirs *were* the sonship and the glory and the covenants ...'. Prior to 1965, English translations were predominantly in the past tense, reflecting the received legacy of supersessionism. The Council's decision to render this passage in the present tense thus asserts an important theological principle: modern Jews continue to live in relationship with God.[2] *Nostra Aetate* reiterated this point with a further citation from Romans (11.28-29): 'God holds the Jews most dear for the sake of their

---

1.   Second Vatican Council, *Nostra Aetate* (1965), ch. 4.
2.   For more on NA's use of the present tense for Rom. 9.4-5, see Eugene J. Fisher, 'Official Roman Catholic Teaching on Jews and Judaism: Commentary and Context', in Eugene J. Fisher and Leon Klenicki, eds, *In Our Time: The Flowering of Jewish-Catholic Dialogue* (New York/Mahwah: Paulist Press, 1990), p. 6.

Fathers; He does not repent of the gifts He makes or of the calls He issues –
such is the witness of the Apostle.'[3]

The Council made a related methodological decision when it drew upon
Paul's metaphor of the olive tree in Rom. 11.17-24, notably linking it with
Eph. 2.14-16:

> Nor can [the Church] forget that she draws sustenance from the root of that well-
> cultivated olive tree onto which have been grafted the wild shoots, the Gentiles (Cf.
> Rom 11.17-24). Indeed, the Church believes that by His cross Christ, Our Peace,
> reconciled Jews and Gentiles, making both one in Himself (Cf. Eph. 2.14-16).[4]

By associating Romans' in-grafting of the gentiles with Ephesians'
reconciliation between Jews and gentiles, the Council actualized a reading of
Paul's olive tree metaphor that sees today's Jews ('theirs are ... the covenants')
and Christians as related people of faith in covenant with God, both drawing
sustenance from their common roots in biblical Israel. Thus, Pope Benedict
XVI concluded his May 2009 trip to Israel by invoking the olive tree metaphor
in this way:

> Mr. President [Israeli President Shimon Peres], you and I planted an olive tree at your
> residence on the day that I arrived in Israel. The olive tree, as you know, is an image
> used by Saint Paul to describe the very close relations between Christians and Jews.
> Paul describes in his Letter to the Romans how the Church of the Gentiles is like
> a wild olive shoot, grafted onto the cultivated olive tree which is the People of the
> Covenant (cf. 11.17-24). We are nourished from the same spiritual roots. We meet as
> brothers, brothers who at times in our history have had a tense relationship, but now
> are firmly committed to building bridges of lasting friendship.[5]

Nostra Aetate fosters such positive actualizations of Romans 9–11 partially
because it overlooked aspects of the olive tree metaphor that are less conducive
to interfaith rapprochement. As Daniel J. Harrington has noted:

> The document leaves out all the 'unfriendly' things that Paul said about Israel. Now, a
> conciliar document is not intended to be a biblical exegesis. And so, the writers had no
> obligation to include the negative side of Paul's view on the mystery of Israel. However,
> one recognizes quickly that the biblical text offers a more complicated vision, and that
> the council's statement gives only one side of it ... To be fair, Christians and Jews must
> also look at the other, negative elements in Paul's exploration of the mystery of Israel,
> and try to understand the fullness of Paul's view.[6]

To hit the hermeneutical nail on the head, if 'all the preaching of the Church,
as indeed the entire Christian religion, should be nourished and ruled by

3.   *Nostra Aetate*, ch. 4.
4.   Ibid.
5.   Farewell Ceremony Address, Ben Gurion Airport, Tel Aviv, Israel, 15 May
2009. Available at: http://www.vatican.va/holy_father/benedict_xvi/speeches/2009/may/
documents/hf_ben-xvi_spe_20090515_farewell-tel-aviv_en.html.
6.   D. J. Harrington, *Paul on the Mystery of Israel* (Collegeville, MN: Liturgical Press,
1992), pp. 90–1.

the sacred Scripture',[7] then how is the negative side of Paul's reflections to be handled? Obviously the Council did not intend for twenty-first-century Christians to be bound by the Pauline metaphor that Jews not 'in Christ' are like dead branches that have been lopped off from God's holy olive tree. The Council clearly wished to discourage this sort of negative perspective when it declared that 'Jews should not be spoken of as rejected or accursed as if this followed from holy Scripture'.[8] The question is how to account hermeneutically for this disallowance of Paul's 'unfriendly' ideas. In addition to the pruned olive branches of unbaptized Jews, these most notably include the 'veiled' Jewish reading of Israel's Scriptures in 2 Cor. 3, descriptions of the Torah as mediating a curse in Gal. 3.10-14, and the claim that God is angry with 'the Jews, who killed both the Lord Jesus and the prophets' in 1 Thess. 2.14-16.

2. A Dialectical Biblical Hermeneutic

The 1993 study by the Pontifical Biblical Commission, 'The Interpretation of the Bible in the Church', provides a helpful point of departure. It saw the need for a hermeneutical approach that overcomes 'the distance between the time of the authors and first addressees of the biblical texts, and our own contemporary age, and of doing so in a way that permits a correct actualization of the Scriptural message so that the Christian life of faith may find nourishment'.[9] The PBC thus understood biblical interpretation as a kind of conversation:

> Sacred Scripture is in dialogue with communities of believers: It has come from their traditions of faith ... Dialogue with Scripture in its entirety, which means dialogue with the understanding of the faith prevailing in earlier times, must be matched by a dialogue with the generation of today. Such dialogue will mean establishing a relationship of continuity. It will also involve acknowledging differences. Hence the interpretation of Scripture involves a work of sifting and setting aside; it stands in continuity with earlier exegetical traditions, many elements of which it preserves and makes its own; but in other matters it will go its own way, seeking to make further progress.[10]

Furthermore, because Christian faith 'has had to renew itself continually in order to meet new situations ... the interpretation of the Bible should likewise

7   Second Vatican Council, *Dei Verbum* (1965), p. 21.

8.   *Nostra Aetate*, ch. 4. See also the Pontifical Biblical Commission, *The Interpretation of the Bible in the Church* (1993), IV, A, 3. 'Particular attention is necessary, according to the spirit of the Second Vatican Council (*Nostra Aetate*, 4), to avoid absolutely any actualization of certain texts of the New Testament which could provoke or reinforce unfavorable attitudes to the Jewish people. The tragic events of the past must, on the contrary, impel all to keep unceasingly in mind that, according to the New Testament, the Jews remain "beloved" of God, "since the gifts and calling of God are irrevocable" (Rom. 11.28-29).'

9.   Ibid., II, A, 2.

10.   Ibid., III, A, 3.

involve an aspect of creativity; it also ought to confront new questions so as to respond to them out of the Bible'.[11]

Historically, the nature of the Church's relationship to Jews and Judaism did not receive any sustained study from New Testament times up until the aftermath of the Shoah. For nearly two millennia the prevailing supersessionist model was not seriously critiqued.[12] In this context, supersessionism can be defined as a network of related theological claims predicated on the assertion that the Jewish people had been replaced by Christians as the People of God (or at best relegated to a very subordinate status) because God's wrath was upon them for their alleged rejection of Christ.[13] However, as Walter Cardinal Kasper, past president of the Vatican's Commission for Religious Relations with the Jews, has remarked: '[T]he old theory of substitution is gone since the Second Vatican Council. For us Christians today the covenant with the Jewish people is a living heritage, a living reality.'[14] With *Nostra Aetate*'s repudiation of the idea of a biblically-justified divine curse on Jews, and with its recognition that Jews remain in covenant with God, the Catholic Church has found itself in a theological context that is virtually unprecedented in history. Such a reform from a negative to a positive stance toward Judaism unavoidably has repercussions for Christian self-understanding. A dialogical approach to interpreting biblical writers such as Paul can be helpful in mapping out the dynamics of the interaction that occurs between the scriptural texts and readers of today who are grappling with the radically 'new situation' after the Shoah and after *Nostra Aetate*.

---

11.   Ibid.

12   This explains why *Nostra Aetate*, ch. 4, could not cite any ecclesiastical councils or papal declarations to counteract supersessionism, but had to reach back to New Testament texts, especially its earliest books, Paul's epistles.

13.   Bruce Longenecker, 'On Israel's God and God's Israel: Assessing Supersessionism in Paul', *Journal of Theological Studies* 58/1 (April 2007): 26-44, argues that from 'the perspective of (what might be called) "christo-theocentric faith"', Paul considered the solely theocentric faith of mainstream forms of Judaism to be underdeveloped, unenlightened and salvifically deficient and therein lies his supersessionism. But from the perspective of the grand sweep of God's acts in history, Paul imagined ethnic Israel to play the role of God's specially chosen instrument in the course of salvation history (p. 39). Therefore, Longenecker concludes, Paul's 'christocentric supersessionism was not necessarily and inevitably a form of anti-Judaism or anti-Semitism – although it clearly can be one or both, and all too often has been' (p. 40). This viewpoint has some merit in the context of Paul's imminent eschatological horizon (see below), but for later Christians who did not share Paul's eschatology, a Judaism that was 'underdeveloped, unenlightened, and salvifically deficient' was dangerous to Christians and really ought not to exist after having been replaced by Christ and the Church. On the basis of history, one has to wonder if a somewhat benign 'christocentric supersessionism' can really exist for any length of time without becoming anti-Jewish. In addition, thinking of Judaism only 'ethnically' today (which Longenecker does not suggest) would disparage the value of Jewish religious life over the centuries. The issue of how to 'actualize' Paul remains.

14.   '*Dominus Iesus*'. Paper given at the 17th meeting of the International Catholic–Jewish Liaison Committee (1 May 2001), p. 3.

Also indebted to the work of scholars such as Hans Georg Gadamer and Paul Ricoeur, Sandra M. Schneiders has offered a comprehensive biblical hermeneutic that complements and more comprehensively examines the principles more sketchily expressed by the PBC in 1993. She sees biblical interpretation as a dialectic between the *explanation* of what a text says and an *understanding* of the implications of the text for our own world of today.[15] To use the letters of Paul as an illustration, the activity of explanation, which could also be called exegesis, uses an array of historically critical methods to explore 'the World behind the Text', the world that gave rise to Paul's various epistles. Combined with literary critical analyses of the 'World of the Text', for example, how Paul rhetorically tries to convince his intended readers of his assertions, the reader of today can arrive at multifaceted 'ideal meanings' of the text, which should ground any interpretations of the text.

In Schneiders' system, the ideal meanings of the text must then be put into dialogue with or actualized in our own world. By entering into 'the World before the Text', the reality that the text imperfectly projects, modern faith engages biblical faith, constructs a cognitive 'Meaning of the Work' for today, and, as a result, the transformative power of God may be unleashed. An examination of the significance of Paul's olive tree metaphor might for our post-Shoah, post-*Nostra Aetate* world be an example of the process of actualization.

In our conversation with the biblical text we may find ourselves disagreeing with part of what a biblical author like Paul says because of our different knowledge (e.g., Gen. 1's depiction of a flat earth), or because we don't share the urgent emotions of the writers (e.g., Ps. 137.19; Jn 8.44). Today's readers also have a different 'effective history' than the biblical authors if for no other reason than two thousand years have intervened. 'By effective history is meant historical reality not only as initiating event but also as modified and amplified by all that the initiating event has produced ... The past is not ontologically or epistemologically stationary; it is constantly being reconstituted within its own effective history.'[16] Thus, readers in a post-*Nostra Aetate* Church may be aware of how debates among the first Jewish members of the earliest churches over the requirements for gentile admission contributed to a later caricature of Torah-observance as mindless legalism. They will likely react quite differently to Paul's words about 'the curse of the Law' (Gal. 3.13) than either his original intended readers or all the intervening generations of readers until 1965. In addition, modern readers will likely bring to the text questions that were not on the mind of the biblical author.

On the other hand, by getting to know the scriptural writers as human beings who encountered God amid all the ambiguities of human history and society, today's readers may find themselves transformed by being challenged

---

15.   See her *The Revelatory Text: Interpreting the New Testament as Sacred Scripture* (San Francisco: Harper, 1991), pp. 17–18, 157–61.

16.   Ibid., 159–60.

by the biblical vision – even if that vision is only imperfectly realized in the Bible itself.

This flowchart graphically summarizes the movements of this dialectical biblical hermeneutic:

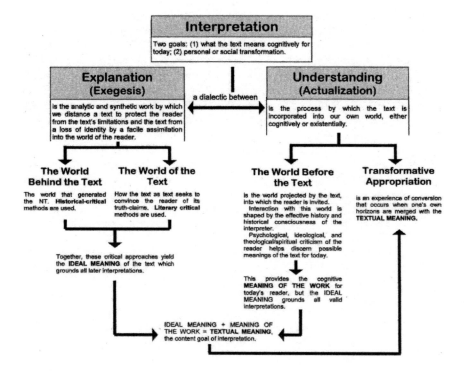

This essay follows this dialectical process in discussing the pertinence of Paul's letters for twenty-first-century relations between Christians and Jews. The Letter to the Romans will figure prominently because it is the only one of Paul's epistles, and perhaps the only New Testament book, that grapples in a sustained fashion with the subject of Jews outside of the Church. As the Jewish apostle to the gentiles, Paul struggles with questions that have been bothering him: why are his Jewish kinfolk proving to be less receptive to the gospel of Jesus Christ than God-fearing gentiles? Does this emerging demographic suggest that God has not been faithful to the people of Israel? Are unbaptized Jews doomed to condemnation at the approaching time of God's judgement on the world? In pondering these matters, Paul develops various ideas that may or may not be helpful for post-Shoah Christians.

3. *The World behind Paul's Letter to the Church*[17] *in Rome*

The Letter to Romans is also unique because it is the only letter Paul sent to a church community that he did not personally establish. Moreover, the church in Rome had many Jewish members, unlike the gentile communities in Corinth, Galatia or Thessalonica to which Paul wrote.

House churches among Jews in Rome probably came into being in the mid-40s, possibly as a result of the efforts of Jewish apostles from Judea. The Roman church would therefore have had a strongly Jewish orientation, even after gentiles began to participate.

In 49 CE, the Emperor Claudius banished some Jews from Rome because of a commotion over someone named 'Chrestus', probably a reference to Christ.[18] Some of those expelled were Jewish apostles such as Prisca and Aquila whom Paul met in Corinth (Acts 18), but it seems unlikely that the church in Rome was bereft of all its Jewish members. After Claudius' death (54 CE), prominent figures likes Prisca and Aquila could return to Rome, enabling Paul to greet them in his letter (Rom. 16.3-5a).[19]

By the end of the 50s, Paul was planning on ending his apostolic work in the eastern Roman Empire. He intended eventually to travel to Spain to begin a mission in the west, and planned to stop in Rome in order to organize this expedition (15.23-24, 28-29). His activity in the eastern Mediterranean had been controversial. His advocacy of Torah-free admittance of gentiles into the Church led to a public clash with Peter in Antioch (Gal. 2.11-14), caused a rift with his partner Barnabas (2.13), prompted him to look upon the leaders of the Jerusalem church with sarcasm (2.6), and provoked hostility with other apostles who desired some gentile prerequisites for baptism (2.4). His claims

17.   For the sake of convenience, I refer to the Roman church in the singular, even though it is likely that there were a number of small 'house churches' in the city. This scenario is vigorously pursued in Mark D. Nanos, *The Mystery of Romans: The Jewish Context of Paul's Letter* (Minneapolis: Fortress Press, 1996). 'Church' is capitalized to refer to believers in the lordship of Jesus universally, while lower case 'church' refers to a local community.

18.   According to the Roman writer Suetonius, Claudius 'expelled Jews from Rome because of their constant disturbances impelled by Chrestus'. Some scholars, following Acts 18.2, conclude that Claudius had ordered all Jews to leave Rome. Since this would banish perhaps 50,000 people, an eviction attested to nowhere else in contemporary literature, this seems highly improbable. Perhaps only Jews in the church were exiled. But, again, this seems unlikely owing to Roman difficulties in distinguishing among different types of Jews. Most likely, the edict expelled those who were the most outspoken in their debates over 'Chrestus' – people like Prisca and Aquila. See Raymond E. Brown, 'The Roman Church Near the End of the First Christian Generation', in idem and John P. Meier (eds), *Antioch and Rome: New Testament Cradles of Catholic Christianity* (New York/Ramsey: Paulist Press, 1983), pp. 100–2, 107–9. Brown's insights greatly inform this section of this essay.

19.   It is debated whether Romans 16 is part of the original letter. The observation by Brown and others (ibid., pp. 108–9) that Paul ends his letter with an exercise in name-dropping in order to introduce himself to the Roman church and also to acquire its support for his collection for the Jerusalem church is a convincing argument that Romans 16 is integral to the original.

that gentiles must not take on Torah observance gave rise to the claim that Paul was encouraging baptized Jews to abandon Torah observance (Acts 21.21), a view not to be found in Paul's own letters.

Partially in an effort to dispel this cloud over his ministry, Paul encouraged each of the gentile churches he founded to appoint delegates to represent them in carrying a donation for the well-being of the 'mother church' in Jerusalem (1 Cor. 16.1-4; 2 Cor. 8.1-24). If this embassy was accepted by the leaders in Jerusalem, it would be a sign of solidarity between Jewish and gentile churches and powerful evidence of the Spirit's presence in Paul's apostleship.

Before journeying westward to Rome, Paul planned to travel to Jerusalem to accompany the delegates with their contribution (Rom. 15.25-32). He wrote to the church in Rome before setting out both to introduce himself and Phoebe, a church official from the eastern seaport of Corinth, who may have carried the letter to Rome (16.1-2). Paul may have hoped that Phoebe, presumably a skilled businesswoman, would receive aid from the Roman church in mounting the expedition to Spain. Paul was also counting on Rome's prayers and support for the success of his mission to Jerusalem (15.30-32).

This provides a significant clue to the situation of the church community in Rome. Although by this time the Roman church was already predominantly gentile (e.g., Rom. 1.13), and although it might have been composed of a number of smaller house-churches (e.g., 16.5), in general it must have been sufficiently akin to the more Torah-observant Jerusalem church to be able to offer Paul some credible support with its leaders. In other words, 'the dominant Christianity at Rome had been shaped by the Jerusalem Christianity associated with James and Peter, and hence was a Christianity appreciative of Judaism and loyal to its customs'.[20] By writing to the church in Rome, Paul was both trying to disabuse its believers of any distorted versions of his preaching that they might have heard, and also showing them that his ministry was compatible with the outlook of the Jerusalem assembly, which Rome resembled.[21]

Scholars who seek to reconstruct the setting of the Roman church find especially important Paul's written comments concerning the eating of meat which had been sanctified to idols and about the attitudes of the 'strong' and 'weak' toward such meat (14.1-15, 13). Some scholars simply identify the 'strong' and 'weak' as gentile and Jewish believers, respectively. They detect an internal debate within the Roman church between dominant gentiles and the returning expelled Jews.[22] Others contest this identification, arguing

20. Ibid., p. 110.
21. Ibid., p. 111. Jacob Jervell, 'The Letter to Jerusalem', in Karl P. Donfried, ed., *The Romans Debate* (rev. exp. edn; Peabody, MA: Hendrickson Press, 1991), pp. 53–64.
22. For example, Harrington, *Paul on the Mystery of Israel* (Collegeville, MN: Liturgical Press, 1992), pp. 41–2; Francis Watson, 'The Two Roman Congregations: Romans 14.1–15.13', in Donfried, ed., *The Romans Debate*, pp. 203–15.

that there are not neatly defined 'groups' in the Roman church, but simply varieties of faith practice.[23]

It is probably best not to simply equate the 'weak' and 'strong' with Jews and gentiles. There were Jews and gentiles in Christ who no longer felt bound by kosher laws (and hence could eat meat offered to idols without hesitation), and there were Jews and gentiles in Christ who felt obligated not to consume idol-meat. More important is Paul's lack of enthusiasm for either position; instead he insists on unity. He seems more interested in distinguishing his opinions from extreme ideas that might have been erroneously associated with him.[24]

To summarize, Paul's aim in Romans is to offer an accurate and balanced summary of his preaching in order to win Rome's support for him personally, for his delicate diplomatic gesture to the Jerusalem church and for his planned mission to Spain. He also seeks to promote oneness between Jews and gentiles in the Church, including the church in Rome. While Paul may have heard of some squabbles among Roman house churches over questions of practice, such wrangles cannot be neatly characterized as Jew in Christ versus gentile in Christ. Paul avoids becoming immersed in such local exchanges, and instead tactfully focuses on the main theme of his preaching: the greater issues of unity and fellowship.

In furthering his purposes, Paul often seems concerned about the issue of boasting. He wants no boasting of strong over weak (Rom. 14.1; 15.1), of weak over strong (14.3b-4), of Jew over gentile (2.17ff.), or of gentile over Jew (1.18ff.). Boasting seems to function for Paul as a sign of failure to realize one's dependence on God's mercy (3.9, 27; 5.1-5). It also shows a lack of concern for the unity of the Body of Christ (12.1-21). For Paul, boasting demonstrates inadequate faith.

In his reflections on boasting, he focuses on the boasting of gentiles in the Church over Jews outside the Church (11.13-14, 25-26). This leads him for the first time to write about the status of unbaptized Jews and of the apostles' overall failure to successfully preach the gospel to them.

4. *The World of the Text of Romans 11*

The problem of boasting is one which Paul had encountered before, especially in Corinth (e.g., 1 Cor. 1.26-31; 3.21; 4.7; 5.2, 6; etc.). In Rome the subject takes on a new twist because of the Jewish legacy and presence there. Thus a side of Paul not visible in his other letters is revealed; he not only desires gentiles as gentiles to be admitted into the Church on an equal basis with Jews; in Romans it becomes clear that he also wants Jews as Jews to be accorded equal dignity in the Church with gentiles. It is also evident that Paul expects gentile believers to respect even Jews not in the Church. He gives many reasons why gentiles in Christ have no grounds for boasting.

---

23. For example, Robert J. Karris, 'Romans 14.1–15.13 and the Occasion of Romans', in Donfried, ed., *The Romans Debate*, pp. 65–84.

24. Brown, 'First Generation': 119–20.

4.1. *All people depend on the generosity of God*

Because all sin, Jew and gentile alike, all are dependent on God's mercy (Rom. 3.9; 11.6, 30-32). No one can earn a right relationship with God. It can only be humbly accepted as an undeserved gift, as grace. This precludes anyone from boasting about a status they didn't merit in the first place.

4.2. *Gentile believers are indebted to Jews*

Gentiles have been admitted into Christ only because of the faith of the Jews in Christ. Paul expresses this through a series of metaphors. Gentiles have been sanctified by a holy dough and are grounded in a root which brings them to holiness (11.16). It is the 'remnant', Jews in Christ, graced by God with the faith of Christ (11.5-6), who have mediated to the gentiles God's promises to Israel. Since 'wild' gentile branches can only bear fruit by being grafted onto the domesticated olive plant (11.17ff.), they must recognize their ongoing debt to the Jewish tradition.[25] Gentiles in Christ have no justification to boast over either Jews in Christ or outsiders.

4.3. *God has caused Jews to oppose the gospel in order to save gentiles*

Although he was at a loss to explain the lack of Jewish responsiveness to apostolic preaching about Jesus, Paul was convinced that gentiles in Christ could not degrade Jews either inside or outside the church. Paul had become convinced that God, in Christ, was bringing to fulfilment all the Torah promises that gentiles would come to share in the blessings of Abraham. He hoped that his fellow Jews would readily perceive this wondrous culmination and longed for their assent to the gospel proclamation (Rom. 9.3).

In trying to comprehend Jewish ambivalence or hostility to the apostles, Paul found assistance in the biblical concept of the hardening of one's heart. Jewish tunnel-vision must be God's doing![26] The purpose of God's action was

---

25.   It should be noted that there is scholarly debate over who Paul means by 'the root' (11.16). Some have seen it as referring to Christ, while others to the 'remnant', Jews-in-Christ such as Paul himself. Other commentators understand the root to mean the patriarchs or biblical Israel. See Joseph A. Fitzmyer, *Romans* (Anchor Yale Bible Commentary; New Haven: Yale University Press, 1992), pp. 609–10. See also his article 'Romans' in Raymond E. Brown, Joseph A. Fitzmyer and Roland E. Murphy, *The New Jerome Biblical Commentary* (Englewood Cliffs, NJ: Prentice Hall, 1990), p. 861.

26.   Paradoxically, the failure to perceive God's actions in Christ is Paul's principal criticism of his Jewish kinfolk throughout Romans, even though he can simultaneously attribute such blindness to God. This is evidence of the painfulness this subject had for Paul, a pain intensified by Paul's imminent eschatological expectations. His struggle with this matter also lies behind his metaphor of the veil over Jewish eyes in 2 Cor. 3. (His comments there on Jewish biblical interpretation would need to be actualized today along the lines of

to catalyze the apostolic mission to the gentiles in the short time left before the dawning of the Age to Come (11.25).

Therefore, baptized gentiles had still less reason to look contemptuously on Jews outside the Church. Rapid gentile admission to the Church had been made possible only by God's intervening to make most Jews blind to the importance of Christ. As a result, gentiles could only marvel at God's gracious activity on their behalf.[27]

4.4. *Jews more naturally belong in God's plans than gentiles*

Jews not in the Church, to whom Paul refers as 'branches that were broken off' (11.19), will have a much easier time being reintroduced to their natural status as God's People than did the gentile believers who were unnaturally grafted onto an alien tradition. Again, gentiles have little ground for feelings of superiority.

4.5. *Gentiles in Christ must demonstrate God's presence with the Church*

Jews and gentiles in the Church have a responsibility to make Israel 'jealous' (11.11). By this, Paul means that the ethical life of the baptized must clearly manifest the presence of God. Paul expects that by seeing God at work among former pagans, his Jewish kinfolk would come to perceive the reality of what God had done in Christ. Gentile believers, then, cannot boast because by doing so they diminish their witness to God's activity among them.

PBC 2001's statements that both rabbinic and Christian 're-readings' of the Scriptures of ancient Israel are 'retrospective' readings, which are analogous and parallel processes (see II, A, 6-7).)

In Rom. 3.27-31, he asserts that since God is the God of gentiles as well as Jews, God can enter into relationship with gentiles on the basis of gentile faith. This for Paul does not upturn the Torah (3.31) because, he argues, the Law itself anticipated this divine outreach to the nations independent of itself (3.21). In this way, Christ is the *telos*, the end or goal or climax of the Torah (10.4). Israel, in Paul's judgement, has failed to perceive this because they have come to identify only Torah observance, not faith, as the mark of relationship with God (9.30-32a).

27. This was not Paul's first effort to grapple with the apparent failure of God's promises to an Israel sceptical of the preaching of the apostles. First, he explored what makes a true Jew, hypothesizing that there were Jews who seemed so only superficially but really were not (Rom. 9.6ff.). Then he invoked the biblical image of the faithful remnant of Israel, applying it to Jews in Christ. God's promises were being realized in the fidelity to Christ of baptized Jews (9.27; 11.1-6). One gets the sense that Paul is groping for a way to maintain both the election of Israel and the need for faith in Christ. He comes to consider the role of God's will and grace (9.14-18; 11.6) and this led him to his most developed conception: God's (temporary) hardening of Jewish hearts catalyzed the mission to gentiles.

4.6. It is inevitable that all Israel will be saved

Jews not in Christ are, for Paul, apparently in some sort of 'theological limbo', to use Daniel Harrington's phrase.[28] Although currently 'broken off' from the mainstream of God's covenantal actions, they are irrevocably destined for inclusion in God's salvation because of God's faithfulness to divine promises (11.28-29). *All* Israel will be saved (11.26). Jews not in Christ have 'stumbled' in order to make way for the gentiles, but they have not 'fallen' into perdition (11.11). Paul hopes to 'save some of them' from their blindness (11.14), but the inevitable Jewish recognition of God's actions in Christ will mean nothing less than life from the dead (11.15).

Once more, baptized gentiles can only respond with humble awe to the supreme graciousness of God. Despite Israel's (divinely-caused) hostility to the gospel, unbaptized Jews maintain their honourable standing as the Chosen People (9.4-5; 11.28-29), and are predestined to be included in the Age to Come. Gentiles, the beneficiaries of a similar divine generosity, can have no legitimate behaviour other than to praise God (11.30-36).

All of the above arguments against gentile boasting, especially the last one, must be understood in the context of Paul's expectations for the future. Paul believed that the New Creation, or the Age to Come, was in the final throes of erupting into human history (e.g., Rom. 8.18-25). The definitive establishment of the New Age would occur with the triumphant return of Christ enthroned in glory (e.g., 1 Cor. 15.23-28). Paul fully expected that Christ's return, his *parousia*, would occur within his own lifetime (1 Thess. 4.15) or, at least, shortly thereafter (Phil. 1.21-26; 3.20; 4.5). Indeed, Paul's perception that time was so short (e.g., 1 Cor. 7.26, 29) was probably the primary reason for the urgency with which he sought to save as many gentiles as possible. Unless rescued from their idolatrous habits by faith in Christ, they would feel God's judgement and wrath as the present age ends (Rom. 1.18–2.11).[29]

With this imminent eschatological, or end-times, horizon, it is understandable why Paul could be comfortable imagining his unbaptized Jewish kinfolk in a sort of theological stasis. During the present transitory 'ripple in time'[30] between the Present Age and the Age to Come (or between Christ's raising and return), God had frozen Jewish hearts in order to direct the efforts of the apostles toward the saving of the gentiles.

This is why Paul speaks about 'life from the dead' (Rom. 11.15) in connection with the acceptance by unbaptized Jews of God's deeds in Christ. Although the sequence of events is probably not fixed in Paul's mind, the return of Christ in glory, the inauguration of the New Creation, and the unity

---

28.   Harrington, *Mystery of Israel*, pp. 55, 81.
29.   That urgency may also explain the noxious rhetoric used by Paul in 1 Thess. 2.14-16, if those verses are not a later interpolation. Frustrated by assaults on the faith of the Thessalonian believers and on his own mission to gentiles, he lashes out angrily.
30.   I am indebted to Paula Fredriksen for this phrase.

of Jews and gentiles were all anticipated to be roughly contemporaneous events.

By thinking this way, Paul was able to reconcile several incongruous concepts: (1) the irrevocable election of all the People of Israel and the inevitable fulfilment of God's promises to them; (2) Israel's current failure to perceive these promises as being fulfilled in Christ; (3) the significance of Christ for all humanity; and (4) Christ's imminent *parousia* and the dawning of the New Creation.

5. *Actualizing Paul in a Post-Shoah,* Post-Nostra Aetate *Church*

With this hasty 'explanation' of Romans 11 in terms of the worlds behind and of the text, we turn to the 'understanding' side of Schneiders' dialectical model and consider the actualization of Paul's ideas in our different world of today. We are asking how the world before the text, the world projected by the text, sheds light on a post-Shoah, post-*Nostra Aetate* Church two thousand years after Paul. To begin, some differences between Paul's vision and our own must be considered.

First, it should be observed that most twenty-first-century Christians do not share Paul's end-times expectations. The vast majority of Christians do not expect the return of Jesus and the ultimate establishment of God's reign to occur within their own lifetimes. Given the lapse of two millennia since Paul's day, most Christians today have consciously or unconsciously postponed the eschaton into the indefinite future. Similarly, few modern Jews anticipate the dawn of the messianic age very soon. Rather, God's People are thought to have a duty to work with God in bringing the world to its eventual completion.

Not sharing in Paul's sense that 'all our futures are so foreshortened … for the present scheme of things is rapidly passing away',[31] his efforts to hold together discordant theological convictions about Israel and Christ can seem to us to be strained.

In addition to living in a world with a different eschatological outlook, twenty-first-century Jews and Christians are heirs to a shared two-millennia history that Paul did not dream would continue to unfold. In Schneiders' phrasing, we have a radically different 'effective history' which shapes our consciousness, perceptions and dreams.

For Catholics, this means that Paul's words are read today in a Church community that has authoritatively renounced its history of anti-Jewish preaching, that is struggling to come to grips with the dreadful reality of the Shoah, that seeks to reform earlier anti-Jewish theologies, and that recognizes the ongoing spiritual vitality of the Jewish people and tradition.

---

31. J. B. Phillips's dramatic rendering of 1 Cor. 7.29b, 31b. See his *The New Testament in Modern English* (rev. edn; New York: Macmillan, 1972).

This last point is a major divergence of the thinking of modern Catholics from that of Paul. Post-*Nostra Aetate* Catholic ecclesial instructions have stressed that 'the history of Judaism did not end with the destruction of Jerusalem, but rather went on to develop a religious tradition ... rich in religious values'.[32] Jewish history is seen to continue especially in the diaspora, 'which allowed Israel to carry on to the whole world a witness – often heroic – of its fidelity to the one God and to "exalt God in the presence of all the living" (Tb. 13.4)'.[33] The recognition of such spiritual faithfulness enabled John Paul II to declare that a 'better understanding of certain aspects of the Church's life can be gained by ... taking into account the faith and religious life of the Jewish people as professed and lived now as well'. Likewise, Catholic preachers have been advised to 'draw on Jewish sources (rabbinic, medieval and modern) in expounding the meaning of the Hebrew Scriptures and the apostolic writings',[34] and the Pontifical Biblical Commission has observed that Catholics can 'learn much from Jewish exegesis practiced for more than two thousand years'.[35]

These and numerous other possible examples demonstrate current Catholic appreciation of the theological richness of the post-New Testament Jewish tradition. Since Paul pre-dated the writing of the Mishnah and Talmuds, he did not know that post-Jesus Jewish creative vitality would renew Jewish life in a world without the Jerusalem temple. With our different historical perspective, modern Catholics cannot relate to Paul's ideas about unbaptized Jews being in a theological limbo, waiting for the eschaton to be reattached to the ongoing activity of God in the world. Paul could imagine this very temporary state of affairs in his eschatological enthusiasm, but we, who two thousand years later have personally experienced the spiritual dynamism of Jewish friends, cannot agree that Judaism languishes in such stasis.

Another difference between Paul's day and our own can be seen in the nature and composition of the Church. When Paul wrote his letters, the Church was a movement within the diverse world of late Second Temple Judaism. The fact that Paul never uses the word 'Christian' or 'Christianity' reflects the reality that followers of Jesus Christ did not yet see themselves as a religion clearly distinct from Judaism. Moreover, Jews were still in the majority among those baptized into Christ. Gentiles were becoming members, too, but their numbers were initially small. The ratio of Jews to gentiles in Christ varied widely from place to place (compare the Jerusalem church to the Corinthian church, for example).

---

32.   Commission for Religious Relations with the Jews, 'Guidelines and Suggestions for Implementing the Conciliar Declaration *Nostra Aetate*, 4' (1974), p. III.

33.   Idem, 'Notes on the Correct Way to Present Jews and Judaism in Preaching and Teaching in the Roman Catholic Church' (1985), pp. VI, 25.

34.   Bishops' Committee on the Liturgy, National Conference of Catholic Bishops, *God's Mercy Endures Forever: Guidelines on the Presentation of Jews and Judaism in Catholic Preaching* (Washington, DC: USCC, 1988), p. 31i.

35.   Pontifical Biblical Commission, *The Jewish People and Their Sacred Scriptures in the Christian Bible* (2001), II, A, 7.

Today, however, the Christian religion can be called the gentile Church. The tiny fraction of Christians who are of Jewish heritage are not encouraged by most Christians to maintain Jewish practices and they are considered non-Jews by their former co-religionists. This difference in self-understanding between Paul and us also influences the actualization of Paul's ideas today.

Taking such discrepancies into account, Romans 11 can be actualized for modern Catholic-Jewish relations (Schneiders' cognitive 'Meaning of the Work') in several ways.

5.1. *Gentile Christians still have no ground for boasting*

A main Pauline theme in Romans (and other letters) is that boasting is contradictory to gratitude for God's graciousness. Among other things, he was concerned about baptized gentiles bragging or feeling superior to Jews whether baptized or unbaptized.

One can only imagine Paul's reactions if somehow he were to learn the ensuing history of relations between Jews and the later gentile Church. His hope that his gentile converts would live such ethical lives that his Jewish kinfolk would become 'jealous' of God's obvious presence among them failed miserably as history unfolded; indeed Christian conduct often had the opposite effect on Jews. If, over the centuries, Jews have at times been able 'to serve God without fear in holiness' (Lk. 1.74-75):

> ... then it is certainly only in exceptional cases that this has been due to the behavior of Christians. The Jewish no to Jesus Christ, and even more to the Church, has therefore been legitimated countless times by the obedient behavior of Jews and the disobedient behavior of Christians. The Christian churches will only be what they are called to be for the People of God, as far as is humanly possible, when they have testified convincingly through their life and behavior for just as long a period as they filled the Jews with apprehension, that for Israel they are a reason not for fear but for fearlessness and perhaps even for confidence.[36]

This leads to the conclusion that Paul's explanation for widespread Jewish rejection of apostolic preaching (God's hardening of Jewish hearts to save gentiles) is inapt today. We Christians must admit that historical Jewish resistance to the Good News reflects less on Jewish hearts than on Christian ones.

5.2. *The relationship between Jews and Christians is a mystery*

Paul's uses the term 'mystery' in his grappling with the difficult question of the relationship between the people of Israel and the people of the Church (Rom.

---

36. Peter von der Osten-Sacken, *Christian-Jewish Dialogue: Theological Foundations* (Philadelphia: Fortress Press, 1986), p. 81.

11.25). He then concludes his ruminations by citing Isa. 40.13 and Job 35.7; 41.11, in a doxological exclamation, apparently expressing dissatisfaction with his ability to fully grasp God's plans and activities:

> O the depth of the riches and wisdom and knowledge of God! How unsearchable are his judgements and inscrutable his ways! 'For who has known the mind of the Lord? Or who has been his counsellor?' 'Or who has given a gift to him, to receive a gift in return?' For from him and through him and to him are all things. To him be the glory forever. Amen. (11.33-36)

'Mystery' is a word rich with theological meaning and potential. It refers to the presence of the divine in human life that can be perceived but not fully compassed by limited human understanding. There is always more to be discovered. The 'mystery' of the Jewish and Christian relationship, for instance, was a theme in the 1974 Vatican Guidelines: '... it is when [the Church is] "pondering her own mystery" that she encounters the mystery of Israel'.[37]

Underlying Paul's use of the word mystery is his conviction that God is at work in the relationship between Israel and the Church. The passage of twenty centuries suggests that God intends for the two communities to have complementary, if different, roles in the world. The same intuition is probably at work in Pope John Paul II's words: 'As Christians and Jews, following the example of the faith of Abraham, we are called to be a blessing for the world [cf. Gen. 12.2ff.]. This is the common task awaiting us. It is therefore necessary for us, Christians and Jews, to be first a blessing to one another.'[38]

5.3. Both Jews and Christians dwell in covenant with God

As noted earlier, *Nostra Aetate* reaffirmed the covenantal bonding between God and the Jewish people, citing Romans 9.4-5 and 11.26, 28. Paul sought to maintain this fundamental conviction even in the light of his incomparable, transcending experience of Christ (Phil. 3.8). His perhaps personally unsatisfying solution was to relegate unbaptized Jews to a temporary 'twilight zone' of irrelevance until the eschaton brought salvation to 'all Israel' (Rom. 11.26). As mentioned earlier, Christians today do not expect the *parousia* in their lifetimes and after two millennia can hardly think of Jewish religious life as moribund. However, Paul's eschatological understanding of salvation has important implications today.

Paul spoke of salvation mostly in terms of being found in right relationship with God (righteous), at the eschaton. Thus, he prayed for one of his gentile churches that God would 'so strengthen your hearts in holiness that you may

---

37.   Vatican, 'Guidelines' (1974), ch. V.
38.   'Address on the Fiftieth Anniversary of the Warsaw Ghetto Uprising', 6 April 1993.

be blameless before our God and Father at the coming of the Lord Jesus with all his saints' (1 Thess. 3.13; cf. 5.23; Phil. 1.9-11; 2.16-17; Rom. 8.18-25). Although over the centuries Christians have naturally developed many different definitions of salvation,[39] its intrinsically eschatological aspect has been preserved in traditions such as the Lord's Prayer, 'Thy kingdom come'.

If twenty-first-century Christians accept Paul's declaration that 'all Israel will be saved' (Rom. 11.26) and understand salvation as culminating at the End of Days, then:

> ... in underlining the eschatological dimension of Christianity we shall reach a greater awareness that the people of God of the Old and the New Testament are tending towards a like end in the future: the coming or return of the Messiah – even if they start from two different points of view. It is more clearly understood that the person of the Messiah is not only a point of division for the people of God but also a point of convergence. Thus is can be said that Jews and Christians meet in a comparable hope, founded on the same promise made to Abraham (cf. Gen 12.1-3; Heb. 6.13-18).[40]

In terms of Jewish salvation, such considerations lead to the conclusion that Christians should not seek to baptize Jews in pre-eschatological historical time. Rather, the Church has a mission alongside Jews, not to Jews. Walter Cardinal Kasper has explained this in very Pauline terms:

> Such petitions for the coming of the Kingdom of God and for the realization of the mystery of salvation are not by nature a call to the Church to undertake missionary action to the Jews. Rather, they respect the whole depth of the *Deus absconditus*, of his election through grace, of the hardening and of his infinite mercy. So in this prayer the Church does not take it upon herself to orchestrate the realization of the unfathomable mystery. She cannot do so. Instead, she lays the *when* and the *how* entirely in God's hands. God alone can bring about the Kingdom of God in which the whole of Israel is saved and eschatological peace is bestowed on the world.[41]

This means that for twenty-first-century Catholics there are two faith communities who experience covenantal bonding with God. While there has been much theological discussion about whether there is one overarching covenant, two separate Sinai and New covenants, multiple covenantal moments, or covenantal life lived in two modalities (my own preference), it must now be understood as a basic tenet of Christian faith, witnessed to by Paul, that God has entered into a saving relationship with Jews and Christians alike.

39. See, for example, Clark Williamson, 'What Does It Mean to Be Saved?', in Philip A. Cunningham, ed., *Pondering the Passion: What's at Stake for Christians and Jews?* (Lanham, MD: Rowan and Littlefield, 2004), pp. 119–28.

40. Vatican, 'Notes' (1985), pp. II, 10. Note also PBC, 'Jewish People' (2001): 'Jewish messianic expectation is not in vain. It can become for us Christians a powerful stimulus to keep alive the eschatological dimension of our faith. Like them, we too live in expectation' (II, A, 5).

41. 'Striving for Mutual Respect in Modes of Prayer', *L'Osservatore Romano*, 16 April 2008: 8–9.

In some ways, this reopens for today's Christians the paradox with which Paul was trying to wrestle. The permanency of God's relationship with Israel must be related to Christian conviction of the universal significance of Christ. If Jews are in a saving, covenantal bonding with God, independently of Christ, then how is Christ universally significant? This question is the subject of the recently published *Christ Jesus and the Jewish People Today: New Explorations of Theological Interrelationships* (Eerdmans, Gregorian and Biblical Presses, 2011)

5.4. *The relationship between Jews and Christians is an organic one*

Additionally, it can be suggested that Paul's olive tree metaphor was based on a sound intuition; whatever the covenantal configuration, the relationship between the two faith communities is an organic one. It is one which touches on the very essences of the two traditions. Without advocating any kind of syncretism, the relationship might even be described as symbiotic.

This understanding has frequently been voiced in Catholic documents since *Nostra Aetate*, which have taken note of 'the spiritual ties which link the people of the New Covenant to the stock of Abraham'.[42] John Paul II spoke eloquently of the bonds between Judaism and Christianity, stating that 'our two religious communities are connected and closely related at the very level of their respective identities',[43] and that 'the Jewish religion is not "extrinsic" to us, but in a certain way is "intrinsic" to our own religion. With Judaism we have a relationship which we do not have with any other religion. You [Jews] are our dearly beloved brothers and, in a certain way, it could be said that you are our elder brothers.'[44] The Pope's use of such familial language is indicative of the intimacy which post-*Nostra Aetate* Catholics are able to feel for the Jewish community. This would seem to be a modern actualization of Paul's organic imagery.

How this spiritual closeness is to manifest itself in Catholic practice remains to be seen. The recognition of our rapport with the Jewish spiritual heritage must be reflected in Catholic liturgy, music, education, self-definition and christology. Much has been accomplished in this regard, but there is much that remains to be done.

It ought to be mentioned that while this attitude is new for Christians, it is also a novel experience for Jews to hear themselves referred to in such positive and familial ways. Given past history, it is only natural for Jews to wonder if this unprecedented tone is only some temporary aberration from the Christian norm, or if it is one more, even if unintentional, effort to assimilate Jews into Christianity. Some Jews are opposed to entering into interreligious dialogue for these and other reasons:

42.   *Nostra Aetate*, ch. 4.
43.   'Address to Representatives of Jewish Organizations', 12 March 1979.
44.   Idem, 'Address at the Great Synagogue of Rome', 13 April 1986.

We feel that, emotionally, we are not as yet ready to enter into a fraternal dialogue with a church, a religion, that has been responsible for so much suffering, and which is ultimately responsible for the murder of our fathers and mothers, brothers and sisters in the present generation ... All we want of Christians is that they keep their hands off us and our children![45]

Christians certainly have little basis to be offended by such sentiments. Our mutual history has been too painful and prolonged to anticipate the immediate establishment of *shalom* between the two communities. All that we Christians can do is undertake to reform our tradition's failure to heed Paul's warnings against arrogance and to commit ourselves to behaving as a covenanted people should. However, if God graces us with any measure of success, and we Christians succeed in reconfiguring our self-definitions accordingly, then, sooner or later, Jews will also be confronted with re-evaluating their views of Christianity. If such Jewish reflection sees validity in some sort of organic spiritual relationship between the two faiths, then Jewish, as well as Christian, communal self-definition will be affected.

Assimilation need not be the inevitable result of a Jewish recognition of an organic link with Christianity. The Pauline metaphor of the olive tree can serve as the inspiration for a model which sees modern rabbinic Judaism and contemporary Christianity as both being branches of the biblical Hebrew root.[46] Both traditions are thereby related, although remaining distinctive.

5.5. *The gentile Church is nourished by its holy Jewish roots*

Another Pauline theme that can readily be actualized among Christians today was explicitly applied in *Nostra Aetate*: 'nor can [the Church] forget that she draws nourishment from that good olive tree onto which the wild olive branches of the Gentiles have been grafted (cf. Rom. 11.17-24)'. Significantly, whereas Paul could have been thinking of Jews in Christ, such as himself, as the ones who mediated holiness to gentile believers, such a construct is impossible in the virtually entirely gentile Church of the present day. It is noteworthy, therefore, that the Vatican Council used Paul's image in relation to the Jewish tradition as whole. The Church is continuously enriched by the Jewish tradition, and, as several Catholic statements indicate, that enrichment

---

45.   Eliezer Berkovits, 'Judaism in the Post-Christian Era', in F. E. Talmage, ed., *Disputation and Dialogue: Readings in the Jewish-Christian Encounter* (New York: KTAV, 1975), pp. 290, 293. For a contrary viewpoint, see David Novak, *Jewish–Christian Dialogue: A Jewish Justification* (New York/Oxford: Oxford University Press, 1989), and a special issue of *CCAR Journal*, Spring 2005.

46.   For example, Leon Klenicki and Eugene J. Fisher, eds, *Root and Branches: Biblical Judaism, Rabbinic Judaism, and Early Christianity* (Winona, MN: Saint Mary's Press, 1987).

is not limited to biblical Jews, but includes the Jewish contemporaries of the Church today.[47]

Indeed, it could be said that the reverse is also true: the Church suffers when it forgets its Jewish roots. In the words of the bishops of the United States:

> By the third century ... a de-Judaizing process had set in which tended to undervalue the Jewish origins of the Church ... Most essential concepts in the Christian creed grew at first in Judaic soil. Uprooted from that soil, these basic concepts cannot be perfectly understood. It is for this reason that *Nostra Aetate* recommends joint 'theological and biblical studies' with Jews.[48]

Such collaborative ventures have occurred in the past several decades, and have produced much new insight. New lines of discussion are emerging especially in the areas of Scripture, christology, liturgy and ethics. Future efforts in this regard should continue, but, following the principle that Catholics need nourishment from the Jewish tradition, they should also increasingly move beyond academic and clerical circles and into the lives of the average believer. Some ways to do this are to encourage Jews and Catholics to visit each other's houses of worship, to experience dialogue with one another on the local level, to pray together to the Creator of all, and to collaborate together in addressing social needs.[49]

The prayers and songs raised in Catholic worship must also reflect the Church's new awareness of its connectedness to Judaism. References to Jews as dwelling in continuing covenant with God must replace supersessionist allusions or comments about Jews only in the past tense.

Additionally, 'Jews and Judaism should not occupy an occasional or marginal place in [Christian] catechesis: their presence is essential and should be organically integrated.'[50] Sustained and thorough education on Judaism is an important priority for Catholics today.[51]

This is probably the best place to observe that similar questions arise regarding typical Jewish knowledge of Christianity. Although Jews are obviously not nourished by any Christian roots, stereotypical views of 'the other' are probably as common among them as they are among Christians.[52]

---

47.   For example, Vatican, 'Guidelines' (1974), Preamble; Vatican, 'Notes' (1985), pp. VI, 25; and John Paul II, 'Address to Christian Experts in Jewish-Christian Relations' (1975).

48.   National Conference of Catholic Bishops, 'Statement on Catholic–Jewish Relations' (1975).

49.   Bishops' Committee on Ecumenical and Interreligious Affairs, National Conference of Catholic Bishops (USA), 'Guidelines for Catholic–Jewish Relations' (1985 revision), Recommended Programs.

50.   Vatican, 'Notes' (1985), pp. I, 2.

51.   Ibid., Conclusion, p. 27.

52.   See John T. Pawlikowski, 'Rethinking Christianity: A Challenge to Jewish Attitudes', *Moment* 15/4 (Aug. 1990): 36–9.

As one Jewish commentator has put it, 'Jews have thought little about the spiritual dignity of other faiths.'[53]

5.6. *Jews and Christians must witness to the Age to Come together*

Finally, Paul's eschatological concerns have an additional implication in the present day, albeit with some adaptations. Like Jesus before him, everything that Paul did was ultimately directed toward the arrival of the Reign of God, the New Creation, when God 'will be all in all' (1 Cor. 15.28). Although we don't share Paul's urgent timetable in this regard, Jews and Christians both believe that they must work on behalf of the Age to Come. It is a vocation that they can fulfil together.[54]

In an era beset with interreligious conflict, Christians and Jews can offer a badly needed model of collaboration and a vision of God's desires for the world. This is perhaps the strongest instruction that Paul would have for gentile Christians today. We have been grafted, through Christ, onto God's plans for the world through no merit of our own. In humble thanks for that gift, we should join with the elder People of God in witnessing to and working toward God's New Creation.

6. *Conclusion*

This essay has shown that Paul's letters, particularly the Letter to the Romans as actualized by *Nostra Aetate*, have proven to be an enormous stimulus for dialogue between Jews and Christians. Yet the Pauline epistles, in common with all Scripture, cannot simply be lifted out of their originating contexts and dropped into the very different contexts of Christians in the twenty-first century. Consequently, there are limits to the applicability of Paul's perspectives in today's world.

Yet the temptation remains strong to use the New Testament as a 'proof-text' by avoiding a dialectical process to actualize it. Recently, for example, some writers have sought to minimize the full significance of *Nostra Aetate*, chapter 4, by trying to uncritically read Romans 9–11 through the lenses of the non-Pauline Letter to the Hebrews, whose very different circumstances and genre are left unexplored. Thus, Avery Cardinal Dulles has written that *Nostra Aetate* 'left open the question whether the Old Covenant remains in force today'[55] and that 'The most formal statement on the status of the Sinai

---

53. Ibid., Irving Greenberg, 'Response to John T. Pawlikowski', 39. See also Eugene J. Fisher, 'Typical Jewish Misunderstandings of Christianity', *Judaism* 22 (1973): 21–32.

54. Vatican, 'Guidelines' (1974), ch. IV: Vatican, 'Notes' (1985), ch. II, pp. 10–11; BCEIA, 'Guidelines' (1985), Recommended Programs, p. 7.

55. 'The Covenant with Israel', *First Things* (Nov. 2005); http://www.firstthings.com/article.php3?id_article=256.

covenant under Christianity appears in the Letter to the Hebrews, which points out that ... the first covenant is "obsolete" and "ready to vanish away" (Heb. 8.13).' [56] Similarly, Albert Cardinal Vanhoye had recourse to Hebrews in discussing 'the permanent validity of the "covenant-promise of God," which is not a bilateral pact such as the Sinai Covenant, often broken by the Israelites ... In this [non-Sinaitic] sense, according to the New Testament, "Israel continues to be in a covenant relationship with God."'[57]

Space prohibits a discussion here of the interesting topic of intertextuality, relating different biblical authors to one another in the process of actualizing them. It must suffice to observe that the unknown author of Hebrews did not pursue the question of God's relationship with unbaptized Jews that Paul pondered in Rom. 9–11. It was therefore perfectly appropriate for the authors of *Nostra Aetate* to give priority to Paul in speaking about the Church's relations with Jews today.

More relevant to this essay is the observation that Romans, Hebrews and all biblical texts must be engaged dialectically, not tendentiously 'proof-texted'. In a recent commentary, Luke Timothy Johnson stresses this point with regard to the Letter to the Hebrews, but, mutatis mutandis, his words are just as pertinent for the subject of Paul's letters and the relationship between the People of Israel and the Church today:

> [P]resent-day theologians who are tempted to discourse about Jewish and Christian relations should not make Hebrews speak absolutely or anachronistically, but should recognize the gap between the situation faced by Hebrews and the questions posted by circumstances today, and therefore hear Hebrews (and all other scriptural witnesses) with a certain degree of subtlety. Theologians today might do well to focus less on what Hebrews says about the first covenant than on what Hebrews insists is the rigorous demand of obedience imposed by the new covenant, and rather than seek to discourse about the fate of Jews in God's plan, might seek to discover the dimensions of following the fidelity of Jesus to God's plan.[58]

56.   'Covenant and Mission', *America* 187/12 (10/21/02): 10.

57.   Zenit.org, 'Cardinal Vanhoye on Jews and Scripture' (7 October 2008); http://www.zenit.org/article-23841?l=english.

58.   *Hebrews: A Commentary*, The New Testament Library (Louisville, London: Westminster John Knox Press, 2006), p. 212.

Chapter 7

A CHRISTIAN-JEWISH DIALOGICAL MODEL IN LIGHT OF NEW RESEARCH ON PAUL'S RELATIONSHIP WITH JUDAISM

John T. Pawlikowski

The last decade or so has witnessed considerable evolution in terms of models for the Jewish-Christian relationship. As Christian theologians began to reflect on the relationship between the Church and the Jewish people in light of Vatican II's decree *Nostra Aetate* and parallel Protestant document, their first proposals tended to fall within two basic categories usually termed the 'single covenant' and the 'double covenant' models. These models exhibited a variety of approaches.[1]

The 'single covenant' model generally holds that Jews and Christians basically belong to one covenantal tradition that began at Sinai. In this perspective, the Christ event represented the decisive moment when the gentiles were able to enter fully into the special relationship with God which Jews already enjoyed and in which they continued. Some holding this viewpoint maintain that the decisive features of the Christ event have universal application, including to the Jews. The statement on the Jewish Scriptures in the New Testament released in 2001 by the Pontifical Biblical Commission[2] appears to argue that within historical times Jews legitimately await the Messiah through their own covenant. There is no need for Jews to convert to Christianity. Cardinal Walter Kasper has articulated this position in some of his writings a few years ago when he insisted that the Jewish-Christian relationship is sui generis because Jews share in authentic revelation from the standpoint of Christian theology. Hence they do not need to convert and they will achieve salvation if they remain faithful to their particular path.[3] Kasper,

---

1.   For a description of these varied approaches, cf. John Pawlikowski, *Jesus and the Theology of Israel* (Wilmington, DE: Michael Glazier, 1989).

2.   Pontifical Biblical Commission, *The Jewish People and Their Sacred Scriptures in the Christian Bible* (Vatican City: Libreria Editrice Vaticana, 2002). For a discussion of this document, including my reflections, cf. a special issue of *The Bible Today*, May/June 2003.

3.   Walter Cardinal Kasper, 'The Good Olive Tree', *America* 185.7 (17 September 2001) and 'Christians, Jews and the Thorny Question of Mission', *Origins* 32.28 (19 December 2002): 464; also cf. Avery Cardinal Dulles, 'Evangelization and the Jews', with a response by Mary C. Boys, Philip A. Cunningham and John T. Pawlikowski, *America* 187.12 (21 October 2002): 8–16, and Christoph Schonborn, 'Judaism's Way to Salvation', *The Tablet*, 29 March 2008.

however, has not returned to this perspective in more recent times. It is clear that the prevailing Vatican position is that of a 'single covenant' without the nuances added by Kasper.

The 'double covenant theory', favoured by some theologians,[4] begins at the same point as its 'single covenant' counterpart, namely, with a strong affirmation of the continuing bond between Christians and Jews. But then it prefers to underline the distinctiveness of the two traditions and communities, particularly in terms of their experiences after the final separation between church and synagogue. Christians associated with this perspective insist on maintaining the view that through the ministry, teachings and person of Jesus a vision of God emerged that was distinctly new in terms of some of its central features. Even though there may have been important groundwork laid for this emergence in Second Temple or Middle Judaism, especially in Jewish mystical literature, what came to be understood regarding the divine-human relationship as a result of Jesus has to be regarded as a quantum leap.

Many scholars, including myself, now feel dissatisfied both with the single and double covenant options. This dissatisfaction stems from new research on the nature of Judaism in the first century CE as well as new insights into the process of church–synagogue separation resulting from what has been termed the 'parting of the ways' scholarship.[5]

The scholarship continuing to emerge from the 'Parting of the Ways' research is doing much to reintegrate Jesus and the early church within the wide tent that constituted the Jewish people in the first and second centuries of the Common Era. It has clearly tended to push back the date for significant separation between church and the Jewish people well beyond the end of the first century and even later as we move to the Christian East. And even when the separation did occur this scholarship has brought forth evidence of some continuing constructive interaction. To emphasize this point one important collection of essays looking at this question has been titled *The Ways That Never Parted.*[6]

Early on in the 'Parting of the Ways' research my former colleague in the cluster of theological schools at the University of Chicago, Dr Robin Scroggs, offered a concise summary of the directions in which this research was taking us.[7] His analysis was favourably quoted by the late Cardinal Joseph Bernardin of Chicago, an episcopal leader in the Christian-Jewish dialogue, in his own writings on the relationship between the Church and the Jewish people.[8]

---

4.   I personally subscribed to this position initially.

5.   Cf. Adam H. Becker and Annette Yoshiro Reed, eds, *The Ways That Never Parted: Jews and Christians in Late Antiquity and the Early Middle Ages*, Texts and Studies in Judaism, no. 95 (Tubingen: Mohr Siebeck, 2003); Matt Jackson-McCabe, *Jewish Christianity Reconsidered: Rethinking Ancient Groups and Texts* (Minneapolis: Fortress, 2007).

6.   Ibid.

7.   Robin Scroggs, 'The Judaizing of the New Testament', *Chicago Theological Seminary Register* (Winter 1986): 1.

8.   Cardinal Joseph Bernardin, *A Blessing to Each Other. Cardinal Joseph Bernardin and Jewish-Catholic Dialogue* (Chicago: Liturgy Training Publications, 1996), pp. 78–9.

Scroggs made the following affirmations in his distillation of the new scholarship on Jesus' relationship with Judaism and on the Jewish setting of early Christianity: 1. The movement begun by Jesus and continued after his death in Palestine can best be described as a reform movement within Judaism. There is little extant evidence during this period that Christians had a separate identity from the Jews. 2. The Pauline missionary movement, as Paul understood it, was a Jewish mission which focused on the gentiles as the proper object of God's call to his people. 3. Prior to the end of the Jewish war with the Romans, which ended in 70 CE, there was no such reality as Christianity. Followers of Jesus did not have a self-understanding of themselves as a religion over against Judaism. A distinctive Christian identity only began to emerge after the Jewish-Roman war. 4. The later sections of the New Testament all show some signs of a movement towards separation, but they also generally retain some contact with their Jewish matrix.

Another pioneering scholar in the initial phase of the 'Parting of the Ways' discussion was the late Saldarini. In various essays he underlined the continuing presence of the 'followers of the Way' in the wide tent of Judaism over the first few centuries. Saldarini especially underscored the ongoing nexus between Christian communities and their Jewish neighbours in Eastern Christianity whose theological outlook is most often ignored in presentations about the early church within Western Christian theology.[9]

As the profound re-evaluation of the church's origins begun by scholars such as Scroggs and Saldarini has continued, we see further development of its initial themes. The biblical scholar John Meier, in the third volume of his comprehensive study of New Testament understandings of Jesus, argues that from a careful examination of the New Testament evidence Jesus must be seen as presenting himself to the Jewish community of his time as an eschatological prophet and miracle worker in the likeness of Elijah. He was not interested in creating a separatist sect or holy remnant along the lines of the Qumran community. But he did envision the development of a special religious community within Israel. The idea that this community 'within Israel would slowly undergo a process of separation from Israel as it pursued a mission to the Gentiles in this present world – the long-term result being that his community would become predominantly Gentile itself – finds no place in Jesus' message or practice'.[10]

In a more recent study, David Frankfurter adds further to the notion of significant intertwining between Christians and Jews for a period well after Jesus' own lifetime. He has insisted that within the various 'clusters' of

9.   Anthony J. Saldarini, 'Jews and Christians in the First Two Centuries: The Changing Paradigm', *Shofar* 10 (1992): 32–43; 'Christian Anti-Judaism: The First Century Speaks to the Twenty-First Century', The Joseph Cardinal Jerusalem Lecture 1999 (Chicago: Archdiocese of Chicago, The American Jewish Committee, Spertus Institute of Jewish Studies and the Jewish United Fund/Jewish Community Relations Council, 1999).
10.   John P. Meier, *Companions and Competitors* (New York: Doubleday, 2001), p. 251.

groups that included Jews and Christians there existed a 'mutual influence persisting through late antiquity. There is evidence for a degree of overlap that, all things considered, threatens every construction of an historically distinct "Christianity" before at least the mid-second century.'[11]

The growing number of biblical scholars who have become engaged in this 'Parting of the Ways' discussion all stress the great difficulty in locating Jesus within the ever-changing Jewish context in the first century. Some speak of 'Judaisms' and 'Christianities' in this period, almost all involving some mixture of continued Jewish practice with new insights drawn from the ministry and preaching of Jesus. For scholars such as Paula Fredriksen, even speaking of 'the parting of the ways' is unhelpful because it implies two solid blocks of believers.[12] The various groups in fact were entangled for at least a couple of centuries. So, as Daniel Boyarin has rightly insisted, we cannot speak of Judaism as the 'mother' or 'the elder brother' of Christianity.[13] These are essentially 'linear' images that this new scholarship has discredited as superficial in terms of the actual reality. Rather, what eventually came to be known as 'Judaism' and 'Christianity' in the Common Era resulted from a complicated, parallel 'co-emergence' process over an extended period of time during which various themes became predominantly associated with one or two major focal points. Many factors contributed to this eventual differentiation, including Roman retaliation against 'the Jews' for the late first century revolt against the occupation of Palestine and the development of a strong 'against the Jews' teaching during the patristic era. The 'conversion' of Emperor Constantine also proved decisive for the eventual split into two distinctive religious communities.

Within the overall 'Parting of the Ways' scholarship one of the most important results has been the significant re-evaluation of Paul's outlook on Judaism. Traditionally Paul has been viewed both in popular and scholarly circles in Christianity as in many ways its founder. He has been credited with bringing about the decisive break with Judaism through his rejection of any Torah obligations for gentile converts in the first century at the so-called Council of Jerusalem. Paul has often been portrayed as espousing a view in which Christianity clearly holds a position of theological superiority over Judaism.

Much of this fundamentally anti-Jewish perspective on Paul has been due to the dominance of a master narrative in Christian circles rooted in the book of Acts. This master narrative begins with Stephen's decisive break with Judaism in chapter 7 of Acts. So-called Jewish Christians then begin to disappear from this master narrative until chapter 11 when they are totally

---

11. David Frankfurter, 'Beyond "Jewish-Christianity": Continuing Religious Sub-cultures of the Second and Third Centuries and Their Documents', in Becker and Reed, p. 132.

12. Paula Fredriksen, 'What "Parting of the Ways"? Jews, Gentiles and the ancient Mediterranean City', in Becker and Reed, pp. 35–64.

13. Daniel Boyarin, 'Semantic Differences on "Judaism/Christianity"', in Becker and Reed, pp. 65–86.

removed from the story following Peter's revelatory vision whereby he is convinced to abandon his previous adherence to continued Jewish observance. From that point onwards the master narrative focuses exclusively on gentiles as the new people of God and moves the geographic centre of Christianity to Rome in place of Jerusalem. Thus in the account of Christian origins that has tended to dominate Christianity's perspective, Judaism is superseded and even annulled, with Paul being viewed as the primary messenger for this teaching. This master narrative from Acts has been especially pronounced during the Easter season in the Catholic liturgy where readings from Acts are used extensively.

This classical perspective on Paul and Judaism was significantly reinforced in the mid-nineteenth century in the writings of F. C. Baur. In his classical work *Paul the Apostle*, written in 1845,[14] Baur argued for the existence of only two factions in the early church. One was the Jewish Christians whose leader was Peter and the other gentile Christians who looked to Paul for spiritual guidance. The Jewish Christians, in Baur's perspective, stood mired in a narrow legalism that blinded them to the universalistic elements in Jesus' teachings supposedly championed by Paul.

Increasingly Paul is being seen as an integral part of the complicated Jewish-Christian scene brought to the surface through the 'Parting of the Ways' scholarship rather than someone who stood totally apart from this scene and repudiated its basic orientation. Shortly before his death the prominent New Testament scholar Raymond Brown said in a public speech in Chicago that he had now become convinced that Paul had a very high regard for Torah, including its ritual dimensions, and that, if he had had a son, would likely have had him circumcised. Even Paul's 'christological' reflections are now seen by some as having links to parts of the Jewish mystical tradition of the time, a view first propounded in a scholarly conference held at Catholic Theological Union in Chicago in 1991 under the direction of Hayim Perelmuter of CTU and Wilhelm Wuellner of the Lutheran faculty at the Graduate Theological Union in Berkeley.[15] This Jewish 'mystical' approach to Paul has been further developed in recent years, including in a volume by Benjamin D. Sommer of Jewish Theological Seminary in New York titled *The Bodies of God and the World of Ancient Israel*.[16]

The new thinking on Paul's outlook on Judaism in terms of the Christian faith began with the late Harvard biblical scholar, and subsequently Lutheran bishop of Stockholm, Krister Stendahl. In a seminal article in the *Harvard Theological Review* in 1963, entitled 'The Apostle Paul and the Introspective Conscience of the West',[17] Stendahl began to undercut the dominance of

14. F. C. Baur, *Paul the Apostle of Jesus Christ: His Life and Works, His Epistles and Teachings* (Peabody, MA: Hendrickson, 2003).

15. Cf. Hayim Goren Perelmuter and Wilhelm Wuellner, eds, *Proceedings: Conference on the Question of the Letters of Paul Viewed from the Perspective of The Jewish Response Mode* (Chicago: Catholic Theological Union, 15–18 November 1991).

16. Benjamin D. Sommer, *The Bodies of God and the World of Ancient Israel* (Cambridge: Cambridge University Press, 2009).

17. K. Stendahl, 'Paul and the Introspective Conscience of the West', *The Harvard Theological Review* 56(3) (1963): 199–215.

the Baur perspective in Christian scholarship, a perspective that depicted Paul as fundamentally anti-Torah. This interpretation played a central role in Christian theological self-definition in Protestant theology in particular. Stendahl persuasively argued that such an anti-Torah understanding of Paul bears little resemblance to what Paul actually believed about the continued practice of Jewish ritual by Christians. His work has been picked up by an impressive list of scholars who include, among others, E. P. Sanders, Peter Tomson, James D. G. Dunn, John Lager, Daniel Harrington, Jerry L. Sumney and Lloyd Gaston. They have been joined of late by several Jewish scholars, most notably Alan Segal.

What is beginning to emerge in important sectors of Pauline scholarship is the picture of a Paul still very much a Jew, still quite appreciative of Jewish Torah, with seemingly no objection to its continued practice by Jewish Christians so long as their basic orientation is founded in Christ and his teachings, and still struggling at the end of his ministry to balance his understanding of the newness implied in the Christ event with the continuity of the Jewish covenant, something quite apparent in the famous chapters 9–11 of Romans which Vatican II used as the cornerstone of its declaration on continuing Jewish covenantal inclusion in chapter 4 of *Nostra Aetate*. A few of the biblical scholars involved in this new Pauline research even go so far as to maintain that Paul regarded Torah observance so highly that he feared that if gentiles tried to practise it they would only corrupt its authentic spirit. Such a view admittedly pushes the envelope of scholarly evidence a bit far, but it is presently under discussion in some scholarly circles.

One of the scholars at the centre of the new picture of Paul is John G. Gager. He is founder of the important Oxford–Princeton continuing study group on the 'Parting of the Ways'. In an essay, Gager[18] has summarized the new vision of Paul that in his judgement must replace the dominance of the picture from Acts that has held sway in Christian theology and worship for very long. Gager's summary includes the following points: 1. He strongly emphasizes the plurality of practice among followers of Jesus who continued to observe Torah. They were far from uniform in their continued observance of Jewish practices. 2. Jewish Christians in fact did not disappear from the scene after Peter's so-called revelatory vision as the author of Acts would have us believe. They remained a significant force in Christian churches for many centuries, especially in the regions of Syria and beyond where they were far from a tiny minority and were not seen as heretical in their outlook or practices. 3. Early Christianity, unlike what is presented in Acts, did not simplistically reorient its geographic focus uni-directionally towards Rome. Rather, it moved multi-directionally into every area of the Mediterranean region and beyond. In places such as Syria, Jewish Christianity appeared in fact to occupy the dominant position in the church. 4. Together with other scholars such as Brown, Gager repudiates any notion that Paul rejected

18.   John Gager, 'Did Jewish Christians See the Rise of Islam?', in Becker and Reed, pp. 366–7.

Judaism and those we term Jewish Christians. Rather, he chose to devote his energies to the outreach to gentile believers whom, for whatever reason, he felt did not have the obligation to pick up on Torah observance in their faith expression. The author of Acts, Gager insists, enlisted Paul in the effort to downgrade Jewish Christianity. Gager thus implies, though he does not say it explicitly, that the author of Acts rather than Paul is in fact the founder of the anti-Jewish form of Christianity that has been so powerful (and negative) a force throughout Christian history. Paul in fact advocates a 'two door' policy in terms of salvation with distinctive paths for Jews and gentiles. 5. Largely due to the image of Paul created by the author of Acts, Paul became known as the arch-enemy of Jewish Christians, as the person who totally undermined their legitimacy as an authentic expression of Christianity. This image also infected Jewish circles where Paul also traditionally has been regarded, even by scholars favourably disposed towards Jesus and his teachings, as the founder of a Christian church that became anti-Jewish at its core. The Jewish philosopher Hannah Arendt once spoke of the chasm she felt between the teachings of Jesus in the gospels and the Christ of the Pauline texts.

Gager also adds a point relative to the revelatory experience which, according to Acts 2, led to a change of heart on the part of Peter regarding the continuation of Jewish practices by followers of Jesus. He questions the actual historicity of this account, believing it was a story developed by the author of the text to buttress his own anti-Judaic perspective. Gager argues this view from a section in the later Pseudo-Clementine writings where Peter complains that 'some have undertaken to distort my words, by certain intricate interpretations, into an abolition of the Law, as if I myself thought such a thing – God forbid! For to take such a position is to act against the Law of God which was spoken through Moses and whose eternal endurance was attested to by Our Lord.'[19]

In light of this new research on Paul, the question arises, was he the founder of Christianity or merely a faithful Jew? In some ways the answer is he was both. There is little doubt that Paul took a very positive attitude towards Judaism and its Torah, though he had important criticisms about its mode of application.[20] He himself likely continued to adhere to many of its provisions and would have been aghast at the 'denuded' form of Christianity separated from its Jewish soul that eventually emerged in so many quarters of the church where in the light of the strong 'against the Jews' theology in much of patristic theology it became laced with outright contempt for the Jewish people and their faith. In that sense he remained a 'faithful Jew'. But he did believe that the coming of Christ had resulted in a fundamental reorientation of faith into a system of belief rooted in the experience of Christ. For Paul,

19.   Cf. the translation and discussion in Wayne Meeks, ed., *The Writings of St. Paul* (New York: Norton, 1972), p. 178ff. Gager interprets this passage as 'Peter's wrath' against the author of Acts.

20.   As Emmanuel Nathan of the Catholic University of Leuven's Pauline Project rightly pointed out to me, if we retain an understanding of Paul as a faithful Jew, we shall have to deal with his critique of Judaism as well.

the experience of the resurrected Christ was personally transforming. Paul certainly wanted Jews to recognize Jesus as the Messiah of Israel as well of the nations, but this did not mean any repudiation of the Torah. In fact, from the Pauline perspective, a contradiction between Jesus as the Messiah and the Torah would in fact be rather ridiculous as he sometimes appears to draw a parallel and even identify the Law with the gospel of God's acts in Jesus Christ.

Paul's battle with the so-called 'Jewish Christians', which Baur erroneously built into a fundamental confrontation, was in fact a much more limited dispute restricted to those Jewish Christians who refused to accept Paul's view of a fundamental reorientation for believers in Christ. For Paul, the Jewish Torah genuinely mattered; but Christ mattered more. And this was why he felt he could extend covenantal membership to gentiles without requiring of them a commitment to Jewish ritual practices as highly as Paul regarded those practices. For Paul, Israel will ultimately be saved through God's eschatological Messiah. Romans 9–11 clearly shows that Paul expected all Israel to attain salvation. He appeared to regard the present 'disobedience' of the Jewish people as in fact an integral part of the divine plan for human salvation. There was even a way in which the Jewish rejection of Jesus as the expected Messiah of Israel could be seen as a 'christological sacrifice', paralleling Jesus' separation from God the Father on Calvary. In this sense Paul can be termed the founder of Christianity, but in a far different way than the classical portrayal of him in this regard as one who expunged Judaism and its practices from Christian faith, who favoured Christ over Torah in an absolute sense.

In light of this analysis of Paul and Judaism, the question remains, what does this scholarship have to say to us today regarding an understanding of the relationship between the Church and the Jewish people. In terms of more recent attempts to move the discussion away from the earlier 'single covenant– double covenant' categories to a model where exclusivism, inclusivism and pluralism are the dominant motifs, we can say that Paul's view brings us to an 'inclusivist' model in terms of the Christian-Jewish relationship without settling the tensions that such a model continues to generate. Paul clearly asserts some revelatory 'newness' through his understanding of Christ. But he equally asserts continued Jewish covenantal inclusion after the Christ event as well as a root connectedness between the two religious communities.

Cardinal Walter Kasper some years ago began to bring these tensions to the surface without offering any clear resolution. He argued on the one hand for the continued salvific validity of the Jewish path to salvation: 'If they [i.e., the Jews] follow their own conscience and believe in God's promises as they understand them in their religious tradition they are in line with God's plan.'[21] Hence, Kasper has insisted, there is no need to proselytize Jews because they are already in a covenantal relationship with God. The theological

---

21.   Cf. n. 3.

justification for such a position lies in the fact that Jews are the only non-Christian religious community with authentic revelation from the Christian perspective. Hence, the Christian-Jewish relationship is sui generis.[22] For Kasper, and he strongly insists on this, there are two distinctive but not totally distinct paths to salvation. The paths remain integrated, particularly with respect to their eschatological conclusion. What Kasper has failed to do is offer any explanation of how his equally strong insistence on the universality of Christ relates to this vision of two distinctive paths. He does not say that Jews in the end must give an explicit recognition to Christ. But neither does he eliminate such a possibility. Hence his position remains ambiguous and in definite need of further development. I suspect that the current climate in the Church, particularly the late Cardinal Avery Dulles' direct challenge to much of post-*Nostra Aetate* theological reflection, may be responsible for the lack of any further development of Kasper's thinking, much of which comes from the first period of his tenure as President of the Holy See's Commission for Religious Relations with Jews.

Trying to build on what we have learned from the 'Parting of the Ways' scholarship, including that related to the Paul-and-Judaism question and from Cardinal Kasper, I would want to maintain several key notions as building blocks for a model of the Christian-Jewish relationship. Speaking of distinctive, but not totally distinct, paths to salvation seems to me to be the best current linguistic option, far better than the earlier 'single and double covenants'. This option depends fundamentally on a 'parallel' understanding of the emergence of Judaism and Christianity rather than the older linear understanding. The relationship ought to be seen as sui generis. But Kasper's argument from 'authentic revelation' with regard to Judaism remains incomplete for it relies solely on biblical Judaism. And, as Jewish scholars such as Reuven Firestone have persuasively argued, biblical Judaism was in serious decline at the time of Jesus and the Judaism that emerged from the religious revolution within the Jewish community in this period produced a new Jewish religious reality still linked to biblical Judaism but significantly transformed in many areas.[23] This new model can best be placed in the 'inclusivist' category but still remains open to some 'pluralistic' redirection, at least with regard to Islam.

In my current, still evolving, theological perspective I would want to argue that Jews will not be required to explicitly pick up christological language, even at the end time, as part of their redemptive process. Hence I would make it clearer than Kasper that the distinctive paths followed by Jews and

---

22.   This was also the clear position of Pope John Paul II. Also, Archbishop Michael Fitzgerald when he served as President of the Pontifical Council for Interreligious Dialogue supported the sui generis view of the Christian-Jewish relationship. The Church's relationship to Islam he regarded as the first among the other relationships with world religions.

23.   Reuven Firestone, *Who Are the Real Chosen People? The Meaning of Chosenness in Judaism, Christianity, and Islam* (Woodstock, VT: Skylight Paths, 2008), pp. 60–2.

24.   Cf. n. 2.

Christians stand on an equal footing. The Christian path is not inherently superior to the Jewish one. This seems the implication of the Pontifical Biblical Commission's assertion (explicitly endorsed by Cardinal Ratzinger in his Introduction to that document) that Jewish messianic hopes are not in vain.[24] And though the PBC document later speaks of the eschatological Messiah of the Jews as the One who will exhibit traits Christians have already seen and acknowledged in the Jesus who has already come and remains in the Church, there is an opening, albeit small, for arguing that 'the One' need not be spoken of in expressly christological terms.

With Paul I would want to argue for significant 'newness' in the revelation in Christ. This 'newness', as I have argued in previous writings,[25] relies heavily on an incarnational approach to christology whereby humanity saw with greater transparency than before the intimate link between humanity and divinity. We will need to continue to explore whether such incarnational awareness has any resonance in Jewish theology. A few years ago the response might have been absolutely *not*. But scholars such as Michael Wyschogrod, Elliot Wolfson and Benjamin Sommer have begun to explore this question in recent years.[26]

In addition, in the lengthy process of emergent separate paths for Christianity and Judaism, Christianity, as it became an essentially gentile religion without much appreciation of its Jewish roots and saw its theology translated into Greek philosophical language, lost an important revelatory dimension rooted in Torah which Jesus himself manifested and which Paul struggled to maintain even though it was a struggle that he would eventually lose thanks in part to the author of Acts. Thus Judaism as well preserves a distinctive revelation rooted in history and creation, something that R. Kendall Soulen has correctly identified as the hallmark of the Jewish covenantal tradition.[27] Christians will need to recover this Jewish revelation as part of eschatological completeness.

The Jewish and Christian revelatory cores cannot be merged all that easily. That is why we speak of distinctive paths. In the pre-eschatological age I see them continuing to play off each other, both 'blessed' by God (to embrace the term used by Mary Boys), until the end of days. This represents a far from complete model but I do think it responds to some of the questions left unanswered by Cardinal Kasper. Certainly we shall have to continue

---

25.   Cf. John Pawlikowski, *Christ in the Light of Christian-Jewish Dialogue* (New York: Paulist, 1982; rpr. Eugene, OR: Wipf and Stock, 2001); and 'Christology and the Jewish-Christian Dialogue: A Personal Theological Journey', *ITQ*, 72.2 (2007): 147–67.

26.   Cf. Michael Wyschogrod, *The Body of Faith: God and the People* Israel (Northvale, NJ: Jason Aronson, 1995); Elliot R. Wolfson, 'Gazing Beneath the Veil: Apocalyptic Envisioning the End', in John T. Pawlikowski and Hayim Goren Perelmuter, eds, *Reinterpreting Revelation and Tradition: Jews and Christians in Conversation* (Franklin, WI: Sheed & Ward, 1997), pp. 77–103. On Sommer, cf. n. 16.

27.   R. Kendall Soulen, *The God of Israel and Christian Theology* (Minneapolis: Fortress, 1996).

its development, including whether there is a possibility of opening up the essentially inclusivist Christian-Jewish relationship to a wider pluralistic model without endangering the former.

New research on the so-called 'Parting of the Ways', together with the papers presented here, have resulted in a significantly new perspective on the Pauline outlook on Jews and Judaism. We now appear to in fact be moving into a second phase of the discussion about Paul and Judaism launched by scholars such as E. P. Sanders. While we are far from a scholarly consensus regarding a new image of Paul and the Jewish community and its religious tradition, clearly we have moved away from the picture in which he was seen as deeply opposed to Judaism and its practice of Torah to one which sees him as likely a Torah-observer throughout his life and struggling to come to grips with the relationship between Judaism and Christianity from a theological point of view. I would now contend that his perspective on the Jewish-Christian relationship remained in flux until his death and hence it is our responsibility today to pick up where he left off in terms of new research and experiences.

So where does this emerging picture leave us with regard to developing a contemporary model for Jewish-Christian relations? I have tried to sketch an outline of such a model as I see it emerging from the new scholarship. Two points, however, are becoming clear. Contemporary research on Paul, including that presented here, undermines the classical view of him as a major author of supersessionist theology. Secondly, we cannot claim that Paul provided any final, definitive model for us simply to follow today. Positively, a theology of the Jewish-Christian relationship today must be built around a notion of simultaneous linkage and diversity. There is a permanent bonding between the two faith traditions. But, especially since their eventual parting, they each maintain distinctive approaches to the understanding of the God–community relationship. Hence I have proposed a model of distinctive, but not totally distinct, paths for Judaism and Christianity prior to the eschaton. These paths, while essentially parallel, have to be seen as intersecting at some key points. I now prefer such a model to the earlier single and double covenant perspectives.

Chapter 8

SHARING GOD WITH OTHERS OR DIVIDING GOD FROM POWERLESSNESS: A LATE-MODERN CHALLENGE BY THE HETEROTOPIAN EXPERIENCE OF THE NEW PAUL

Hans-Joachim Sander

You may have seen this commercial with George Clooney on TV. In the video clip Clooney drinks a certain type of coffee which, in fact, doesn't taste very well but which gives you the impression that you get a flavour of him personally. In the clip, an attractive woman – in fact the actress Camilla Belle – approaches Clooney standing right by the coffee-machine where he sips a cup of coffee. And she says to him 'Excuse me. I am sorry, do you mind if I am ...'. Clooney, of course, thinks that she wants to get an autograph after having recognized him. And so, he is searching for his pen but then he has to confess 'I'm sorry I don't have a pen.' She looks pretty surprised and then she says 'I just want a Nespresso.' As soon as Clooney realizes that it's not him who is the real star on the scene, he sips again at his cup issuing the commercial's trailer: 'Nespresso. What else?'

Clooney tunes this line with a sound of such surprised deception that one is almost immediately inclined to give him merciful support for not being recognized as he deserves it. This is of course a very sophisticated advertisement. It plays with irony and with self-relativization. And the irony of a relativity confessed by Clooney himself even increases his appeal as one of the most attractive men on earth.

Looking to what has happened to Paul in the last two decades, sometimes this George Clooney clip is crossing my mind. Christian theology – or at least Christian systematic theology – is standing since centuries in front of Paul and of course this theology thinks it's her who has the real say about Paul. Whoever wants to approach Paul has to deal with her positions like 'Paul, the real inventor of Christian message about God', 'Paul, the founder of personal justification', 'Paul, the source for subjective sovereignty'. And it's these positions which really matter about Paul.

But now two very attractive ideas are approaching Paul and obviously they are not in favour of these ideas at all. They tell something about him that is a heavy relativization of what seemed to be obvious facts for which Christian systematic theology is claiming copyright. They demonstrate that these are not facts but fiction. The first attractive approach comes from exegesis and its New Perspective on Paul demonstrates that even if he may have become a Christian he certainly remained a Jew. And looking closer to this hypothesis one has to confess: 'Paul, the Jew. What else?' The second attractive approach comes from contemporary philosophy and its dealings with Paul demonstrate how much his presentation of powerlessness is politically valid for subjects endangered by the fluidity and flexibility of late modernity we are going through. And looking closer to these philosophies opening up a new Paul never seen before one has to confess: 'Paul, the political thinker of powerlessness. What else?'

But unfortunately Christian systematic theology is not George Clooney. It is not that attractive at all and nobody will book systematic theologians for a highly paid job in a commercial. So, it's pretty hard to answer to these relativizing views on the new Paul with irony and with a humorous understanding of faults concerning Paul's positions. They force us to rethink basics in Christian convictions. But it seems to me that these relativities on Paul by the New Perspective and by the new philosophies are unavoidable. The only task of systematic theology is to bring forward arguments which enable us to realize with affirmation and admiration these various 'what elses?'. But I hope, the flavour of the arguments will be better than Clooney's capsules of coffee.

1. The New Perspective on Paul – A Relativization of the Faithful Subject by Justification of the Relevant Other

In exegetical contexts the New Perspective on Paul is already very well know und thoroughly discussed.[1] Within systematic theology the picture is different. This is due to the fact that systematic discussions are in the second row concerning biblical matters and so, they are always coming late. And it has something to do with the dispositions of discourse in relation to Paul. He is used as a representative figure for modern discourses in theology. This is the reason why the New Perspective has triggered some discussion about Luther's ability to get a correct picture of Paul's intentions and theological issues.[2] Especially Protestant systematic theologians are trying hard to prove that there are no misunderstandings of Paul in Luther's theology but that there is a basic misunderstanding of Luther by the New Perspective.[3]

---

1.   Cf. James Dunn's response to the complex variety of arguments in the debate 'The New Perspective: whence, what and whither?' in James Dunn, *The New Perspective on Paul* (Tübingen: Mohr Siebeck, 2005), pp. 1–88; I also rely on: N. T. Wright, *Paul. In Fresh Perspective* (Minneapolis, MN: Fortress, 2005).

2   Michael Bachmann (ed.), *Lutherische und neue Paulusperspektive. Beiträge zu einem Schlüsselproblem der gegenwärtigen exegetischen Diskussion* (Tübingen: Mohr Siebeck, 2005).

3.   Cf. Wilfried Härle, 'Paulus und Luther. Ein kritischer Blick auf die "New Perspective"', in *Spurensuche nach Gott. Studien zur Fundamentaltheologie und Gotteslehre* (Berlin: de Gruyter, 2008), pp. 202–39 (also in *ZThK*, 103 (2006): 362–93). Härle is

Continuity from Paul to Luther is much more than a hermeneutical question because the Reformation's idea of justification has very much shaped modern civilization. It is not the question how much of Luther representatives of the New Perspective have read in their academic life but how stable the ground proves to be Luther has built his theology on. If this ground is a logical progress from the basic Christian narratives then the secular offspring of the modern idea about justification by faith alone do represent a culture which should be defended with all the power Christian religion is able to accumulate. One may theologically rethink the modern story shaped by the Reformation's interpretation of the Christian narratives if these narratives point in a different direction.

There is a question of power involved in this theological problem. It comes out of the grammar modern justification is built on. The use Luther made of Paul is the very source for important binary codes in modern life and these binary codes provide with power and divide power from powerlessness. In this sense, the New Perspective on Paul effects more than purely exegetical problems. Its different view affects the platform on which modern life was built, the justification of the singular subject before God and in relation to social institutions, especially the Church. It would have an impact on the modern power structure if a discontinuity from Paul to Luther must be conceded. The binary codes of this structure would become fragile by that.

Luther's view on Paul's theological achievements has liberated the medieval world from an overwhelming divine power being a force constantly putting pressure on one's own personal life, on society and culture, on economy and politics. This has opened up the door to modernity in the sense that the single subject seized position after position which put it in the very centre of life. A vision continuously looked realistic that the whole life of a person

---

challenging E. P. Sanders' view on Luther and attacking it as a complete misconception in the very core of Luther's theology: 'Anhand dieses Zusammenhangs zwischen Gerechtigkeit und Glauben macht Luther eine exegetische bzw. philologische Entdeckung von größter Bedeutung: Die Prämisse, von der er bei alledem ausgegangen war, nämlich sein Verständnis von "Gerechtigkeit Gottes ist dem Text – ja dem ganzen biblischen Kanon – unangemessen. Mit dieser verkehrten Prämisse bricht aber das ganze schreckliche Gebäude von unerfüllbarer Forderung und gleichwohl bestehender Strafandrohung wie ein Kartenhaus in sich zusammen. Wenn Gottes Gerechtigkeit seine Barmherzigkeit ist, durch die er im Menschen Vertrauen weckt, dann ist nicht nur dieser Teufelskreis durchbrochen, sondern dann geschieht durch die Verkündigung des Evangeliums genau das, wozu das Gesetz – als Forderung und Drohung – nicht in der Lage war: Der Mensch kann und wird nun Gott und seinen Nächsten lieben, die Gebote erfüllen, weil er es nicht mehr aus Angst vor Strafe zu tun versucht, sondern aus Dankbarkeit für die ihm zuteilgewordene Barmherzigkeit Gottes tut. Bei allem Respekt: Diese Einsichten Luthers haben sich E. P. Sanders auch nicht von ferne erschlossen. Er sieht in Luther einen Menschen, der Schuld- und Gewissensprobleme hat und sich darum durch den Gedanken einer zugerechneten, fiktiven Gerechtigkeit eine Lösung zurechtlegt, an die er glauben kann, die ihm hilft, mit seinen Schuld- und Gewissensproblemen zu leben und die ihn doch nicht nötigt, sein Leben radikal zu ändern und am Willen Gottes auszurichten. Das alles hat mit Luther – klar und deutlich gesagt – nichts zu tun' (226/227).

depends on the talents and decisions of his own or her own – no matter what circumstances of birth, family, ethnic context, culture, gender and age one is confronted with by existence. The justified subject got the chance of being master of the universe and in the process of modern civilizations mankind has taken this chance. The subject's mastership is built on a different knowledge about God's justice. This justice is full of fairness and it is not a demonstration of almightiness at the cost of the individual.

Here, God's power was transformed into a force for personal hope based on God's grace by and through faith in Christ. This has humanized God and it has modernized his power as a source of cultural progress. God is a power for progressing mankind's living conditions. His justice is not a force of checking men into very tight borders. There is a positive link between God's power and men's power – and finally women's power as well – in modern times. They depend on each other and human civilized culture is the locus where this interdependency can be experienced. This culture is not a religious one, it is a secular phenomenon and the more secular it is the more it is in the line of the interdependency of God and men. There is no religious precondition to keep this culture on a progressive track.

On the contrary, if God's power is proven to be an obstacle for the living conditions of mankind or of personal life then a person is set free to get rid of this power. A negative relation between God's power and human development is not on the agenda. Then God's power has to fade away.

If there is no such thing as self-salvation but nevertheless good reasons to hope for a final triumph of salvific history, also in the case of one's own existence then one is set free to concentrate on earthly matters and to develop them to their very best. It is in God's will to discipline one's life for the sake of one's own existence. And it is certainly not God's will that one doesn't care for what will be this life's final result. This discipline is the essential tool of the subject's mastery and it is for the sake of one's own life and for the lives of others.

The human progress made possible by this liberation may not be enough before God because everybody always remains a sinner – however hard he or she may try to go along with God's will. There is always concupiscence lurking in inner life. But this is not the most important issue. There is no reason to be constantly in fear of God because one has to face personal failure. Each one of my failures gives reason to try better the next time.

On the other hand, God is set free from being a sort of permanent persecutor. This role is taken over by conscience. Authority by inner life is efficient enough for the sake of God's providence and so, God can concentrate his powers to salvific history. Grace is solely given by God on his terms and I must not be bothered pushing God into a direction of my personal favour. I am set free not to be occupied by what God is doing with his singular power of salvation for others and not even for myself. It is proven by Christ that he has no intention to use it against mankind. So, I can have positive expectations for my existence because God has positive expectations with mankind. His plans may be in favour of my own self here and now.

This means a deep relativization for the Church which was very much felt by the Catholic Church in modern times. For almost five hundred years it opposed the central meaning of justification by faith alone.[4]

For Luther's discovery of justification by faith alone the Church and the religious community as a whole is put into the second row. The Church is still very important for the gospel's presence in history, in society, in front of the state. But she is not decisive for personal salvation any more. This is decided between God and a human being personally. One may establish a good relation between God and oneself but nevertheless each one of these two partners has their own business in this process. One may work hard for the gospel's importance in earthly matters but it is basically God who has to take care for his final importance in daily life and in history. And this is also the case for the person's existence – my life is my responsibility, I cannot put God in charge neither of my personal matters nor for existential decisions of others. A person is set free by justification to take care for her own self and this person cannot be held responsible for the final result of somebody else's life – however close these persons may be. I may help somebody else but basically and finally it's his business or her business.

At the same time if I am *'simul iustus et peccator'* then it is my personal responsibility to care for the very best of my existence and to stimulate others to do the same. I have to enlarge the distance to the sinful part of my life and to close the gap to the justified mode of my existence, because God has set me free to experience faith in Christ as justification of life. Although I will never be able to overcome sin in my life, there is no reason to be pessimistic about a possible justification. This possibility alone gives me the power to look for a life in the line of God's will. It is not enough that I may develop myself – I have to do so because this is the very realm of my own powers. If I am not able to develop myself I will not be able to be useful for others. My own existence is a demonstration of my power and this demonstration is a possible locus for God's presence by justification.

So, I have to concentrate on my personal matters to improve them as much as possible – no matter how bad the living conditions may be. They can never be that bad that I cannot take advantage of them for my own sake. God is standing on my side – and this improves the conditions for my life decisively.

---

4.   And even when the Lutheran and the Catholic denominations of Christian religion found an agreement by the Joint Declaration on the Doctrine of Justification, in 1999 there was fierce opposition by German Lutheran theologians because the Official Common Statement by the Lutheran World Federation and the Catholic Church didn't agree on an essential in Luther's theology, the nature of sin in *concupiscentia*. The Catholic Church couldn't agree that concupiscence is already sin as expressed in Rom. 7.7-8. This position would give the individual human subject the central meaning on the side of man in the process of justification. The Catholic Church, eager to keep her own meaning for justification towards every human being, wanted to embody the subject in a position where sin means a sort of breaking peace with the Church which is the place of God's presence in history. In justification by faith peace with the Church is restored and for that the sacrament of penitence is so important. For a Lutheran position penitence is not put into a central position for man's inner relations with God.

It is impossible to give myself up without destroying the chance to reach the very best which is possible in my life and by which I will be judged. A person is basically responsible for her or his existence; nobody can claim that it's God who is responsible instead.

Consequently, theodicy doesn't relieve a person from his or her existence by charging God for her or his fate. The problem of theodicy charges one's own life to decide if one may still go along with God's importance for oneself – or if one has to decide it's in one's own best interest to get rid of God's existence. If God cannot be of good use in my personal suffering then I may improve my capability to take care for myself by pushing him out of my life. In this case this power to push him out is the last service God's power can provide for my personal improvement. And it may also be a help for others not yet capable to keep him out of their lives if I can demonstrate that life will be improved by No-God. By justification the relevant subject is set free to work for his or her personal progress and this may include that there is no justification by God needed for the pursuit of one's own happiness. The atheist option to deny God's existence due to the power included in it is yet another example of the positive relation between God's power and the modern subject's power.

This was of course not the intention of the Reformation's theologians but this result cannot be excluded from liberation achieved by theologies of justification. But in the midst of justification there is a chance to relativize God and especially God's power. This power has no necessary existence for modern times but a pragmatic existence. It is useful in any respect for strengthening one's own power. As soon as it is not able to deliver this empowerment it has to be relativized.

To sum up: two powers are relativized by the theological progress achieved by the thesis of justification, the Church and God. And a third power is strengthened by it – the power of the subject. In modern times God, Church and subject are combined in a sort of imbalanced trinity of power. Two of them are engaged in empowering the third one, the subject, and this subject takes all of the power it can get from the other two.

This threefold imbalanced nexus between relativization and empowering is attacked by the New Perspective on Paul. It is not re-powering the Church and it is not giving God new power to overcome any attempt to relativize his importance. It is introducing the logical relativization of the last partner in the modern trinity of power – the subject is relativized. It cannot claim any longer that everything has to be useful for it. On the contrary it is put into a position where its fate virtually depends on others. If a person cannot share God's justice to him or to her with others then the whole idea of justification will lead to bankruptcy of this person. This sharing does not rely on conditions set by this person but by the others. There are no means based on one's own subjectivity and owned by me personally which provides me with a decisive advantage before God. This is an important new clue of the New Perspective on Paul. He has discovered justification by faith in Christ under conditions set by others. This explains his resistance against a purely self-related esteem of ethnic Jews believing at the same time in Christ and to be the chosen ones above others, especially above other believers in Christ. Such a pride at the cost of others is attacked by Paul in Gal. 2 and Rom. 9.

Justification is granted by faith; it is not a result of ethnic, moral, cultural or personal specification. In the name of such justification a binary code between 'us' and 'them' has no effect. It must be overcome. Without respect for others one cannot claim to be in the realm of God's grace. Paul's theology is not simply following a grammar to decide between Law and gospel. 'The point, I repeat, if the new perspective is to be properly appreciated, is to recognize that the way by which such "attitudes", such "misunderstandings" of God's concern for the "other", the "outsider", were challenged was by means of Paul's gospel of justification, of God's acceptance, for *all* who believe, and on no other condition – not ethnicity, not colour, not race, not class, not creed, not denomination. It is crucial to the health of the churches that this aspect of Paul's doctrine of justification by faith alone be not neglected – as it has been frequently neglected in the history of Christianity, and still today in many parts of the "Christian West". There is something ironic in the fact that in pushing so hard to the more fundamental need of humankind before God, so many commentators ignore or play down the seriousness of the issue which actually brought the more fundamental point to such vital and all-consuming relevance for Paul.'[5]

From a systematic point of view, the position of that which Dunn calls 'faith', is crucial here. Faith doesn't mean a position of power before God and in relation to other human beings. It stands for a position of powerlessness in relation to others. If those who believe in Christ are embodied in the justification by the covenant of God with his people then they have no reason to exclude others from this justification simply because they are different to the Jews and to themselves. There is no advantage against others based on God's justification by Christ – not even the advantage to have the true faith. True faith in Christ leads to the due respect of God's possible justification of others on the basis of their lives and their human values. In 1 Cor. 9 Paul is using this connection as basis for his missionary strategy.

Justification by faith and not by merit has basically a social and political dimension because it empowers others and it depowers the power claims of those who believe in being justified against others. Justification by faith is a sort of relativity theory for believers in Christ. In this sense the New Perspective doesn't simply take a stand different to theologies coming out of reformation and it doesn't simply provide with hermeneutics for a 'true Paul'. It opens Paul's theology for a current problem of life and society. Systematically seen, the New Perspective is a theological theory developed in the context of a liquid modernity where theologies cannot avoid dealing with all sorts of relativizations. The contextualized character of the New Perspective is its strong point; it is not an argument against it. Therefore, Dunn can point to the social and ethnic dimension of his 'new perspective' on

5.   Dunn, *New Perspective*, p. 33.

Paul and he can deny the goal to turn around historical developments within Protestant theology: 'It [the New Perspective] does *not* set this understanding of justification by faith in antithesis to the justification of the individual by faith. It is *not* opposed to the classic Reformed doctrine of justification. It simply observes that a social and ethnic dimension was part of the doctrine from its first formulation, was indeed integral to the first recorded exposition and defence of the doctrine – "Jew first but also Greek". These are the slogans which we should use to summarise Paul's gospel – "to all who believe Jew first but also Greek", "no distinction between Jew and Greek … to all who call upon him" (Rom. 1.16; 10.12) – not the dogmatically logical "from plight to solution", still less Sanders' somewhat contrived antitheses, "from solution to plight". This is the lost theological dimension of the doctrine which needs to be brought afresh into the light, *not* to diminish the traditional doctrine, but to enrich the doctrine from its biblical roots and to recover the wholeness of Paul's teaching on the subject.'[6]

Jews and Greeks are a binary code Paul has to overcome in order to make his point against adversaries claiming that being Jews they have to separate from the Greeks in order to keep the justification God has chosen them to get access to. These Jews and Greeks are, of course, real human beings being Jews or being Greeks and they belong to the groups Paul is engaged with by his mission. But at the same time they are simply assigned to positions within Paul's theory of justification and these positions may be filled with other people or other groups. The only necessary element for the assignment is the binary code by which these groups are bound to each other within the normal order of things. By this code real justification has to be decided between two positions and only one of these two stands for it. As soon as one side is chosen the other is excluded. This coding was radically denied by Paul's theology of justification and this is the major systematic claim coming out of the New Perspective.

Whoever comes first in justification has no advantage compared to others bound to him or her by a binary code because these others may be given the same chance by God. Justification is a common ground with others before God. Relevant others are unavoidable for one's own way to come to terms with existence before God and with other human beings. Whoever these Jews and those Greeks may actually be, there is not a position 'Jew' which could be separated from the position 'Greek'. One can only get to first position in attributing the same chance of justification to the other position. Without respecting the other in the binary code the access to the position one wants to be assigned to is denied. So, one side depends on the position of the other for the final goal. This relativity is a *conditio sine qua non* for both sides.

Binary codes are not simply taxonomies for ordering problems. They are mechanisms to create power. If the position of Jew is relevant for justification then those at the position of Greek have to be excluded. Power becomes available which overpowers the Greek and for the Greek only powerlessness

6.   Dunn, *New Perspective*, p. 33.

is left. In modern times various binary codes have ruled societies, politics, culture, religions like friend–foe, left–right, black–white, male–female, barbarians–men of culture, true believers–non-believers, and so on. At least the binary code of Law and gospel as being identical with the binary code of Christians and Jews was invented by the Reformation. It was one of the major power mechanisms in the nineteenth and twentieth centuries for Christians.

In this sense the New Perspective urges us to relativize the Reformation by a new Paul which stands firmly against binary codes in terms of justification. But it is not a relativization claiming that one has to overcome Reformation. This is simply impossible. The claims are reaching out to the modern grammar for which the Reformation's opposition between believing in Law and faith in the gospel is a major example. Claims of its essential continuity with Paul are arguing that the grammar of the modern civilization must be continued. But then the New Perspective is a major obstacle. So, the debate around its theses is a struggle which way one should go for in current civilization. Without substantial respect for the other claims of singularity, we fall short of Paul's insight in the process of justification.

Something quite similar to the relativization of singularity can be observed by the other 'new perspective on Paul', the claims of new philosophies on Paul. Here, it is universality which comes under pressure.

2. The New Philosophies on Paul – A Relativization of Political Power by Powerlessness of Excluded Subjects

The New Perspective on Paul on exegetical grounds has brought a different understanding of the universality of justification. The new philosophical perspective on Paul leads to a different understanding of the importance of the human subject. It turns out to be a political statement of a special sort. But it is not the subject's power which is politically relevant. It is powerlessness subjects cannot avoid which enables them to resist against any political power. Within the new philosophies on Paul the subject's powerlessness takes the position the process of justification holds for the New Perspective on Paul. In exegetical terms the subject is relativized by respect towards the other before God – whoever this other may be in concrete history. In philosophical terms the subject is relativized by the lack of sovereignty. It is unable to be the very ground for universality claimed by political, cultural, religious ambitions and so, this inability is a cornerstone to resist political powers. These philosophies on Paul have different reasons for their arguments and they are critical against each other. But they agree on Paul as holding a firm stand against universal claims based on the sovereignty of the subject. This gives him a surprising political impact not to be expected from a theologian whose name is taken to be responsible for Rom. 13.[7]

---

7.   I rely heavily here on the excellent book by Dominik Finkelde, *Politische Eschatologie nach Paulus. Badiou-Agamben-Žižek-Santner* (Wien: Turia+Kant, 2007): for a

For Alain Badiou a mathematical theory is the starting point. He is taking up Cantor's deliberations about the infinite. For Cantor infinity is not only a potential infinity, that is, a set which is basically finite but whose fullness cannot be conceived here and now. Infinity may also be an actual infinity, that is, a set which is definitely endless and which is present as a reality here and now. In consequence to actual infinity the finitude of life may be considered not as the normal order of things but as the great exception. On the contrary, it is actual infinitude which is building up normality. The many and not the one is grounding reality, that is, the Greek hope for universality based on unity is dismissed. There is no way to avoid or overcome plurality. Every oneness is relative to the infinitude of others.

Badiou transforms this into an ontological reversal for the relation of transcendence and immanence. Transcendence as being boundless infinity is not the great exception to the normal experiences but it can break into finitude at any moment and at any place. Immanence as a set of objects of any sort is located within an infinite set of transcendence not being objectified within this set.[8] Each set, be it a numerical one, a sociological one, a political one, is grounded in a void which is a set of itself and which is part of the situation of the objectified set. This void is not conceivable within the locus of this set but it is present in an excess which is going beyond the objectified set. This void expressed by an excess from objectified finitude is the clue to singularity. Any order of things, the status of a finite set controlled by a power excluding the excess, can be relativized by void being an excess from infinity. And this relativization if it happens cannot be avoided and it cannot be controlled by the power ordering the finite set. This excess is transcending the ordered status and so, it cannot be proofed within its order. But it can be believed as a reality present at any moment and at any time. This *site de l'événement* is the locus of a novelty changing the whole situation. It has revolutionary impact.

For Badiou, the messianic event of Christ as proclaimed by Paul takes up this locus. It is pure transcendence marking real infinitude and by that it is the very source of truth. At the other side, the Jewish Law and the Greek philosophies are simply systems of order opposing transcendence or excluding its revolutionary infinitude from normality in order to preserve their powers. They cannot represent real truth because in cosmic terms they represent the exception, not the reality of infinitude. For the messianic event as being an excess necessary to wipe out the powers of normality Paul cannot rely on this philosophy or that law. He has nothing else than his subjectivity which could

new interpretation of Rom. 13, see Wright, *Paul*, pp. 59–82. Wright sees in Paul a 'counter-imperial theology' which gives God all power to overpower the empire of the state. The empire is a tool in God's hands which can be terminated as soon as God wishes to do so. Up to this point one may respect the state to avoid chaos. But the empire of the state is relativized by faith in God's justice.

8.   Alain Badiou, *Das Sein und das Ereignis* (Zürich: Diaphanes, 2005): 'Es ist folglich der nichtseiende Punkt, von dem aus begründet werden kann, dass es *eine* Präsentation des Seins gibt' (p. 59).

ground the event seen as unprecedented both by Greek philosophies and Jewish Law. This is what happens to Paul before Damascus. Here, messianic power overpowers the burden of philosophical and religious order in the mode of a founding subjectivism. For Badiou, this is a subjective gesture having unmatched power by its powerlessness. 'Paul's unprecedented gesture consists in subtracting truth from the communitarian grasp, be it that of people, a city, an empire, a territory or a social class. What is true cannot be reduced to any objective aggregate.'[9] The singularity of this gesture is the only universality possible. It resists universalism and relativism by the sudden emergence exceeding any order. 'Consequently, a universal singularity is not of the order of being, but of the order of a sudden emergence.'[10]

Badiou's idea of a universal singularity is strictly declined by Giorgio Agamben because there is no universality in Paul.[11] Nevertheless, like Badiou Agamben is using Paul as a major example for his own theory of messianic time. Its basic idea is the division of division. The code which divides the chosen people from the pagan people is divided by Paul according to Agamben. This excludes the binary mode by which one has to decide to which part the relevant object is subjected. There are Jews chosen by God's grace and there are non-Jews chosen by God's grace. The first are not living outside the Law, the second are not living within the Law, but both are included in that which grace means. They are included in that which is excluded by parting the chosen people from the pagan people. Inclusion in exclusion is Agamben's major idea in his project of *homo sacer* for which the Muselman of the Nazi death camps is a striking reality in history. Whoever is included in exclusion is revealing an alternative to the ruling order which is precarious for this order. In this sense the division of the division is bringing in resistance against the power produced by the division of the ruling order. As in the position of *homo sacer*, Agamben has to find a category resisting the ruling power of the division caused by Law and this category has to have some reality in history.

For this, Agamben might refer to Paul. Especially in Rom. 11.1-26 a third category is put into the division of am/gojim: the remnant. The division based on the Law is undercut by another division – a remnant will remain in this time 'according to the election of grace' (Rom. 11.5). This is not a finite set or a vision of the end of time. It is happening now and here as the reality of the messianic time we are living in grounded in Christ. It is the position of those who cannot identify themselves by the division am/gojim without possessing a higher position. By the remnant the binary code of am/gojim is falling apart. So, the remnant is not the great alternative. It cannot be a finite set or an assurance against the end of time. It is the site of those who cannot

9.   Alain Badiou, *Saint Paul. The Foundation of Universalism* (trans. by R. Brassier, Stanford: Stanford University Press, 2003), p. 5.

10.   Alain Badiou, *Eight Theses on the Universal*, http://www.lacan.com/badeight.htm, thesis 2.

11.   Giorgio Agamben, *Die Zeit, die bleibt. Ein Kommentar zum Römerbrief* (Frankfurt: Suhrkamp, 2006), p. 65.

be identical with themselves and who, by this non-identity, can exclude themselves from any power including them into an order ruled by its divisions. Only here, at an inclusion by exclusion, salvation is possible. It happens here and now and this is the messianic time. In this sense the remnant, living the messianic time, endures all time because it is saved by excluding the division of the Law. 'Als Rest machen wir, die Lebenden, die *en to nyn kairo* bleiben, die Rettung möglich. Als Rest sind wir ihre "Erstlingsgabe" (Röm 11,16: *aparche*), sind wir sozusagen schon gerettet: Gerade deshalb aber werden wir nur als Rest gerettet werden. Der messianische Rest überschreitet unrettbar das eschatologische Ganze, er ist das Unrettbare, das die Rettung möglich macht.'[12]

Messianic time turns time into a relativization of history. It is the time which time needs to come to its end in the sense that we terminate our idea of time. By messianic time we cannot objectify time any more. Its division into past, present, future becomes obsolete; this division is divided by messianic time and a remnant of time occurs. The time that is left transforms time into a permanent locus for the Messiah's return. Life cannot be lived any more as an existential project through past, present and future. It is no project but the time that is left to overcome the division of time. In this sense one is living in Christ. By this status something is given up and something else is given. Sovereignty of a subject in time is a fake, a mere idea but no existential reality. But this relativizes every power, such as, for example, the power of the state. Its state of the emergency is no demonstration of sovereignty but of dividing time. This division is divided in messianic time. At any moment every situation can change completely – the Messiah returns – and everything in life is changed from bottom up. No power has a lasting grip on such a subject living messianic time.

For Slavoj Žižek there is still a hidden universalistic agenda in Agamben's messianic remnant. The thirdness of this remnant in opposition to the binary code of chosen people versus pagans is yet at the same time dependent on the universalism of this code. Otherwise it couldn't function as alternative. For Žižek one cannot get the power quest out of abtract ideas and this is missing in Agamben's messianic remnant. 'Allgemeinheit ist nicht der neutrale Behälter für besondere Gestalten oder deren gemeinsames Maß und auch nicht der passive (Hinter-)Grund, auf dem die Besonderheiten ihre Schlachten austragen, sondern sie ist *diese Schlacht selbst*, der von einer zur anderen besonderen Gestalt führende Kampf.'[13] In Žižek's view the exclusion is the more important position than the remnant and by that he incorporates Agamben's view of the inclusion of the excluded. Only at the position of being excluded one can claim universality – which is, of course, a relativistic universality, that is, its claims are coming out of powerlessness and not by power. On the basis of the Nicean Creed, Žižek is taking up from Paul the

12.   Agamben, *Zeit*, p. 69.
13.   Slavoj Žižek, *Parallaxe. Aus dem Engl. von Frank Born* (Frankfurt: Suhrkamp, 2006), p. 41.

death of Christ which is missing in Badiou's philosophy. So, death and God are combined on the basis of powerlessness. Only powerlessness by sacrifice as demonstrated in Christ's death is able to give us meaning in a world without meaning and to guarantee some sort of freedom. This is Paul's most significant insight.

Christ is sacrificing his life without gift in return. By existing in Christ one is subjected to the meaning of this sacrifice and one should not expect a gift in return for this existence. In some sense a believer risks everything for nothing.[14] But this is true power – it is a power able to transform all other powers. It is almighty power. Christ is not dying at the cross to leave humanity and to come back to divinity. He is dying exactly because he is God.[15] It is an ability of divine nature to give everything for nothing. If a subject is living a life according to this kenosis it cannot be broken by other powers. In giving up sovereignty this subjectivity is a political power par excellence. Peter Paik calls it a 'Kierkegaardian conceptualization of radical politics'[16] and Paul is its role-model.

Eric Santner, the last of the new philosophers on Paul I would like to refer to,[17] is picking up Paul's existential insight in Rom. 7: 'What shall we say then? Is the law sin? God forbid. Howbeit, I had not known sin, except through the law: for I had not known coveting, except the law had said, Thou shalt not covet: but sin, finding occasion, wrought in me through the commandment all manner of coveting: for apart from the law sin is dead … For I know that in me, that is, in my flesh, dwelleth no good thing: for to will is present with me, but to do that which is good *is* not. For the good which I would I do not: but the evil which I would not, that I practise. But if what I would not, that I do, it is no more I that do it, but sin which dwelleth in me' (Rom. 7.7s.18-20). There are powers in a person's inner life and a human being is subjected to these powers. By social, political and religious institutions mankind is trying to keep these powers under control. They balance their uncanny nature by building up symbolic identities. This gives legitimacy to personal life – a sort of relief which enables human beings to work with reality. One's life looks like a 'normal life'. But at the same time these institutions create constantly excesses of meaning – 'remnants' in Santner's diction – which are uncanny and making precarious demands. They seem to be grounded in an otherness we cannot avoid and this can build up to the very big Other. This is what the Law is about and what Paul's theology is dealing with. We accept demands of this surplus in meaning by building up fantasies giving human life stability and providing it with forms to face reality. 'Fantasy organizes or "binds" the

---

14.   Ibid., p. 97.

15.   Ibid., p. 116.

16.   'The Pessimist Rearmed: Žižek on Christianity and Revolution', *Theory & Event* 8 (2005) (quoted from Finkelde, *Eschatologie* 9).

17.   Eric Santner, 'Miracles Happen: Benjamin, Rosenzweig, Freud and the Matter of the Neighbor', in Slavoj Žižek, Erich Santner and Kenneth Reinhard (eds), *The Neighbor. Three Inquiries in Political Theology* (Chicago, IL: Chicago University Press, 2005), pp. 76–134.

surplus into a schema, a distinctive "torsion" or spin that colors/distorts the shape of our universe.'[18]

But nevertheless this constantly creates uneasiness with one's own identity. You can never be sure if this symbolic identity meets the demands and if it is really one's own identity. The reason that Santner considers to be beyond these doubts is that all institutions are groundless and that they simply cover their fragility up by claiming authority. At the same time we are banned by that because we urgently need such authority to keep up legitimacy in our lives. Otherwise the whole system of symbolic forms would be in deep trouble. In modernity the lack of legitimacy in these institutions became obvious. We know that they do not deliver what they promise. Nevertheless we cannot give up the symbolic identity they provide us with. And so, we opt for keeping a 'validity without meaning'.[19] Paul's insisting that the Law is not given up by the Christ-event reflects this human condition. 'The mind is ... haunted, under the "ban" of something that profoundly matters without being a full-fledged thought or emotion.'[20] We are living in this ban without consciously fighting to be banned.

Paul's remarks about the relation of Law and sin in Rom. 7.7 are uncovering this constellation. Without Law there is no sin but we cannot claim the Law to be sin. We have to claim us to be sinner because we cannot avoid being confronted by Law. For Santner this analysis is a criticism of the ban in human condition. It is not simply the Torah which is attacked here but the symbolic identity which depends on groundless institutions claiming power and which cannot be simply left by us. It is a political act to leave the power of the institutions behind. This empowers us without giving us power. And Paul's God is a source of energy for this process because he is turning the human dependency around. His power is a counterpower to utopias of sovereignty inherent in the human condition created by groundless institutions: 'if indeed the Jewish God is a kind of Master, he is one that, paradoxically, suspends the sovereign relation'.[21]

Finkelde transforms Santner's position into a new interpretation of Paul's 'being in Christ'. His discovery that the Law is still in rule but it is not decisive any more gives Paul the chance to leave the institutions of the Jewish Law and the Hellenistic philosophy as a believer in Christ. He is not creating a new institution to replace the old ones but simply overriding any personal symbolic identity. Paul prefers to be a fool than to submit to the symbolic order of groundless institutions. 'Ein Ende des "Dramas der Legitimität" findet Paulus allein in Christus. Die permanente, ja krankmachende Suche nach Legitimität in einer illegitim bleibenden, symbolischen Schimären produzierenden Welt, scheint beendet. Letzte Legitimität erlangt das Subjekt

---

18. Eric Santner, *The Psychotheology of Everyday Life. Reflections on Freud and Rosenzweig* (Chicago, IL: Chicago University Press, 2005), p. 39.

19. Ibid.

20. Ibid.

21. Ibid., p. 27.

Paulus nur in seiner Offenheit gegenüber göttlicher Offenbarung, nicht gegenüber den Institutionen der Welt.'[22] Hence, resurrection would be a sort of exodus from the ban of a groundless symbolic identity. It could be seen as 'a release from the fantasies that keep us in the thrall of some sort of exceptional "beyond"'.[23]

These philosophies create a new Paul never seen before in theology. It is a Paul alienated from the mainstreams of the Christian religious community and of scholarly traditions. This Paul is not simply a highly respected source from the past but a contemporary in the fluid surroundings of late modernity. He is living with us and he cooperates in destruction of the subject's fictions about sovereignty which is harsh but unavoidable. This has a wide range for theology. Paul's authority is no more at hand for those who want to keep the normal religious order of Christian faith. This new Paul has a destabilizing power. Is he capable of being respected theologically?

3. From Utopia to Heterotopia –
Christian Mission in Front of the New Paul

The New Perspective on Paul and the new philosophies on Paul endanger more than simply traditions of interpretation. The Church's traditional mission is no longer backed by the greatest missionary the Church ever had if there is truth in these new views. And it is enough if there is some truth in them which indeed there is. The New Perspective brings logic to Paul's debate with Peter and the other representatives of the Christian community in Jerusalem on the one hand and his continuing support for Jewish religious positions on the other hand. The new philosophy brings forward the revolutionary power in Paul's powerless identity quest which was demonstrated in the Reformation. Whatever can be brought forward against these new views the basic shift they give to an understanding of Paul will hold. So, it would be irrational to expect that these views will perish in the near future and theology simply has to wait for that.

But then there are precarious theological consequences based on this new Paul. At least the formula 'singularity of faith in Christ plus universality of the subject longing for universal claims of Christian singularity = necessity for Christian mission towards everybody everywhere at every time' becomes very doubtful. Paul's central place for Christian mission does not support this formula.

We are used to the fact that Jesus was not only a Jew but that he is a Jew. His goal was to transform his fellow Jews, and even to call those he might have thought to be sent to 'Jews' may already be an anachronism. He certainly didn't found a different religious community in the sense of a faith essentially different from faith in Jhwh as Christian trinity is. But the Christian main

22.   Finkelde, *Eschatologie*, p. 114.
23.   Santner, *Psychotheology*, p. 30.

line holds it to be evident that Paul developed the path towards a different religious community and that this religious community thinks of herself as the true believers before God. And now the New Perspective says: 'be cautious that we Christians do not make the same mistake as Paul presented to his fellow Jews'. Paul may have been a Christian but he certainly remained a Jew – religiously and theologically. One cannot use a binary code and putting Paul in the position of the principal witness for that. His basic beliefs are issued against separation between Christ and the Jewish people. He is following an anti-binary agenda in his theology. There he firmly stood against dividing justification by an essential difference between people from Judea believing in Christ and people from the diaspora believing in Christ. Paul was even convinced that believers in Christ must be very careful in their relation to religious others not to make the same mistake he made in his Jewish life against Christians. Believing in Christ is no reason to look to others as inferior to one's own position before God – whoever these others may be. Belief in Christ is rather a reason to search for one's own sinfulness in order to overcome divisions inflicted by one's own power over others.

If Paul firmly stood against any division in terms of salvation between Jews and Christians which would put those who invent this division in a theological advantage before God, then he cannot be the mastermind of a mission to the Jews which sets the Jews in a second row before God and other people in a third, a fourth, and so on. Then the mission to the Jews is essentially an attack on the universality of the gospel whose grace is granted by God on his terms alone because this mission denies God the freedom to save them on his grounds and not on the grounds of Christian religious claims. Then a Christian mission of the Jews even proves that Christians picturing themselves as religiously superior to the other are not justified before God. They miss the very point of justification by faith alone and they look to faith as a sort of personal work. A mission which explicitly or implicitly leads to these consequences cannot refer to Paul as its role-model.

The result of the new philosophies on Paul comes close to this precarious result from a different angle. Christian mission with the goal to convince people of the salvific meaning of the gospel is addressed to individual human beings. A person is not yet converted if representatives of its own people decide to convert to Christianity – although this was for a long time the leading strategy of Christian missionaries after the striking successes with Constantine and Clovis. A person has to decide out of herself because in matters of belief Christian faith cannot accept anything else but sovereignty of the individual subject. It may be that this subject is not sovereign at all in terms of social status, political will, economic means, and so on, but before God only existential sovereignty of one's own soul can hold. You cannot believe for somebody else and nobody else can do it for you. To be a Christian means to be a self-conscious person decided on one's own grounds.

But the new philosophy on Paul says that Paul is not the chief witness for such sovereignty; on the contrary, he is a heavy critic of its modes of thought which is the main line of modern thinking, especially modern political thinking. Paul's theology gets political importance because it is a clear vote for overriding, relativizing, denouncing the possibility of such a position in front of God. Paul's theology is strengthening people by powerlessness they cannot avoid in the very centre of their existence, be it the non-normality of his or her singularity, be it an alternative time to time's usual divisions, be it a fate struck by violence or be it a devaluation of various symbolic identities. In this powerlessness Paul discovers the very key for a life of subjects able to resist powers alienating them from the very source of their personal existence. A Christian mission which favours personal sovereignty in matters of belief may be a very powerful enterprise but it cannot refer to Paul as its finest example. As in the case of justification the subject a Christian mission addresses remains an otherness who cannot be put into the powerful position this mission has at hand to convince him or her. This other continues to be a vulnerable person, subjected to all sorts of power which try and do get a hand on her existence.

Christian mission is in danger just of being another of these powers, especially when it follows a project of increasing religious power by converting people. Against such projects Paul reminds Christians that powerlessness on the side of the concrete other empowers him or her to resist that this mission gets a hold on this concrete existence. For Paul, this is backed by the same God this mission wants people to believe in. So, Paul, the greatest missionary in Christian religious history, is relativizing this mission by pointing to powerlessness at its very centre.

In both new views – the New Perspective and the new philosophy on Paul – there is a significant change for Paul's importance in Christian theology in general and especially in Christian mission. They touch on utopias bound with this mission which are using binary codes. I will mention only four. First, there is the expectation that in the end everybody will become a Christian – if not in historical time then in eschatological time. To be a Christian means the chance to be saved; not to become a Christian means not to be saved for sure. From an eschatological point of view no other religion will prevail before God than the Christian religion, because this religion is the chosen one. Second, there is the expectation that those who refuse to become Christians finally will regret this unwillingness, and this expectation is giving security for those who are already Christians and who have to suffer because of their religious conviction. Third, there is hope that even the Jews – or to put it more correctly: especially the Jews – will in the end agree that the Messiah did already come and that he was Jesus. The messianic nature of Christ does not depend on acceptance by Jews but the fate of the Jewish people finally depends on this fact. To be pro-Christ means to be pro-Messiah, and to be against Christ means to be against the Messiah. Fourth, for every human being whoever he or she may be it is the best choice to become or to be a Christian. Christian existence is the peak-point of human nature, so that to be a human being means to long implicitly for Christian existence. Christianity means humanity and to be against Christianity means to be against humanity.

Such utopias are overridden by the new Paul. Paul is rather a factor to denounce such Christian projects as obstacles for the mission of the gospel. This mission is not following binary codes but it is breaking them up. Utopias are very modern disciplinary methods which enable people and communities to accumulate power by clearly knowing which ways are wrong and who is misled. In this sense the Christian utopias for the mission of the Church have accelerated power claims by the Church and by Christian groups, not the least against the Jews in secular societies like in the assimilation of secular Jews from the eigtheenth to the twentieth century.

Paul's letters have a canonical authority. They are a *locus theologicus* for Christian theology and for the Church's official teaching. If the results of the new perspectives can be held true then this *locus theologicus* will become a precarious site for arguments. This locus is denouncing binary codes as useful tools for Christian mission. By the New Perspective and by the new philosophy on Paul, Paul's canonical letters are turned into a heterotopos. They are sites of arguments nobody in the Church and in theology can avoid but this *locus theologicus* demonstrates how much traditional missionary praxis is alienated from the beliefs these letters put into an agenda of Christian faith because this praxis needs binary codes in order to function.

Heterotopias are sites which are really there but which reveal the authority of a locus which is concealed by utopias having the power to shape the relevant order of things.[24] In this sense Paul's letters arguing against binary codes are really there and they confront Christian praxis with its constant use of such coding procedures. Heterotopias put precarious processes into action. To be confronted with one's own utopias one has to give up power claims which have dominated one's own action even in cases where one didn't want to use power. In this sense heterotopias create powerlessness. But this is the very source of the mission Paul has subjected his faith to. So, the new Paul has a liberating effect for theology, the Church and her mission. It has to take a New Perspective destroying their binary codes. This creates powerlessness for this mission, but just this powerlessness will bring it back to Paul as one of their major sources.

24.   Michel Foucault, 'Andere Räume', in *Schriften in vier Bänden. Dits et Ecrits* (Bd. 4, Frankfurt: Suhrkamp, 2005), pp. 931–42; English version: '"Different Spaces"', in M. Foucault, R. Hurley, J. D. Faubion and P. Rabinow (eds), *Aesthetics, Method, and Epistemology: Essential Works of Foucault 1954–1984* (London, 2000), pp. 175–85.

Chapter 9

Paul at the Intersection between Continuity and Discontinuity: On Paul's Place in early Judaism and Christianity as well as in Christian-Jewish Dialogue Today

Hans Hermann Henrix

In present-day theology and Christian-Jewish dialogue, some very remarkable developments can be observed. In these, questions regarding Paul have a status of their own. Paul is being situated more within the multifaceted Judaism of the Second Temple period than was the case over a long a period of time in exegetical tradition. In situating him in early Judaism and Christianity, the fundamental word is continuity. At the same time, Paul is a decisive factor of discontinuity in the two communities' process of separation, which took longer and was more complex than exegesis and theology argued for a long time. Thus a new openness for Paul has come about in Christian-Jewish dialogue, and some very remarkable Jewish statements are part of this development.

If, guided by fundamental theology, one looks at the present state of the discussion as a Catholic ecumenical theologian in particular with reference to the keyword on the 'New Perspective on Paul', the systematic theologian very soon discovers two things: 1. Systematic theology is only very gradually perceiving the systematic relevance of insights in the 'New Perspective on Paul' that are finding exegetical expression.[1] 2. The hermeneutic problem, which Phil Cunningham formulated as 'interaction that occurs between the scriptural texts and readers of today who are grappling with the radically "new situation" after the Shoah and after *Nostra Aetate*', comes to the fore.[2]

In the following attempt to discuss the systematic relevance of a few of the aspects of the current discussion on the 'New Perspective on Paul', I shall concentrate on the contributions to the 2009 Leuven colloquium,

---

1. Similarly Hans-Joachim Sander, 'Sharing God with Others or Dividing God from Powerlessness: A Late-Modern Challenge by the Heterotopian Experience of the New Paul', in this volume.

2. Cf. Philip A. Cunningham, 'Paul's Letters and the Relationship between the People of Israel and the Church Today', in this volume.

'New Perspectives on Paul and the Jews', without entirely neglecting other literature. I do not conceal the fact that I am not inclined to see symmetry in the relationship between continuity and discontinuity where 'Paul and Judaism' are concerned. My tendency is rather to assume that continuity dominates and is the foundation.[3] My own hermeneutic option is close to Phil Cunningham's approach, but will be further developed.

1. A Hermeneutic Reassurance

Just as in general, many theological voices and positions and even theologies found expression in the whole of the Christian Bible made up of the Tenach and the New Testament, so in the Pauline writings there is also a pluralism of statements about Israel, the Jews and the Torah that are in tension with one another. The exegesis of the Pauline writings has to find the meaning of each of the individual passages in itself and in its context in the respective letter. When exegesis refers to the whole body of Pauline writings, the statements in 1 Thess. 2.14-16 and Rom. 9f.; 11.1, 11, 18, 26, for example, stand out in sharp tension with one another. Their meaning for us is not already given by showing the individual biographical context of Paul and the very different situations of the community in Thessalonica and in Rome, which he is addressing. So is it necessary to look at the whole of Pauline writings, of the New Testament and finally of the entire Bible when interpreting theologically the abiding tension between Paul's two statements?[4] But what could this 'whole' be? It seems that the interpretation of Scripture as a whole can only be done by turning the old rule of interpretation, according to which the Scriptures must be *interpreted* by the Scriptures, more precisely into the instruction to *criticize* the Scriptures by means of the Scriptures. During the previous Leuven colloquium on 'Anti-Judaism and the Fourth Gospel' in the year 2000, Hendrik Hoet went in the direction of this principle with a hermeneutic assurance,[5] which linked exegesis and Christian-Jewish dialogue in a double way: the study of the New Testament calls upon every honest exegete to dialogue with Jewish colleagues, just as present-day dialogue with

3.   In its content, this thesis is close to Mark D. Nanos' 'working hypothesis that Paul was probably Torah-observant', in 'Paul's Relationship to Torah in Light of His Strategy "to Become Everything to Everyone" (1 Corinthians 9.19-23)', in this volume. The Catholic systematic theologian accepted the admonition of Michael Bachmann, a Protestant colleague and exegete, in 'Paulus, Israel und die Völker. Hermeneutische und exegetische Notizen', *Manuscript* (June 2009), 2–4, that exegetical work on details can discuss all too general evaluations.

4.   Cf., e.g., the sketch of the 'exegetical issues' in Nanos, 'Paul's Relationship to Torah'.

5.   Hendrik Hoet, '"Abraham is our Father" (John 8:39). The Gospel of John and the Jewish-Christian Dialogue', in Reimund Bieringer, Didier Pollefeyt and Frederique Vandecasteele-Vanneuville (eds), *Anti-Judaism and the Fourth Gospel. Papers of the Leuven Colloquium, 2000* (Royal Van Gorcum: Assen/Netherlands, 2001), pp. 187–201.

Jewish colleagues demands renewed study of the New Testament. Respect for Jewish companions on the way forbids every anti-Jewish interpretation of the New Testament. It forces present-day exegesis and theology to revise traditional statements, which were often marked by anti-Jewish feelings. Hoet suggests placing the text that is burdened by anti-Judaism into the 'dynamic of the Spirit' as a way out of the dilemma of any anti-Judaism found in the New Testament or nourished by the New Testament: 'Every word of the Scriptures must be understood against the horizon of the whole "dynamic" of the entire Bible. But who will define that? ... We are not looking for a canon inside the canon, which might function as a criterion of the right interpretation of the Scriptures, but we do plead for due consideration of the inner coherence of the entire Scriptures – and the coherence is the God of life and love. Does the God we get to know through the Scriptures not teach us that true and just is everything that leads to the life of all God's beloved?'[6] Hoet expresses his conviction 'that a scientific, honest and open-minded literary study of the Bible, in dialogue with Jews, Christians ... can help to trace the "dynamic" and the inner coherence of the entire Old and New Testament even better'.[7] As far as it goes, his approach is a valid attempt. Hoet finally describes the Bible's coherence and centre of meaning as follows: 'One may say that the Biblical logic reasons fundamentally in terms of family relations of father and children, of brothers and sisters: man is revealed as "God child" called to live together with those from other people's as one big family of God's children. The "logic" seems to me to be the ground of the "inner coherence" or the "dynamic" and the "spirit" of the Bible.'[8]

But could the biblical family logic with its hermeneutic function as the Bible's centre of meaning not also turn against a text such as 1 Thess. 2.14-16? Perhaps after all one must look at this more energetically. In biblical thinking, doing has priority: fulfilling the law, practising the good, love. This love contains a wisdom that has to do with fundamental respect in the face of the otherness of the Other.[9] When in the history of their interpretation, certain passages such as 1 Thess. 2.14-16 and their interpretations have led to disregard of the Other, they must be exposed to criticism. Can we deny that this is the case for the passage in the First Letter to the Thessalonians?[10] The danger that Christian exegesis and theology has a hidden latent disposition towards anti-Judaism, at times with fine ramifications, still exists. This requires a 'hermeneutics of distrust'. It can be experienced, for example, when

6.   Ibid. 196f: On further acceptance of this criterion, cf. Hans Hermann Henrix, 'Canon – Revelation – Reception', 534–48, especially 541–6.

7.   Ibid., 197.

8.   Ibid.

9.   Sander, 'Sharing God with Others', 179, expresses this in his style of language as follows: 'If a person cannot share God's justice to him or to her with others then the whole idea of justification will lead to bankruptcy of this person.'

10.   Roger Burggraeve argued analogously at the 2000 Leuven colloquium: 'Biblical Thinking As The Wisdom of Love', in Bieringer et al., *Anti-Judaism and the Fourth Gospel*, pp. 202–25, 209 on Jn 8.31-59.

statements in the New Testament that are critical of Jews and their intensified Christian interpretation are discussed in dialogue with Jewish colleagues or when they are read by them in virtual dialogue with the Christian history of interpretation. Then it is possible to encounter – as for example with Amy-Jill Levine – a Jewish way of reading that experiences a passage such as 1 Thess. 2.14-16 as a 'slap in the face'.[11]

At the 2000 Leuven colloquium, James D. G. Dunn warned not to take the issue of anti-Judaism, for example, in the gospel according to John, too lightly. The issue may not be denied or suppressed. Rather, serious work must be done on it. And this not only because it reminds us of the still virulent anti-Judaism of the Christian tradition that followed it, but also because 'it reminds us that revelation comes through dirty hands and inadequate human language, and that the all too vigorous altercations of the first century were an integral part of the emerging identity of Christianity and remain fundamental to its continuing self-understanding'.[12]

What does it mean that revelation – put harshly – came to us 'through dirty hands'? The acknowledgement of Scripture's historical conditioning and thus also of that of the Pauline texts includes the recognition of the historical conditioning of revelation, which is embodied in the texts of Scripture. Revelation cannot be separated from its historically conditioned form. It is not accessible in a 'timeless core' that can be cut out of its historical conditioning. There is no such thing as 'pure' revelation. The Bible is at one and the same time the Word of God and the word of human beings. Revelation 'plays' in the pluralism of statements within the Bible, in the 'vis-à-vis' of the biblical text and its post-biblical interpretation, in the dialogue between the canonical Scripture and the community in Judaism and Christianity that reads and lives it as canon. And in the relationship between the canonical text and the reading, studying and proclaiming community there is something other, something that is 'beyond'. The canonical text comes from 'somewhere else'; its meaning or significance has become manifest in human experience, and at the same time, it is 'broken'. This is borne out in the insight 'that revelation never happens in a straightforward way, but always takes place in and through interpretation that needs to be critically questioned, which in turn will give cause for shifting, even contradictory, interpretations'.[13]

Theologically, the efforts regarding the 'New Perspective on Paul' have a part in preparing the way for revelation to us today. Precisely through their

---

11. Amy-Jill Levine, *The Misunderstood Jew. The Church and the Scandal of the Jewish Jesus* (New York: HarperCollins, 2007), pp. 95–9: At the 2000 Leuven colloquium, Adele Reinartz spoke of the 'slap in the face' through Johannine talk about 'the Jews': '"Jews" and Jews in the Fourth Gospel', in Bieringer et al., *Anti-Judaism and the Fourth Gospel*, pp. 341–56, 341: 'in my own initial encounters this … the term "Jew" (in its Johannine use) felt like a slap in the face'.

12. James D. G. Dunn, 'The Embarrassment of History: Reflections on the Problem of "Anti-Judaism" in the Fourth Gospel', in Bieringer et al., *Anti-Judaism and the Fourth Gospel*, pp. 47–67, 66.

13. Burggraeve, 'Biblical Thinking as the Wisdom of Love', 213.

critical objection against conventional perspectives in interpreting Paul, they draw attention to an 'inappropriate human language' and perhaps also to the 'dirty hands', through which revelation came.[14] This must be kept in mind.

2. *'Call rather than Conversion' – Continuity's Fundamental Category*

In his enlightening outline of the emergence of Jewish interest in Paul, Daniel Langton draws attention to the fact that Robert Travers-Herford drew a parallel between the rabbinic story of the stubborn Gehazi, whose master visits Damascus in order to bring him back on the right path, and the report on the 'conversion' of Paul to Christianity in Damascus.[15] By speaking of the apostle Paul's experience close to Damascus as 'conversion', Travers-Herford corresponds with a broad consensus in Christian understanding of Paul. The three reports in the Acts of the Apostles on Paul's experience outside of Damascus (Acts 9.1-19; 22.4-16; and 26.9-19), as well as Paul's own description of it in Gal. 1.11-17, have generally been read under the title 'conversion'. This word normally characterized Paul's experience as a change of religion from 'Judaism' to 'Christianity'. It was said that Paul turned away from 'Judaism', turned his back on it, and turned towards a different religion, Christianity. And in fact, the event that has been transmitted does testify to a dramatic change: the Jew Saul is so attached to his Jewish faith that he zealously persecutes those who believe in Christ, for which his agreement to the killing of Stephen, mentioned in the Acts of the Apostles (Acts 8.1) stands, as does his intention to persecute those in Damascus who believe in Christ (Acts 9.1-2). The nature of the Damascus experience as Paul's being suddenly overwhelmed seems to justify even more understanding it as 'conversion'.

And yet, in a whole chapter precisely on the Damascus experience, entitled antithetically as 'Call rather than Conversion', Krister Stendahl, who prepared the way and opened up the 'New Perspective on Paul', corrects what 'we often think we hear or recognize in Paul'.[16] According to Stendahl, if one reads the reports mentioned more closely one discovers 'a greater continuity between "before" and "after". Here is not that change of "religion" that we commonly associate with the word *conversion*. Serving the one and same God, Paul receives a new and special calling in God's service to bring his message to the nations. All the reports emphasize this commission, not the

14.   Nanos, 'Paul's Relationship to Torah', draws attention to this in his constant argument around ethical problems in the dominant interpretation of Paul in 1 Cor. 9.19-23.

15.   David Langton, 'Some Historical Observations Regarding the Emergence of a Jewish Interest in the Apostle Paul and its Relation to Christian Pauline Scholarship', (unpublished manuscript), 1 (the rabbinic story can be found in Sotah 47a and Sanhedrin 107b).

16.   Krister Stendahl, *Der Jude Paulus und wir Heiden. Anfragen an das abendländische Christentum*, (München: Kaiser, 1978), p. 17; the chapter 'Eher Berufung als Bekehrung' ['Call rather than Conversion']: pp. 17–37.

conversion. Rather than being "converted", Paul was called to the specific task – made clear to him by his experience of the risen Lord – of apostleship for the Gentiles, one hand-picked through Jesus Christ on behalf of the one God of Jews and Gentiles.'[17] In his exegetical study of Paul's report of his call in Gal. 1.13-16, Stendahl draws attention to the fact that the apostle describes his experience, for example with the phrase about his having been chosen 'from his mother's womb', in 'concepts belonging to a prophetic vocation' in Isaiah (49.1 and 6) and Jeremiah (1.5). Just as there is no break in the prophetic vocation, the Damascus experience does not give rise to a break from 'Judaism' in Paul. The concept of conversion stands for the break and the mode of thinking where a change of religion is concerned. For Thomas Blanton, the model of 'conversion to Christianity' is linked to polemic against Judaism, from which he firmly excludes Paul in his analysis of the Second Letter to the Corinthians.[18] So instead of a break and a change of religion, there is with Paul 'a great continuity between "before" and "after"'. Together with Stendahl, I believe that calling the Damascus experience 'call/vocation' rather than 'conversion' is an appropriate short phrase that expresses the fundamental flow of continuity which is there, even with all the drama and change that this event and its consequences contain.[19]

Nevertheless, in his very perspicacious contribution, 'Salvation in Paul's Judaism', Michael F. Bird spoke of a 'pre-conversion life in pharisaic Judaism' and thought: 'His conversion was, in its immediate setting, a transference from one Jewish sect to another.'[20] And in what follows, he again returns to the concept of 'conversion'.[21] However, Bird does not use the term 'conversion' in an uninhibited way that lacks all questions, but rather rejects its possible misunderstanding in the sense of a complete discontinuity; he speaks of 'a transference from one Jewish sect to another'. And he precedes his study of

17. Ibid., p. 18.
18. Thomas R. Blanton, 'Paul's Covenantal Theology in 2 Cor. 2.14–7.4', in this volume, particularly p. 69, footnote 26.
19. Langton, 'Some Historical Observations', draws attention to Leo Baeck who in his understanding of Paul also rejected calling the Damascus event 'conversion': 'In general, one speaks of Paul's conversion. But this expression is insufficient. What happened in Paul's life was not a conversion in the usual sense of the word, but rather a revolution, a transformation': Leo Baeck, *Paulus, die Pharisäer und das Neue Testament* (Frankfurt am Main: Ner-Tamid Verlag, 1961), pp. 7–37 (= *Der Glaube des Paulus*, 1952), 9. In analogy to Stendahl, the German New Testament scholar Josef Blank explained Gal. 1.15f. 'within the category of "prophetic vocation"', and he considered it to be 'problematic to speak of the "conversion" of Paul and to place this aspect unilaterally in the forefront'. He continued: 'Paul did not convert from lack of faith to faith, he was not an unbeliever ... nor did he convert from an immoral way of life to a moral way of life; Paul was not a bad, immoral human being; it is not even possible to say that he converted from Judaism to Christianity, because at that time, Christianity did not yet exist as an independent reality separate from Judaism.' Josef Blank, 'Paulus – Jude und Völkerapostel. Als Frage an Juden und Christen', in Markus Barth et al., *Paulus – Apostat oder Apostel? Jüdische und christliche Antworten* (Regensburg: Pustet, 1977), pp. 147–72, 152.
20. Michael F. Bird, 'Salvation in Paul's Judaism?' in this volume.
21. Ibid.

Paul's identity and of the socio-religious place of the Pauline communities with the question that needs to be clarified: 'In his conversion/call did Paul simply shift from a pharisaic sect to a messianic sect *within Judaism*, or has he now been dislocated, religiously and socially, *from Judaism?*'[22] Bird speaks at the same time of 'conversion' and 'call'. He considers the apostle's biography to be 'a matter of seismic changes in personal identity'. For him, Paul's identity underwent significant transformations in thought, and yet Bird does not deny continuity. For he notes, 'that the new identity is continuous with his Israelite ancestry', to which of course he immediately adds, 'but also consciously distinct from it'.[23] I understand Bird as meaning that for him the continuity remains important; but I doubt that it is also an (asymmetrical) fundamental category for him. And calling the Damascus event 'vocation/call' rather than 'conversion', stands for continuity as a fundamental category.

3. A Jewish Missionary to the Nations – Discontinuity in Continuity

John Pawlikowski sums up the understanding of the Pauline vocation as follows, referring thereby to his Chicago colleague Robin Scroggs' important research results: 'The Pauline missionary movement, as Paul understood it, was a Jewish mission which focused on the Gentiles as the proper object of God's call to his people.'[24] One could apply Paul's declaration of intention for redemption through Jesus Christ in Gal. 3.14 to his apostolic service: 'in order that in Christ Jesus the blessing of Abraham might come to the Gentiles'. Paul is called to go to the gentiles and to announce to them that they are included in the 'salvation of the people of God'. His apostolate is characterized by the 'inclusion in the community of salvation' of the gentiles. According to Michael Bachmann, the gentiles should 'be included in the community of salvation precisely as non-Jews'.[25] Paul is the 'apostle of the Gentiles; in the Letter to the Romans, he speaks of his obligation to both, to Greeks and to Barbarians, but in fulfilling this obligation, he is very conscious of the Jews and of their role in God's plan (Rom. 1.14-16). In the Acts of the Apostles, a programmatic picture is drawn of the Jew Paul, the former

---

22. Ibid. Similarly, Thomas Söding also vacillates between conversion and call/vocation: 'Ich lebe, aber nicht ich, ...' (Gal. 2.19). 'Die theologische Physiognomie des Paulus', *Communio: Internationale katholische Zeitschrift* 38 (2009), 119–34, 133: 'Paul looks back (2 Cor. 4) to the vision of Damascus ... but he characterizes his conversion and vocation in such a way that all Christians' formative insight of faith can be mirrored in it.' Similarly, Jens Schröter, 'Paulus in der Apostelgeschichte', *Communio: Internationale katholische Zeitschrift* 38 (2009), 135–48, 138, uses both 'conversion' and 'vocation' and says in a note: '"Conversion" and "vocation" mean two perspectives of this event, which must not be played out against one another' (146).

23. Bird, 'Salvation in Paul's Judaism?'.

24. John T. Pawlikowski, 'A Christian-Jewish Dialogue Model in Light of New Research on Paul's Relationship with Judaism,' in this volume.

25. Michael Bachmann, 'Paul, Israel, and the Gentiles'.

Pharisee, who brings the Gospel to the world of the Gentiles, and this only ends when Paul reaches Rome, the center of power of the Gentile world.' Paul is interested above all 'in ensuring the rights of the Gentile converts to be entirely and truly heirs of God's promises to Israel. Their rights are based solely on faith in Jesus Christ.'[26] His 'apostolate for the Gentiles' means that he was called and chosen by Jesus Christ for the sake of the one God of Jews and gentiles. This apostolate was carried by the 'conviction that the Gentiles become part of God's people without having to pass through the Law. This is Paul's secret revelation and his knowledge.'[27] Stendahl even sees in the change of name from Saul to Paul – often cited in favour of understanding the Damascus event as a 'conversion' – an indication of Paul's apostleship to the gentiles. The call outside of Damascus is not what triggered the change of name. Rather, the report in Acts 13 about the conflict with a magician who passed himself off as a prophet by the name of Bar Jesus/Elymas before the Roman proconsul Sergius Paulus of Cyprus, combines the two names when verse 9 says: 'But Saul, also known as Paul, filled with the Holy Spirit ... said'. From this event on, the apostle is always called Paul in the Acts of the Apostles, and this name accompanies him on his further journey of bringing the gospel from Jerusalem to Rome. For Stendahl the change of name symbolizes 'this move of the focal point ... From now on, Rome is the "magnet"'.[28] And Rome stands for the world of the gentiles.

Paul is a missionary for Jesus Christ because he recognized the God of Israel, 'his' God, working in the Christ event, and in fidelity to this God of Israel, he proclaimed the gospel to the gentiles as an 'Israelite'.[29] He did this in 'Jewish categories'.[30] Thus Phil Cunningham and Michael Bird have good reason to formulate Paul's call/vocation and task as that of the 'Jewish Apostle to the gentiles' and the 'Jewish Christian Apostle of Jesus Christ to the gentiles'.[31]

4. Law or Torah and Christ – An Antithesis in Paul's Writing?

The letters of the 'Jewish Apostle to the Gentiles' are so full of tension that – as Michael Bachmann soberly notes – even in the discussion under the title of 'New Perspective on Paul' no 'far reaching consensus' has been reached. Something analogous can also be said about the contributions to the 2009 Leuven colloquium. On the one hand, for example, Michael Bird in his contribution, after all his underlining of Paul's continuity with

---

26.   Stendahl, *Der Jude Paulus und wir Heiden*, pp. 10–11.
27.   Ibid., p. 20.
28.   Ibid., 23; similarly Schröter, 'Paulus in der Apostelgeschichte', p. 137.
29.   Karl-Wilhelm Niebuhr, 'Paulus im Judentum seiner Zeit. Der Heidenapostel aus Israel in "neuer Sicht"', *Communio: Internationale katholische Zeitschrift* 38 (2009), 108–118, 111.
30.   Franz Mußner, *Traktat über die Juden*, (München: Kösel, 1979), p. 235.
31.   Cunningham, 'Paul's Letters', and Bird, 'Salvation in Paul's Judaism?'.

Judaism ultimately marks quite strongly the discontinuity. He offered an interpretation of 2 Cor. 3 and of Rom. 10.4 according to which he believes it to be obvious 'that Paul emphasized the discontinuity between the epochs of Christ and Torah/Moses'.[32] Indeed, between the two, the 'antithesis' reigns, so that the statement in the Letter to the Romans saying that *telos gar nomou Christos* 10.4 must be understood as the end of the Law. On the other hand, Michael Bachmann presented a Pauline result with a very different emphasis. According to him, the appearance of the concept of *nomos* 118 times in the *corpus paulinum* certainly does include harsh comments criticizing the Law and without question statements on the Law that are not positive. But with all that, Paul also speaks very positively about the Mosaic Law, so that the often expressed impression of a 'radical criticism of the Law' is not in accord with the Pauline statements themselves. According to Bachmann, Paul is not talking about 'complete "freedom from the Law"'. 'There is no question' regarding the emphasis in Rom. 10.4 on 'the Christ event', but for Bachmann this can 'hardly be translated as the "end/ending of the Law"'; instead, Paul is talking about a teleological reality, so that Christ (is) rather to be understood as 'the goal of the Law'.[33]

Mark Nanos' contribution to Paul's understanding of the Law and the Torah is full of pathos when he says that an antithesis exists neither between the Torah and Jesus nor between the Torah and Paul. Right at the beginning he says: 'The traditional and almost undisputed answer is that he renounced Torah-observance for disciples of Christ – except to imitate Jewish behaviour to evangelize among Jews. Yet to me it seems more logical that a Jew, such as Paul claims to be (2 Cor. 11.22; Phil. 3.5-6), who is seeking to convince fellow Jews as well as gentiles to turn to Jesus as the one representing the ideals and promises of Torah, would uphold the quintessential basis of that message, that is, he would observe Torah (cf. Rom. 1.1-5; 3; 9.32–11.36; 15.8-9; 1 Cor. 15.1-28; Gal. 3.19; 5.14).'[34] And Nanos develops this position, saying that he considers interpreting the phrase, 'I have become all things to all people', in 1 Cor. 9.22 in the sense of a 'rhetorical adaptability' to be a better solution.

Not only the positive statements in Rom. 13.9f. or Gal. 5.13f. alluding to the commandment to love, give Bachmann as well reason to see it as problematic when exegetical understanding considers Paul's criticism of the Law to be a 'call to (complete) "freedom from the law"'.[35] Bachmann understands the passage in Gal. 3.19f., that is often cited as a radical criticism

32. Ibid.
33. Bachmann, 'Paul, Israel, and the Gentiles'.
34. Nanos, 'Paul's Relationship to Torah'. Analogously, Sander, 'Sharing God with Others', can say: 'The New Perspective brings logic to Paul's debate with Peter and the other representatives of the Christian community in Jerusalem on the one hand and his continuing support for Jewish religious positions on the other hand.'
35. The same understanding can be found with Nanos, 'The Myth of the "Law-Free" Paul Standing Between Christians and Jews': www.marknanos.com/Myth-Lawfree-12-3-08. pdf (10 December 2008), p. 6, when he speaks of 'the ideals of Torah that Paul upholds to be central, the love of one's neighbor as oneself (Lev. 19:18; Rom. 13:8; Gal. 5:14)'.

of the Law by Paul, contextually in the sense that it is the 'one' God who causes 'the Christ event as well as the law, and since according to v. 8 the Christ event ... applies to "all nations", the God of the Law (or of the legislation) is at the same time the God of the whole world'. What Bachmann says is thereby in accordance with the fact that God's oneness is also the basis for Paul's proclamation.[36] Of course, the Law that came from the one and only God cannot give life, which the Christ event can (Gal. 2.1f.).[37] Bachmann sums up his results on the concept of *nomos* by saying: 'The term *nomos* is normally really not used negatively by Paul. But the Christ event makes it possible to see that being convinced that the Law itself can transmit "life" is an illusion ... On the other hand, the Christ event (which somehow has to do with the love of Jesus (see e.g. Gal. 2.20) leads to the Christians loving correspondence with the Torah – at least that is what Paul thinks! (see again e.g. Gal. 5.13f.).'[38] In his detailed examination of the Pauline phrase *erga nomou*, in the context of which Paul speaks of the commandment of circumcision, Bachmann also comes to this result. The negative connotation of this phrase aims at not imposing upon gentiles or gentile Christians rules such as that of circumcision. 'It is precisely not a condition for inclusion in the community of salvation that such halakhot be accepted by non-Jews and thus also not that non-Jews become Jews. The condition is rather Christ alone or faith in Christ (cf. e.g. Gal. 2.16f.).' Bachmann distinguishes very firmly between the halakhot mentioned as rules or ritual regulations in the sense of 'boundary markers', and doing, so that he sums up his thinking on the Pauline understanding of 'justification' as follows: '"Justification" does not demand of gentiles or Gentile-Christians the acceptance of Jewish "boundary markers", as if these also applied to non-Jews; inclusion in the community of salvation does not go by way of the detour of halakhically regulated inclusion in Judaism and is in this respect universally possible.'[39]

Bachmann's situating the Law and Christ does not turn their position towards one another into an 'antithesis' but rather, with all clear distinction, also emphasizes proximity and positivity between the Law or the Torah and Christ. For a Catholic ecumenical theologian, this position brings to mind a current discussion which began with the Jesus book by Pope Benedict XVI.

After causing irritations in the Catholic-Jewish relationship through his 2008 Good Friday prayer and the decree lifting the excommunication of the auxiliary bishops of the Society of Pius X, Pope Benedict in his book *Jesus of*

---

36.   On this, cf. Hans Hermann Henrix, *Gottes Ja zu Israel. Ökumenische Studien christlicher Theologie* (Berlin, Aachen: Institut Kirche und Judentum, 2005), pp. 103–20 (= 'Für uns der einzige Gott, der Vater ... und der einzige Kyrios Jesus Christus' [1 Kor 8,6]. Zur christlichen Rede von Gott und Jesus Christus), as well as Hubert Frankemölle, *Frühjudentum und Urchristentum. Vorgeschichte – Verlauf – Auswirkungen* (4. Jahrhundert v.Chr. bis 4. Jahrhundert n. Chr.), (Stuttgart: Kohlhammer, 2006), pp. 286–9.

37.   Bachmann, 'Paul, Israel, and the Gentiles'.

38.   Ibid.

39.   Ibid.

Nazareth has a literary dialogue with Rabbi Jacob Neusner.[40] The subject of this dialogue is the Sermon on the Mount. For the Pope, 'the majority of the Sermon on the Mount (Mt. 5.17–7.27)' after the 'programmatic introduction by the Beatitudes ... gives so to speak the Messiah's Torah' (p. 132). 'The title and interpretative key' to this Torah of the Messiah is 'a word that surprises us over and over again and that clearly and unequivocally states God's fidelity to God's own self and the fidelity of Jesus to the faith of Israel: "Do not think that I have come to abolish the law or the prophets; I have come not to abolish but to fulfil ..." (Mt. 5.17-19)' (p. 133). In the first part of his conversation with Neusner on the question regarding the Sabbath, the Pope explains what the expression concerning the Sermon on the Mount as Torah of the Messiah means. Here the Pope first corrects a misunderstanding that has often come up, as if by his saying that 'the Sabbath exists for man and not man for the Sabbath', Jesus had 'broken open a blinkered legalistic praxis and given instead a more generous and liberated view' (p. 138). In the conflict around the Sabbath, the issue is 'not a form of morality, but rather a highly theological, or to say it more precisely, a Christological text' (p. 142). Benedict is brought to this result by Neusner's sharp objection to seeing Jesus taking 'the place of the Torah'. Benedict picks up Neusner's objection: 'With this, the real core of the conflict is laid bare. Jesus understands himself as the Torah – as the Word of God in person' (p. 143). And picking up both Matthew's word, 'Here is something greater than the temple' (Mt. 12.6, p. 140), and that of Neusner, Pope Benedict speaks of Jesus' claim 'to be himself the Torah and the Temple in person' (p. 144). He takes up other expressions concerning Jesus as Torah from his dialogue with Jacob Neusner and seems to be en route, so to speak, to an unusual key category or even to a new title for Christ: 'the living Torah of God' (p. 206), or 'Jesus is the Torah itself' (p. 364). When Benedict says that 'Jesus sees himself as the Torah', and when he reaffirms his statement by adding, '– as the Word of God in person', his statement is transparent in view of the 'mighty prologue to the Gospel according to John' (p. 143). By calling Jesus Christ the 'Torah in person', the 'living Torah of God' or the 'Torah itself' – one could also speak of the Torah incarnate – Benedict traced a path that should be continued in theological discussion, if it is to be kept free of positions of substitution and supersessionism. Thus, when confronted with the fact that Rom. 9–11, for example, does not appear in Pope Benedict's book on Jesus, one must examine whether the characterization of Jesus Christ as the Torah in person is close to Pauline statements. But one must also assess whether this characterization contains a potentially critical question to exegesis, theology and the Church. Over and beyond that, reflection on soteriology could raise

---

40.   Joseph Ratzinger/Benedikt XVI., *Jesus von Nazareth. Erster Teil von der Taufe im Jordan bis zur Verklärung* (Freiburg: Herder, 2007); the Pope's conversation with Jacob Neusner and his book, *Ein Rabbi spricht mit Jesus. Ein jüdisch-christlicher Dialog* (München: Herder, 1997), is on pages 131–60. The passages quoted from it will be indicated in the text in parentheses.

the question whether the Christian certainty is correct in believing that Jewish life according to Israel's Torah stands under God's blessing and is thus salvific, which would raise theological questions as regards 'mission towards the Jews'. Here, let me simply allude to the theological *opinio* that in further reflection on Jesus Christ as the living Torah and on Paul's championing for hope as regards Israel, it seems possible to justify this, particularly based on the Letters to the Galatians and the Romans.[41]

5. Jesus Christ as the 'Torah in Person': A Systematic Characterization in Proximity to Paul?

Understanding Jesus Christ as 'living Torah', as the 'Torah in person', contains a statement about continuity with Israel, about the abiding reference to Israel. For the Torah is Israel's Torah, which the God of Israel entrusted and gave to his chosen people Israel as his covenantal partner. At the same time, a markedly christological finality is inscribed into the Torah, which in its content is close to Rom. 10.4, where Paul – thus with Michael Bachmann – speaks of Christ with a teleological tendency as the 'goal of the law'.[42] In his contribution, Mark Nanos not only recapitulated the Pauline understanding of Jesus as the 'goal' of the Torah – agreeing exegetically (as a Jewish exegete), not as a profession of faith; he also alluded indirectly to Rom. 10.4 and spoke of Jesus 'as the one representing the ideals and promises of Torah'.[43] In characterizing Jesus Christ as the 'Torah in person', one can hear a call that is influenced by Paul.

What the Jewish interpreter Mark Nanos sees as exegetically possible based on Paul, is alarming to Jacob Neusner in his exegesis of the relationship between Jesus and the Torah in the gospel according to Matthew. For Neusner sees Jesus taking the place of the Torah and standing at the height of God in the Sermon on the Mount. Pope Benedict uses this Jewish way of reading the Jesus of Matthew by taking it up affirmatively: Jesus has the authority of the Torah and of the giver of the Torah. His Torah is the 'Torah of the Messiah'. Jesus as the Torah become a person may 'interpret the Mosaic order of God's commandments in such a radically new way as only the lawgiver – God himself – does' (148). It is a new interpretation, the transmission of which to the gentiles was the subject of 'the conflict between Paul and the so-called Judaists' (150). The Pope supports its right to this by quoting Paul in Gal. 5.13: 'You are called to freedom' (151). For those who follow Jesus, 'the search for the will of God in communion with Jesus is an orientation' in understanding and living the teachings of the Torah of Moses (cf. 152).

41. Hans Hermann Henrix, 'The Son of God became a Human Being as a Jew. On Taking the Jewishness of Jesus Seriously for Christology' (as yet unpublished manuscript) examines in what way this title should be taken up in soteriological discussion.
42. Bachmann, 'Paul, Israel, and the Gentiles'.
43. Nanos, 'Paul's Relationship to Torah'.

Communion with Jesus then brings clearly into view the 'word that surprises us over and over again and that clearly and unequivocally states God's fidelity to God's own self and the fidelity of Jesus to the faith of Israel: "Do not think that I have come to abolish the law or the prophets; I have come not to abolish but to fulfill ..." (Mt. 5.17-19)' (133). According to Paul this would mean that he who was born of a woman is 'subject to the law' (Gal. 4.4). Thus we may understand the characterization of Jesus Christ as the 'Torah in person' in proximity to important fundamental Pauline statements.

6. *Jesus Christ as the Torah Incarnate – A Title Critical of Tradition*

The characterization of Jesus as the Torah in person, which seems to be a title, means positively that Jesus fulfilled the Torah of God, that he was a son of Israel who faithfully adhered to the Torah, and that the Torah became incarnate in him and has its 'goal' in him. Over and beyond this central positive content, however, the title also has considerable critical significance. For it shows the problematic nature of a tradition in theology and the Church that was and is in danger of a persistent or fundamental 'no' to Israel's Torah, not least through recourse to Paul. This is not only the danger of a proclamation and a theology with slogans like 'freedom from the law' and a 'Torah-free' gospel when these are exaggerated and turned into a radical antithesis. It is also the danger of a relative lack of relationship, which separates Jesus and the Torah by saying that the Torah belongs to the Jews, Jesus to the Christians.

Thomas Aquinas could acknowledge, '*lex vetus manifestabat praecepta legis naturae*', in other words, that the old law contains natural law; but 'the old law' is only valid insofar as it belongs to natural law; however, the supplements in the 'old law' that go beyond natural law and are not imposed upon the other nations for their observance are only binding for the Jewish people and aim at preparing it for the coming of Christ; with the coming of Christ, these laws are dead, and for Christians they even bring death (cf. *Summa theologica* 1/II q. 98,5; q. 103,4 or 104,3).[44] A long position in theology and the Church corresponds with Aquinas' position, which only acknowledged the Torah as God's teaching insofar as it was of a universal nature. In such a tradition, the Decalogue was not qualified as God's teaching because it was God's teaching from Sinai to Moses and his people, but because it is in accord with natural law. However, not only the Decalogue's relationship to revelation and its nature as a document and seal of the Sinai covenant were thereby forfeited, but also its relationship to Jesus as a follower of the Torah and of the Decalogue. The theological

---

44. For the discussion on this position cf., e.g., Klaus Müller, *Tora für die Völker. Die noachidischen Gebote und Ansätze zu ihrer Rezeption im Christentum* (Berlin: Institut Kirche und Judentum, 1994), pp. 210–13, as well as Michael Wyschogrod, *Abraham's Promise. Judaism and Jewish-Christian Relations* (Grand Rapids, MI: Eerdmans, 2004), p. 208.

understanding of Jesus Christ as the Torah in person claims precisely this relationship between Jesus and the Torah.

Thus, understanding Jesus as the Torah in person does not work as an uncritical connecting motive. For it not only stands critically against a tradition of separation between Jesus and the Torah. It also challenges the present-day Christian-Jewish encounter to clarify the understanding of Torah. The discussion around the 'New Perspective on Paul' applies not least to this question. The scope of that discussion on how *nomos* is to be understood was already mentioned. And I cannot conceal that what Michael Bird said about 'Paul's matrix of ... Torah-free gentile mission'[45] does not quite convince me. Here, the weight of Mark Nanos' objection against a 'Torah-free lifestyle' in Paul's writing should be given greater attention. And here I feel closer to Michael Bachmann's recourse to the positive statements in Rom. 13.9f. or Gal. 5.13f., which allude to the commandment to love and which call upon Christians to be in 'loving correspondence with the Torah'. His theocentric way of reading Gal. 3.19-22 in view of the one and only God who 'caused the Christ event as well as the law' also seems to me to have an affinity with talk of Christ as the Torah in person. Circumcision is thereby not imposed on the Christians from among the gentiles, and 'non-Jews becoming Jews' is not made a condition.

The Torah is impressed upon Christians and their Church by their Jesus Christ according to Mt. 5.17f., but according to Rom. 13.9f. and Gal. 5.13f., it is also suggested to them paraenetically by the Jewish apostle to the gentile Paul. Perhaps one could say: just as the written Torah is mediated to the Jewish people through the oral Torah of the Talmud, the Torah is mediated to the Church through Jesus and his apostle Paul. Paul Van Buren hints at this idea in an inversion of the argument: 'we could say that the story of Jesus is the church's Talmud that takes us to Torah. That is why the church can recite the Shema, for Jesus teaches the church to love the Lord our God with all its heart and strength, and to love the neighbor as oneself.' Because he takes Jesus seriously as teacher of the Torah, Paul Van Buren comes to the ecclesiological conclusion: 'The connection between the Torah and the church is and should be fundamental, because Christians can never relate to the real, the living Jesus without the Torah. A Jesus apart from Torah is not the real Jesus ... but a figment of pious imagination. Set the church adrift from Torah and you set the church adrift, not merely from its foundations in Israel, but adrift from its foundation in Jesus Christ. The future for the church, if it is to have a future as the church of the God and Father of Jesus Christ, lies in its discovering, precisely as Gentiles and not Israel, the priority of the Torah and so of its Old Testament in its liturgy and for life, and so of its learning to re-read its New Testament always in the light of the Old Testament.'[46] In his conclusion from a Pauline point of view, Michael Bachmann for his part

---

45. Bird, 'Salvation in Paul's Judaism?'.

46. Paul Van Buren, 'Torah, Israel, Jesus, Church – Today': http://www.jcrelations.net/en/?item=791.

maintains as ecclesiologically relevant: 'Paul does not understand the Church (of God) as something anti-Jewish; rather, it comes into being in Judaism and out of Judaism, and is thus according to him something like a universalization of the Jewish people – in any case, a more universal reality, which for this reason is precisely not bound to Jewish "boundary markers", to *erga nomou*. Aside from these regulations, the ethical stimulus of the Law of Moses as well remains with the Christ event and the love of neighbour connected with it, at least in principle.'[47] The all too pithy talk of a Torah-free gospel in theology and the Church must be countered with this.

7. Conclusion

Through their thoughts on the more Johannine characterization of Jesus Christ as the Torah in person, these reflections in the context of the 'New Perspective on Paul' seemed rather to lead away from Paul. However, in actual fact, the exegetical discussion of Paul gave rise to them and in their own way, they looked at the issue of continuity and discontinuity between Judaism and Christianity that is discussed in that context. They emphasized the weight of continuity without denying that Paul also was a decisive factor of discontinuity in the drawn-out process of separation between the two communities. To express this, John Pawlikowski used the appealing sentence: 'With Paul I would want to argue for significant "newness" in the revelation in Christ.'[48] Thus Paul represents the double reality of continuity and separation between the Church and Judaism. The discussion of the 'New Perspective on Paul' shows clearly that Paul's separation from Judaism was sharpened by a questionable exegesis of Paul in history and tradition. This sharpening must be corrected and overcome. And Paul gives double support to saying that the separation of those who differ must in no case become rigid as constitutive enmity: first of all through his repeated warning to the Christian community against boasting, not least in the face of Israel, out of which Phil Cunningham in particular spoke;[49] and then through his admonition in Rom. 13.9f. or Gal. 5.13f. to really live the commandment of love, which is the main point of the Torah. What certainly applies to the individual Christians has its own relevance for their Churches. In connecting the 'new perspective and the new philosophy on Paul', Hans-Joachim Sander thought about this not least from the point of view of the theology of mission and came thereby to the following surprising thesis that also merits agreement: 'If Paul firmly stood against any division in terms of salvation between Jews and Christians which would put those who invent this division in a theological advantage before God then he cannot be the mastermind of a mission to the Jews which sets the Jews in a second row before God and other people in a third, a fourth, and

47.   Bachmann, 'Paul, Israel, and the Gentiles'.
48.   Pawlikowski, 'A Christian-Jewish Dialogue Model'.
49.   Cunningham, 'Paul's Letters'.

so on. Then the mission to the Jews is essentially an attack on the universality of the gospel whose grace is granted by God on his terms alone because this mission denies God the freedom to save them on his grounds and not on the grounds of Christian religious claims. Then a Christian mission of the Jews even proves that Christians picturing themselves as religiously superior to the other is not justified before God. They miss the very point of justification by faith alone and they look to faith as a sort of personal work. A mission which explicitly or implicitly leads to these consequences cannot refer to Paul as its role-model.'[50] In other words: all of us and all of our communities are on probation where our practice of the ethics of the Torah's main point is concerned; and at the same time, in relation to this lived probation, Paul's 'justification through faith alone' is always an 'over and beyond'.

(Translated by Sr Dr Katherine Wolff nds, Kiryat Yearim/Israel.)

50.   Sander, 'Sharing God with Others': Along with the literature cited by Sander on the philosophy regarding Paul, cf. particularly Gregor Maria Hoff, 'Die paulinische Inversion. Die dekonstruktiven Paulus-Lektüren Slavoy Žižeks und Giorgio Agambens', *Communio: Internationale katholische Zeitschrift* 38 (2009): 179–90.

EPILOGUE

James D. G. Dunn

It was a great sadness to me that my house removal from Durham to Chichester and the attendant ramifications made it impossible for me to join the conference on 'Paul and Judaism'. The invitation by Reimund Bieringer to contribute an 'Epilogue' both increased the regret that I had been unable to participate more directly and helped to assuage it. The above chapters no doubt give a good feel for the vibrancy and interaction of the conference itself and leave me somewhat tantalized over the contribution I might have made in person, and whether it might have added much of value to the conference and its outcome.

In reading the essays several issues became immediately obvious, several of them taken up in more than one essay. Perhaps the most useful contribution I can make to the project at this epilogical stage is to take up these same issues and to comment on them briefly. Most of the comments are on the need for a greater nuancing in formulation of the issues, with the hope that a greater sensitivity to what Paul actually wrote will at least sometimes point the way to a more positive handling of the issues, perhaps even to their resolution![1]

1. Judaism

A feature of the essays which immediately caught my attention was what may be best described as too casual references to 'Judaism'. So the first thing I would have liked to draw attention to is the importance of more careful use of the term 'Judaism', bearing in mind that the term 'Judaism' itself has several referents. When the issue is Paul's 'continuity/discontinuity' with 'Judaism', we must always ask, what Judaism are we referring to? For if we are to avoid confusion we must always appreciate that 'Judaism' in such a discussion can have three or four different referents, with further subdivisions within each referent:

1.   Since the discussion of the above essays focuses principally on Paul, including not least the impact of 'the new perspective' on Pauline studies, I should perhaps refer to my *The Theology of Paul the Apostle* (Grand Rapids, MI: Eerdmans/Edinburgh: T&T Clark, 1988), and *The New Perspective on Paul* (Tübingen: Mohr Siebeck, 2005; rev., Grand Rapids, MI: Eerdmans, 2008), on which most of my following observations are based.

1. Present-day Judaism, in direct continuity with the emerging rabbinic Judaism of the post-70 and post-200 period; within this Judaism there is, of course, a number of subdivisions – Orthodox, Conservative, Reform, Liberal, and so on.
2. Second Temple Judaism, which almost coincides with the post-biblical (post-Hebrew Bible) period; the diversity of Second Temple Judaism is well recognized today – including notably the 'sects (*haireseis*)' of Sadducees, Pharisees, Essenes, the Nazarenes, but also the rather amorphous category of 'diaspora Judaism' (preferable to the older term 'Hellenistic Judaism').
3. Within Second Temple Judaism should be recognized the 'Judaism' of which Paul speaks in Gal. 1.13-14, a usage most probably in direct continuity with the earliest usage (indeed, so far as we can tell, the creation) of the term, as attested in 2 Maccabees, to refer to the religio-nationalist resistance to Hellenism,[2] as Paul's own characterization ('much more of a zealot for the traditions of the fathers') strongly suggests.
4. 'Biblical Judaism' could be used to distinguish the religion of Israel as attested in the Hebrew Bible, though since the term 'Judaism' here would be anachronistic, the category would better be referred to as 'biblical Israel'.

It is important, then, to avoid the impression that continuity/discontinuity between Paul and Judaism is the same as continuity/discontinuity between (present-day) Christianity and (present-day) Judaism. The issue can better be expressed as the continuity/discontinuity of *both* rabbinic Judaism *and* early Christianity with Second Temple Judaism. A key issue, not least in Jewish/Christian dialogue, is the degree to which both rabbinic Judaism and Christianity are willing truly to recognize *both* their own *and* the other's roots in Second Temple Judaism, and both to recognize the degree to which their continuing character was shaped by that Second Temple matrix. Since the final de facto parting of the ways between Christianity and Judaism did not take place until the fourth century, the mutually growing hostility between emerging Christianity and emerging rabbinic Judaism from the second century onwards, and in particular the growing anti-Judaeos tradition within that Christianity, should not diminish the common roots of both religions, 'Rebecca's children', in Second Temple Judaism.[3]

2. The Greek term *Ioudaismos* first appears in literature in 2 Maccabees, in three passages – 2.21, 8.1 and 14.38. The first of these, 2.21, describes the Maccabean rebels as 'those who fought bravely for Judaism' (*huper tou Ioudaismou*); 8.1 describes their supporters as 'those who had continued in Judaism' (*tou memenêkotas en tô Ioudaismô*); and 14.38 describes the martyr Razis as one who had formerly been accused of Judaism and who had eagerly risked body and life *huper tou Ioudaismou*. It is also notable that in 2 Maccabees the term was obviously coined as a counter to *hellênismos*, 'Hellenism' (2 Macc. 4.13) and *allophulismos*, 'foreignness' (2 Macc. 4.13; 6.25).

3. See particularly D. Boyarin, *Border Lines: The Partition of Judaeo-Christianity* (Philadelphia, PA: University of Pennsylvania, 2004); I may refer also to my *The Partings of the Ways between Christianity and Judaism and their Significance for the Character of Christianity* (London: SCM, 2nd edn, 2006).

As for the historical Paul, the importance of Gal. 1.13-14 is its clear testimony that Paul himself saw and spoke of a discontinuity between his Christian stance and his former modus operandi 'within Judaism' – 'Judaism' was the space and context within which he conducted his pre-Christian life. But if by 'Judaism' here Paul actually meant what could more accurately be referred to as 'Pharisaic Judaism', as I believe to be the case, then the implied discontinuity was with only one subset of Second Temple Judaism. To the extent that Pharisaic Judaism was the subset of Second Temple Judaism which led more or less directly into rabbinic Judaism, then, of course, Paul's affirmation of discontinuity with Pharisaic Judaism helps explain the degree to which rabbinic, and present-day Judaism, have regarded Paul as an apostate. So too, if by 'Judaism' we mean Pharisaic Judaism, then one could speak of Paul's 'conversion' from 'Judaism', and even of his 'anti-Judaism', and could understand why his devaluation of his previous Judaism (Phil. 3.2-8) is readily transposable in Jewish perspective into an anti-(rabbinic) Judaism.[4]

However, if Second Temple Judaism was much broader than Pharisaic Judaism, and is to be recognized as nevertheless authentic Judaism, then to speak of Paul as anti-Jewish is at best misleading. Moreover, the issue of whether Paul can or should be recognized as a Jew, as an authentically Jewish voice within Second Temple Judaism, has to be posed much more firmly than the majority of both Jews and Christians want or feel comfortable with. For if the Sadducees were Jews, if the Essenes were Jews, if Jews living in the diaspora (unable ever to attend the temple, even the pilgrim feasts) were Jews, then Paul was a Jew, however much he antagonized most of his fellow Jews. Michael Bird is right: we must beware of turning intra-Jewish debates into anti-Jewish encounters.

The degree to which Paul's gospel was Jewish hardly needs to be restated. The one God he proclaimed in the face of the many gods of the Greco-Roman world was the God of Israel. Although the titular significance of 'Messiah/Christ' had largely faded in Paul's usage, the fact that the title had become so firmly attached to the name of Jesus ('Jesus Christ, Christ Jesus') defined Jesus forever as the divinely commissioned saviour hoped for by the Jewish people. The fact that Paul's gentile converts soon became known as 'Christians' implies that these gentile believers identified themselves by reference to this Jewish Messiah. Nor should we ever allow both sides of the Jewish/Christian dialogue to forget that the Scriptures for Paul were Israel's Scriptures. Paul's understanding of the significance of Jesus' death draws heavily on Israel's sacrificial cult, that he 'died for our sins in accordance with the scriptures' (1 Cor. 15.3). His understanding of Jesus' resurrection was rooted in early Judaism's refusal to allow that the Maccabean martyrs' death was the end of

---

4.   Typical of passages which gave me some disquiet regarding the too casual use of the term 'Judaism' was John Pawlikowski's comment: 'There is little doubt that Paul took a very positive attitude towards Judaism', which reads oddly in the light of Paul's only references to 'Judaism' (Gal. 1.13-14).

their story (2 Macc. 7). And Paul's usual term for the gatherings of his gentile converts as *ekklêsia* owed less to the citizen assembly of the Hellenistic city and much more to the LXX's translation of the *qahal Israel* or *qahal Yahweh* by the term *ekklêsia* – the 'church' in direct continuity with the 'assembly' of Israel.

If, then, the focusing issue is the continuity/discontinuity between Paul and 'Judaism', where does the continuity/discontinuity stress come?

2. Covenant

One stress-point is in the motif of the *covenant*, as the essays of Bill Campbell, Thomas Blanton and John Pawlikowski make clear: in particular, whether Paul's gospel can properly be described as 'covenant theology' and whether in that case we should be speaking of one covenant or two. I have elsewhere argued that to describe Paul's gospel as 'covenant theology' is at best misleading.[5] So let me start there.

As we shall see, Paul's use of *diathêkê* to refer to his own gospel is not characteristic and may be described as at best incidental, so that any attempt to build Paul's theology of covenant solely on his use of the term in one or other passage is likely to be lopsided.

- Paul uses *diathêkê* in Gal. 3 to refer to the promise made to Abraham, but in the sense of 'will or testament' (3.17), with 'the Law' coming later and making no difference to the promise (3.17-18). But the contrast is actually between *promise* and Law,[6] not between covenant and Law, as further indicated by Paul's readiness to speak of 'two covenants', where Sinai (the Law) is one (4.24) and the other is again better characterized in terms of promise (4.23, 28). The casualness of his use of *diathêkê* here indicates that for Paul *diathêkê* was a convenient term to draw into a differently expressed contrast between the phases of God's purpose.
- In the Corinthian letters, Paul draws on the last supper tradition to speak of 'the new covenant' (1 Cor. 11.25), and in 2 Cor. 3.5-14 on the contrast between old covenant (Sinai) and new covenant given by Jer. 31.31-34. This latter contrast is between the ministry of Moses (characterized by Sinai) and his own ministry. Here it should be noted that Paul avoids the word 'Law' (*nomos*) and uses instead the term *gramma* ('letter') (3.6-7), presumably reflecting the contrast between 'stone tablets' and 'fleshly heart' = 'new spirit' in Ezek. 11.19 and

---

5. 'Did Paul have a Covenant Theology? Reflections on Romans 9.4 and 11.27', in S. E. Porter and J. C. R. de Roo, eds, *The Concept of the Covenant in the Second Temple Period* (Leiden: Brill, 2003), pp. 287–307; also in S. E. McGinn, ed., *Celebrating Romans: Template for Pauline Theology*, R. Jewett FS (Grand Rapids, MI: Eerdmans, 2004), pp. 3–19; reprinted in my *New Perspective on Paul*, ch. 20.

6. Paul uses both terms, 'promise' and 'law', eight times in the sequence Gal. 3.14-28.

36.26-27 (2 Cor. 3.3). But it is equally important to note that Paul's use of the Jeremiah and Ezekiel passages carries with it the implication that the new covenant/the new spirit was a way of writing the Law in the heart and thus of ensuring a more effective obedience of the Law (Jer. 31.32-33; Ezek. 36.27).

- Most striking is Paul's use of *diathêkê* in Romans, where he refers it only to Israel's covenant(s) and to God's covenant with Israel for Israel's salvation (Rom. 9.3-5; 11.25-27). Paul does not use 'covenant' as a term for his own understanding of God's purpose to include gentiles. On the contrary, he takes pains to insist that the covenants are still Israel's, and that God remains faithful to his (covenant) commitment to Israel (11.28-29). If Paul's theology can be justly described as 'covenant theology', as reflecting his own use of the term in Romans, the reference can only be to his theologizing on God's faithfulness to his covenant with Israel.

An important conclusion follows from this: to focus any debate about Paul's theology on the term 'covenant' is liable to distract attention from Paul's primary contrast (in Galatians and Romans) between 'promise' and 'Law'. That there is continuity for Paul between 'before' and 'now' is undeniable. But to put it in terms of covenant is at best misleading. The continuity is with the *promise* God made to Abraham and the fathers. And the continuity with Israel is in large part that Israel likewise traced its understanding of its covenant relation with God back to the same promises. It is the fact that, as demonstrated by Deuteronomy and the prophets on the one hand, and by Paul on the other, Christianity and Judaism both identify themselves by reference back to the divine initiative of the promise to Abraham, which is the primary root of continuity between Christianity and Judaism.

To understand Paul aright, it is crucial to appreciate that he saw his own commissioning as apostle to the gentiles as rooted in these promises. He can even describe one of the three strands of the promise to Abraham (that all the nations would be blessed in Abraham) as already the 'gospel' (Gal. 3.8). Acts makes the same point (Acts 3.25). And both Paul and Acts take some pains to insist that what we refer to primarily as Paul's conversion, they regarded primarily as Paul's prophetic commissioning to preach Christ to the gentiles in fulfilment of and as enacting out Israel's own commission to be a light to the gentiles (Acts 13.47; Gal. 1.15; Isa. 49.1-6).[7] This is why Paul can/should be regarded as an authentically Jewish voice within Second Temple Judaism: he defined his apostolic calling by reference to the Scriptures of his people; he saw Jesus and the movement he and his resurrection had given birth to as fulfilling a role for Israel hitherto unfulfilled.

This is also why continuity with Israel is so important for Christianity's own identity and self-understanding. To be noted is the fact that Paul sees

---

7.   See also Henrix's reflection above on Stendahl's 'Call rather than Conversion' thesis.

the continuity in relation to Israel, not in relation to Judaism;[8] indeed, we may say that 'Israel' rather than 'Judaism' correlates to 'promise' rather than 'covenant'. Here I find it hard to understand why Bill Campbell reacts so negatively to my observation that 'A Christianity which does not understand itself in some proper sense as "Israel" forfeits its claim to the scriptures of Israel.' It is hard to read Romans 9–11 in any other sense ('some proper sense'). The subject of these chapters is not, as so often mis-entitled, 'Israel and the Church'; the subject of Rom. 9–11 is only 'Israel'. Paul attempts to redefine Israel as 'the called of God' (9.6-12), a definition which again roots Israel's identity in the promises of God, and which can include gentiles (9.24-25). But he never resiles from the fundamental conviction that Israel, the nation of Israel, is included in that call; though at present in part hardened, nevertheless 'all Israel will be saved' (11.25-26); God is faithful to his covenant promises (11.27-32).[9] And integral to this reflection on Israel's identity and future he includes the image of Israel the olive tree (11.17-24). What has happened is that gentile branches have been grafted into this tree – that is, into Israel. The gentile branches are not grafted into a shoot replanted from and complementary to the main tree of Israel; they are grafted into Israel, and only so are they able to share in the richness of the tree's root (11.17).[10]

This again makes reversion to a two-covenant model a quite unsuitable one for interpreting Paul's hope. It was in fulfilment of God's promise to Abraham that the gospel was going to gentiles (Gal. 3.6-14; Rom. 15.8-12 underscores the same point).[11] It was by being grafted into the same olive tree that both gentile and unbelieving Jewish branches would be saved. Whether John Pawlikowski's 'inclusivist' language, and 'distinctive but not distinct' formulation are adequate reformulations of Paul's vision, I am not clear;[12]

---

8. Michael Bachmann's assertion that Paul uses 'Israel' 'exclusively with regard to real Judaism' only muddies the waters; though Paul could speak in effect of the 'real Jew' (Rom. 2.28-29). Similarly Mark Nanos's assertion that Paul's movement was 'best approached as Judaism' needs a more nuanced statement.

9. It is 'Israel' in this sense which Paul seems to have in mind in Gal. 6.16, discussed so fully by Michael Bachmann.

10. Philip Cunningham justifiably draws attention to *Nostra Aetate* 4 in this connection.

11. Bill Campbell comments that Rom. 15.8 shows that the purpose that 'the gentiles might glorify God for his mercy' was only secondary to the primary purpose of confirming the promises given to the patriarchs. I do not think Paul would have agreed with such a formulation. For Paul it was of first importance that the promise to the patriarchs included the promise of blessing to the gentiles. Paul was steward of the great 'mystery', hidden from the ages, that God always intended to draw the gentiles in to be one with his people Israel (Rom. 11.25; Col. 1.25-27; Eph. 3.1-6; Paul would have agreed more with the James of Acts 15.14-18); Rom. 15.8-12, as the summation of his most careful statement on the subject, makes the point clearly.

12. Michael Bird's caution over use of an 'inclusivist/exclusivist' contrast is justified, though I question his confidence that Paul already conceived Christians as a *tertium genus*, a third race.

but they are certainly a positive advance on the old supersessionist tradition, and are superior to the two-covenant solution.

The failure of Paul's vision to be realized – the imminence of the deliverer's coming from Zion (11.26) and of the end-time resurrection of the dead (11.15) – does not change Paul's basic theology of gospel (fulfilment of the promise to Abraham) and church (integrated into Israel). The intervening 2,000 years do change the terms of Jewish–Christian relations and dialogue – both the 'Judaism' and the 'Christianity' now in dialogue are very different from the biblical and Second Temple Judaism(s) and the sect of the Nazarenes with which Paul had to deal. But when we try to bring Paul into the contemporary dialogue we should at least start by doing so in Paul's own terms.

3. *Law*

A second point of stress in the continuity/discontinuity debate is, of course, *the Law*. I found encouraging the reaction in several of the above essays against the too strict antithesis between gospel and Law which has for too long motivated particularly Lutheran exegesis of Jesus and Paul to find both Jesus and Paul making an outright breach with the Law.[13] Because 'gospel' and 'Law' were posed as polar opposites, even the developed doctrine of the 'third use of the Law (*tertius usus legis*)' could hardly prevent the charge of antinomianism being levelled against Protestantism. And the problem of how to integrate Paul's 'justification by faith' teaching with his teaching that judgement will be 'according to works' (Rom. 2.6-16; 2 Cor. 5.10) remains unresolved for many Protestant expositors to this day.

So it does need to be reasserted once again that Paul saw a positive role for the Law within the saving purpose of God. Its role as *paidagôgos* of Israel was now passé (Gal. 3.19–4.11); life before God was/need no longer be 'under the Law'. Its weakness in the face of the flesh and its abuse by sin did not amount to a condemnation of the Law – Paul takes pains to mount a defence of the Law in Rom. 7.7–8.4 on precisely these issues. On the contrary, Paul does not hesitate to say that the coming and death of Christ had as its purpose that those who walk according to the Spirit could thus fulfil the just requirements of the Law (8.4). Paul could even talk of the 'Law of the Spirit of life' in the same context (8.2), that is, the Law itself, liberated from the abusive power of sin and death, able to liberate those who found their motivation in following

13.   H. M. Müller, '"Evangelium latuit in lege": Luthers Kreuzespredigt als Schlüssel seiner Bibelhermeneutik', in C. Landmesser, et al. (eds), *Jesus Christus als die Mitte der Schrift*, O. Hofius FS (BZNW 86; Berlin: de Gruyter, 1997), pp. 101–26: 'the distinction between law and gospel grew out of Luther's exegetical work in his conversation with the apostle . . . the distinction between law and gospel as basis for the teaching of justification by faith'. 'Only he who takes up this distinction and lets his thinking be led by it is, according to Luther, a good theologian' (pp. 101–2; also 107–9). E. Lohse, *Paulus* (München: C. H. Beck, 1996): 'It is justified to point out, however, that one may not conclude from Luther's sharp confrontation against mediaeval works righteousness to a correspondingly dark background of the Judaism of Paul's time, as has happened not seldom in the older discussion' (p. 285).

the lead of the Spirit rather than in satisfying the appetites of the flesh. In the same way, Paul had been ready to set what elsewhere was an antithesis between faith and Law into a conjunction – the Law of faith (Rom. 3.27) – faith as that reliance on God[14] out of which genuine obedience from the heart springs, faith as 'establishing' the Law (3.31), enabling the Law to exercise its true function; faith, that is, as the corollary to the new covenant law written on the heart.

This raises again, as with Michael Bird and Thomas Blanton, the question whether 'covenantal nomism' is an appropriate term to be drawn into the discussion. The criticism of E. P. Sanders' introduction of the term, as characterizing Israel's/Judaism's 'pattern of religion',[15] has largely missed the point. It can be fairly claimed that Sanders overemphasized the 'covenant' side of the term and underemphasized the 'nomism' side. This was understandable, after all, since traditionally it had been the 'nomism' side on which the emphasis had been placed in the criticism of Judaism as being essentially 'legalistic' in character. So Sanders could be excused for his attempt to redress the balance. The point is, however, that the phrase 'covenantal nomism' well indicates that there are two/twin aspects of Israel's/Judaism's understanding of the divine/human relationship. That relationship starts from and is based on the divine initiative of election and gratuitous promise; and it looks for a human response of obedience and faithfulness. The balance between these twin emphases is different in different writings; in various situations, for example, the responsibility of Israel to maintain the covenant and to be more faithful had to be more heavily urged and stressed than, say, in the Psalms. But it can be fairly generalized that both aspects are present or assumed in every biblical and Second Temple Jewish writing.

The more challenging issue is whether *Paul's* 'pattern of religion' can also be described as 'covenantal nomism' or its Christian equivalent. And if we take Paul's attitude to the Law, and his teaching on judgement according to works seriously, then the answer has to be yes. For in Christianity the equivalent to the 'covenant' emphasis in Israel/Judaism is the grace expressed in Christ and received through faith. And equivalent to the 'nomism' emphasis in Israel/Judaism is 'the obedience of faith' which Paul characterized his apostleship as seeking to bring about among the gentiles (Rom. 1.5). As Morna Hooker observed in her review of Sanders' *Paul and Palestinian Judaism*, 'In many ways, the pattern which Sanders insists is the basis of Palestinian Judaism fits exactly the Pauline pattern of Christian experience: God's saving grace evokes man's answering obedience.'[16]

---

14. Cf. Hans-Joachim Sander's reformulation of faith in terms of 'powerlessness', as both reflecting the powerlessness of Jesus' crucifixion, and indicating the gospel's openness to the powerless (unprivileged, uncovenanted) other.

15. Particularly D. A. Carson, et al., eds, *Justification and Variegate Nomism. Vol. 1: The Complexities of Second Temple Judaism* (WUNT 2.140; Tübingen: Mohr Siebeck, 2001).

16. M. D. Hooker, 'Paul and "Covenantal Nomism"' (1982), in *From Adam to Christ: Essays on Paul* (Cambridge: Cambridge University Press, 1990), pp. 155–64 (157).

One of the features of Paul's treatment of the Law which is often neglected or inadequately appreciated is that Paul differentiated within the Law. He neither regarded the Law as a wholly negative factor, nor did he reject or downgrade its commandments as a whole. The fact that he was as much against idolatry and *porneia* as the Scriptures, and that he rooted his hostility to these practices in the Law, should not be disregarded as irrelevant to the 'Paul and the Law' debate. The fact that Paul could regard the love command, drawing no doubt on Jesus' own teaching, as the fulfilment of the Law (Rom. 13.8-10), as the summation of 'the whole Law' (Gal. 5.14), should likewise not be downplayed. So Paul's refusal to require obedience (from his gentile converts) of the laws of circumcision, clean and unclean and Sabbath (Gal. 5.2-4; Rom. 14) should not be taken as indicative of his wholesale rejection of the Law. He regarded *some* of the Law's commandments as no longer relevant, no longer binding. The point is nowhere clearer than in 1 Cor. 7.19, where Paul can say *both* that 'circumcision and uncircumcision no longer count for anything' *and* that 'what matters is keeping the commandments of God'. Of course Paul would have been well aware that the obligation of circumcision was one of 'the commandments of God'. His statement, however, indicates clearly that for him circumcision no longer counted as a commandment to be observed by all, gentile members of the new (Jewish) sect as well as Jews.[17]

I confess to some surprise that Mark Nanos in his lengthy discussion of 1 Cor. 9.19-23 does not make more reference to 7.19. For 7.19 seems to express the same Pauline attitude towards the Law as does 9.19-23; and he does so in a way which helps clarify the theological rationale behind what to so many has come across as 'Paul's inconsistent and morally suspect behaviour'. For 7.19 made it clear that Paul neither rejected the Law holus-bolus, nor can be described simply as 'Torah observant'. Rather, he thought that some commandments of the Torah no longer mattered, while still being committed to observing the commandments of God. Taking up the language he uses in Romans, Paul no longer thought that the Law straightforwardly instructed him to 'know the will of God and discern the things which matter' (Rom. 2.18). Now it was the renewal of his mind which enabled him to 'discern the will of God' (Rom. 12.2), that is, to discern what really mattered *within* the Law, that some commandments were far more important than others and not all requiring obedience of gentile believers. It was the recognition that circumcision and non-circumcision no longer mattered, that observance or non-observance of laws of clean and unclean no longer really counted for anything before God, which left Paul free to observe or not to observe as his circumstances made appropriate – but still to count doing the will of God and keeping his commandments as one of his top priorities.

17.   Reflecting on Philip Cunningham's and Hans Hermann Henrix's essays, it occurs to me that as changing circumstances (phases in God's purpose) caused Paul to discount various Torah commandments, a similar argument could be mounted with regard to the more negative references to 'the Jews' within the NT, such as John 8.44 and 1 Thess. 2.14-16.

It was the need for an exegesis of Paul which explained how he was thus able/free to distinguish *within* the Law, between different commandments of the Law, which led me to distinguish the role of the Law as a 'boundary marker' as that aspect of the Law for which Paul saw no continuing function – the boundary role so clearly articulated in the *Letter of Aristeas* 139–42, a role in fact similar to the protective role of the *paidagôgos* in Gal. 3.[18] It is surely no mere coincidence that the commandments of the Law which Paul regarded as passé are precisely the practices which marked out Second Temple Judaism and made it so distinctive, as Christianity began to emerge – circumcision, laws of clean and unclean, and Sabbath. These were the principal boundary markers which distinguished Jews from gentiles and kept Jews separate from gentiles. My contribution to 'the new perspective of Paul' was the insight that this observation could be linked to the (basic New Perspective) recognition that Paul's teaching on justification through faith grew out of his mission to the gentiles (Stendahl). The link could be made by recognizing that Paul saw breaking down the boundary between Jew and gentile as fundamental to his apostleship to the gentiles, breaking down the social boundary function of the Law as central to his gospel, removing the requirements particularly of circumcision and laws of clean and unclean as nodal points of his understanding of justification by *faith*. A large part of the genius and value of Ephesians is that it expresses this central element in Paul's theology and mission so clearly – Eph. 2.11–3.7.[19]

It is here, I suppose, that I ought to say a little on the *erga nomou* theme, posed afresh by Michael Bachmann, although in linking *erga nomou* and 'boundary markers' as he does, he confuses the boundary *function* of certain laws with the laws themselves and their observance. Since we have traversed the same ground on several occasions, I hesitate to go round the mulberry bush yet again. So perhaps it will suffice to make the point that when Paul first uses the phrase (Gal. 2.16), the most obvious interpretation is that his use of the phrase was prompted by Peter's (and the other Jewish believers') separation from the gentile believers in Antioch. The 'works of the Law' which Peter was trying to 'compel' the gentile believers to observe, were the laws of clean and unclean and other commandments (and *halakhoth*) which determined whether Jew and gentile could eat together; I still think Lev. 20.24-26 expresses most clearly the theological rationale behind Peter's withdrawal from table fellowship. Paul denounced Peter at the time (or later, as he recalled the episode when writing Galatians) because he believed that

18.   This probably provides the clue for the interpretation of Rom. 10.4. In the sequence of Rom. 9.30–10.4, Paul rebukes Israel for pursuing 'the law of righteousness' 'as if it was from works' (9.31-32), and for regarding righteousness as peculiarly 'their own' (that is, their's and not anyone else's) (10.3). Christ has brought an 'end' to the Law in that function, the Law as thought so to function (cf. Gal. 3.23-25).

19.   Hans-Joachim Sander's essay re-expresses the point in terms of justification overcoming the 'us' and 'them/the other/the outsider' dichotomy and rightly notes the danger of Christians today making the same mistake with regard to the Jews that the Jews made with regard to 'the (other) nations/gentiles'.

Peter was trying to 'compel the gentiles to judaize' (2.14), that is to live according to Jewish customs/rules.[20] It was not the fact that Peter still held to such *halakhoth* to which Paul objected; it was the fact that Peter believed it necessary to *obey* these laws and rulings, that he actually 'separated' from other believers (as Lev. 20.24-26 insisted). That was treating 'works of the Law' as an essential addition to faith in Christ.

So I still cannot see how Michael can make such a sharp distinction between the rule in itself and the practising of that rule. For example, 4QMMT did not want the Jerusalemites simply to affirm the halakhic rules which it laid out; the letter-writer wanted them to *observe* these halakhoth; affirmation without observance would amount to denial. And when Paul asks whether the Galatians received the Spirit from the 'hearing of faith' or from 'works of the Law' (Gal. 3.2-5), he was not suggesting that knowledge of or respect for 'works of the Law' might be regarded as a possible way to receive the Spirit; he was denying that the Galatians had had to submit to or observe certain or various Torah commandments in order to receive the Spirit.[21] Since the theological logic behind both the insistence on 'works of the Law' and Paul's resistance is so clear I remain puzzled why Michael continues to insist that *erga nomou* in all these passages refer only to 'regulations' and not to the observance of such regulations.

4. Christ

Although Michael Bird concludes by provocatively asserting that 'for Paul, salvation is of Judaism only in so far as Judaism is of Jesus Christ', I was somewhat surprised that the continuity/discontinuity issue did not find more focus on Christ and on his status/significance for Christians. The point of stress in the essays does not come on the issue of Jesus' Jewishness; that is a given. Nor does it come on the anomaly of believing in a crucified Messiah, which was a point of stress for the earliest believers, if 1 Cor. 1.23 and Gal. 3.13 are any guide; but Messiah Jesus Jews continued to prosper in Jerusalem, it would appear, more or less up until the outbreak of the Jewish revolt. Nor does the point of stress become evident in the christological claims for Jesus, which subsequent Judaism certainly regarded as a threat to its foundational belief in God as one; but again, despite claims to the

20.   Reverting to Mark Nanos's discussion of 1 Cor. 9.17-23, Paul's objection to Peter at Antioch was not that he (Peter) 'lived like a Jew', or indeed that he (Peter) had 'lived like a Gentile', but that he (Peter) had tried to 'compel' gentile believers 'to judaize', as though crossing the Jew/gentile boundary should be deemed essential for gentile believers, as though such observance of the Law really mattered.

21.   Michael Bird seems to acknowledge the point when he writes, that for Paul the inclusion of gentile believers 'in the community of salvation does not entail the acceptance of such halakhot by non-Jews, and therefore does not request their conversion to Judaism'; 'acceptance of such halakhot' means acting in accord with such halakhot, as 'conversion to Judaism' would certainly imply.

contrary, there is no evidence that Paul's use of Wisdom language to refer to Jesus, or his talk of Jesus as Lord sharing in acclamations due to God, provoked any marked hostility or persecution from his fellow Jews. It would have been good, perhaps salutary, to know how Paul's fellow Jews reacted to his application of Ps. 110.1 to the risen Jesus in 1 Cor. 15.24-28. All that said, of course, it should be freely acknowledged that the christology which Paul articulated was well on the way towards the Christian creedal statements regarding Christ which subsequently proved anathema to rabbinic Judaism. Nevertheless, the point remains that Paul's reflections on the significance and status of Jesus remained almost entirely within the categories and range of reflection on divine immanence already current in Second Temple Judaism.

The point of stress that comes in the continuity/discontinuity debate as expressed in the above essays is almost wholly limited to the question of the relation of Christ to Torah, particularly in the essay of Hans Hermann Henrix. Here I don't find it very helpful to describe Christ as 'the living Torah', 'the Torah in person', or 'the Torah incarnate' (Joseph Ratzinger). I would find it more helpful to follow Paul's line of thought: that Christ can be identified with divine Wisdom, as in Rom. 10.6-10[22] and 1 Cor. 8.6. As Israel's wisdom tradition identified Wisdom with the Torah (Sir. 24.23; Bar. 4.1), so Paul identified Christ with Wisdom. As Israel saw the wisdom by which God created and sustains the world embodied (incarnated) in Torah, so Paul (and John) saw the same Wisdom embodied/incarnated in Jesus. That is not to say that Christ is Torah incarnate, or Torah in person. It is rather to recognize that both Israel and Paul saw the mysterious immensity of God's creative, revelatory and redemptive power most clearly expressed in and through, in one case, Torah, and in the other, Christ. The line of continuity between Judaism and Christianity at this point is not through Torah as such, but through the endless reflection on the part of both as to the way the one God has manifested his will and himself most fully. The comparison and dialogue between some of the more stupendous rabbinic claims for Torah and Christian claims for Christ should be one of the most intriguing and potentially enriching experiences for both Jew and Christian.

On the related question as to whether Paul believed that Israel's salvation would be through their coming to faith in Christ (the one covenant or two issue), I still think that this is what Paul believed. But here, too, nuance is required. The Paul who saw Christ as the embodiment of the mysterious immensity of God's immanence was certainly open to the possibility that the eschatological outworking of God's purpose could be in unexpected terms. As the coming of Jesus fulfilled messianic hopes in an unexpected but still recognizable way, perhaps the hopes for Christ's return and Israel's salvation would be similarly fulfilled. When I was writing my commentary on Romans I was impressed by the fact that Paul seems to have expressed his hope for

---

22. Romans 10.6-10 shares its interest in reflecting on Deut. 30.11-14 with Bar. 3.29-30 and *Targum Neofiti* on Deut. 30; see my *Romans* (WBC 38, 2 vols; Dallas: Word, 1988), 2.603-5.

Israel (in Rom. 11), the resolution of the mystery, in non-explicitly Christian terms – simply that 'Out of Zion the Deliverer will come' (Rom. 11.26). It is almost as though Paul did not want to predetermine how God would resolve the puzzle of his faithfulness to Israel and the openness of his grace to all. So he expressed his hope in broad terms, his assurance that God's ultimate motivation, as Israel had learned from the beginning, was determined by 'mercy' – sure that God would be 'merciful to all', even if he had no clear idea of who the 'all' would include.

A final thought: if the 'new perspective' is one of the motivations behind the above discussion, there is another aspect which I would have thought could involve Paul's christology more fully – that is, not simply in the strong influence of Jesus' ethical teaching on Paul's catechetical teaching. Such an influence almost certainly determined Paul's basic attitude to the Law as fulfilled in the love command. And 'the law of Christ' (Gal. 6.2) can most plausibly be understood as the traditions of Jesus' mission and teaching showing Paul's converts how they should fulfil the Law's commands. To that extent Christ can be described as 'the living Torah'. But more important here is the fact that Paul's christological soteriology provides a link between Paul's teaching on justification and his teaching on how gentiles too can be heirs of the promise made to Abraham. The key link is provided by Paul's 'in Christ' motif. As Paul argues in Gal. 3, it is by being 'in Christ' that gentiles can be counted as Abraham's seed. 'In Christ' is another reason why ethnic and social differences no longer count for anything (Gal. 3.28), as circumcision and uncircumcision no longer count for anything. 'In Christ' provides the link between justification by faith and judgement according to works. For 'in Christ' describes also the process by which the justified sinner is transformed more and more into the image of Christ, the eldest brother (for example, Rom. 8.29; 2 Cor. 3.18). Despite the insistence of some Reformed, Paul did not see a straightforward transfer of status accepted as conversion-initiation through faith to final judgement (initial acquittal guaranteeing final acquittal). He saw also a process of transformation and conformation, in which his other images and effecters of salvation (Christ and the Spirit) played an ongoing role, always as an outcome of that same trust and reliance with which the process began.

I find it ever stimulating, indeed exciting, that Paul the apostle, speaking nearly 2,000 years ago, can still provoke such discussion, still call in question so many of our presuppositions and traditions, and still challenge us to deeper thought and reflection on our relationships with God and with one another. Thus we may hope to help realize Pope Benedict's goal in declaring 2008–9 the bimillennial year of Paul – to *rediscover* Paul, or as a Roman Catholic friend re-expressed it, to *discover* Paul, as for the first time!

BIBLIOGRAPHY

Agamben, Giorgio. *Die Zeit, die bleibt. Ein Kommentar zum Römerbrief*. Frankfurt: Suhrkamp, 2006.

Aletti, Jean-Noël. 'Où en sont les études sur Saint Paul? Enjeux et proposition'. *RSR* 90 (2002): 329–52.

Avemarie, Friedrich. 'Tension Between God's Command and Israel's Obedience as Reflected in the Early Rabbinic Literature'. In *Divine and Human Agency in Paul and his Cultural Environment*, eds John Barclay and Simon Gathercole; London: T&T Clark, 2007, 50–70.

Bachmann, Michael. *Von Paulus zur Apokalypse – und weiter. Exegetische und rezeptionsgeschichtliche Studien zum Neuen Testament* (samt englischsprachigen *summaries*) (NTOA/StUNT 91), Göttingen: Vandenhoeck & Ruprecht, 2011.

———. *Anti-Judaism in Galatians? Exegetical Studies on a Polemical Letter and on Paul's Theology*. Trans. R. L. Brawley; Grand Rapids, MI: Eerdmans, 2009.

———. 'Bemerkungen zur Auslegung zweier Genitivverbindungen des Galaterbriefs: "Werke des Gesetzes" (Gal. 2,16 u. ö.) und "Israel Gottes" (Gal. 6,16)'. In *Umstrittener Galaterbrief. Studien zur Situierung und Theologie des Paulus-Schreibens*, eds idem and Bernd Kollmann (BThSt 106), Neukirchen-Vluyn: Neukirchener Verlag, 2009, 95–118.

———. 'Biblische Didaktik ohne historische Rechenschaft? Einige Notizen und das Beispiel der (paulinischen) Rechtfertigungsbotschaft'. In *Erstaunlich lebendig und bestürzend verständlich? Studien und Impulse zur Bibeldidaktik*, eds idem and Johannes Woyke; Neukirchen-Vluyn: Neukirchener Verlag, 2009, 1–25.

———. 'Neue Zugänge zu Paulus – und ihre ökumenische Relevanz'. *Cath(M)* 63 (2009): 241–61.

———. 'Was für Praktiken? Zur jüngsten Diskussion um die ἔργα νόμου'. *NTS* 55 (2009): 35–54.

———. 'Neutestamentliche Hinweise auf halakhische Regelungen'. In *Nuovo Testamento: Teologie in dialogo culturale. Scritti in onore di Romano Penna nel suo 70° compleanno* (SRivBiB 50), eds N. Ciola and G. Pulcinelli; Bologna, 2008, 449–62.

———. 'Auseinandersetzungen um Verhaltensregeln im frühen Christentum als Indizien eines Ringens um Identität und Universalisierung der Religionsgemeinschaft'. In Jörg Rüpke, ed. (in cooperation with Franca Fabricius), *Religionsgeschichte in räumlicher Perspektive. Abschlussbericht zum Schwerpunktprogramm 1080 der Deutschen Forschungsgemeinschaft 'Römische Reichsreligion und Provinzialreligion'*. Tübingen: Mohr Siebeck, 2007, 213–22.

———. 'Christus, "das Ende des Gesetzes, des Dekalogs und des Liebesgebots"?'. *ThZ* 63 (2007): 171–4.

———. 'J. D. G. Dunn und die Neue Paulusperspektive'. *ThZ* 63 (2007): 25–43.

———. 'Zur Argumentation in Gal 3.10-12'. *NTS* 53 (2007): 524–44.

———. 'Zur Rezeptions- und Traditionsgeschichte des paulinischen Ausdrucks ἔργα νόμου: Notizen im Blick auf Verhaltensregeln im frühen Christentum als einer "Gruppenreligion"'. In *Gruppenreligionen im römischen Reich. Sozialformen, Grenzziehungen und Leistungen* (StTAC 43), ed. Jörg Rüpke; Tübingen: Mohr Siebeck, 2007, 69–86.

————. 'Keil oder Mikroskop. Zur jüngeren Diskussion um den Ausdruck "'Werke' des Gesetzes"'. In Bachmann, *Lutherische und Neue Paulusperspektive. Beiträge zu einem Schlüsselproblem der gegenwärtigen exegetischen Diskussion* (WUNT 182), Tübingen: Mohr Siebeck, 2005, 69–134.

————. 'Von den Schwierigkeiten des exegetischen Verstehens. Erwägungen am Beispiel der Interpretation des paulinischen Ausdrucks "Werke des Gesetzes"'. In *Kontexte der Schrift I: Text, Ethik, Judentum und Christentum, Gesellschaft. Ekkehard W. Stegemann zum 60. Geburtstag*, ed. Gabriella Gelardini; Stuttgart: Kohlhammer, 2005, 49–59.

————. 'Die Botschaft für alle und der Antijudaismus: Nachdenken über Paulus und die Folgen'. In *Ernstfall Frieden. Biblisch-theologische Perspektiven*, eds Marco Hofheinz and Georg Plasger; Wuppertal: Foedus-Verlag, 2002, 57–74.

————. '*Verus Israel*: Ein Vorschlag zu einer "mengentheoretischen" Neubeschreibung der betreffenden paulinischen Terminologie'. *NTS* 48 (2002): 500–12.

————. 'Zur Entstehung (und zur Überwindung) des christlichen Antijudaismus'. *ZNT* 10 (2002): 44–52.

————. *Antijudaismus im Galaterbrief? Exegetische Studien zu einem polemischen Schreiben und zur Theologie des Apostels Paulus*. Göttingen: Vandenhoeck & Ruprecht, 1999.

————. 'Rechtfertigung und Gesetzeswerke bei Paulus'. In idem, *Antijudaismus im Galaterbrief? Exegetische Studien zu einem polemischen Schreiben und zur Theologie des Apostels Paulus* (NTOA 40), Freiburg (Schweiz)/Göttingen: Universitätsverlag, 1999, 1–31.

————. '4QMMT und Galaterbrief, מעשי התורה und ΕΡΓΑ ΝΟΜΟΥ'. In idem, *Antijudaismus im Galaterbrief? Exegetische Studien zu einem polemischen Schreiben und zur Theologie des Apostels Paulus* (NTOA 40), Freiburg (Schweiz)/Göttingen: Universitätsverlag, 1999, 33–56.

————. 'Ermittlungen zum Mittler: Gal 3,20 und der Charakter des mosaischen Gesetzes'. In idem, *Antijudaismus im Galaterbrief? Exegetische Studien zu einem polemischen Schreiben und zur Theologie des Apostels Paulus* (NTOA 40), Freiburg (Schweiz)/Göttingen: Universitätsverlag, 1999, 81–126.

————. 'Die andere Frau. Synchrone und diachrone Beobachtungen zu Gal 4.21–5.1'. In idem, *Antijudaismus im Galaterbrief? Exegetische Studien zu einem polemischen Schreiben und zur Theologie des Apostels Paulus* (NTOA 40), Freiburg (Schweiz)/Göttingen: Universitätsverlag, 1999, 127–58.

————. 'Kirche und Israel Gottes. Zur Bedeutung und ekklesiologischen Relevanz des Segenswortes am Schluß des Galaterbriefs'. In idem, *Antijudaismus im Galaterbrief? Exegetische Studien zu einem polemischen Schreiben und zur Theologie des Apostels Paulus* (NTOA 40), Freiburg (Schweiz)/Göttingen: Universitätsverlag, 1999, 159–89.

————. 'Jüdischer Bundesnomismus und paulinisches Gesetzesverständnis, das Fußbodenmosaik von Bet Alfa und das Textsegment Gal 3,15-29'. In idem, *Antijudaismus im Galaterbrief? Exegetische Studien zu einem polemischen Schreiben und zur Theologie des Apostels Paulus* (NTOA 40), Freiburg (Schweiz)/Göttingen: Universitätsverlag, 1999, 57–77/80.

————. *Sünder oder Übertreter. Studien zur Argumentation in Gal 2,15ff.* (WUNT 59), Tübingen: Mohr Siebeck 1992.

Bachmann, Michael, ed. *Lutherische und neue Paulusperspektive. Beiträge zu einem Schlüsselproblem der gegenwärtigen exegetischen Diskussion* (WUNT 182), Tübingen: Mohr Siebeck, 2005.

Badenas, Robert. *Christ the End of the Law: Romans 10.4 in Pauline Perspective*. Sheffield: JSOT Press, 1985.

Badiou, Alain. *Saint Paul. The Foundation of Universalism*. Trans. R. Brassier. Stanford: Stanford University Press, 2003. German translation: *Paulus. Die Begründung des Universalismus*, trans. H. Jath; München 2002, Zürich/Berlin, 2009.

————. *Das Sein und das Ereignis*. Zürich: Diaphanes, 2005.

Baeck, Leo. *Paulus, die Pharisäer und das Neue Testament*. Frankfurt am Main: Ner-Tamid Verlag, 1961.

Baltes, Matthias. 'Mixed Monotheism? The Areopagos Speech of Paul'. In *With Unperfumed Voice: Studies in Plutarch, in Greek Literature, Religion and Philosophy, and in the New Testament Background*, ed. Frederick E. Brenk; Stuttgart: Franz Steiner, 2007, 470–94.

Barclay, John M. G. '"Do We Undermine the Law?": A Study of Romans 14.1–15.6'. In *Paul and the Mosaic Law*, ed. James D. G. Dunn; rev. edn, Grand Rapids and Cambridge: Eerdmans, 2001, 287–308.

———. *Jews in the Mediterranean Diaspora: from Alexander to Trajan (323 BCE–117 CE)*. Edinburgh: T&T Clark, 1996.

———. 'Paul among Diaspora Jews: Anomaly or Apostate?' *JSNT* 60 (1995): 89–120.

Barth, Markus. 'Der gute Jude Paulus'. In *Richte unsere Füsse auf den Weg des Friedens*. FS Helmut Gollwitzer, eds Andreas Baudis et al.; München: Kaiser, 1979.

Barton, Stephen C. '"All Things to All People": Paul and the Law in the Light of 1 Corinthians 9.19-23'. In *Paul and the Mosaic Law*, ed. James D. G. Dunn; rev. edn, Grand Rapids and Cambridge: Eerdmans, 2001, 271–85.

Bauckham, Richard. 'Apocalypses'. In *Justification and Variegated Nomism: Volume 1 – The Complexities of Second Temple Judaism*, eds D. A. Carson, Peter T. O'Brien and Mark Seifrid; Grand Rapids, MI: Baker, 2001.

Baur, F. C. *Paul the Apostle of Jesus Christ: His Life and Works, His Epistles and Teachings*. Peabody, MA: Hendrickson, 2003.

Becker, Adam H. and Annette Yoshiro Reed, eds. *The Ways That Never Parted: Jews and Christians in Late Antiquity and the Early Middle Ages* (TSJ 95), Tübingen: Mohr Siebeck, 2003.

Beißer, Friedrich. 'Was heißt bei Paulus "Jesus Christus ist das Ende des Gesetzes"?'. *KuD* 51 (2005): 52–4.

Beker, J. Christiaan. 'The Faithfulness of God and the Priority of Israel in Paul's Letter to the Romans'. In *Christians Among Jews and Gentiles: Essays in Honor of Krister Stendahl on His Sixty-fifth Birthday*, eds George W. E. Nickelsburg and George W. MacRae; Philadelphia, PA: Fortress, 1986, 10–16.

———. *Paul the Apostle: The Triumph of God in Life and Thought*. Edinburgh: T&T Clark, 1980.

Bell, Richard H. *The Irrevocable Call of God* (WUNT 184), Tübingen: Mohr Siebeck, 2005, 238–43.

———. *Provoked to Jealousy: The Origin and Purpose of the Jealousy Motif in Romans 9–11* (WUNT 2.63), Tübingen: Mohr Siebeck, 1994.

Bendemann, Reinhard. von. *Heinrich Schlier: Eine kritische Analyse seiner Interpretation paulinischer Theologie* (BEvTh 115), Gütersloh: Kaiser, 1995.

Bergmeier, Roland. 'Vom Tun der Tora'. In Michael Bachmann (ed. in cooperation with Johannes Woyke), *Lutherische und Neue Paulusperspektive. Beiträge zu einem Schlüsselproblem der gegenwärtigen exegetischen Diskussion* (WUNT 182), Tübingen: Mohr Siebeck, 2005, 161–81.

Berkovits, Eliezer. 'Judaism in the Post-Christian Era'. In *Disputation and Dialogue: Readings in the Jewish-Christian Encounter*, ed. F. E. Talmage; New York: KTAV, 1975.

Bernardin, Cardinal Joseph. *A Blessing to Each Other. Cardinal Joseph Bernardin and Jewish-Catholic Dialogue*. Chicago: Liturgy Training Publications, 1996.

Bernat, David A. *Sign of the Covenant: Circumcision in the Priestly Tradition*. Atlanta, GA: SBL, 2009.

Betz, Hans Dieter. 'The Concept of the "Inner Human Being" (ὁ ἔσω ἄνθρωπος) in the Anthropology of Paul'. *NTS* 46 (2000): 315–41.

———. *2 Corinthians 8 and 9. A Commentary on Two Administrative Letters of the Apostle Paul*. Hermeneia; Philadelphia, PA: Fortress Press, 1985.

————. *Galatians: A Commentary on Paul's Letter to the Churches in Galatia.* Hermeneia; Philadelphia PA: Fortress, 1979.

Beyer, Klaus. *Die aramäischen Texte vom Toten Meer samt den Inschriften aus Palästina, dem Testament Levis aus der Kairoer Genisa, der Fastenrolle und den alten, talmudischen Zitaten. Ergänzungsband.* Göttingen: Vandenhoeck & Ruprecht, 1994.

Bieringer, Reimund. 'Biblical Revelation and Exegetical Interpretation According to *Dei Verbum* 12'. In *Vatican II and Its Legacy*, eds M. Lamberigts and L. Kenis (BETL 166), Leuven – Dudley, MA: Peeters, 2002, 25–58.

————. 'Teilungshypothesen zum 2. Korintherbrief. Ein Forschungsüberblick'. In idem and Jan Lambrecht, *Studies on 2 Corinthians* (BETL 112), Leuven: Leuven University Press – Peeters, 1994, 67–105.

Bieringer, Reimund and Mary Elsbernd. 'Introduction: The "Normativity of the Future" Approach: Its Roots, Development, Current State and Challenges'. In Bieringer and Elsbernd, *Normativity of the Future: Reading Biblical and Other Authoritative Texts in an Eschatological Perspective*, Leuven: Peeters, 2010, 3–25.

Bird, Michael F. *Crossing Over Sea and Land: Jewish Proselytizing Activity in the Second Temple Period.* Peabody, MA: Hendrickson, 2009.

————. 'What if Martin Luther Had Read the Dead Sea Scrolls? Historical Particularity and Theological Interpretation in Pauline Theology: Galatians as a Test Case'. *JTI* 3 (2009): 107–25.

————. *The Saving Righteousness of God: Studies on Paul, Justification, and the New Perspective.* Carlisle, UK: Paternoster, 2007.

————. *Colossians and Philemon* (NCCS), Eugene, OR: Cascade, 1999.

Bird, Michael F. and Preston M. Sprinkle. 'Jewish Interpretation of Paul in the Last Thirty Years'. *CBR* 6 (2008): 355–76.

Birnbaum, Ellen. *The Place of Judaism in Philo's Thought: Israel, Jews, and Proselytes.* Providence, RI: Brown University Press, 1996.

Bishops' Committee on the Liturgy, National Conference of Catholic Bishops, *God's Mercy Endures Forever: Guidelines on the Presentation of Jews and Judaism in Catholic Preaching.* Washington, DC: USCC, 1988.

Blank, Josef. 'Paulus – Jude und Völkerapostel. Als Frage an Juden und Christen'. In *Paulus – Apostat oder Apostel? Jüdische und christliche Antworten*, eds Markus Barth et al.; Regensburg: Pustet, 1977, 147–72.

Blanton, Thomas R. IV. 'Spirit and Covenant Renewal: A Theologoumenon of Paul's Opponents in Second Corinthians'. *JBL* 129 (2010): 129–51.

————. *Constructing a New Covenant: Discursive Strategies in the Damascus Document and Second Corinthians* (WUNT 2.233), Tübingen: Mohr Siebeck, 2007.

Bockmuehl, Marcus. *The Epistle to the Philippians.* London: Black, 1997.

Bornkamm, Günther. 'The Missionary Stance of Paul in 1 Corinthians 9 and in Acts'. In *Studies in Luke–Acts*, eds Leander E. Keck and J. Louis Martyn; Philadelphia, PA: Fortress Press, 1980, 194–207.

————. *Paul.* Trans. D. M. G. Stalker; New York: Harper & Row, 1971.

Boyarin, Daniel. *Border Lines: The Partition of Judaeo-Christianity.* Philadelphia, PA: University of Pennsylvania, 2004.

————. 'Semantic Differences on "Judaism/Christianity"'. In *The Ways That Never Parted: Jews and Christians in Late Antiquity and the Early Middle Ages* (TSJ 95), eds Adam H. Becker and Annette Yoshiro Reed; Tübingen: Mohr Siebeck, 2003, 65–86.

————. *A Radical Jew: Paul and the Politics of Identity.* Berkeley, CA: University of California, 1994.

Brawley, Robert. 'Contextuality, Intertextuality, and the Hendiadic Relationship of Promise and Law in Galatians'. *ZNW* 93 (2002): 99–119.

Brown, Raymond E. 'The Roman Church Near the End of the First Christian Generation'. In idem and John P. Meier, *Antioch and Rome: New Testament Cradles of Catholic*

Christianity, New York and Ramsey, NJ: Paulist Press, 1983.

Bruce, Frederick Fyvie. *The Acts of the Apostles: The Greek Text with Introduction and Commentary*. 3rd revised and enlarged edn, Grand Rapids, MI, and Leicester, UK: Eerdmans and Apollos, 1990.

Bultmann, Rudolf. *Primitive Christianity in its Contemporary Setting*. Trans. R. H. Fuller; London: Thames and Hudson, 1956.

Burchard, Christoph. 'Nicht aus Werken des Gesetzes gerecht, sondern aus Glauben an Jesus Christus – seit wann?'. In idem, *Studien zur Theologie, Sprache und Umwelt des Neuen Testaments* (WUNT 107), ed. Dieter Sänger; Tübingen Mohr Siebeck, 1998, 230–40.

Burggraeve, Roger. 'Biblical Thinking As The Wisdom of Love'. In Reimund Bieringer, Didier Pollefeyt, Frederique Vandecasteele-Vanneuville, eds, *Anti-Judaism and the Fourth Gospel. Papers of the Leuven Colloquium, 2000*, Assen/Netherlands: Royal Van Gorcum, 2001, 202–25.

Byrne, Brendan. 'Interpreting Romans: The New Perspective and Beyond'. *Int* 58 (2004): 241–52.

———. 'Interpreting Romans in a Post-"New Perspective" Perspective'. *HTR* 49 (2001): 227–41.

Campbell, Douglas A. *The Quest for Paul's Gospel: A Suggested Strategy*. London: T&T Clark, 2005.

Campbell, William S. '"I Rate All Things as Loss": Paul's Puzzling Accounting System: Judaism as Loss or The Re-Evaluation of All things in Christ'. In *Celebrating Paul: Festschrift in Honour of J.A.Fitzmyer and J.Murphy-O'Connor*, ed. Peter Spitaler; CBQ Monograph Series, Washington: Catholic Biblical Association of America, 2011.

———. 'Religion, Identity and Ethnicity: The Contribution of Paul the Apostle'. *Journal of Beliefs and Values* 29 (2008): 139–50.

———. 'Unity and Diversity in the Church: Transformed Identities and the Peace of Christ in Ephesians'. *Transformation: An International Journal of Holistic Mission Studies* 25 (2008): 15–31.

———. '"As Having and as not Having": Paul and Indifferent Things in 1 Corinthians 7.17-32a'. Unpublished paper, SNTS Annual General Meeting, Aberdeen, 2006.

———. *Paul and the Creation of Christian Identity* (LNTS 322), London and New York, 2006.

———. 'Perceptions of Compatibility Between Christianity and Judaism in Pauline Interpretation'. *BibInt* 13 (2005): 298–316.

———. 'Divergent Images of Paul and His Mission'. In *Reading Israel in Romans: Legitimacy and Plausibility of Divergent Interpretations*, eds Cristina Grenholm and Daniel Patte; Harrisburg, PA: Trinity Press International, 1999, 187–211.

———. 'Christ the End of the Law: Rom. 10.4'. In *Paul's Gospel in an Intercultural Context: Jew and Gentile in the Letter to the Romans*, Bern, Frankfurt, New York: Peter Lang, 1992, 60–7.

Carson, D. A. 'Mystery and Fulfillment: Toward a More Comprehensive Paradigm of Paul's Understanding of the Old and the New'. In *Justification and Variegated Nomism: Vol. 2: The Paradoxes of Paul*, eds D. A. Carson et al.; Tübingen and Grand Rapids, MI: Mohr Siebeck and Baker Academic, 2004, 393–436.

———. 'Summaries and Conclusions'. In *Justification and Variegated Nomism: Volume 1 – The Complexities of Second Temple Judaism*, eds D. A. Carson, Peter T. O'Brien and Mark Seifrid; Grand Rapids, MI: Baker, 2001.

Carson, D. A. et al., eds. *Justification and Variegated Nomism. Vol. 1: The Complexities of Second Temple Judaism* (WUNT 2.140), Tübingen: Mohr Siebeck, 2001.

Chadwick, Henry. *The Enigma of St Paul*. London: University of London, The Athlone Press, 1969.

————. 'St. Paul and Philo of Alexandria'. In *History and Thought of the Early Church*, ed. Henry Chadwick; London: Variorum Reprints, 1982, Original: *BJRL* 48 (1965–6), 286–307.

————. '"All Things to All Men" (1 Cor. IX.22)'. *NTS* 1 (1954–5): 261–75.

Cheung, Alex T. *Idol Food in Corinth: Jewish Background and Pauline Legacy* (JSNTSup 176), Sheffield: Sheffield Academic Press, 1999.

Chun Park, Eung. *Either Jew or Gentile: Paul's Unfolding Theology of Inclusivity*. Louisville, KY: Westminster John Knox, 2003.

Cohen, S. J. D. *The Beginnings of Jewishness: Boundaries, Varieties, Uncertainties*. Berkeley, CA: University of California, 1999.

Conzelmann, Hans. 'The Address of Paul on the Areopagus'. In *Studies in Luke–Acts*, eds Leander E. Keck and J. Louis Martyn; Philadelphia, PA: Fortress Press, 1980.

Coppins, Wayne. *The Interpretation of Freedom in the Letters of Paul. With Special Reference to the 'German' Tradition* (WUNT 2.261), Tübingen: Mohr Siebeck, 2009.

Crafer, T. W. *The Apocriticus of Macarius Magnes* (Translations of Christian Literature, Series 1: Greek Texts), London: SPCK, and New York: Macmillan, 1919.

Crossley, James. 'Mark 7.1-23: Revisiting the Question of "All Foods Clean"'. In *Torah in the New Testament*, eds Michael Tait and Peter Oakes; London and New York: T&T Clark, 2009, 8–20.

Crüsemann, Frank. *Kanon und Sozialgeschichte: Beiträge zum Alten Testament*. Gütersloh: Kaiser/Gütersloher Verlag, 2003.

Dahl, Nils Alstrup. 'The One God of Jews and Gentiles (Rom. 3.29-30)'. In idem, *Studies in Paul: Theology for the Early Christian Mission*, Minneapolis, MN: Augsburg, 1977. Reprinted: Eugene, OR: Wipf & Stock Publishers, 2002.

————. 'Zur Auslegung von Gal. 6.16'. *Jud.* 6 (1950): 161–70.

Daube, David. *The New Testament and Rabbinic Judaism*. Peabody, MA: Hendrickson, 1990. Original: London, 1956.

Davies, W. D. 'Paul and the People of Israel'. *Jewish and Pauline Studies*. Philadelphia, PA: Fortress Press, 1984, 123–52.

————. *Paul and Rabbinic Judaism. Some Rabbinic Elements in Pauline Theology*. 2nd edn (with additional notes), London: SPCK, 1955.

Deines, Roland. 'The Pharisees Between "Judaisms" and "Common Judaism"'. In *Justification and Variegated Nomism: The Complexities of Second Temple Judaism*, eds D. A. Carson, Peter T. O'Brien and Mark A. Seifrid; Grand Rapids, MI: Baker, 2001.

Desmond, William D. *Cynics*. Ancient Philosophies, Berkeley CA: University of California Press, 2008.

The Dogmatic Constitution on Divine Revelation (*Dei Verbum*, 18 November, 1965), no. 2. Available online http://www.vatican.va/archive/hist_councils/ii_vatican_council/ documents/vat-ii_const_19651118_dei-verbum_en.html (accessed 26 October 2010).

Donaldson, Terence L. *Jews and Anti-Judaism in the New Testament: Decision Points and Interpretations*. London: SPCK, and Waco, TX: Baylor University Press, 2010.

————. *Judaism and the Gentiles: Jewish Patterns of Universalism (to 135 CE)*. Waco, TX: Baylor University Press, 2007.

————. 'Jewish Christianity, Israel's Stumbling and the *Sonderweg* Reading of Paul'. *JSNT* 29 (2006): 27–54.

————. *Paul and the Gentiles: Remapping the Apostle's Conviction World*. Minneapolis, MN: Fortress, 1997.

————. 'The "Curse of the Law" and the Inclusion of the Gentiles: Galatians 3.13-14'. *NTS* 32 (1986): 94–112.

Downing, Francis Gerald. *God with Everything: The Divine in the Discourse of the First Christian Century* (The Social World of Biblical Antiquity, Second Series 2), Sheffield: Sheffield Phoenix Press, 2008.

Downs, David J. *The Offering of the Gentiles. Paul's Collection for Jerusalem in Its Chronological, Cultural, and Cultic Contexts* (WUNT 2.248), Tübingen: Mohr Siebeck, 2008.

Dreher, Matthias. 'Luther als Paulus-Interpret bei Adolf Schlatter und Wilhelm Heitmüller. Ein forschungsgeschichtlicher Beitrag zur "New Perspective on Paul"'. *Luther* 79 (2008): 109–25.

Duff, Paul B. '"Transformed from Glory to Glory:" Paul's Appeal to the Experience of His Readers in 2 Corinthians 3.18'. *JBL* 127 (2008): 759–80.

———. 'Glory in the Ministry of Death: Gentile Condemnation and Letters of Recommendation in 2 Cor. 3.6-18'. *NovT* 46 (2004): 313–37.

———. 'The Concept of Covenant in Paul'. In *The Concept of the Covenant in the Second Temple Period*, eds Stanley E. Porter and Jacqueline C. R. de Roo; Atlanta, GA: SBL, 2003, 269–85.

Dulles, Avery Cardinal. 'Evangelization and the Jews'. With a response by Mary C. Boys, Philip A. Cunningham and John T. Pawlikowski, *America* 187.12 (21 October 2002): 8–16.

Dunn, James D. G. *The New Perspective on Paul*. Tübingen: Mohr Siebeck, 2005; rev. edn, Grand Rapids, MI: Eerdmans, 2008.

———. *The Partings of the Ways between Christianity and Judaism and their Significance for the Character of Christianity*. London: SCM, 2nd edn, 2006.

———. 'The Dialogue Progresses'. In Michael Bachmann, *Lutherische und Neue Paulusperspektive. Beiträge zu einem Schlüsselproblem der gegenwärtigen exegetischen Diskussion* (WUNT 182), Tübingen: Mohr Siebeck, 2005, 389–430.

———. 'The New Perspective: whence, what and whither?' In idem, *The New Perspective on Paul* (WUNT 185), Tübingen: Mohr Siebeck, 2005, 1–88.

———. 'Noch einmal "Works of the Law": The Dialogue Continues'. In idem, *The New Perspective on Paul: Collected Essays* (WUNT 185), Tübingen: Mohr Siebeck, 2005, 407–22.

———. 'Did Paul have a Covenant Theology? Reflections on Romans 9.4 and 11.27'. In *The Concept of the Covenant in the Second Temple Period*, eds Stanley E. Porter and Jacqueline C. R. de Roo; Atlanta, GA: SBL, 2003, 287–307.

———. 'The Embarrassment of History: Reflections on the Problem of "Anti-Judaism" in the Fourth Gospel'. In Reimund Bieringer, Didier Pollefeyt, Frederique Vandecasteele-Vanneuville (eds), *Anti-Judaism and the Fourth Gospel. Papers of the Leuven Colloquium, 2000*, Assen/Netherlands: Royal Van Gorcum, 2001, 47–67.

———. 'Who Did Paul Think He Was? A Study of Jewish-Christian Identity'. *NTS* 45 (1999): 174–93.

———. *The Theology of Paul the Apostle*. Grand Rapids, MI: Eerdmans, 1998.

———. 'Two Covenants or One? The Interdependence of Jewish and Christian Identity'. In *Geschichte-Tradition-Reflexion*, eds Hubert Cancik, Hermann Lichtenberger and Peter Schäfer, FS M. Hengel; Tübingen: Mohr Siebeck, 1996, 97–122.

———. *Jesus, Paul and the Law: Studies in Mark and Galatians*. London: SPCK, 1990.

———. 'The Theology of Galatians'. In idem, *Jesus, Paul, and the Law. Studies in Mark and Galatians*, London: SPCK, 1990, 240–64.

———. *Romans* (WBC 38), 2 vols, Dallas TX: Word, 1988.

———. *The Theology of Paul the Apostle*. Grand Rapids, MI: Eerdmans and Edinburgh: T&T Clark, 1988.

———. 'The New Perspective on Paul'. *BJRL* 65 (1983): 95–122.

Eastman, Susan Grove. 'Israel and the Mercy of God: A reading of Galatians 6.16 and Romans 9-11'. *NTS* 56 (2010): 367–95.

Ebner, Martin. 'Die Rechtfertigungslehre des Paulus in soziologisch-sozialgeschichtlicher Perspektive'. In *Paulus. Identität und Universalität des Evangeliums*, ed. N. Kleyboldt; Münster: Dialog-Verlag, 2009.

Ehrensperger, Kathy. '"Nothing is profane" and "everything is indeed pure": Hospitality and Paul's Discussion of κοινός and καθαρός in Romans 14.14 and 14.20'. Short paper presented at the SNTS General Meeting, Vienna, 2009.

———. 'Paul and the Authority of Scripture: A Feminist Perspective'. In *As It is Written: Studying Paul's Use of Scripture*, eds Christopher D. Stanley and Stanley N. Porter; Atlanta, GA: SBL, 2008, 281–308.

———. 'Reading Romans in the Face of the "Other": Levinas, the Jewish Philosopher, Meets Paul, the Jewish Apostle'. In *Reading Romans with Contemporary Philosophers and Theologians*, ed. David Odell-Scott; London and New York: T&T Clark International, 2007, 115–54.

Eisenbaum, Pamela. *Paul Was Not a Christian: The Original Message of a Misunderstood Apostle*. New York: HarperCollins, 2009.

Ellison, H. L. 'Paul and the Law – "All Things to All Men"'. In *Apostolic History and the Gospel: Biblical and Historical Essays Presented to F. F. Bruce on his 60th Birthday*, eds W. Ward Gasque and Ralph P. Martin; Grand Rapids, MI: Eerdmans, 1970, 195–202.

Engberg-Pedersen, Troels, ed. *Paul Beyond the Judaism/Hellenism Divide*. Louisville, KY: Westminster John Knox, 2001.

Eriksson, Anders. *Traditions as Rhetorical Proof: Pauline Argumentation in 1 Corinthians*, (CBNT 29), Stockholm: Almqvist & Wiksell International, 1998.

Eskola, Timo. *Theodicy and Predestination in Pauline Theology* (WUNT 2.100), Tübingen: Mohr Siebeck, 1998.

Fee, Gordon D. *The First Epistle to the Corinthians* (New International Commentary on the New Testament), Grand Rapids, MI: Eerdmans, 1987.

Finkelde, Dominik. *Politische Eschatologie nach Paulus. Badiou-Agamben-Žižek-Santner*. Wien: Turia+Kant, 2007.

Firestone, Reuven. *Who Are the Real Chosen People? The Meaning of Chosenness in Judaism, Christianity, and Islam*. Woodstock, VT: Skylight Paths, 2008.

Fishbane, Michael. *Text and Texture*. New York: Schocken, 1979.

Fisher, Eugene J. 'Official Roman Catholic Teaching on Jews and Judaism: Commentary and Context'. In *In Our Time: The Flowering of Jewish-Catholic Dialogue*, eds idem and Leon Klenicki; New York and Mahwah, NJ: Paulist Press, 1990.

———. 'Typical Jewish Misunderstandings of Christianity'. *Judaism* 22 (1973): 21–32.

Fitzmyer, Joseph A. *First Corinthians: A New Translation with Introduction and Commentary* (AB 32), New Haven, CT and London: Yale University Press, 2008.

———. *Romans* (AYBC), New Haven, CT: Yale University Press, 1992.

———. 'Romans'. In *The New Jerome Biblical Commentary*, eds Raymond E. Brown, Joseph A. Fitzmyer and Roland E. Murphy; Englewood Cliffs, NJ: Prentice Hall, 1990.

Flusser, D. 'Paul's Jewish-Christian Opponents in the Didache'. In *Gilgul. Essays on Transformation, Revolution and Permanence in the History of Religion, dedicated to R.J. Zwi Werblowsky* (SHR 50), eds Shaul Shaked et al.; Leiden: Brill, 1987, 71–90.

Flynn, T. R. 'Das Ereignis lesen: Žižek liest Badiou über den Heiligen Paulus'. in *Über Žižek. Perspektiven und Kritiken*, eds Erik M. Voigt and Hugh J. Silverman; Wien: Turia+Kant, 2004, 191–209.

Fotopoulos, John. *Food Offered to Idols in Roman Corinth: A Social-rhetorical Reconsideration of 1 Corinthians 8.1–11.1* (WUNT 2.151), Tübingen: Mohr Siebeck, 2003.

Foucault, Michel. 'Andere Räume'. In *Schriften in vier Bänden. Dits et Ecrits*, vol. 4, Frankfurt: Suhrkamp, 2005, 931–42; English version: '"Different Spaces"', in Michel Foucault, James D. Faubion and Paul Rabinow, *Aesthetics, Method, and Epistemology: Essential Works of Foucault 1954–1984*, London: New Press, 2000, 175–85.

Fowl, Stephen. 'Learning to Be a Gentile'. In *Christology and Scripture: Interdisciplinary Perspectives*, eds Andrew T. Lincoln and Angus Paddison; London and New York: T&T Clark, 2007, 22–40.

Frankemölle, Hubert. *Frühjudentum und Urchristentum. Vorgeschichte – Verlauf – Auswirkungen* (4. Jahrhundert v.Chr. bis 4. Jahrhundert n. Chr.), Stuttgart: Kohlhammer, 2006.

Frankfurter, David. 'Beyond "Jewish-Christianity": Continuing Religious sub-cultures of the second and third centuries and their documents'. In *The Ways That Never Parted: Jews and Christians in Late Antiquity and the Early Middle Ages*, Texts and Studies in Judaism, no. 95, eds Adam H. Becker and Annette Yoshiro Reed; Tübingen: Mohr Siebeck, 2003.

Fredriksen, Paula. 'Judaizing the Nations: The Ritual Demands of Paul's Gospel'. *NTS* 56 (2010): 232–52.

———. 'Paul, Purity, and *Ekklesia* of the Gentiles'. In *The Beginnings of Christianity: A Collection of Articles*, eds Jack Pastor and Menahem Mor; Jerusalem: Yad Ben-Zvi Press, 2005, 205–17.

———. 'What "Parting of the Ways"? Jews, Gentiles and the Ancient Mediterranean City'. In *The Ways That Never Parted: Jews and Christians in Late Antiquity and the Early Middle Ages* (TSJ 95), eds Adam H. Becker and Annette Yoshiro Reed; Tübingen: Mohr Siebeck, 2003, 35–64.

———. 'Judaism, the Circumcision of Gentiles, and Apocalyptic Hope'. *JTS* 42 (1991): 532–64.

Freitag, J. 'Werke II: Systematisch-theologisch'. In *LThK*³ 10 (2001): 1097–8

Frey, Jörg. 'Paul's Jewish Identity'. In *Jewish Identity in the Greco-Roman World*, eds Jörg Frey, Daniel R. Schwartz and Stephanie Gripentrog (AGJU 71), Leiden: Brill, 2007.

———. 'Das Judentum des Paulus'. In *Paulus. Leben – Umwelt – Werke – Briefe*, ed. O. Wischmeyer (UTB 2767), Tübingen/Basel, 2006, 5–43.

Frey, Jörg, Daniel R. Schwartz and Stephanie Gripentrog, eds. *Jewish Identity in the Greco-Roman World* (AGJU 71), Leiden: Brill, 2007.

Fuchs-Kreimer, Nancy. 'The "Essential Heresy": Paul's View of the Law According to Jewish Writers: 1886–1986'. PhD dissertation, Temple University, 1990.

Funke, Hermann. 'Antisthenes bei Paulus'. *Hermes* 98 (1970): 459–71.

Furnish, Victor Paul. *The Theology of the First Letter to the Corinthians*. New Testament Theology, Cambridge and New York: Cambridge University Press, 1999.

———. *II Corinthians* (AB), New York and London: Doubleday, 1984.

Gadenz, Pablo T. *Called from the Jews and from the Gentiles. Pauline Ecclesiology in Romans 9–11* (WUNT 2.267), Tübingen: Mohr Siebeck, 2009.

Gager, John. 'Did Jewish Christians See the Rise of Islam?'. In *The Ways That Never Parted: Jews and Christians in Late Antiquity and the Early Middle Ages* (TSJ 95), eds Adam H. Becker and Annette Yoshiro Reed; Tübingen: Mohr Siebeck, 2003, 366–7.

———. *Reinventing Paul*. Oxford: Oxford University Press, 2000.

Garland, David E. 'The Dispute Over Food Sacrificed to Idols (1 Cor. 8.1–11.1)'. *PrST* 30.2 (2003): 173–97.

Gaston, Lloyd. *Paul and the Torah*. Vancouver: University of British Columbia Press, 1987.

Georgi, Dieter. 'The Early Church: Internal Jewish Migration or New Religion?'. *HTR* 88 (1995): 35–68.

Gerdmar, Anders. *Rethinking the Judaism-Hellenism Dichotomy: A Historiographical Case Study of Second Peter and Jude* (CBNT 36), Stockholm: Almqvist & Wiksell, 2001.

Giesen, Heinz. 'Befreiung des Gesetzes aus der Sklaverei als Ermöglichung der Gesetzeserfüllung (Röm 8,1-4)'. *BZ NF* 53 (2009): 179–211.

Gill, David W. J. and Conrad H. Gempf, eds. *The Book of Acts in its Graeco-Roman Setting* (Book of Acts in its First Century Setting), Grand Rapids, MI and Carlisle, UK: Eerdmans and Paternoster Press, 1994.

Given, Mark Douglas. *Paul's True Rhetoric: Ambiguity, Cunning, and Deception in Greece and Rome* (Emory Studies in Early Christianity 7), Harrisburg, PA: Trinity Press International, 2001.

Glad, Clarence E. 'Paul and Adaptability'. In *Paul in the Greco-Roman World: A Handbook.* ed. J. Paul Sampley; Harrisburg, PA: Trinity Press International, 2003, 17–41.

———. *Paul and Philodemus: Adaptability in Epicurean and Early Christian Psychagogy.* Supplements to Novum Testamentum 81. Leiden and New York: E.J. Brill, 1995.

Gooch, Paul W. 'The Ethics of Accommodation: A Study in Paul'. *TynBul* 29 (1978): 93–117.

Gooch, Peter David. *Dangerous Food: I Corinthians 8-10 in its Context.* SCJ 5. Waterloo, Ontario: Wilfrid Laurier University Press, 1993.

Gundry, Robert H. *The Old is Better: New Testament Essays in Support of Traditional Interpretations* (WUNT 178), Tübingen: Mohr Siebeck, 2005, 195–224.

Haacker, Klaus. 'Verdienste und Grenzen der "neuen Perspektive" der Paulus-Auslegung'. In Michael Bachmann, ed. (in cooperation with J. Woyke), *Lutherische und Neue Paulusperspektive. Beiträge zu einem Schlüsselproblem der gegenwärtigen exegetischen Diskussion* (WUNT 182), Tübingen: Mohr Siebeck, 2005, 1–15.

———. *Der Brief des Paulus an die Römer* (ThHK 6), 2nd, corrected edn, Leipzig: EVA, 2002.

———. 'Umkehr zu Israel und "Heimholung ins Judentum"'. Schritte zur Versöhnung zwischen Christen und Juden'. In idem, *Versöhnung mit Israel. Exegetische Beiträge* (Veröffentlichungen der Kirchlichen Hochschule Wuppertal 5), Neukirchen-Vluyn: Neukirchener Verlag, 2002, 191–208.

———. '"Ende des Gesetzes" und kein Ende? Zur Diskussion über te,loj no,mou in Röm 10,4'. In *Ja und nein. Christliche Theologie im Angesicht Israels. Festschrift zum 70. Geburtstag von Wolfgang Schrage*, eds K. Wengst and G. Saß (in cooperation with K. Kriener and R. Stuhlmann); Neukirchen-Vluyn: Neukirchener Verlag, 1998, 127–38.

———. 'Das Evangelium Gottes und die Erwählung Israels. Zum Beitrag des Römerbriefs zur Erneuerung des Verhältnisses zwischen Christen und Juden'. *TBei* 13 (1982): 70–1.

Hafemann, Scott J. *Paul, Moses, and the History of Israel.* Peabody, MA: Hendrickson, 1995.

———. *Paul, Moses, and the History of Israel: The Letter/Spirit Contrast and the Argument from Scripture in 2 Corinthians 3* (WUNT 81), Tübingen: Mohr Siebeck, 1995.

Hagner, Donald A. 'Paul as a Jewish Believer – According to his Letters'. In *Jewish Believers in Jesus: The Early Centuries*, eds Oskar Skarsaune and Reidar Hvalvik; Peabody, MA: Hendrickson, 2007, 97–120.

Hall, Barbara. 'All Things to All People: A Study of 1 Corinthians 9.19-23'. In *The Conversation Continues: Studies in Paul & John In Honor of J. Louis Martyn*, eds Robert T. Fortna and Beverly R. Gaventa; Nashville, TN: Abingdon Press, 1990, 137–57.

Harink, Douglas. *Paul Among the Postliberals: Pauline Theology Beyond Christendom and Modernity.* Grand Rapids, MI: Brazos Press, 2003.

Harkins, Paul W. *Saint John Chrysostom: Discourses Against Judaizing Christians* (The Fathers of the Church: A New Translation 68), Washington, DC: Catholic University Press of America, 1979.

Härle, Wilfried. 'Paulus und Luther. Ein kritischer Blick auf die "New Perspective"'. In *Spurensuche nach Gott. Studien zur Fundamentaltheologie und Gotteslehre*, Berlin: de Gruyter, 2008, 202–39.

———. 'Paulus und Luther. Ein kritischer Blick auf die "New Perspective"'. *ZThK* 103 (2006): 326–39.

Harrington, Daniel J. *Paul on the Mystery of Israel.* Collegeville, MN: Liturgical Press, 1992.

Hays, Richard B. *First Corinthians* (Interpretation), Louisville, KY: John Knox Press, 1997.

Heath, Malcolm. 'Invention'. In *Handbook of Classical Rhetoric in the Hellenistic Period: 330 B.C.–A.D. 400*, ed. Stanley E. Porter; Boston and Leiden: Brill, 2001, 89–119.

Heckel, Ulrich. 'Das Bild der Heiden und die Identität der Christen bei Paulus'. In *Die*

Heiden: Juden, Christen und das Problem des Fremden, eds Reinhard Feldmeier, Ulrich Heckel and Martin Hengel; Tübingen: Mohr Siebeck, 1994, 269–96.

Hengel, Martin. *Judaism and Hellenism*. 2 vols, trans. John Bowden; London: SCM, 1974.

Henrix, Hans Hermann. *Gottes Ja zu Israel. Ökumenische Studien christlicher Theologie*. Berlin: Aachen, 2005.

Hodge, Caroline Johnson. *If Sons, Then Heirs: A Study of Kinship and Ethnicity in the Letters of Paul*. New York: Oxford University Press, 2007.

———. 'Apostle to the Gentiles: Constructions of Paul's Identity'. *BibInt* 13 (2005): 270–88.

Hoet, Hendrik. '"Abraham is our Father" (John 8:39). The Gospel of John and the Jewish-Christian Dialogue'. In *Anti-Judaism and the Fourth Gospel. Papers of the Leuven Colloquium, 2000*, eds Reimund Bieringer, Didier Pollefeyt, Frederique Vandecasteele-Vanneuville; Assen/Netherlands: Royal Van Gorcum, 2001, 187–201.

Hoff, Gregor Maria. 'Die paulinische Inversion. Die dekonstruktiven Paulus-Lektüren Slavoy Žižeks und Giorgio Agambens'. *Communio: Internationale katholische Zeitschrift* 38 (2009): 179–90.

Hofius, Otfried. '"Werke des Gesetzes". Untersuchungen zu der paulinischen Rede von den ἔργα νόμου'. In idem, *Exegetische Studien* (WUNT 223), Tübingen: Mohr Siebeck 2008, 49–88.

———. 'Gesetz und Evangelium nach 2. Korinther 3'. In idem, *Paulusstudien* (WUNT 51), Tübingen: Mohr Siebeck, 1994.

Hogan, Pauline Nigh. *'No Longer Male and Female': Interpreting Galatians 3:28 in Early Christianity* (LNTS 380), London: T&T Clark, 2008.

Holmberg, Bengt. *Exploring Early Christian Identity*. Tübingen: Mohr Siebeck, 2008.

Hooker, Morna D. *From Adam to Christ*. Cambridge: Cambridge University Press, 1990.

———. 'Paul and "Covenantal Nomism"' (1982). In idem, *From Adam to Christ: Essays on Paul*, Cambridge: Cambridge University Press, 1990, 155–64.

Horn, Friedrich. W. 'Die Darstellung und Begründung der Ethik des Apostels Paulus in der *new perspective*'. In idem and Ruben Zimmermann (eds), *Jenseits von Indikativ und Imperativ. Kontexte und Normen neutestamentlicher Ethik I* (WUNT 238), Tübingen, 2009, 213–31.

———. 'Juden und Heiden. Aspekte der Verhältnisbestimmung in den paulinischen Briefen. Ein Gespräch mit Krister Stendahl'. In Michael Bachmann, *Lutherische und Neue Paulusperspektive. Beiträge zu einem Schlüsselproblem der gegenwärtigen exegetischen Diskussion* (WUNT 182), Tübingen: Mohr Siebeck, 2005, 17–39.

Horsley, Richard. *Wisdom and Spiritual Transcendence at Corinth: Studies in First Corinthians*. Eugene, OR: Cascade Books, 2008.

Hubbard, Moyer. *New Creation in Paul's Letters and Thought*. Cambridge: Cambridge University Press, 2002.

Hübner, Hans. *Das Gesetz bei Paulus. Ein Beitrag zum Werden der paulinischen Theologie* (FRLANT 119). Göttingen: Vandenhoeck and Ruprecht, 3rd edn, 1982.

———. 'νόμος'. *EWNT* 2 (1981): 1158–72.

Huttunen, Niko. 'Greco-Roman Philosophy and Paul's Teaching on the Law'. In *The Nordic Paul: Finnish Approaches to Pauline Theology*, eds Lars Aejmelaeus and Antti Mustakallio; London and New York: T&T Clark, 2008.

Hvalvik, Reidar. 'A "Sonderweg" for Israel: A Critical Examination of Current Interpretation of Romans 11.25-27'. *JSNT* 38 (1990): 87–107.

Jackson-McCabe, Matt. *Jewish Christianity Reconsidered: Rethinking Ancient Groups and Texts*. Minneapolis: Fortress, 2007.

Jaubert, Annie. *La notion d'alliance dans le judaïsme aux abords de l'ère chrétienne* (Patristica Sorboniensia 6), Paris: Éditions du Seuil, 1963.

Jervell, Jacob. 'The Letter to Jerusalem'. In *The Romans Debate*, ed. Karl P. Donfried, rev. and exp. edn; Peabody, MA: Hendrickson, 1991, 53–64.

————. *The Unknown Paul: Essays on Luke–Acts and Early Christian History*. Minneapolis, MN: Augsburg, 1984.

————. *Luke and the People of God: A New Look at Luke–Acts*. Minneapolis, MN: Augsburg, 1972.

Johnson, Luke Timothy. *Hebrews: A Commentary* (NTL), Louisville, KY, and London: Westminster John Knox Press, 2006.

Jossa, Giorgio. *Jews or Christians? The Followers of Jesus in Search of their own Identity* (WUNT 202), Tübingen: Mohr Siebeck, 2006.

Käsemann, Ernst. *Commentary on Romans*. London: SCM, 1980.

————. 'The Righteousness of God in Paul'. In idem, *New Testament Questions of Today*, London: SCM, 1969, 168–82.

Kasper, Walter Cardinal. 'Striving for Mutual Respect in Modes of Prayer'. *L'Osservatore Romano*, 16 April 2008: 8–9.

————. 'Christians, Jews and the Thorny Question of Mission'. *Origins* 32.28 (19 December 2002).

————. 'The Good Olive Tree'. *America* 185.7 (17 September 2001).

Kauppi, Lynn Allan. *Foreign but Familiar Gods: Greco-Romans Read Religion in Acts* (LNTS 277), London and New York: T&T Clark, 2006.

Keesmaat, Sylvia C. 'Paul and his Story. Exodus and Tradition in Galatians'. In *Early Christian Interpretation of the Scriptures of Israel. Investigations and Proposals*, eds Craig A. Evans and James A. Sanders (JSNTSup 148), Sheffield: Academic Press, 1997, 301–33.

Kellermann, Ulrich. *Das Achtzehn-Bitten-Gebet. Jüdischer Glaube in neutestamentlicher Zeit. Ein Kommentar*. Neukirchen-Vluyn: Neukirchener, 2007.

Kertelge, Karl. *Rechtfertigung bei Paulus*. Münster: Aschendorff, 1967.

Klausner, Joseph. *From Jesus to Paul*. Boston, MA: Beacon, 1939.

Klenicki, Leon and Eugene J. Fisher, eds. *Root and Branches: Biblical Judaism, Rabbinic Judaism, and Early Christianity*. Winona, MN: Saint Mary's Press, 1987.

Klinghoffer, David. *Why the Jews Rejected Jesus: The Turning Point in Western History*. New York: Doubleday, 2005.

Knox, Wilfred L. *St. Paul and the Church of Jerusalem*. Cambridge: Cambridge University Press, 1925.

Kotsko, Adam. *Žižek and Theology*. London and New York: T&T Clark, 2008.

Kottsieper, Ingo. 'Hebräische, transjordanische und aramäische Briefe'. *TUAT.NF* 3 (2006): 357–83.

Kraus, W. *Das Volk Gottes. Zur Grundlegung der Ekklesiologie bei Paulus* (WUNT 85), Tübingen: Mohr Siebeck, 1996.

Krötke, W. 'Gute Werke II: Dogmatisch'. *RGG⁴* 3 (2000): 1344–5.

Kuula, Kari. *The Law, the Covenant and God's Plan*. Vol. 2: *Paul's Treatment of the Law and Israel in Romans* (FES 85), Göttingen: Vandenhoeck & Ruprecht, 2002.

Lake, Kirsopp. '"Your Own Poets": Note XX'. In *The Acts of the Apostles: Part 1, Vol. 5*. eds idem and Henry Joel Cadbury, *The Beginnings of Christianity*, London: Macmillan, 1920, 246–51.

Lambrecht, Jan. 'Transformation in 2 Cor. 3.18'. In Reimund Bieringer and Jan Lambrecht, *Studies on 2 Corinthians* (BETL 112), Leuven: Leuven University Press – Peeters, 1994, 295–307.

Langton, Daniel R. 'The Myth of the "Traditional View of Paul" and the Role of the Apostle in Modern Jewish-Christian Polemics'. *JSNT* 28.1 (2005): 69–104.

Lausberg, Heinrich. *Handbook of Literary Rhetoric: A Foundation for Literary Study*. Leiden, Boston, Köln: Brill, 1998, trans. by M. T. Bliss, A. Jansen and D. E. Orton of *Handbuch der literarischen Rhetorik. Eine Grundlegung der Literaturwissenschaft*. München: Max Hueber, 1973.

Levine, Amy-Jill. *The Misunderstood Jew: The Church and the Scandal of the Jewish Jesus*. New York: HarperSanFranscisco, Harper Collins, 2006, 2007.

Lichtenberger, Hermann and Stefan Schreiner. 'Der neue Bund in jüdischer Überlieferung'. *Theologische Quartalschrift* 176.4 (1996): 272–90.

Lieu, Judith. *Christian Identity in the Jewish and Graeco-Roman World*. Oxford: Oxford University Press, 2004.

Lohmeyer, Ernst. *Probleme paulinischer Theologie*. Stuttgart: Kohlhammer, s.d.; Darmstadt: Wissenschaftliche Buchgesellschaft, 1954.

———. 'Gesetzeswerke'. *ZNW* 28 (1929): 177–207.

Löhr, Helmut. 'Paulus unter den Philosophen. Eine Besinnung auf den Zweck paulinischer Theologie'. *GlLern* 23 (2008): 150–63.

Lohse, Eduard. *Paulus*. München: C.H. Beck, 1996.

Longenecker, Bruce. 'On Israel's God and God's Israel: Assessing Supersessionism in Paul'. *JTS* 58 (2007): 26–44.

———. 'On Critiquing the "New Perspective" on Paul: A Case Study'. *ZNW* 96 (2005): 266–9.

———. *The Triumph of Abraham's God: The Transformation of Identity in Galatians*. Nashville, TN: Abingdon, 1998.

———. *Eschatology and the Covenant: A Comparison of 4 Ezra and Romans 9–11*. Sheffield: Sheffield Academic Press, 1991.

Longenecker, Richard Norman. *Paul, Apostle of Liberty*. New York: Harper & Row, 1964.

Luz, Menahem. 'Salam, Meleager!'. *Studi italiani di filologia classica* 6 (1988): 222–31.

Macarius Magnes. *Apocritus* 3.31. Trans. R. Joseph Hoffmann, *Porphyry's Against the Christians: The Literary Remains*. New York: Prometheus Books, 1994.

Maccoby, Hyam. *Paul and Hellenism*. London: SCM, 1991.

———. *The Mythmaker: Paul and the Invention of Christianity*. New York: Harper & Row, 1986.

Malherbe, Abraham J. *Paul and the Popular Philosophers*. Minneapolis, MN: Fortress Press, 1989.

Marshall, I. Howard. 'Palestinian and Hellenistic Christian: Some Critical Comments'. *NTS* 19 (1973): 271–87.

Martin, Dale B. *Slavery as Salvation: The Metaphor of Slavery in Pauline Christianity*. New Haven, CT: Yale University Press, 1990.

Martyn, J. Louis. *Galatians: A New Translation with Introduction and Commentary* (AB 33), New York: Doubleday, 1997.

Mayer, Bernhard. *Unter Gottes Heilsratschluss. Prädestinationaussagen bei Paulus*. Würzburg: Echter, 1974.

McGinn, S. E., ed. *Celebrating Romans: Template for Pauline Theology*, FS Robert Jewett; Grand Rapids, MI: Eerdmans, 2004.

Meeks, Wayne. *Christ Is the Question*. Louisville, KY: Westminster/John Knox Press, 2006.

———. 'Breaking Away: Three New Testament Pictures of Christianity's Separation from Jewish Communities'. In *'To See Ourselves as Others see Us': Christians, Jews, and 'Others' in Late Antiquity*, eds J. Neusner and E. S. Frerich; Chico, CA: Scholars, 1985.

Meeks, Wayne, ed. *The Writings of St. Paul*. New York: Norton, 1972.

Meier, John P. *Companions and Competitors*. New York: Doubleday, 2001.

Meiser, Martin. 'Vom Nutzen der patristischen Exegese für die neutestamentliche Schriftauslegung (am Beispiel des Galaterbriefes)'. In *Paulus und die antike Welt. Beiträge zur zeit- und religionskundlichen Erforschung des paulinischen Christentums. Festgabe für Dietrich-Alex Koch zum 65. Geburtstag* (FRLANT 222), eds David C. Bienert, Joachim Jeska and Thomas Witulski; Göttingen: Vandenhoeck und Ruprecht, 2008, 189–209.

———. *Galater* (Novum Testamentum Patristicum 9), Göttingen: Vandenhoeck und Ruprecht, 2007.

Meißner, Stefan. *Die Heimholung des Ketzers: Studien zur jüdischen Auseinandersetzung mit Paulus* (WUNT 2.87), Tübingen: Mohr Siebeck, 1996.

Merklein, Helmut. 'Die Ekklesia Gottes. "Der Kirchenbegriff bei Paulus und in Jerusalem"'. In idem, *Studien zu Jesus und Paulus* (WUNT 43), Tübingen: Mohr Siebeck, 1987, 296–318.

Mitchell, Margaret M. 'Pauline Accommodation and "Condescension" (συγκατάβασις): 1 Cor. 9.19-23 and the History of Influence'. In *Paul Beyond the Judaism/Hellenism Divide*, ed. Troels Engberg-Pedersen; Louisville, KY: Westminster John Knox Press, 2001, 197–214 .

———. '"A Variable and Many-sorted Man": John Chrysostom's Treatment of Pauline Inconsistency'. *Journal of Early Christian Studies* 6.1 (1998): 93–111.

———. *Paul and the Rhetoric of Reconciliation: An Exegetical Investigation of the Language and Composition of 1 Corinthians*. Louisville, KY: Westminster/John Knox Press, 1992.

Montefiore, C. G. *Judaism and St. Paul: Two Essays*. New York: Dutton, 1915.

Moo, Douglas J. *The Epistle to the Romans* (NICNT), Grand Rapids, MI: Eerdmans, 1996.

Moule, C. F. D. 'Jesus, Judaism, and Paul'. In *Tradition and Interpretation in the New Testament*, eds G. F. Hawthorne and O. Betz; Grand Rapids, MI: Eerdmans, 1987.

Müller, Klaus and Peter von der Osten-Sacken, eds. *Tora für die Völker. Die noachidischen Gebote und Ansätze zu ihrer Rezeption im Christentum* (SKI 15), Berlin: Institut Kirche und Judentum, 1994.

Müller, M. 'Aufhören oder Vollendung des Gesetzes? Eine Antwort an Friedrich Beißer'. *KuD* 53 (2005): 308–9.

———. 'Jesus und das Gesetz. Eine Skizze im Licht der Rezeptionen'. *KuD* 50 (2004): 208–25.

———. '"Evangelium latuit in lege": Luthers Kreuzespredigt als Schlüssel seiner Bibelhermeneutik'. In Christoph Landmesser, et al., eds, *Jesus Christus als die Mitte der Schrift*, FS Otfried Hofius (BZNW 86), Berlin: de Gruyter, 1997, 101–26.

Murphy-O'Connor, Jerome. 'A Ministry Beyond the Letter (2 Cor. 3.1-6)'. In Lorenzo de Lorenzi, ed., *Paolo Ministro del nuovo Testamento (2 Co 2,14–4,6)* (Serie Monographica di 'Benedictina': Sezione Biblico Ecumenica 9), Rome: Benedictina, 1987, 105–57.

Mußner, Franz. *Traktat über die Juden*. München: Kösel, 1979.

Nanos, Mark D. 'The Myth of the "Law-Free" Paul Standing Between Christians and Jews'. *Studies in Christian–Jewish Relations* 4 (2009): 1–21.

———. 'Paul and Judaism: Why Not Paul's Judaism?'. In *Paul Unbound: Other Perspectives on the Apostle*, ed. Mark Douglas Given; Peabody, MA: Hendrickson, 2009, 117–60.

———. 'Paul's Reversal of Jews Calling Gentiles "Dogs" (Philippians 3.2): 1600 Years of an Ideological Tale Wagging an Exegetical Dog?'. *BibInt* 17 (2009): 448–82.

———. 'The Polytheist Identity of the "Weak," And Paul's Strategy to "Gain" Them: A New Reading of 1 Corinthians 8.1–11.1'. In *Paul: Jew, Greek, and Roman*, ed. Stanley E. Porter; Pauline Studies 5, Leiden and Boston: Brill, 2008, 179–210.

———. 'Paul between Jews and Christians'. *BibInt* 13 (2005): 221–316.

———. 'How inter-Christian approaches to Paul's rhetoric can perpetuate negative valuations of Jewishness – Although proposing to avoid that outcome'. *BibInt* 13 (2002): 255–69.

———. *The Irony of Galatians: Paul's Letter in First-Century Context*. Minneapolis, MN: Fortress Press, 2002.

———. 'What Was at Stake in Peter's "Eating with Gentiles" at Antioch?'. In idem, ed., *The Galatians Debate: Contemporary Issues in Rhetorical and Historical Interpretation*, Peabody, MA: Hendrickson, 2002, 282–318.

———. 'The Jewish Context of the Gentile Audience Addressed in Paul's Letter to the Romans'. *CBQ* 61 (1999): 283–304.

———. *The Mystery of Romans: The Jewish Context of Paul's Letter*. Minneapolis, MN: Fortress Press, 1996.

Nasuti, Harry P. 'The Woes of the Prophets and the Rights of the Apostle: The Internal Dynamics of 1 Corinthians 9'. *CBQ* 50 (1988): 246–64.

Nathan, Emmanuel. 'Paul Between Coherence and Contingency: Taking a Closer Look at Paul's Language in 2 Cor. 3'. *Pauline Theology in the Making Seminar*, SBL Annual Meeting, New Orleans, 2009, 1–8.

Navia, Luis E. *Antisthenes of Athens: Setting the World Aright* (Contributions in Philosophy 80), Westport, CT: Greenwood Press, 2001.

Neubrand, Maria. *Israel, die Völker und die Kirche. Eine exegetische Studie zu Apg 15*. SBB 55. Stuttgart, 2006.

Neusner, Jacob. *The Emergence of Judaism*. Louisville, KY: Westminster John Knox, 2004.

———. *Ein Rabbi spricht mit Jesus. Ein jüdisch-christlicher Dialog*. München: Herder, 1997.

Niebuhr, Karl-Wilhelm. 'Paulus im Judentum seiner Zeit. Der Heidenapostel aus Israel in "neuer Sicht"'. *Communio: Internationale katholische Zeitschrift* 38 (2009): 108–118.

———. *Heidenapostel aus Israel: Die jüdische Identität des Paulus nach ihrer Darstellung in seinen Briefen* (WUNT 62), Tübingen: Mohr/Siebeck, 1992.

Novak, David. *Jewish–Christian Dialogue: A Jewish Justification*. New York and Oxford: Oxford University Press, 1989.

O'Brien, Peter T. 'Was Paul a Covenantal Nomist?'. In *Justification and Variegated Nomism: Volume 2 – The Paradoxes of Paul*, eds D. A. Carson, Peter T. O'Brien and Mark Seifrid; Grand Rapids, MI: Baker, 2004.

Osten-Sacken, Peter von der. *Christian-Jewish Dialogue: Theological Foundations*. Philadelphia, PA: Fortress Press, 1986.

Pardee, Dennis. *Handbook of Ancient Hebrew Letters*. SBL.SBibSt 15, Chico, CA: Scholars, 1982.

Partington, Angela, ed. *The Oxford Dictionary of Quotations*, 4th edn, Oxford: Oxford University Press, 1992.

Pawlikowski, John. 'Christology and the Jewish-Christian Dialogue: A Personal Theological Journey'. *ITQ* 72.2 (2007): 147–67.

———. *Christ in the Light of Christian-Jewish Dialogue*. New York: Paulist, 1982; repr. Eugene, OR: Wipf and Stock, 2001.

———. 'Rethinking Christianity: A Challenge to Jewish Attitudes'. *Moment* 15/4 (Aug. 1990): 36–9.

———. *Jesus and the Theology of Israel*. Wilmington, DE: Michael Glazier, 1989.

Penna, Romano. 'L'évolution de l'attitude de Paul envers les Juifs'. In Albert Vanhoye, ed., *L'apôtre Paul. Personnalité, style et conception du ministère* (BETL 73), Leuven: Leuven University Press – Peeters, 1986, 390–421.

Perelmuter, Hayim Goren and Wilhelm Wuellner (eds), *Proceedings: Conference on the Question of the Letters of Paul Viewed from the Perspective of The Jewish Response Mode*. Chicago: Catholic Theological Union, 15–18 November 1991.

Phillips J. B. *The New Testament in Modern English*. Rev. edn. New York: Macmillan, 1972.

Pontifical Biblical Commission. *The Jewish People and Their Sacred Scriptures in the Christian Bible*. Vatican City: Libreria Editrice Vaticana, 2002.

Pope Benedict XVI/Joseph Ratzinger. *Jesus von Nazareth. Erster Teil von der Taufe im Jordan bis zur Verklärung*. Freiburg: Herder, 2007.

———. *Farewell Ceremony Address, Ben Gurion Airport*, Tel Aviv, Israel, 15 May 2009. Available at: http://www.vatican.va/holy_father/benedict_xvi/speeches/2009/may/documents/hf_ben-xvi_spe_20090515_farewell-tel-aviv_en.html.

Porter, Stanley E. 'Was Paul a Good Jew? Fundamental Issues in a Current Debate'. In *Christian-Jewish Relations Through the Centuries*, eds idem and B. W. R. Pearson; JSNTSup 192, Sheffield: Sheffield Academic Press, 2000, 148–74.

Qimron E. and J. Strugnell. *Qumran Cave 4. Vol. V: Miqṣat Maʿaśe Ha-Torah* (DJD X), Oxford: Clarendon, 1994.

――――. 'An Unpublished Halakhic Letter from Qumran'. In *Biblical Archaeology Today. Proceedings of the International Congress on Biblical Archaeology, Jerusalem, April 1984*, eds J. Aviram et al., Jerusalem, 1985, 400–7.

Räisänen, Heikki. *Paul and the Law*. Philadelphia, PA: Fortress Press, 1986.

――――. 'Galatians 2.16 and Paul's Break with Judaism'. *NTS* 31 (1985): 543–53.

Rapa, Robert K. *The Meaning of 'Works of the Law' in Galatians and Romans* (Studies in Biblical Literature 31), New York et al.: Lang, 2001.

Reinhartz, Adele. '"Jews" and Jews in the Fourth Gospel'. In *Anti-Judaism and the Fourth Gospel. Papers of the Leuven Colloquium, 2000*, eds Reimund Bieringer, Didier Pollefeyt and Frederique Vandecasteele-Vanneuville; Assen/Netherlands: Royal Van Gorcum, 2001, 341–56.

Reis, David. 'Flip-Flop?: John Chrysostom's Polytropic Paul'. *JGRChJ* 4 (2007): 9–31.

Rendtorff, Rolf. 'Ein gemeinsamer Bund fur Juden und Christen? Auf der Suche nach einer neuen Bestimmung der christlich Identität'. *Kirche und Israel* 1 (1994): 3–20.

――――. *Hat denn Gott sein Volk verstoßen? Die evangelische Kirche und das Judentum seit 1945. Ein Kommentar* (ACJD 18), München: Kaiser, 1989.

Richardson, P. 'Pauline Inconsistency: 1 Corinthians 9.19-23 and Galatians 2.11-14'. *NTS* 26 (1979): 347–62.

――――. 'Early Christian Sources of an Accommodation Ethic – From Jesus to Paul'. *TynBul* 29 (1978): 118–42.

――――. *Israel in the Apostolic Church*, Cambridge: Cambridge University Press, 1969.

Richardson, Peter and Paul W. Gooch. 'Accommodation Ethics'. *TynBul* 29 (1978): 89–93.

Rissi, Mathias. *Studien zum zweiten Korintherbrief: Der alte Bund – Der Prediger – Der Tod*. ATANT 56; Zürich: Zwingli Verlag, 1969.

Roo, Jacqueline C. R. de. *Works of the Law at Qumran and in Paul*. New Testament Monographs 13; Sheffield: Sheffield Phoenix Press, 2007.

Rudolph, David Jacob. 'A Jew to the Jews: Jewish Contours of Pauline Flexibility in 1 Corinthians 9.19-23'. PhD dissertation: Selwyn College, University of Cambridge, 2006,

Runesson, Anders. 'Particularistic Judaism and Universalistic Christianity?: Some Critical Remarks on Terminology and Theology'. *ST* 54 (2000): 55–75.

Saldarini, Anthony J. 'Christian Anti-Judaism: The First Century Speaks to the Twenty-First Century'. The Joseph Cardinal Jerusalem Lecture 1999. Chicago: Archdiocese of Chicago, The American Jewish Committee, Spertus Institute of Jewish Studies and the Jewish United Fund/Jewish Community Relations Council, 1999.

――――. 'Jews and Christians in the First Two Centuries: The Changing Paradigm'. *Shofar* 10 (1992): 32–43.

Sanders, E. P. 'Covenantal Nomism Revisited'. *JSQ* 16 (2009): 23–55.

――――. 'Jewish Associations with Gentiles and Galatians 2.11-14'. In *The Conversation Continues: Studies in Paul and John in Honor of J. Louis Martyn*, eds Robert T. Fortna and Beverly R. Gaventa; Nashville, TN: Abingdon, 1990.

――――. *Paul, the Law, and the Jewish People*. Philadelphia, PA: Fortress, 1983.

――――. *Paul and Palestinian Judaism: A Comparison of Patterns of Religion*. Minneapolis, MN: Fortress, 1977. German translation: *Paulus und das palästinische Judentum. Ein Vergleich zweier Religionsstrukturen* (StUNT 17), Göttingen: Vandenhoeck und Ruprecht, 1985.

Sanders E. P. et al., eds. *Jewish and Christian Self-Definition: Vol. 2: Aspects of Judaism in the Graeco-Roman Period*. London: SCM, 1981.

Sandmel, Samuel. *The Genius of Paul*. Philadelphia, PA: Fortress, 1979.

――――. *Judaism and Christian Beginnings*. Oxford: Oxford University Press, 1978.

Sänger, Dieter. 'Review of G. Harvey, *The True Israel. Uses of the Names Jew, Hebrew and*

Israel in Ancient Jewish and Early Christian Literature (AGJU 35), Leiden et al. 1996'. *ThLZ* 123 (1998): 737–40.

Santner, Eric. 'Miracles Happen: Benjamin, Rosenzweig, Freud and the Matter of the Neighbor'. In *The Neighbor. Three Inquiries in Political Theolog*, eds Slavoj Žižek, Erich Santner, Kenneth Reinhard; Chicago: Chicago University Press 2005, 76–134.

———. *The Psychotheology of Everyday Life. Reflections on Freud and Rosenzweig.* Chicago: Chicago University Press, 2005.

Schaff, Philip, ed. *A Select Library of the Nicene and Post-Nicene Fathers of the Christian Church.* First Series. Vol. XII: *Saint Chrysostom: Homilies on the Epistles of Paul to the Corinthians.* Grand Rapids, MI: Eerdmans, 1978.

Schaller, Bernd. '"Christus, der Diener der Beschneidung ... auf ihn werden die Völker hoffen": Zu Charakter und Funktion der Schriftzitate in Röm. 15.7-13'. In *Das Gesetz im frühen Judentum und im Neuen Testament*, eds Dieter Sänger and Matthias Konradt; Göttingen: Vandenhoeck & Ruprecht, 2006, 261–85.

Schewe, Susanne. *Die Galater zurückgewinnen. Paulinische Strategien in Gal 5 und 6.* FRLANT 208; Göttingen: Vandenhoeck & Ruprecht, 2005, 199–200.

Schippan, Thea. *Einführung in die Semasiologie.* 2nd, rev. edn; Leipzig: VEB, 1975.

Schlier, Heinrich. *Der Brief an die Galater* (KEK 7), 10th edn; Göttingen: Vandenhoeck und Ruprecht, 1949.

Schneiders, Sandra M. *The Revelatory Text: Interpreting the New Testament as Sacred Scripture.* San Francisco, CA: HarperCollins, 1991.

Schnelle, Udo. 'Paulus und das Gesetz. Biographisches und Konstruktives'. In *Biographie und Persönlichkeit des Paulus*, eds Eve-Marie Becker and Peter Pilhofer (WUNT 187), Tübingen: Mohr Siebeck, 2005, 245–70.

Schoeps, Hans Joachim. *Paul: The Theology of the Apostle in the Light of Jewish Religious History.* Philadelphia, PA: Westminster, 1961.

Schönborn, Christoph. 'Judaism's Way to Salvation'. *The Tablet*, 29 March 2008.

Schrage, Wolfgang. *Der erste Brief an die Korinther.* 4 vols. Neukirchen-Vluyn: Neukirchener Verlag, 1991–9.

———. '"Israel nach dem Fleisch" (1Kor 10,18)'. In *'Wenn nicht jetzt, wann dann?'. Aufsätze für Hans-Joachim Kraus zum 65. Geburtstag*, ed. H.-G. Geyer et al.; Neukirchen-Vluyn: Neukirchener Verlag, 1983, 143–51.

Schreiber, Stefan. 'Paulus und die Tradition. Zur Hermeneutik der "Rechtfertigung" in neuer Perspektive'. *ThRv* 105 (2009): 91–102.

Schrenk, G. 'Der Segenswunsch nach der Kampfepistel'. *Jud.* 6 (1950): 170–90.

———. 'Was bedeutet "Israel Gottes"?'. *Jud.* 5 (1949): 81–94.

Schröter, Jens. 'Paulus in der Apostelgeschichte'. *Communio: Internationale katholische Zeitschrift* 38 (2009): 135–48.

———. 'Die Universalisierung des Gesetzes im Galaterbrief. Ein Beitrag zum Gesetzesverständnis des Paulus'. In idem, *Von Jesus zum Neuen Testament. Studien zur urchristlichen Theologiegeschichte und zur Entstehung des neutestamentlichen Kanons* (WUNT 204), Tübingen: Mohr Siebeck, 2007, 171–201.

Scroggs, Robin. 'The Judaizing of the New Testament'. *Chicago Theological Seminary Register* 75 (Winter 1986).

Segal, Alan. *Paul, the Convert: The Apostolate and Apostasy of Saul the Pharisee.* New Haven, CT, and London: Yale University Press, 1990.

Segal, Alan F. 'Paul's Religious Experience in the Eyes of Jewish Scholars'. In *Israel's God and Rebecca's Children: Christology and Community in Early Judaism and Christianity: Essays in Honor of Larry W. Hurtado and Alan F. Segal*, eds David B. Capes et al.; Waco, TX: Baylor University Press, 2007, 321–43.

———. 'Conversion and Messianism: Outline for a New Approach'. In *The Messiah:*

Developments in Earliest Judaism and Christianity, ed. James H. Charlesworth; Minneapolis, MN: Fortress, 1992.

Seifrid, Mark. 'For the Jew first: Paul's Nota Bene for his Gentile Readers'. In *To the Jew First: The Case for Jewish Evangelism in Scripture and History*, Grand Rapids, MI: Kregel, 2008.

———. *Christ, Our Righteousness: Paul's Theology of Justification* (NSBT 9), Downers Grove, IL: IVP, 2000.

Senk, R. *Das 'Israel Gottes'. Die Frage nach dem Volk Gottes im Neuen Testament* (Reformatorische Paperbacks 24), 2nd rev. edn, Hamburg, 2006.

Smit, Joop. *'About the Idol Offerings': Rhetoric, Social Context, and Theology of Paul's Discourse in First Corinthians 8.1–11.1* (CBET27), Leuven and Sterling, VA: Peeters, 2000.

Smith, Jonathan Z. 'Fences and Neighbors: Some Contours of Early Judaism'. Repr. in idem, *Imagining Religion: From Jonestown to Babylon*, Chicago and London: University of Chicago Press, 1982, 1–18.

Söding, Thomas. 'Die theologische Physiognomie des Paulus'. *Communio: Internationale katholische Zeitschrift* 38 (2009): 119–134.

Sommer, Benjamin D. *The Bodies of God and the World of Ancient Israel* (Cambridge: Cambridge University Press, 2009).

Soulen, R. Kendall. *The God of Israel and Christian Theology*. Minneapolis, MN: Fortress, 1996.

Spinnler, Rolf. 'Ein Sieg über das Siegen. Radikal im Denken, extrem in der Hoffnung: Warum der Apostel Paulus aktueller ist denn je und sich selbst die wichtigsten Philosophen der Gegegenwart für ihn begeistern'. *Die Zeit* no. 52 (17.12.2008): 54–5.

Sprinkle, Preston M. *Law and Life. The Interpretation of Leviticus 18:5 in Early Judaism and in Paul* (WUNT 2.241), Tübingen: Mohr Siebeck, 2008.

Stanford, William Bedell. *The Ulysses Theme: A Study in the Adaptability of a Traditional Hero*. Dallas, TX: Spring Publications, 1992.

Stegemann, Ekkehard. W. 'Die befristete Zeit. Der Philosoph Giorgio Agamben über den Römerbrief des Paulus'. *Neue Zürcher Zeitung* no. 50 (1.3.2007): 55.

———. 'Zwischen Juden und Heiden, aber "mehr" als Juden und Heiden? Neutestamentliche Anmerkungen zur Identitätsproblematik des frühen Christentums'. In idem, *Paulus und die Welt. Aufsätze*, selected and ed. by Christina Tuor and Peter Wick; Zürich: Theologischer Verlag, 2005, 73–92.

Stendahl, Krister. *Das Vermächtnis des Paulus. Eine neue Sicht auf den Römerbrief*. Zürich: Theologischer Verlag, 2001.

———. *Der Jude Paulus und wir Heiden. Anfragen an das abendländische Christentum*. München: Kaiser, 1978.

———. *Paul among Jews and Gentiles and Other Essays*. Philadelphia, PA: Fortress, 1976. German translation by W. Stegemann: 'Paulus und das introspektive Gewissen des Westens'. In *KuI* 11 (1996): 19–33.

———. 'The Apostle Paul and the Introspective Conscience of the West'. *HTR* 56 (1963): 199–215.

Stolle, Volker. 'Nomos zwischen Tora und Lex. Der paulinische Gesetzesbegriff und seine Interpretation durch Luther in der zweiten Disputation gegen die Antinomer vom 12. Januar 1538'. In Michael Bachmann, *Lutherische und Neue Paulusperspektive. Beiträge zu einem Schlüsselproblem der gegenwärtigen exegetischen Diskussion* (WUNT 182), Tübingen: Mohr Siebeck, 2005, 41–67.

———. *Luther und Paulus. Die exegetischen und hermeneutischen Grundlagen der lutherischen Rechtfertigungslehre im Paulinismus Luthers*. Arbeiten zur Bibel und ihrer Geschichte 10, Leipzig: Evangelische Verlagsanstalt, 2002.

Stowers, Stanley K. *A Rereading of Romans: Justice, Jews, Gentiles*. New Haven, CT: Yale University Press, 1994.

————. 'Paul on the Use and Abuse of Reason'. In David L. Balch, Everett Ferguson and Wayne A. Meeks, eds, *Greeks, Romans, and Christians: Essays in Honor of Abraham J. Malherbe*, Minneapolis, MN: Fortress Press, 1990, 253–86.

Strack Herman L. and Paul Billerbeck. *Kommentar zum Neuen Testament aus Talmud und Midrasch*. Vols I–IV; München: Beck, 1926–8.

Strecker, Georg. *Theology of the New Testament*. Trans. M. Eugene Boring; Louisville, KY: Westminster John Knox, 2000.

————. 'Paulus aus einer "neuen Perspektive". Der Paradigmenwechsel in der jüngeren Paulusforschung'. *KuI* 11 (1996): 3–18.

Stuhlmacher, Peter. 'Erwägungen zum ontologischen Charakter der καινὴ κτίσις bei Paulus'. *EvTh* 27 (1967): 1–35.

Taubes, Jakob. *Die politische Theologie des Paulus. Vorträge, gehalten an der Forschungsstätte der evangelischen Studiengemeinschaft in Heidelberg, 23–27. Feb. 1987*. Eds Aleida and Jan Assmann; München: Fink, 1993 (3rd edn, 2003).

Taylor, N. H. 'Apostolic Identity and the Conflicts in Corinth and Galatia'. In *Paul and His Opponents*, ed. Stanley E. Porter (PAST 2), Leiden: Brill, 2005, 115–22.

Theobald, Michael. *Der Römerbrief* (EdF 294), Darmstadt: Wissenschaftliche Buchgesellschaft, 2000.

Thielman, Frank. *From Plight to Solution: A Jewish Framework for Understanding Paul's View of the Law in Galatians and Romans*. Leiden: Brill, 1989.

Thiselton, Anthony C. *The First Epistle to the Corinthians: A Commentary on the Greek Text* (NIGTC), Grand Rapids, MI, and Carlisle: Eerdmans and Paternoster Press, 2000.

Thrall, Margaret. *The Second Epistle to the Corinthians*. 2 vols (ICC), Edinburgh: T&T Clark, 1994–2000.

Tiwald, Markus. *Hebräer von Hebräern. Paulus auf dem Hintergrund frühjüdischer Argumentation und biblischer Interpretation* (HBS 52), Freiburg: Herder, 2008.

Tobin, Thomas H. *Paul's Rhetoric in Its Contexts: The Argument of Romans*. Peabody, MA: Hendrickson, 2004.

Toit, Andrie Du. *'Paulus Oecumenicus*: Interculturality in the Shaping of Paul's Theology'. *NTS* 55 (2009): 121–43.

Tomson, Peter J. 'Gamaliel's Counsel and the Apologetic Stance of Luke/Acts'. In *The Unity of Luke/Acts*, ed. Joseph Verheyden (BETL 142), Leuven: Leuven University Press and Peeters, 1999, 585–604.

————. *Paul and the Jewish Law: Halakha in the Letters of the Apostle to the Gentiles* (CRINT), Assen and Minneapolis, MN: Van Gorcum and Fortress Press, 1990.

————. 'The Names Israel and Jew in Ancient Judaism and in the New Testament'. *Bijdr.* 47 (1986): 120–40, 268–89.

Trigg, Joseph W. 'Augustine/Jerome, *Correspondence*'. In *Biblical Interpretation*, ed. Michael Glazier (Message of the Fathers of the Church 9), Wilmington, DE: 1988, 250–95.

Vanlandingham, Chris. *Judgement and Justification in Early Judaism and the Apostle Paul*. Peabody, MA: Hendrickson, 2005.

van Unnik, W. C. *Das Selbstverständnis der jüdischen Diaspora in der hellenisticschen-römanischen Zeit*. Leiden: Brill, 1993.

Visscher, Gerhard H. *Romans 4 and the New Perspective on Paul. Faith Embraces the Promise* (Studies in Biblical Literature 122), New York: Peter Lang, 2009.

Vlach, Michael J. *The Church as a Replacement of Israel: An Analysis of Supersessionism* (Edition Israelogie), Frankfurt am Main et al.: Peter Lang, 2009.

Wagner, J. Ross. *Heralds of the Good News: Isaiah and Paul in Concern in the Letter to the Romans*. Leiden: Brill, 2003.

Wander, Bernd. 'Gottesfürchtige und Proselyten'. In Jürgen Zangenberg, ed., *Neues Testament und antike Kultur 3: Weltauffassung – Kult – Ethos*, Neukirchen-Vluyn: Neukirchener, 2005, 50–2.

Watson, Francis. *Paul, Judaism, and the Gentiles: Beyond the New Perspective.* Grand Rapids, MI: Eerdmans, 2007.

Weber, Ferdinand Wilhelm. *System der altsynagogalen palästinischen Theologie aus Targum, Midrasch und Talmud.* Leipzig: Dörffling & Franke, 1880.

Weinfeld, Moshe. *Deuteronomy and the Deuteronomic School.* Oxford: Clarendon Press, 1972.

———. 'The Covenant of Grant in the Old Testament and in the Ancient Near East'. *JAOS* 90.2 (1970): 189.

Welborn, Laurence L. '"Extraction from the Mortal Site": Badiou on the Resurrection in Paul'. *NTS* 55 (2009): 295–314.

———. *Paul, the Fool of Christ: A Study of 1 Corinthians 1-4 in the Comic-Philosophic Tradition* (Early Christianity in Context), London and New York: T&T Clark International, 2005.

Wengst, Klaus. *'Freut euch, ihr Völker, mit Gottes Volk!' Israel und die Völker als Thema des Paulus – ein Gang durch den Römerbrief.* Stuttgart: Kohlhammer, 2008.

Westerholm, Stephen. *Perspectives Old and New on Paul: The 'Lutheran' Paul and his Critics.* Grand Rapids, MI: Eerdmans, 2004.

Williamson, Clark. 'What Does It Mean to Be Saved?'. In *Pondering the Passion: What's at Stake for Christians and Jews?*, ed. Philip A. Cunningham; Lanham, MD: Rowan and Littlefield, 2004.

Willis, Wendell. 'An Apostolic Apologia? The Form and Function of 1 Corinthians 9'. *JSNT* 24 (1985): 33–48.

———. *Idol Meat in Corinth: The Pauline Argument in 1 Corinthians 8 and 10* (SBL DS 68), Chico, CA: Scholars Press, 1985.

Winninge, Mikael. *Sinners and the Righteous: A Comparative Study of the Psalms of Solomon and Paul's Letters.* Stockholm: Almqvist & Wiksell, 1995.

Wolfson, Elliot R. 'Gazing Beneath the Veil: Apocalyptic Envisioning the End'. In *Reinterpreting Revelation and Tradition: Jews and Christians in Conversation*, eds John T. Pawlikowski and Hayim Goren Perelmuter; Franklin, WI: Sheed & Ward, 1997, 77–103.

Wolter, Michael. 'Von der Entmachtung des Buchstabens durch seine Attribute. Eine Spurensuche, ausgehend von Röm 2,29'. In *Sprachgewinn. Festschrift für Günter Bader* (AHST 11), eds Heinrich Assel and Hans Christoph Askani; Berlin and Münster: LIT, 2008, 149–61.

Worman, Nancy Baker. *The Cast of Character: Style in Greek Literature.* Austin, TX: University of Texas Press, 1st edn, 2002.

Wright, N. T. *Paul. In Fresh Perspective.* Minneapolis, MN: Fortress, 2005.

———. 'Romans'. In *NIB*, ed. Leander E. Keck; 12 vols, Nashville: Abingdon, 2002, 10.697.

Wright, Tom. *Paul for Everyone: 1 Corinthians.* London: SPCK, 2003.

Wyschogrod, Michael. *Abraham's Promise. Judaism and Jewish-Christian Relations.* Grand Rapids, MI: Eerdmans, 2004.

———. *The Body of Faith: God and the People Israel.* Northvale, NJ: Jason Aronson, 1995.

Yinger, Kent L. 'Reformation *Redivivus*: Synergism and the New Perspective'. *JTI* 3 (2009): 89–106.

Zenger, Erich. 'Vom christlichen Umgang mit messianischen Texten der hebräischen Bibel'. In *Messias-Vorstellungen bei Juden und Christen*, eds Ekkehard W. Stegemann; Stuttgart: Kohlhammer, 1993, 129–45.

Zetterholm, Magnus. *Approaches to Paul: A Student's Guide to Recent Scholarship.* Minneapolis, MN: Fortress, 2009.

———. 'Purity and Anger: Gentiles and Idolatry in Antioch'. *Interdisciplinary Journal of Research on Religion* (2005): 1–24.

———. *The Formation of Christianity in Antioch.* London: Routledge, 2003.

Žižek, Slavoj. *Parallaxe. Aus dem Engl. von Frank Born*. Frankfurt am Main: Suhrkamp, 2006.

———. *Die gnadenlose Liebe* (stw 1545). Trans. N. G. Schneider; Frankfurt am Main: Suhrkamp, 2001.

———. *Das fragile Absolute. Warum es sich lohnt, das christliche Erbe zu verteidigen.* Trans. N. G. Schneider and J. Hagestedt; Berlin: Volk und Welt Verlag, 2000.

Scripture Index

AUTHOR INDEX